BARRON'S REVIEW COURSE SERIES

Let's Review: Global Studies

Mark Willner
Midwood High School
Brooklyn, New York

Mary Martin
Greene Central School
Greene, New York

Jerry Weiner
Louis Brandeis High School
New York, New York

David Moore
Webster Junior High School
Webster, New York

George Hero
Midwood High School
Brooklyn, New York

BARRON'S

*Robert
LA Sossite*

ACKNOWLEDGMENTS

pp. 357, 358   Marsden, W.E. and V.M., *World in Change*. Copyright © 1983 by Longman Group UK Limited.

pp. 361, 363   Extract taken from WORLD CONTRASTS by Brian Nixon, Copyright © 1986, reproduced by kind permission of Unwin Hyman Ltd.

p. 365   Morrish, M., *Development in the Third World*. Copyright © 1983 by Oxford University Press.

p. 369   MacLean, K. and N. Thompson. *World Environmental Problems*. Copyright © 1981 by John Bartholmew & Sons Ltd.

p. 372   Graves, N., J. Lidstone and M. Naish, *People and Environment: A World Perspective*. Copyright © 1987 by Heinemann Educational Books, Ltd.

All inquiries should be addressed to:
Barron's Educational Series, Inc.
250 Wireless Boulevard
Hauppauge, New York 11788

International Standard Book No. 0-8120-4387-1

Library of Congress Catalog Card No. 90-38445

Library of Congress Cataloging-in-Publication Data

Let's review. Global studies / by Mark Willner...[et al.].
    p.   cm.
   Includes index.
   Summary: A textbook reviewing the physical geography, economic geography, human and cultural geography, and historical and political geography of seven regions of the world.
   ISBN 0-8120-4387-1
   1. Geography—Juvenile literature. [1. Geography.] I. Willner, Mark.
G133.L45   1990
910--dc20   90-38445
                                     CIP
                                       AC

PRINTED IN THE UNITED STATES OF AMERICA

23 880 10 987654

PREFACE

● *For Which Course Was This Book Designed?*

This book was designed to be used as a review text for the New York State course in Regents and RCT Global Studies. The material follows the syllabus in Regents Social Studies: Global Studies, which is used throughout New York State as the basis of a course of study in history on the secondary level. Although the material has been prepared to meet the needs of New York State students, this book can be helpful to students in any secondary-level Global Studies course.

● *What Are the Special Features of This Book?*

The information in this book parallels, for the most part, that of the New York State syllabus in Global Studies. The book has an introductory unit, followed by seven regional units, and an eighth unit, "The World Today." Teachers and students are free to pursue whatever sequence of the seven regional units they wish. However, the sequence in this book follows a specific pattern. That pattern is as follows: I–The Middle East, II–South and Southeast Asia, III–East Asia (China and Japan), IV–Africa, V–Latin America, VI–Western Europe, VII–The Soviet Union and Eastern Europe.

There are several reasons for following the above sequence:
1. The Middle East is a good place to start as it has been, is and will continue to be very much in the news during the last third of this century. As the site of many well-known ancient civilizations as well as the birthplace of Judeo-Christian culture, it is an area to which Americans can easily relate. Indeed, many of the holidays in the fall semester have their roots in the early history of the Middle East.
2. It is important to make global connections as we move from one unit of study to another. Consequently, knowledge of the Middle East becomes useful as we "travel" into South Asia. Indeed, the flow of history in Asia has been from west to east. This is why, for example, Islam, a religion that began in Saudi Arabia, is the major religion of Pakistan and Bangladesh — two South Asian nations. The best-known structure in India is the Taj Mahal, built by a Muslim ruler and containing writing in Arabic. (Also, we should remember that the largest Islamic nation in the world is Indonesia — a Southeast Asian nation, very far away from Islam's birthplace in Saudi Arabia!)
3. Once we are in South Asia, our study of Indian culture helps us learn about Hinduism, Buddhism and Sanskrit. Aspects of these three cultural

patterns spread eastward through a process of cultural diffusion. The Sanskrit language, for example is linked to some Southeast Asian languages. Buddhism spread to China, Korea and Japan. This can partially explain why, in this book, we "travel" to these last three nations in Unit III, having completed our "trip" throughout Unit II.

4. In Unit IV we go to Africa. Its northern half has absorbed much culture and history from the Middle East. Latin America (Unit V) becomes a logical next "stop" after Africa. Indeed, millions of people today in Latin America and the Caribbean can trace their ancestry to West Africa. There is an additional reason for placing Latin America as the fifth and last of the units on non-Western areas. Of all these areas, it is the one that has had the greatest contact with Western Europe. And it is on to Western Europe that we move in to Unit VI, our next unit.

5. Our voyage in Western Europe is very extensive, particularly because knowledge of that area is vital for understanding our own nation's culture, history and government. Knowledge about Western Europe will also help us to understand its many connections and interactions with the areas covered in the next unit, Unit VII—the Soviet Union and Eastern Europe. Indeed, as the 1990's begin, we can see a growing diffusion of Western European economic and political ideas spreading throughout the Soviet Union and Eastern Europe!

Within each unit, we study a particular area in a certain pattern. This pattern can be called a four-fold approach because we look at four features in each area during our "travels" there: *I. Physical Geography; II. Economic Geography; III. Human and Cultural Geography;* and *IV. History and Political Geography.* This kind of area studies and multi-disciplinary approach will be very helpful to us. It is based upon the kinds of questions we would ask if we were actually about to travel in one of the areas. For example if you knew you were going to travel to India next week, you would probably ask a travel agent questions such as these: What clothing should I wear? Can I use American money? Do the people speak English? What kind of government is there? Each of these questions would come under the features in the four-fold approach.

Another reason for using the four-fold approach is because it gives us an easy way to get to know an area. By studying first about the *physical geography* of an area, we get to know its basic land and natural features. We will then be able to understand certain things about its *economy*. A nation's economy is very closely linked to its physical resources. (Consider Saudi Arabia's dependence on oil; Japan's lack of oil and nearness to water.) The *human or cultural* features of a nation have important connections with physical and economic features. And finally, the history and politics of an area are best studied once we know something about its geography, economy and culture. For example, the *history* of the Arab-

Israeli dispute in the Middle East can be examined in light of *physical* features (water and deserts), *economic* issues (oil, shipping routes), and *cultural* factors (Jerusalem's status as a holy city).

The four-fold approach therefore is a good way to study any global area. Into this approach, we can clearly fit the themes of the New York State syllabus:

Physical Geography—The Physical-Historical Setting

Economic Geography—Economic Development

Human and Cultural Geography—Dynamics of Change, Contemporary Cultures

History and Political Geography—Historical Setting, Dynamics of Change, Contemporary Nations and Cultures, Region Within The Global Context

Both the four-fold approach and the sequence of the seven regional units have been used successfully with secondary school classes. They have helped students to learn and teachers to teach about global areas. The sequence of units has also been recommended by the New York City ATSS/UFT (Association of Teachers of Social Studies/United Federation of Teachers).

This book also explains and has references to the various concepts and issues emphasized in the New York State syllabus. The *fifteen key concepts* are as follows: change, choice, citizenship, culture, diversity, empathy, environment, human rights, identity, interdependence, justice, political systems, power, scarcity and technology. The *eleven world issues* are as follows: population, war and peace, terrorism, energy—resources and allocations, human rights, hunger and poverty, world trade and finance, environmental concerns, political and economic refugees, economic growth and development, determination of political and economic systems.

Complementing the text and questions included in each unit are maps, charts, graphs and political cartoons to help portray necessary information.

Finally, three complete Regents Examinations have been reprinted for testing purposes.

● *Who May Use This Book?*

Let's Review: Global Studies provides a valuable supplement to a regular textbook in Global Studies as well as those covering individual regions. For teachers in New York State schools, this book will offer an excellent source of review material to prepare students for the New York State Regents and RCT Examinations in Global Studies.

Although the book has been designed to meet the syllabus of the New York State course in Global Studies, any student taking a course in Global Studies will find it to be a helpful source for review and examination preparation.

● *Taking the Regents and RCT Examinations*

1. Preparation for the Regents Examination begins the first day of class. Good study habits, effective note-taking, completion of all assignments, and a positive attitude throughout the year will make any exam an easier task at the completion of the course.

2. Follow directions closely on the examination itself. Many students are not successful because they do not provide the information asked for, or they leave sections of the question out of their answer. The essays have repeatedly used a format like the following: *Select **two** issues and for each **one** give **three** reasons which led to . . .*" It is imperative that the student provide the information requested. Graders have their "hands tied" by the directions and cannot provide credit for information which is requested and not given.

3. When answering the Part II essay questions, be aware of the scoring breakdown. It will usually be indicated as follows: (5,5,5) or (10) and (5), etc. Keep in mind, especially if time grows short, that some areas are given greater credit than others and therefore should be answered first.

4. Be aware of key terms in the questions, for example, *show, discuss, compare*. Underline key words in the directions to the questions.

5. Budget your time. New York State allows three hours for completion of the Regents exam. You have two parts: Part I (48 multiple-choice questions) worth 55 points and Part II (three essays) worth 45 points (15 points each). Wear a watch and plan out your attack while taking practice examinations.

6. Answer all questions. In the Part I questions, use the process of elimination if necessary. In Part II don't get lazy! You can only be given credit for information provided in your answers.

7. Relax and be confident.

The letters RCT stand for Regents Competency Test. The study and test-taking suggestions for the RCT in Global Studies are the same as those described above for the Regents exam. The RCT, however, is made up in a different style. It has a Part I, containing 50 multiple choice questions. This is worth fifty points. Part II has four essay questions, from which two must be chosen. The essays are worth twenty points, ten points for each one. For a passing score, a student must get 38 points out of 70. On the Regents, a student must get 65 points out of 100.

● *Conclusion*

Whether preparing for the Regents or the RCT exam in Global Studies, this book will be very helpful. Good luck to everyone!

Mark Willner

TABLE OF CONTENTS

INTRODUCTION 1

UNIT ONE   THE MIDDLE EAST   10

I.   Physical Geography (The Physical Setting
      of the Middle East)   12
II.   Economic Geography (Economic
      Development of the Middle East)   17
III. Human and Cultural Geography   22
IV.   History and Political Geography
      (Historical Setting of the Middle East)   27

UNIT TWO   SOUTH AND SOUTHEAST ASIA   48

I.   Physical Geography (The Physical Setting
      of South Asia)   50
II.   Economic Geography (Economic
      Development of South Asia)   54
III. Human and Cultural Geography   60
IV.   History and Political Geography
      (Historical Setting of Southeast Asia)   68

I.   Physical Geography (The Physical Setting
      of Southeast Asia)   77
II.   Economic Geography (Economic
      Development of Southeast Asia)   79
III. Human and Cultural Geography   84
IV.   History and Political Geography
      (Historical Setting of Southeast Asia)   86

UNIT THREE   EAST ASIA   94

I.   Physical Geography (The Physical Setting
      of China)   96
II.   Economic Geography (Economic
      Development of China)   100
III. Human and Cultural Geography   106
IV.   History and Political Geography
      (Historical Setting of China)   112

Contents

I. Physical Geography (The Physical Setting of Japan)   125
II. Economic Geography (Economic Development of Japan)   129
III. Human and Cultural Geography   133
IV. History and Political Geography (Historical Setting of Japan)   140

UNIT FOUR   **AFRICA**   **154**

I. Physical Geography (The Physical Setting of Africa)   156
II. Economic Geography (Economic Development of Africa)   164
III. Human and Cultural Geography   172
IV. History and Political Geography (Historical Setting of Africa)   179

UNIT FIVE   **LATIN AMERICA**   **198**

I. Physical Geography (The Physical Setting of Latin America)   200
II. Economic Geography (Economic Development of Latin America)   206
III. Human and Cultural Geography   215
IV. History and Political Geography (Historical Setting of Latin America)   219

UNIT SIX   **WESTERN EUROPE**   **238**

I. Physical Geography (The Physical Setting of Western Europe)   240
II. Economic Geography (Economic Development of Western Europe)   243
III. Human and Cultural Geography   247
IV. History and Political Geography (Historical Setting of Western Europe)   250

UNIT SEVEN   **THE SOVIET UNION AND EASTERN EUROPE**   **308**

I. Physical Geography (The Physical Setting of the Soviet Union)   310

II. Economic Geography (Economic
Development of the Soviet Union) 315
III. Human and Cultural Geography 318
IV. History and Political Geography
(Historical Setting of Russia) 323

I. Physical Geography (The Physical Setting
of Eastern Europe) 340
II. Economic Geography (Economic
Development of Eastern Europe) 342
III. Human and Cultural Geography 344
IV. History and Political Geography
(Historical Setting of Eastern Europe) 347

UNIT EIGHT   THE WORLD TODAY **354**

ANSWER KEY 382

REGENTS EXAMINATIONS

INDEX

Introduction to Global Studies

The Physical World

Human beings and societies in all regions of the earth share a common *global environment*. This environment is a closed system consisting of a variety of physical features—landforms, bodies of water, vegetation and animal types, and climate regions—which are a result of several natural processes: the rotation and revolution of the earth, geological activity, the water cycle, and biological interactions.

FOUR PARTS OF THE
NATURAL ENVIRONMENT

| Physical features (landforms and bodies of water) | Soil, underground rocks, and underground water. |
| Climate | Living things. |

The environment provides humans with a variety of both renewable and nonrenewable resources, which can be used to meet the needs of both individuals and societies. Though these needs are basic to all humans, the different ways in which they are met are determined by the differences in environment that exist from one part of the earth to another.

The land surface of the earth is generally divided into seven large land masses, called *continents*—North America, Europe, Africa, Australia, and Antarctica. Large bodies of water, called *oceans*—Atlantic, Pacific, Indian, and Arctic—and smaller ones, called seas, cover about 70 percent of the earth's surface. These bodies of water often separate the continents from one another.

In recent centuries, humans have improved their ability to use more of the earth's limited resources, while technology has created closer contacts among peoples of different cultures. This *global interdependence* has made it increasingly important to understand both the similarities and the differences among cultures. Hopefully, such un-

1

derstanding will aid in solving shared problems and resolving disputes between people of different cultures.

Continents and Oceans
THE WORLD

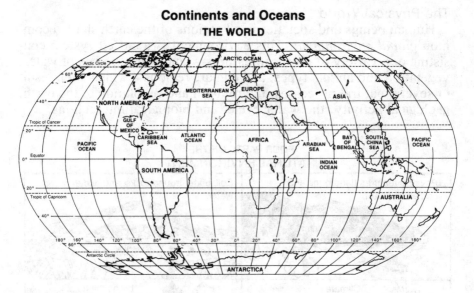

Maps and Their Uses

We can illustrate much information about the world with maps, but we must be aware of their limitations and distortions. Projecting the features of a sphere (the globe) on a flat surface (a map) can distort sizes and distances, especially when we attempt to show the entire world.

Attempting to illustrate the shapes of land masses correctly can distort the sizes of the land masses. Notice the Mercator projection below. On the other hand, trying to accurately show size can distort shape, as in the Peters projection. Thus, maps can convey inaccurate impressions of the importance and influence of certain areas of the world.

Mercator Projection   **Gall-Peters Projection**

2

Placement or location can also create false impressions of the relationships among regions or the relative importance of an area. For example, in the Mercator projection with the Atlantic Ocean in the middle, North America and Europe are located top center. This indicates both their importance and the closeness of their relationship. Compare the Mercator projection with the Japan Airlines map, which centers on the Pacific Ocean, or the MacArthur Corrective Map, which was created by Australians.

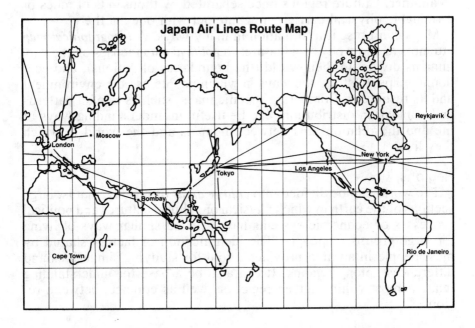

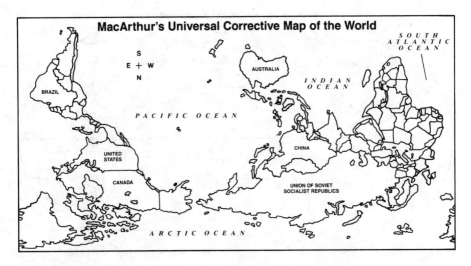

Reading maps requires an understanding of their language. The *scale* provides a tool for determining distances. A map's *legend* provides information about the meaning of lines, symbols, colors, and other markings found on the map itself.

Modern technology has changed how we think about the size of the world. Actual distance (or absolute distance) has become less important than relative distance—how quickly communication and transportation can move ideas and people from one part of the world to another. Culture regions once separated by thousands of miles or formidable physical barriers now interact with one another.

Maps can present information in many ways. A *topographical map* attempts to show physical features, a *political map* focuses on the way humans divide up their world (the boundaries of nations), and economic maps illustrate the ways in which people use the environment and its resources. Comparing specific maps, such as rainfall patterns and population distribution, can be useful in understanding ways of life and the relationships between humans and the world in which they live.

Regions

The world can be divided into *culture areas* or *regions,* that is, large sections of the earth in which physical or cultural features and political processes or economic systems have created similar ways of living for large groups of people. The identification of factors shared by most people in an area provides a tool for studying similarities and differences among regions. It can also be a base for understanding relationships within a given region as well as contacts between regions.

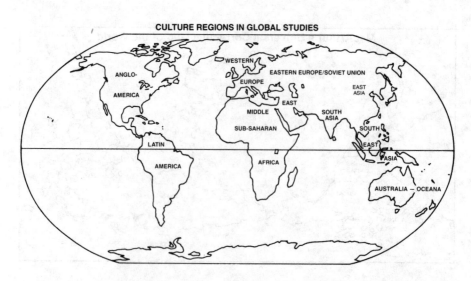

CULTURE REGIONS IN GLOBAL STUDIES

In *Global Studies* we deal with seven of these regions: the Middle East, South and Southeast Asia, East Asia, Africa, Latin America, Western Europe, the Soviet Union and Eastern Europe.

Several factors help to define culture regions. Physical features such as mountains, deserts, or water bodies create sparsely peopled regions between densely populated areas, such as fertile river valleys or coastal plains. Water bodies may also unite groups of islands or coastal areas. Climate patterns and resource bases help to determine life styles within regions, creating distinctive economic systems and resulting social structures.

Location + Separation + Climate + Resources = A Distinctive Culture

World Regions as Used in This Course

Each region possesses a set of factors that sets it apart from the others, starting with its distinctive location. Some factors may be shared by several culture regions, but each region has its own special combination of elements:

Western Europe. Judeo-Christian ethic, Greco-Roman tradition, industrialization, temperate climate, Latin and Germanic languages.

Eastern Europe. Slavic languages, Orthodox Christianity, Communist/Socialist economies, totalitarian political systems undergoing change.

Latin America. Roman Catholicism, Latin-based languages, Spanish/Portugese colonialism, Indian cultural influence.

Sub-Saharan Africa. Tropical climate, triple religious traditions (animism, Christianity, Islam), negroid physical type, oral tradition, ethnic-group social organization, pattern of shifting agriculture.

Middle East. Connecting waterways, crossroads location, Islam, Arabic language and culture, arid climate, mineral (oil) abundance, birthplace of three major religious systems.

South and Southeast Asia. Monsoon climate, Hinduism and Buddhism, flood-plain agriculture, extensive seaborne trade, colonial experience.

East Asia. Confucian/Taoist/Buddhist ethic, hierarchical social system, sense of isolation and uniqueness, character-based alphabet, mongoloid physical type.

Within individual regions, there are great differences. For example, Western Europe consists of more than a dozen countries with differing languages and traditions. In Latin America, the climate varies from tropical in the Amazon to desert on the Altiplano while sub-Sarahan Africa has hundreds of distinct ethnic groups.

Muslims make up a large minority of the population in South and Southeast Asia, and Turkey and Iran are exceptions to the predominantly Arabic culture of the Middle East. In East Asia, Korea provides a bridge between Communist China and capitalist Japan and pre-Communist religious and national variety is beginning to reassert itself in Eastern Europe.

In addition, there are "transition" or "diffusion" zones between the major culture regions, where cultures meet, mix, and produce unique combinations. The Caribbean combines Anglo-European, Latin, and African traditions. Vietnam uses much that is Chinese as well as Indian.

The Impact of Resources, Demography, and History

The natural features of a region create both possibilities and problems, and culture regions today are a product of centuries of history. The rich river plains of India and China have great potential for agricultural production and dense population but also suffer the ravages of flooding. The mineral wealth of Latin America and the Middle East has created great empires but has also attracted conquerors and exploiters.

An imbalance or scarcity of resources can cause conflict and the movement of large groups of people. Both Western and Eastern Europe have experienced widespread and lengthy wars and extensive migration. Most of Japan's large population lives on the non-mountainous 13 percent of that nation's four islands.

The Meaning of Culture

Social scientists use the term *"culture"* to define the total way of life of a group of people. It includes actions and behaviors, tools and techniques, ideas and beliefs. Culture is preserved by the group, taught to and learned by the young, and provides a pattern of interrelationships for the group, as well as a way for them to use their natural environment.

Elements of Culture

Social scientists look at cultures from a variety of viewpoints, concentrating on specific factors as they try to discover the ways in which cultures are similar to and different from one another.

Cultural Diffusion

Ideas and techniques have spread from one culture to another throughout human history, but modern technology and global interdependence have increased both the speed and extent of this cultural diffusion. Some see these recent developments as creating a "global culture" in which similar styles, tastes, and products will be universally acknowledged.

Trade, aid, migration, conquest, slavery, war, and entertainment have all promoted this process, with both positive and negative results. Useful traditions can be destroyed or replaced; social and eco-

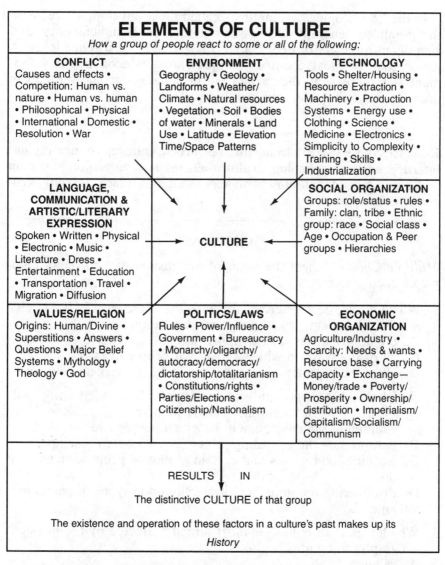

ELEMENTS OF CULTURE
How a group of people react to some or all of the following:

CONFLICT
Causes and effects •
Competition: Human vs.
nature • Human vs. human
• Philosophical • Physical
• International • Domestic •
Resolution • War

ENVIRONMENT
Geography • Geology •
Landforms • Weather/
Climate • Natural resources
• Vegetation • Soil • Bodies
of water • Minerals • Land
Use • Latitude • Elevation
Time/Space Patterns

TECHNOLOGY
Tools • Shelter/Housing •
Resource Extraction •
Machinery • Production
Systems • Energy use •
Clothing • Science •
Medicine • Electronics •
Simplicity to Complexity •
Training • Skills •
Industrialization

LANGUAGE, COMMUNICATION & ARTISTIC/LITERARY EXPRESSION
Spoken • Written • Physical
• Electronic • Music •
Literature • Dress •
Entertainment • Education
• Transportation • Travel •
Migration • Diffusion

CULTURE

SOCIAL ORGANIZATION
Groups: role/status • rules •
Family: clan, tribe • Ethnic
group: race • Social class •
Age • Occupation & Peer
groups • Hierarchies

VALUES/RELIGION
Origins: Human/Divine •
Superstitions • Answers •
Questions • Major Belief
Systems • Mythology •
Theology • God

POLITICS/LAWS
Rules • Power/Influence •
Government • Bureaucracy
• Monarchy/oligarchy/
autocracy/democracy/
dictatorship/totalitarianism
• Constitutions/rights •
Parties/Elections •
Citizenship/Nationalism

ECONOMIC ORGANIZATION
Agriculture/Industry •
Scarcity: Needs & wants •
Resource base • Carrying
Capacity • Exchange—
Money/trade • Poverty/
Prosperity • Ownership/
distribution • Imperialism/
Capitalism/Socialism/
Communism

RESULTS IN

The distinctive CULTURE of that group

The existence and operation of these factors in a culture's past makes up its

History

nomic patterns can be disrupted. But new technology can also bring improvements in standards of living, and new ideas can bring variety and enrichment to any culture.

Increased contact between cultures can also bring about exploitation and help to create or at least emphasize differences in prosperity and standards of living from one culture region to another. The "developed" regions—Europe (East and West), Anglo-America, and Australia/Oceana—have been greatly influenced by the Industrial Revolution. The people of these regions have a more abundant supply of material goods and personal services.

In the "developing" (sometimes called "less developed") regions, the populace generally has fewer comforts and conveniences, and significant numbers of people may survive at a subsistence level. A major goal for most countries in these areas is economic development—an increase in the capacity to produce goods and services in order to make life safer and healthier.

KEY CONCEPTS: Environment, resources, culture, culture region, interdependence, technology, cultural diffusion, map projections, map scales and legends, absolute distance, relative distance, scarcity, economic development.

QUESTIONS

Multiple Choice. Select the letter of the answer that correctly completes each statement.

1. Which phrase best describes the meaning of the term CULTURE?
    A. the advancement and progress of a nation
    B. the ability of humans to appreciate art and music
    C. all of the ways in which a group of people lives
    D. all of the products that a group of humans makes and uses

2. Social scientists who study human culture are called anthropologists. Their work would most likely involve
    A. examining the environment in which people live
    B. determining the operating principles of modern machinery
    C. learning the reasons that certain groups of people live as they do
    D. discovering the influence of climate upon types of plants and animals

3. Which aspect of culture is most directly affected by the physical geography of an area?
    A. religion
    B. language
    C. food
    D. music

4. In dividing the world's population into culture groups, social scientists are most concerned with
    A. weather and climate patterns of different regions
    B. political boundaries separating countries
    C. similarities and differences in styles and patterns of living
    D. present political systems in various nations

5. Below are three different proverbs.

   "Mighty oaks from tiny acorns grow." (United States)
   "The journey of 1000 miles begins with a single step." (China)
   "A little rain each day will fill the river to overflowing." (West Africa)

   Which conclusion is best supported by these proverbs?
   A. Humans in all cultures make excuses for their shortcomings
   B. All cultures are concerned with transportation and conservation
   C. Natural resources are a major concern for people in all cultures
   D. Though cultures may differ humans view many situations in similar ways

6. The popularity of baseball in Japan and karate in the United States are examples of
   A. cultural diffusion
   B. technological development
   C. ethnocentrism
   D. cultural isolation

7. Which of the following statements about maps is NOT correct?
   A. A topographical map would show mountains and water bodies.
   B. Political maps emphasize boundaries between countries.
   C. An economic map might show areas of agricultural production.
   D. Demographic maps generally show types of governments.

8. Culture regions as defined in this course
   A. are for the most part quite small and isolated
   B. usually contain very little cultural variety
   C. have developed as a result of geographic and historical factors
   D. change frequently as political parties and governments change.

9. The so-called "less developed" regions of the world are generally located on which continents?
   A. Asia, Africa, and South America
   B. Europe, Africa and Australia
   C. North and South America and Asia
   D. North America, Australia, and Europe

ESSAY

"The world is at our doorstep." In a concise four to five paragraph essay, explain the meaning of this statement. Be sure to include the following concepts:

A. Global interdependence
B. Cultural diffusion
C. Communications technology

UNIT ONE
THE MIDDLE EAST

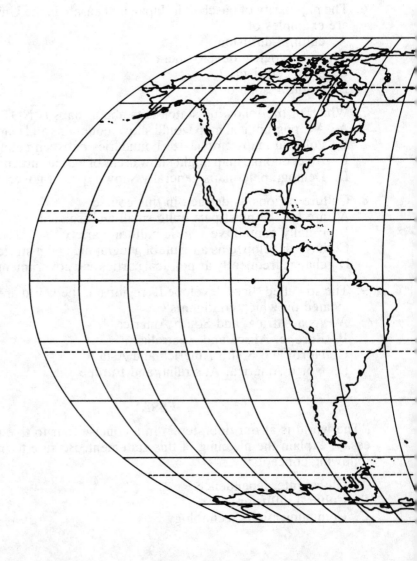

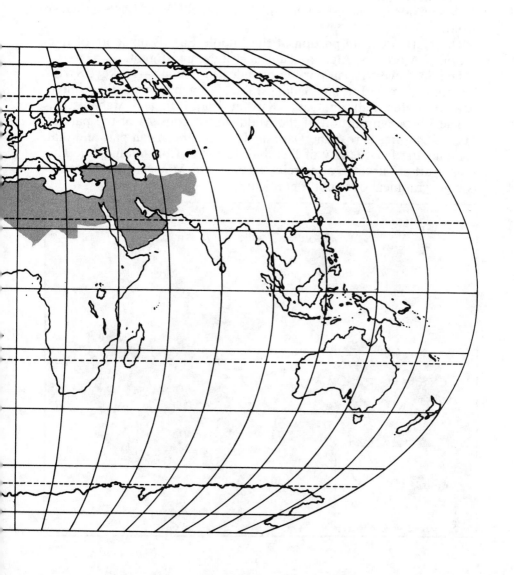

I. Physical Geography (The Physical Setting of the Middle East)

Overview

The region known as the **Middle East** includes parts of three continents—Europe, Africa, and Asia. Because all three continents seem to intersect here, the region has also been called "the crossroads of the world." However, these names, as well as another commonly used name, the **Near East,** seem appropriate only when one looks at a world map with Western Europe at the center. The African portion of the Middle East includes the area known as North Africa, while the Asian portion includes what might be called SWASIA (Southwest Asia).

The North African portion of the Middle East is made up of five nations—Morocco, Algeria, Tunisia, Libya, and Egypt.

The Southwest Asian portion includes 15 nations—Turkey, Syria, Lebanon, Israel, Jordan, Saudi Arabia, Yemen, Oman, the United Arab Emirates, Bahrain, Qatar, Kuwait, Iraq, Iran, and Afghanistan.

The European portion of the Middle East consists of the part of Turkey that lies across the Dardanelles from the Asian part and that contains the famous city of Istanbul (formerly Constantinople). The Asian part of Turkey is often referred to as **Asia Minor.** (This reference is a geographical one, not a political one.)

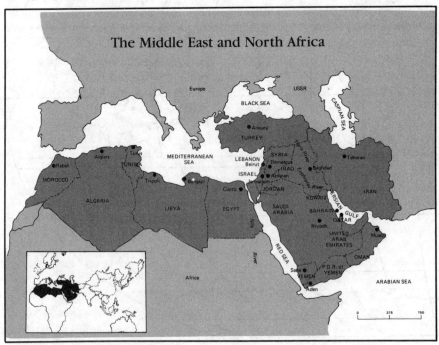

The Middle East and North Africa

Topography

Throughout the Middle East, which is about twice the physical size of the United States, the most common landform is **desert**. The aridity (dryness), lack of vegetation, and barrenness of its desert territories have had profound effects on the history and culture of the Middle East. The **nomadic** (wandering) life styles of such people as the Bedouins, Arabs, and early Israelites put an emphasis on sharing, group values and conformity over individual values. Close family and clan ties, and frugality (thriftiness) were also important. As deserts make up over 80 percent of the land area, population distribution has been uneven. Human settlements were and are still found mainly near the precious water bodies. Armed struggles have occurred throughout history for access to and control over water bodies. The deserts may also have had an impact on the growth of strong religious feelings in the Middle East. A society's religious devotion may become heightened when living amidst harsh natural conditions. Scholars also note that three central religious figures had profound experiences when they were alone in the desert—Moses (Judaism—at Mount Sinai), Jesus (Christianity—in the wilderness), and Mohammed (Islam—in a cave). The major deserts of the Middle East are the **Sahara** in North Africa, which is the largest desert in the world, the **Sinai** in Egypt, the **Rub-al Khali** ("the empty quarter") and the **Nafud** in Saudi Arabia, the **Negev** in Israel, and the **Dasht-i-Kavir** in Iran.

Topographical variety can be seen in the mountain ranges. The **Atlas Mountains** lie in northwest Africa, separating the Sahara Desert from land near the Mediterranean Sea. Since this land area is arable and has a comfortable Mediterranean climate, there are large cities located here, such as Casablanca, Rabat, Algiers, Tunis, and Tripoli. The **Elburz Mountains** in Iran and the **Taurus Mountains** in Turkey are a link between the Himalayas of central Asia to the east and the Alps of Europe to the west.

The **Arabian Peninsula,** sometimes called Arabia, is shaped like a huge boot. It is mostly desert and contains several nations, the largest of which is Saudi Arabia.

Water Bodies

The scarcity of water in the Middle East is an important fact of life and is crucial to understanding the region's history. Apart from their life-sustaining importance, water bodies have also had vital maritime and strategic influence.

The largest bodies of water in the area are the five surrounding seas—the **Caspian, Black, Mediterranean, Red,** and **Arabian.** They have always been a source of fish. The "pathway" provided by the Mediterranean and its Suez Canal link to the Red Sea and then to the Gulf of Aden has brought Europe "closer" to the southwestern, southern, and eastern parts of Asia. The Mediterranean has served as a "highway of conquest, commerce, and culture." In ancient times, Roman legions traveled across the Mediterranean eastward to the Levant (lands touching the eastern Mediterranean, such as modern-day Syria, Lebanon, and Israel), and Phoenician traders traveled westward from the Levant to North Africa. The Persian Gulf, which leads into the Arabian Sea, became a crucial battleground in the Iran-Iraq War of the 1980s. Because the Persian Gulf area contains most of the world's oil reserves, it is a strategic route for oil tankers to pass through—many of them bound for Japan, the United States, and Europe. Finally, the Bosporus—Sea of Mamara—Dardanelles Strait route from the Black Sea has been of paramount importance to the Soviet Union, because it is the only way for Russian ships to reach the warm waters of the Aegean Sea and Mediterranean Sea.

The four major rivers of the Middle East, from ancient times until today, have greatly affected patterns of settlement. They are the **Tigris, Euphrates, Nile,** and **Jordan.** Because of the region's arid climate, these water bodies are very valuable. Except for the coasts of Turkey and the Levant, rainfall is practically nonexistent during the year.

1. The **Tigris** and **Euphrates** rivers originate in the Taurus Mountains of Turkey and flow a few miles apart from each other southeastward. They converge (meet) in Iraq and flow as one, the **Shatt-al-Arab** into the Persian Gulf. The Shatt-al-Arab region, like all delta areas, has rich soil and is also of strategic value because of the nearby oil deposits and ports. Consequently, it witnessed much fighting during the recent Iran-Iraq War.

The area between the Tigris and Euphrates rivers was referred to in ancient times as **Mesopotamia.** It was the site of one of the early river-valley civilizations, as it was well-irrigated and able to support large numbers of people. It was part of an arc-like region called the "fertile crescent," extending from the eastern shores of the Mediterranean Sea to the Persian Gulf. The ancient city of Babylon was in Mesopotamia. Modern-day Baghdad, the capital of Iraq, lies on the Tigris River and is just north of the ruins of Babylon.

2. The other major river-valley civilization in the Middle East arose in ancient Egypt along the **Nile River,** the world's longest river. The Blue Nile, with its source in Central Africa, and the White Nile, with its source in East Africa, converge in the Sudan and flow northward into the Mediterranean Sea. When the Nile waters overflow their banks, they deposit silt and make the nearby land very fertile. The Aswan High Dam was built in 1970 to control the Nile's flood waters. Since over 95 percent of Egypt is desert, the vast majority of Egyptians live along the narrow strip of land along the Nile River. The ancient cities of Thebes and Alexandria (in the delta) are on the river,

as are the present-day capital cities of Egypt (Cairo) and the Sudan (Khartoum).

3. The **Jordan River** is smaller than the other three rivers, but it is vital to the peoples of Lebanon, Syria, Jordan, and Israel. It flows southward from highland areas in Lebanon, Syria, and Israel and makes irrigation possible along its banks. However, use of its waters has led to political quarrels between the nations through which the Jordan River runs.

The Jordan has had historical and political significance. It was an important source of water in ancient times. Jericho, one of the earliest built urban sites in the world, lies only six miles from the Jordan River. Since 1967, the river has been a disputed political boundary between Israel and the nation of Jordan. The land portion just west of the river, now administered by Israel, is called the **West Bank.** It was under Jordanian control until Jordan's attack on Israel during the Six-Day War of June 1967. (See Section IV for further information.) The river is also important because of its biblical significance. For Jews and Christians, the Jordan River is especially noteworthy for beliefs about events that occurred near it concerning such figures as Moses, Joshua, and Jesus.

The Jordan is also economically significant. Its waters flow into the Sea of Galilee and farther south, into the Dead Sea. The Sea of Galilee has been a source of fish from ancient days until the present. The Dead Sea is the lowest point on earth and is the end point for the Jordan's waters. Unique natural conditions have made the Dead Sea area a valuable source of chemicals, such as potash and phosphates. Israel has constructed a major chemical complex there and has invited Jordan's participation.

QUESTIONS

Multiple Choice. Select the letter of the answer that correctly completes each statement.

1. Which is the most likely place for a desert location?
   A. on the windward side of a mountain
   B. on the leeward side of a mountain
   C. near a large body of water
   D. near a capital city

2. Which pair of water bodies is incorrectly matched?
   A. Tigris River-Persian Gulf
   B. Persian Gulf-Strait of Hormuz
   C. Nile River-Arabian Sea
   D. Jordan River-Dead Sea

3. The "fertile crescent" was known historically for the early growth of
   A. manufacturing
   B. civilizations
   C. architecture
   D. water conservation

4. The Rub al Khali refers to a
   A. city
   B. desert
   C. seaport
   D. mountain

5. The Middle East has been described as the "crossroads of the world." Which fact would best support this statement?
   A. Most of the world's oil reserves are there.
   B. The Suez Canal is an important waterway.
   C. Parts of three continents intersect there.
   D. Water bodies surround the region.

6. The area between the Tigris and Euphrates Rivers has been referred to as
   A. Arabia
   B. Palestine
   C. Asia Minor
   D. Mesopotamia

Fact or Opinion. If the statement is a fact, write F. If the statement is an opinion, write O.

1. Desert people live a nomadic lifestyle.

2. The best place to live in the Middle East would be in the Sinai Desert.

3. Peace would come to the Middle East if Jordan and Israel agreed to build a canal between the Mediterranean Sea and the Dead Sea.

ESSAY

Geography can affect the lives of people in many ways. For each geographic feature listed below, explain two ways in which it has affected people in the Middle East:

1. desert

2. water bodies

II. Economic Geography (Economic Development of the Middle East)

Agriculture

It is important to remember that barely 15 percent of the land in the Middle East is arable (good for farming). Moreover, inadequate rainfall, large desert areas, and a scarcity of water bodies are obstacles to agriculture. In addition to these natural obstacles, the traditional system of landownership, with only a very small number of people controlling the little arable land, has also made it difficult to grow enough food to support the increasing population. The major crops are cereal grains, such as wheat and barley, and olives, grapes, and dates, which have been cultivated since ancient times.

Israel's ability to grow oranges and citrus fruits while "making the desert bloom" has enabled it to export food. Egypt has built up a substantial cotton industry. The Aswan High Dam along the Nile has added to Egypt's agricultural productivity.

Over 75 percent of the people in Arab countries are farmers (fellahin), who have traditionally leased the land as tenants from wealthy landowners. However, recent land-reform laws in several countries, including Egypt, Syria, and Iraq, have redistributed the land so that more farmers have become landowners. Nevertheless, primitive farming techniques prevent farmers from getting high crop yields from their lands.

In Israel, a **kibbutz** movement exists whereby land is held collectively by a large group of people who work the land. There are few private landowners. Advanced farming techniques used in Israel have resulted in food surpluses.

Ever since biblical times, sheep herding has been carried on. Consequently, lamb has been a basic part of the diet of the people of the Middle East.

Industrial Production

The major natural resource in the Middle East is oil. Most of this precious resource is found in the Arab nations, such as Saudi Arabia, Kuwait, and Iran, that border the Persian Gulf. It is estimated that most of the world's oil reserves are in the Middle East. Since the oil-rich nations produce more than they need, they are able to export millions of barrels a year. From these exports, the oil-rich nations have gained much money and have become very wealthy.

Growth of the Oil Industry. From about 1900 to 1970, oil production in the Middle East was largely dominated by foreigners—British, French, Dutch, and American. The chief reason for this was that foreigners were able to supply most of the **factors of production.** (The four factors of production are **land, labor, capital,** and **management**—

17

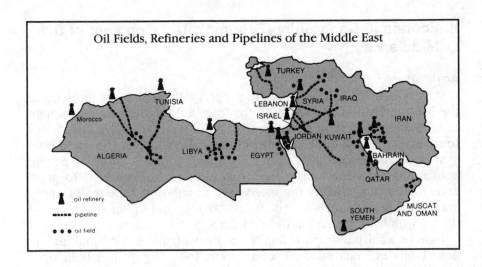

Oil Fields, Refineries and Pipelines of the Middle East

those things that are necessary to make a product.) While the Middle Eastern nations had the land on which oil was first discovered in the early 1900s, they did not have enough of the other three factors of production to produce the oil themselves. Foreigners supplied the other three factors: labor (skilled workers), capital (this refers to both money and machinery, such as oil wells and drills, necessary to produce the oil), and management (skilled managers and engineers).

In any economic relationship, both sides agree to give certain things to each other. By providing labor, capital, and management, the foreigners received **concessions** (permission to use the land) from the oil-rich nations. The foreigners also promised to produce and sell the oil and to give royalties (a percentage of the money earned by selling the oil) to the oil-rich nations. Some foreign companies also agreed to train Arabs from the Middle Eastern nations in oil-production techniques.

By the 1970s, the Arab nations wanted higher royalties and more control over the oil industry. Some nations nationalized (took over) the oil fields. Creation of **OPEC** (Organization of Petroleum Exporting Countries), an organization dominated by the Arab nations, was another step in reducing foreign influence in the oil industry. As the 1990s began, the oil-rich nations had achieved complete control over their oil and had become very wealthy.

Impact of Wealth Gained by Oil. The Arab nations became very wealthy from the large amount of money ("petro-dollars") paid to them by countries that had to import oil. Because they controlled so much oil, the OPEC nations were able to charge almost any price they wanted. The acquisition of vast amounts of money has had im-

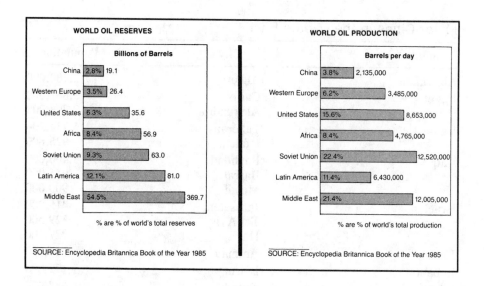

portant consequences both internally (inside these nations) and externally (relations with other countries).

1. **Internal impact.** Although some Arab rulers have used the newly acquired money for themselves, the general tendency has been to use this wealth in ways that would benefit their people. As a result, a dramatic increase in the standard of living has occurred in such nations as Saudi Arabia, where new highways, houses, hospitals, and schools have been built. This rapid increase in modernization has, however, clashed with some traditional values regarding marriages, child-rearing practices, and attitudes towards women in the region. The increased emphasis on material comforts and secular (worldly, non-spiritual) concerns, associated with increasing wealth, has been one reason for the growing influence of Islamic fundamentalists. They are worried about the influence both of modernization and of Western values on traditional Islamic culture.

2. **External impact.** The oil-rich nations of the Middle East have gained more power and respect in international affairs because of their control of oil and because of their newly acquired wealth. For example, by refusing to export oil or by increasing its export of oil to a given nation, an Arab nation can "pressure" that nation to do things a certain way. (Saudi Arabia's embargo [denial] of oil shipments to the United States in 1973 to 1974 was designed to get the United States to behave in a certain way towards Israel.) Many "petro-dollars" have been used by Arab investors to buy up property and businesses in other nations. (An increasing amount of land in New York and London has been sold to Arabs.)

Major Cities in the Middle East

Country	City	Population
Algeria	Algiers	2,200,000
Egypt	Cairo	5,881,000
	Alexandria	2,708,000
Iran	Teheran	5,734,200
	Isfahan	926,600
Iraq	Baghdad	3,400,000
	Basrah	915,000
	Mosul	900,000
Israel	Jerusalem	415,000
	Tel Aviv	329,500
	Haifa	227,400
Jordan	Amman	744,000
Lebanon	Beirut	1,172,000
Libya	Tripoli	587,400
	Benghazi	267,700
Morocco	Casablanca	2,139,200
	Rabat	578,600
Saudi Arabia	Riyadh	1,308,000
	Jidda	1,500,000
	Mecca	366,800
Syria	Damascus	1,178,000
	Aleppo	1,109,100
Tunisia	Tunis	596,600
Turkey	Istanbul	2,772,700
	Ankara	1,877,700
	Izmir	757,800

Source: Encyclopedia Britannica Book of the Year 1985

Current Economic Concerns

1. Many Middle Eastern nations need foreign aid to help them meet economic problems. Egypt and Israel are among the five largest recipients of American aid.

2. Overpopulation and a growth in cities have put a strain on the economy in some areas. Growing numbers of people are demanding that their governments do more to improve living standards. These demands are part of the movement described as a "revolution of rising expectations."

3. Extensive spending on military weapons, especially in Libya, Egypt, Syria, Jordan, Iraq, and Iran, has taken away funds needed

for economic and social development. With the exception of Egypt, the military threat posed by these nations to Israel has forced Israel to spend large amounts of money on arms for defense.

4. Greater regional cooperation could help the nations of the Middle East in finding solutions to common problems. For example, removal of political barriers between Israel and the Arab nations, as well as those between some of the Arab nations themselves, could lead to increased trade, reduction of arms spending, and improved desalinization projects to purify ocean and sea water by removing the salt content.

5. The frequent changes in world oil prices often lowers the income received from "petro-dollars" and affects the region's economy. Also, the search for alternative sources of energy combined with energy-conservation measures may affect the global demand for oil.

QUESTIONS

Multiple Choice. Select the letter of the answer that correctly completes each statement.

1. During the first half of this century, foreign oil companies provided all the factors of production needed in the oil industry EXCEPT for
   A. labor
   B. capital
   C. land
   D. management

2. What did these foreign companies expect in return for their supplying important factors of production?
   A. petro-dollars
   B. territory
   C. pensions
   D. concessions

3. Arable land is land that is good for
   A. growing food
   B. producing oil
   C. manufacturing steel
   D. building highways

4. The Aswan High Dam has increased the agricultural productivity of
   A. Syria
   B. Iran
   C. Egypt
   D. Israel

21

5. Which action by OPEC Nations would most upset foreign oil companies?
   A. desalinization
   B. nationalization
   C. modernization
   D. westernization

6. The decision by Arab governments on how best to use their petro-dollars is an issue that can be described as
   A. human
   B. cultural
   C. physical
   D. economic

7. Most of the oil-producing regions of the Middle East are located around the
   A. Dead Sea
   B. Mediterranean Sea
   C. Persian Gulf
   D. Suez Canal

ESSAY

Describe one way in which each of the following has affected economic activity or productivity in the Middle East:

1. OPEC

2. kibbutz system

3. Aswan High Dam

4. military spending

III. Human and Cultural Geography

Overview

  As a region covering parts of three continents, and often described as "the crossroads of the world," the Middle East contains a variety of people. Three major religions developed here—Judaism, Christianity, and Islam. People live in both small villages and large cities. Over 90 percent of the people of the Middle East can be described as **Semites** or **Semitic.** These terms describe a family of languages that include Arabic and Hebrew. The terms are also used to refer to any-

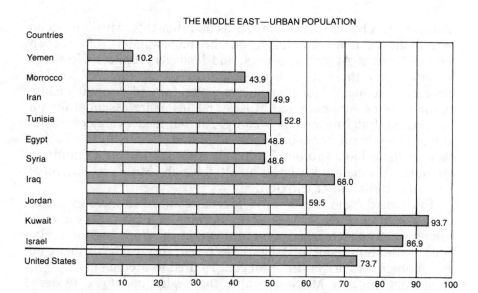

THE MIDDLE EAST—URBAN POPULATION

Countries

Country	
Yemen	10.2
Morrocco	43.9
Iran	49.9
Tunisia	52.8
Egypt	48.8
Syria	48.6
Iraq	68.0
Jordan	59.5
Kuwait	93.7
Israel	86.9
United States	73.7

Percentage of Total Population

Source: Britannica Book of the Year 1986

one who speaks one of these languages and who belongs to an ethnic group that follows certain customs. An Arab is a person who speaks Arabic and who follows traditions associated with an Arab way of life, that is, traditions connected with existence in a desert environment in the Middle East. Although most Muslims in the Middle East are Arabs, the word "Arab" does not refer to a particular religious group. (A small number of people in Egypt, Israel, and Lebanon consider themselves to be Christian Arabs. Muslims in Turkey and Iran do not consider themselves to be Arabs.)

Islam: The Main Religion in the Middle East

Islam is the religion practiced by over 90 percent of the people in the Middle East. It was the third major religion to develop in the area, Judaism being the first and Christianity the second. Many Islamic beliefs come from Judaism and Christianity. The most important belief common to all three religions is **monotheism,** or the belief in the existence of one God, which was first stated by the Jews. The followers of Islam call this one God *Allah.* People who are followers of Islam submit themselves to the will of Allah and are called Muslims. The word "Islam" is defined as "submission."

The Importance of Mohammed. *Mohammed,* the founder of Islam, lived from 570 to 632 in what is now Saudi Arabia. Muslims believe that he was the fourth and most important prophet chosen by God

23

(Allah) to teach and spread holy ideas and thoughts. Muslims accept most of the teachings of Judaism and Christianity and therefore accept the existence of Abraham, Moses, and Jesus as prophets. However, Muslims view these leaders as simply preparing the way for Mohammed. The life of Mohammed is essential for understanding Islam, as the lives of Abraham and Moses and Jesus are essential for understanding Judaism and Christianity. All four leaders are considered to have had direct communication with God. Events in the lives of each of them have profound religious meaning for the faithful; for example, Abraham with Isaac at Mt. Moriah, Moses at Mt. Sinai, Jesus, his birth and crucifixion.

Mohammed, who was born in Mecca, claimed to have had revelations from God and visions while sleeping in a cave. (These revelations were collected and written down in the **Koran**—"the recitations"—the holy book of Islam.) He began to preach his ideas but was scorned and driven from Mecca. He fled to Medina in 622. This flight from Mecca to Medina is called the **Hegira,** and it is considered a very holy event by Muslims. The year 622 marks the first year in the Muslim calendar. Mohammed gained many followers in Medina, raised an army, and was able to take over Mecca. Mecca was an important city because of its economic activity and because it contained a holy shrine, called the **Kabbah.** The Kabbah contains a meteor that Mohammed claimed was sent to earth by Allah. (To this day, Mecca is considered the holiest city to Muslims, with the Kabbah as the holiest site.) Mohammed died in Medina, which is the second holiest city to Muslims. Muslims believe that after death, Mohammed's spirit rode to Jerusalem, where it stepped on a rock and went to heaven. (This rock is the rock on which Jews believed Abraham was going to sacrifice Isaac.) In the 700s, Muslims conquered Jerusalem and built a mosque, called the Mosque of Omar or Dome of the Rock, over this rock. Consequently, Jerusalem is considered Islam's third holiest city.

Basic Beliefs of Muslims. The five basic obligations, or "pillars" of Islam, are described in the chart below, with corresponding similarities in Judaism and Christianity.

The Five Obligations	Islam	Judaism	Christianity
Proclamation of faith	"There is no God but Allah, and Mohammed is his prophet."	"Hear oh Israel, the Lord our God, the Lord is one."	"There is but one God, creator of heaven, earth, and all things."

The Five Obligations	Islam	Judaism	Christianity
Prayer	Five times a day, facing Mecca	Three times a day for some Jews, facing Jerusalem.	Some Christians in the Middle East pray seven times a day.
Fasting	During *Ramadan*, fasting from sunrise to sunset. (Ramadan was the month when the Koran was revealed to Mohammed.)	Fasting on specifically designated days during the year.	
Almsgiving (charity)	"Whoever does not know that his need of the reward for giving is greater than the poor man's need of the gift is donating his charity in vain."	"The poor person does more for the giver than the giver does for the poor man."	"It is more blessed to give than to receive."
Pilgrimage (visit to a holy area)	An obligation to make the *haj* (a visit to Mecca) once in a lifetime. One who makes the haj is called a haji.	Jerusalem is holy because it is the site of the first two Jewish temples and contains the Western Wall.	Bethlehem is holy as the birthplace of Jesus; Jerusalem is important as the site of the crucifixion.
Other Items Holy books	Koran; contains 114 *suras*, or chapters. The *Shari'a* is a code of law based on the Koran.	Old Testament (also called the Tanach, containing the Torah and other writings. The Talmud has commentaries on the Tanach.)	The Bible (contains the Old Testament and the New Testament.)

The Five Obligations	Islam	Judaism	Christianity
Groupings	*Sunni* Muslims and *Shi'ite* Muslims. Sunnis are the larger group. Shi'ites are found mostly in Iran.	Orthodox, Conservative, and Reform	Catholic and Protestant

(For information on the spread of Islam, see the unit on Africa and Southeast Asia; for a comparison between Islam and Hinduism, see the unit on South Asia [India].)

Important Information About Islam

1. Shi'ite Muslims in Iran, as well as scattered groups of Muslims in other countries, claim that many traditional Islamic values are being lost in the 20th century. They would like to see a return to traditional, fundamental values and have thus been called **Islamic fundamentalists.** They are worried about such things as the growth of materialism, introduction of Western values, and changing atittudes on the role of women. Their protests against some Arab governments as well as their preaching have been a source of concern. An example of an Islamic fundamentalist was the former leader of Iran, **Ayatollah Khomeini.**

2. The crescent and the star, symbols of Islam, are found in the flags and currencies of many Islamic nations.

3. There is no central controlling figure for all Muslims, similar to the position of pope for Catholics.

4. Muslims believe that the Koran was revealed to Mohammed in Arabic, and translations are not allowed. In order to read the Koran, one has to know Arabic. Therefore, Arabic became a common language for all Muslims, whether they were Arab such as people in Egypt or non-Arab such as people in Pakistan and Indonesia.

Language

As you read, Arabic is the most widely spoken language in the Middle East. Along with **Hebrew,** spoken mainly in Israel, it is grouped as a Semitic language. Several other languages are also spoken in the Middle East. **Farsi,** or Persian, is spoken mainly in Iran. **Turkish** is spoken in Turkey. The Turkish script is written in Latin letters instead of Arabic, the result of a change made by the Turkish leader **Kemal Ataturk** in 1928. This was a break with tradition, as was his decision to translate the Koran from Arabic into Turkish. European languages are spoken mostly in areas which were under European influence. Thus, English is used in Egypt, while French is used in Lebanon and Syria.

QUESTIONS

Multiple Choice. Select the letter of the answer that correctly completes each statement:

1. Which pair of languages have the most in common?
   A. Arabic and Turkish
   B. Turkish and Hebrew
   C. Hebrew and Arabic
   D. Turkish and Farsi

2. Shi'ites and Sunnis refer to groupings of people who are
   A. Catholics
   B. Jews
   C. Muslims
   D. Protestants

ESSAY

Religion has played a major role in shaping the history and culture of the Middle East. The three major religions in the area are Judaism, Christianity, and Islam.

1. Explain one idea or belief which all three religions share.

2. Describe one idea or belief or practice which each one has that is different from the other two.

3. For each religion, name one person who was extremely important for the growth of that religion.

IV. History and Political Geography (Historical Setting of the Middle East)

Overview
The Middle East has the longest recorded history of any region on the globe. The people who have influenced this history and who have

been affected by it are of diverse backgrounds. Some of these people can trace their roots to the area itself, while others migrated to the Middle East from elsewhere. There are many patterns and periods in Middle Eastern history, and often they overlap; that is, different patterns and movements frequently occurred at the same time in various parts of the area.

The Historical Setting (Pre-History–600 A.D.)

Early Civilizations. The earliest known people in the Middle East settled in the river valleys of the **Nile** and the **Tigris-Euphrates** rivers and built what we call river-valley civilizations (see I. Physical Geography). These two civilizations—the **Egyptian** centered in the Nile River Valley and the **Mesopotamian** in the Tigris-Euphrates River Valley—made many important achievements that influenced human history throughout the world. For this reason, historians call them the "cradles of civilization." (Two other "cradles of civilization" developed in the river valleys of the Huanghe (Yellow) River in South Asia and the Indus River in East Asia.) Several of these early societies conquered territory and grew into empires.

All of these societies were developed by people who were native to the Middle East. However, starting in the 4th century B.C., powerful civilizations from outside the Middle East began to make conquests in the area. They strongly influenced the areas they conquered.

1. After *Alexander the Great* united the Greek city-states, he swept eastward into Asia Minor, Syria, Palestine, and Egypt. Alexander brought Greek culture to the Middle East and therefore **Hellenized** the area. The **Hellenistic** period (the period when Greek culture was brought to the Middle East) lasted from 333 B.C. to 90 B.C.

2. The area called **Palestine** comes from the word "Philistine." The Philistines controlled a small strip of land along the eastern Mediterranean coast in 1200 B.C. This land was first called Palestine by the Romans. The word "Palestine" describes a geographic region and was never the name of a nation. The present-day nation of Israel is located in most of the land that was called Palestine. Israelite kingdoms existed in Palestine from approximately 1000 B.C. to 70 A.D.

3. By 30 B.C., the **Roman Empire** controlled most of the Mediterranean region. Its power extended into all the former Hellenized lands in the Middle East. Roman laws and culture spread in these lands. Christianity began during the Roman period with the birth of Jesus. It started as a reform movement among Jews and gained converts and spread under the leadership of Paul, a Hellenized Jew. Christianity spread throughout the Middle East and other parts of the Roman Empire, although it was persecuted by Rome's emperors. By 313 A.D. Christianity had become so widespread that the **Emperor Constantine** issued the **Edict of Milan,** which granted freedom of worship to all

The Society	The General Area	The Achievements
EGYPTIANS	Egypt	Pyramids, mathematics, control of Nile River waters, hieroglyphics, order maintained by a pharaoh, calendar, medicine, mummification
SUMERIANS	Mesopotamia	Cities, cuneiform, geometry, use of vehicles
BABYLONIANS	Mesopotamia	Hammurabi's code of law, hanging gardens of Babylon
HITTITES	Turkey and Syria	Iron
LYDIANS	Turkey	Coined money
PHOENICIANS	Lebanon	Navigators, traders, alphabet
HEBREWS	Palestine	Monotheism, Ten Commandments, Old Testament
CHALDEANS	Mesopotamia	Astronomy
PERSIANS	Iran	Roads; unified diverse people in a wide empire

Christians in the empire—in both the western part, ruled from Rome, and the eastern part, ruled from the city of Byzantium, on the Bosporus. With the decline of the western part of the Roman Empire, the Emperor Constantine moved to Byzantium, where he built a larger city, known as Constantinople (now the city of Istanbul in Turkey). Constantinople became the capital of the Eastern Roman Empire, also known as the **Byzantine empire.**

4. The Byzantine empire was at its height from 527 to 565, under the **Emperor Justinian** and his wife **Theodora.** It included present-day Greece, Turkey, Israel, Egypt, Jordan, and Syria. The **Justinian Code** set up a legal system based on Roman laws. The beautiful church Hagia Sophia was built under Justinian. Christians in the empire called themselves **Eastern Orthodox** to distinguish themselves from the Catholic Church in Rome. In the years after 600, the Byzantine empire declined as it was subject to attacks from many outsiders. In 1453 the **Ottoman Turks,** who were Muslims, captured Constantinople and ended Christian dominance in the eastern Mediterranean.

The Rise and Spread of Islam, (622–1453)

Islam became a powerful force in the Arabian Peninsula during Mohammed's life and after his death in 632. During the next 100 years, Islam spread from the Arabian Peninsula westward to North Africa and Spain, as well as to other parts of the Middle East. In later years, it was brought to Asia and Africa, south of the Sahara, and by the last half of the 20th century, Islam was a major religion in many nations of Africa (for example, Morocco, Nigeria) and Asia (for example, Bangladesh, Indonesia). There is also a large Muslim community in the Philippines.

Upon Mohammed's death, Muslims chose a leader who was called **caliph.** The first caliph was *Abu Bakr,* the father of Mohammed's wife, Aisha. After his death, control of the **caliphate** (the Muslim-dominated lands in the Arabian Peninsula and those to the immediate west and north) passed eventually to the **Umayyad** clan. Under the **Caliph Muswiyah,** the Umayyads made Damascus the Muslim capital in 661. However, Umayyad leadership was opposed by the followers of **Ali** (the husband of *Fatimah,* Mohammed's daughter), who served as caliph from 656 until he was assassinated in 661. Ali's followers eventually formed the **Shi'ite** branch of Muslims, in opposition to the **Sunni** Muslims.

Shi'ite Muslims drew up their own ideas about Islam. One of these was that the correct interpreters of the Koran were the descendants of Ali, especially twelve leaders known as **imams.** They believe that the twelfth imam, who disappeared about 1,000 years ago, will reappear as the **mahdi** and save the world. Shi'ite Muslims (from the Arabic phrase *Shi'a Ali,* the party of Ali) currently make up 10 percent of the world's approximately 900 million Muslims. The largest group of Shi'ites is in Iran. Ninety percent of the world's Muslims are Sunnis (from the Arabic word *sunna,* customs), who accept individuals other than Ali's descendants as the true successors to Mohammed. The schism (division, split) into two Muslim branches or sects, which began in the late 600s after Ali's assassination, continues into the 1990s, with the growth of many sub-sects and smaller groups.

The Umayyad dynasty lasted from 638 to 750. During that time, its conquests spread Islam throughout three continents.

1. In North Africa and Western Europe (Portugal, Spain, and France) until the Muslims were defeated by Charles Martel in 732 at Tours (in France).

2. In Southwest Asia (in Jerusalem, the Caliph Omar built a mosque over a holy site; see Part III of this unit) and South Asia (people in the Indus River Valley became Muslims; for further information, see Unit II on India).

There were many reasons for the successful territorial expansion of the Umayyads and the spread of Islam. One important reason was

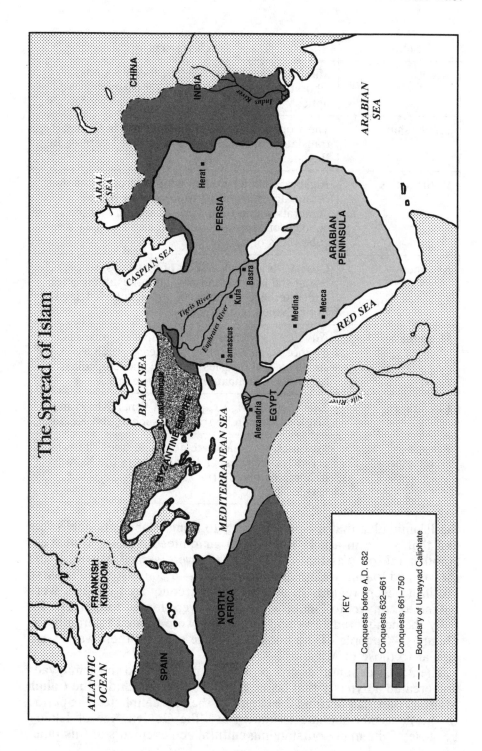

The Spread of Islam

KEY

Conquests before A.D. 632

Conquests, 632–661

Conquests, 661–750

Boundary of Umayyad Caliphate

Subject	Achievement
Science	Manufacture of glass, chemical compounds, laboratory equipment, books on chemistry and optics
Scholarship	The works of Greeks, Persians, and Indians were translated into Arabic; the House of Learning in Baghdad
Mathematics	Algebra; number system adopted from India and eventually transmitted to Europe as Arabic numerals; same for a decimal system and the concept of zero; a system to calculate square and cube roots of numbers
Astronomy	Observatories, calculation of distances in space, use of the astrolabe in navigation, estimating the circumference of the earth and acknowledging it to be shaped like a sphere
Medicine	Advances in surgery and anesthetics, pharmacies, diagnosis and treatment of diseases such as smallpox and measles, medical encyclopedias, hospitals, examinations for physicians
Literature	*The Arabian Nights,* poems of Omar Khayyam, histories written by travelers such as Ibn-Khaldun
Art and architecture	Mosques with elaborate details of trees, flowers, geometric designs, and writing from the Koran; illuminated manuscripts; colorful carpets and textiles

the Islamic idea that it was necessary to bring Islam to nonbelievers and that to die in a **holy war (jihad)** guaranteed a place in heaven. Another reason was that the Umayyads were skilled warriors, and they hoped to gain wealth and fertile lands—a contrast to their harsh life in a desert region. In addition, many conquered peoples were willing to convert to Islam, while others were forced to convert. Finally the conquered Jews and Christians were treated tolerantly (as dhimmis—"people of the book") because some of their ways were similar to those of Muslims.

The **Abbasids,** another group of Muslims, defeated the Umayyads and created a dynasty that lasted from 750 to 1250. Under the **Caliph Mansur, Bahgdad** became the capital of the new caliphate. The period of the Abassid caliphate is known as "the Golden Age of Islam" because of the many outstanding cultural achievements at this time.

The achievements in the Muslim world came at a time when much of Europe was experiencing a period known as the Dark Ages. Accomplishments under the Abbasid caliphate reached Europe through trade and commerce and shaped many features of European culture.

After 1200 the Abbasids declined. Several factors brought about the end of the Golden Age of Islam as well as the Abbasid dynasty. First, it was difficult for the Abbasids to keep control over such a large area. Moreover, many Muslim groups, such as the Arabs, Persians, and Turks, did not get along well with each other. Secondly, the **Crusades** (1095–1200) caused much death and destruction in the Middle East. The Crusades were attempts by Europeans to take over Jerusalem and other Christian holy sites from the Muslims. Eventually, the **Seljuk Turks,** a Muslim people who had taken over Abbasid territory, were able to defeat the European forces. As a result of the Crusades, however, people from both Europe and the Middle East learned much about each other, and trade and commerce between them increased. This process of cultural diffusion enabled Europe to benefit from the Muslim cultural and scientific advances. Finally, the Abbasids were unable to beat back attacks on their lands by the Turks and the Mongols.

The Ottoman Empire, (1453–1918)

The **Ottomans** were one of several Turkish peoples who eventually took over the territory once held by the Abbasids. They also captured Constantinople in 1453, thereby ending the Byzantine empire. All this territory, which consisted of land in North Africa, southeastern Europe, and Southwest Asia, formed the Ottoman Empire. The city of Constantinople was now called **Istanbul,** and it became the center of the empire in what is present-day Turkey. The city's famous Hagia Sophia church was made a mosque.

The name "Ottoman" comes from **Osman,** a Turkish leader in 1300. However, the most famous Ottoman ruler (called sultan) was **Suleiman the Magnificent** (1521–1566), under whom the empire reached the height of its power. He was also called "Suleiman the Lawgiver" because of many legal, educational, and military changes he made. For a time, the empire was well-organized and run, functioning basically as a conquering army constantly at war.

The Ottoman Turks developed a good set of administrators, similar to a civil service, to help run the vast territory in the empire. The attempt by the Ottoman Turks to expand their empire farther into Europe was finally stopped at the Battle of Vienna in 1683.

During the 1800s, the empire began to decline. Reasons for its decline included corruption and inefficiency on the part of the rulers, as well as their inability to hold together so many different peoples. Many of the subject people wished to break free from Ottoman con-

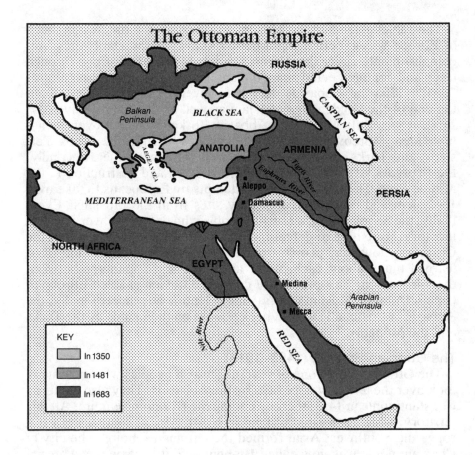

trol. Several short wars with other nations weakened Ottoman rule
and caused a loss of territory. Territorial losses also resulted from
European imperialism. Finally, the Ottomans failed to modernize and
keep up with the growth in industry, technology, learning, science,
weapons, and trade that was occurring in Western Europe. As a result, the declining empire became known as "the sick man of Europe."

The final blow to the empire came in 1918 with the end of World
War I. The Turks fought on the side of Germany and Austria-Hungary
and lost the war. Consequently, the Middle Eastern lands that belonged to the empire were taken away and placed under the control
of the newly formed League of Nations. The League created **mandates**
in these lands (Palestine, Iraq, Syria), which were placed under the
rule of England and France. (A mandate was permission to govern
an area temporarily, until the area was considered ready for independence.) By 1923, all that remained of the Ottoman Empire was
the nation of Turkey. In that year, Turkey was declared a republic

under **Mustapha Kemal Ataturk,** who became the country's first president.

20th-Century Nationalism

The desire of a group of people to establish their own nation in a specific territory can be described as **nationalism.** Nationalist movements in the 20th century have resulted in many new nations.

Turkey. Under President Ataturk, Turkey tried to break away from traditional Middle Eastern ways and become a modernized and Westernized nation. To do this, many changes were carried out. Among them were: abolition of the fez (a headress); ending government support of Islam as the official religion, replacing Islamic laws with a civil law code; ordering that the Turkish language be written in Roman letters instead of Arabic.

Arab Nationalism. The nationalistic desires of different groups of Arabs was evident in both the African and Asian parts of the Middle East.

1. **Algeria.** Algeria came under French control in the 19th century. Algerian nationalism grew in the 20th century and posed a problem for France after the end of World War II in 1945. France's refusal to leave Algeria led to a long and bloody war between 1954 and 1962. Peace talks in 1962 finally brought an end to the war, and Algeria became an independent nation. Its first leader was **Ahmed Ben Bella.**

2. **Lebanon and Syria.** After World War I, France held mandates in Lebanon and Syria. However, after World War II, Lebanon and Syria became free nations when the French left peacefully. Independence came to both nations in 1946.

3. **Iraq and Jordan.** Britain was given mandates over both Iraq and Jordan after World War I. Iraq became independent in 1923, but Britain held on to its mandate in what was then called Trans-Jordan until 1946.

4. **Egypt and Saudi Arabia.** From the late 1800s until 1922, Egypt was a British protectorate. However, in 1922 Egypt became a free constitutional monarchy, although Britain controlled Egypt's foreign affairs. This lasted until 1936, when Egypt gained more self-government. Saudi Arabia, which was formerly colonized, became a nation in 1927. Its name came from **Ibn Saud,** the head of a Muslim sect that had established its power in most of the Arabian Peninsula.

Zionism. This term is used for the nationalistic desire of Jews to re-establish a nation of their own. The Zionist goal was achieved in 1948 with the establishment of **Israel,** which was located in Palestine, with borders somewhat similar to those of the ancient Israelite kingdoms. The territorial goals of Zionists and Arab nationalists conflicted in Palestine, especially while the area was a British mandate from 1920 to 1948. The conflict continues to the present day, with four major wars having been fought between Israel and the Arabs since 1948. (A brief examination of this conflict follows.)

Background of the Arab-Israeli Conflict

The conflict between Israel and the Arab nations is over **sovereignty** (political control) in the land called Palestine. This small strip of land on the eastern shore of the Mediterranean Sea has been inhabited by Jews and Arabs for thousands of years and, as you read earlier, has been under the dominance of different rulers at many times in history.

1. **Jewish sovereignty** in Palestine existed for about 1,000 years. However, with the Roman conquest in 70 A.D., many Jews were forced to leave what for them was "the holy land." This dispersion of Jews, with many eventually settling in Europe, North Africa, Asia, and later in the Americas, is known as the **diaspora.** (The word "diaspora" today can mean any place in the world where a people live outside of their original homeland.) Jews in the diaspora generally led difficult lives, especially in Europe. They were often persecuted for their religious beliefs (such persecution against Jews is referred to as **anti-Semitism**) and were frequently forced to live in separate areas of cities, called **ghettoes.** The ghettoes, as well as village settlements, often suffered from violent attacks, called **pogroms.** By the late 19th century, the majority of Jews lived in the diaspora; yet, there was continuous Jewish habitation in Palestine from the Roman conquest into the 19th century. The movement for the restoration of a Jewish nation in Palestine (Zionism) was sparked in the late 1800s by **Theodore Herzl,** an Austrian Jew and journalist who wrote a book called *The Jewish State*. In the early 1900s, Zionists increased their efforts to help persecuted Jews immigrate to Palestine. At the same time, Zionists tried to get the ruling Ottoman Turks to grant territory for a Jewish state. Jews supported Britain in World War I against the Turks; Chaim Weizmann, the English chemist, contributed to the British war effort with his scientific achievements.

2. **Arab sovereignty** in Palestine can be traced to the **Umayyad conquest** in 638 A.D., which began a long era of Muslim control that lasted until the end of World War I (1918). Different Arab dynasties held power in Palestine from the 7th to the 15th centuries. From 1453 until World War I, sovereignty was held by the Ottoman Turks, who were not Arabs. However, Arab habitation in Palestine was continuous during the period of Ottoman Turkish rule. The Arabs did not like the Turks and wanted to establish their own nation in the area, as did the Jews. Consequently, the Arabs sided with the British in World War I in the struggle against the Turks. With the end of the war, Britain was given temporary control (the British mandate) over Palestine by the League of Nations.

3. During the period when Palestine was under the **British mandate** (1920–1948), Jews and Arabs continued to press their nationalistic claims. Britain made territorial promises to both groups and issued an important document in 1917 called the **Balfour Declaration.** Named after Lord Balfour, the English statesman, the document proposed that Great Britain would view ". . . with favor the establishment in Palestine of a national home for the Jewish people, . . . it being . . . understood that nothing shall be done which may prejudice the civil and religious rights of . . . non-Jewish communities. . . ."

Encouraged by the Balfour Declaration, Jews began to increase their immigration to Palestine, where they bought land from some Arabs and cultivated areas left unused by the Turks. Arab protests against Jews grew into riots and violent confrontations. Britain found it difficult to maintain peace between the two sides and was further weakened by its involvement in World War II (1939–1945). World War II was also the time when persecution against Jews in Europe reach an unprecedented level, with the killing of 6 million Jews by the Germans in the **Holocaust.** This tragedy convinced many Jews that the only safe place for them would be their own nation in Palestine.

At the end of World War II, Britain decided to give up its mandate over Palestine and asked the United Nations to resolve the conflict between the Arabs and Jews in Palestine. In 1947 the UN decided to partition Palestine into two states—a Jewish state and an Arab state. The city of Jerusalem, which was holy to both Jews and Muslims, was to be under UN supervision. Jews accepted this decision and declared their state of Israel in 1948. Arabs both in Palestine and in the new Arab nations outside of Palestine rejected the partition plan. In May 1948, six Arab nations—Egypt, Iraq, Trans-Jordan (later to be called Jordan), Syria, Lebanon, and Saudi Arabia—declared war on Israel. Although the combined Arab forces were larger and better equipped, they were unable to accomplish their goal of destroying Israel. A truce arranged by the UN in 1949 ended the fighting.

The Four Arab-Israeli Wars

1. **The War For Independence, 1948–49.** (This was described above.) Even though the Arabs failed in their goal to drive "the Jews into the sea," they still refused to accept the UN Partition Plan of 1947. In addition, they also refused to recognize the state of Israel even though most of the world recognized the new state.

Israel is the only democracy in the Middle East, and although it was established as a Jewish state, Israel permits religious freedom to all people within its borders. Nevertheless, during the 1948 to 1949 war, over 700,000 Palestinian Arabs fled from Israel to Arab lands, thus becoming refugees. Some of these people fled because they

Israel Before 1967 War

Beirut
LEBANON
Damascus
Tyre
SYRIA
Nahariya
Kuneitra
Akkon
Hadera
Beit Shean
Netanya
JORDAN
Pteah Til
Tel Aviv
Jaffa
Jerusalem
Amman
Gaza
Hebron
El Arish
Kerak
Suez Canal
Ma'an
Suez
SINAI
Eilat
Aqaba
Mudawwara
Gulf of Suez
Gulf of Eilat
Abu Rudeis
SAUDI ARABIA
EGYPT
Dahab

The shaded area shows the boundaries of Israel that existed between 1949 and 1967. At its narrowest point, near the city of Netanya, Israel is only 9 miles wide.

feared the fighting. Many others were urged to leave by Arab armies, who promised to let the Palestinians return once the expected victory over Israel had been achieved.

This first Arab-Israeli war also affected the status of Jerusalem. The Israelis gained control of the western part of the city, while Jordan seized East Jerusalem, which contained the city's important holy sites. Jordan promised to permit equal access to these holy Christian,

Jewish, and Muslim sites for members of the three religions. (However, Jordan never permitted Jews to visit their holy sites.)

2. The 1956 War. Under President **Gamal Abdel Nasser,** Egypt nationalized (took over) from England the Suez Canal in 1956 and prohibited Israel from using the canal. Moreover, terrorist raids into Israel by Egypt and by other Arab nations were causing many deaths. As a result, Egypt and Israel went to war again. However, this time France and England joined with Israel and attacked Egyptian forces along the Suez Canal. Israel defeated the Egyptian army in the Sinai Peninsula and occupied the entire region. The UN arranged a cease-fire ending the war. Egypt kept the Suez Canal and demanded that Israel give back the Sinai Peninsula. Israel agreed to give back the Sinai, hoping that in return Egypt would recognize the state of Israel and agree to peace. A United Nations Emergency Force (UNEF) was sent to keep peace on Israel's borders.

3. The Six-Day War, 1967. Egypt and the other Arab nations continued to refuse to recognize Israel and stepped up their terrorist attacks. Egypt built up its forces in the Sinai Desert, forbade Israel to use the Suez Canal, and closed the Gulf of Aqaba to Israeli shipping. It also ordered the UNEF to leave. These measures, along with Egypt's continued threats to destroy Israel, led the Israelis to strike at Egypt in early June 1967. Although Egypt was well-supplied with Russian equipment and was supported by other Arab nations who attacked Israel, Israel was able to defend itself successfully for the third time in 19 years. Arab armies which attacked Israel from the north, east, and south were thrown back, and Israel took over large amounts of land—the **Sinai Peninsula** and **Gaza** (from Egypt), the **West Bank** of the Jordan River and **East Jerusalem** (from Jordan, who had taken these areas in the 1948 to 1949 war), and the **Golan Heights** (from Syria). The war lasted for six days. Israel annexed East Jerusalem and the Golan Heights, making them part of Israel. Israel offered to negotiate for the other newly won territories if the Arabs would sign a peace treaty and recognize Israel's right to exist.

After the war, Israel held occupied territory, such as the West Bank, that contained a large Arab population. As thousands of people fled, the number of Arab refugees in Arab nations such as Lebanon and Syria increased. Many Arab refugees were forced to live in camps with poor facilities and which served as training grounds for terrorist activity against Israel.

In November 1967 the UN passed Resolution 242 calling for all warring nations to recognize one another and make peace and for Israel to withdraw from the occupied lands. The Arab nations continued their refusal to recognize Israel, and Israel refused to return territory until it received recognition.

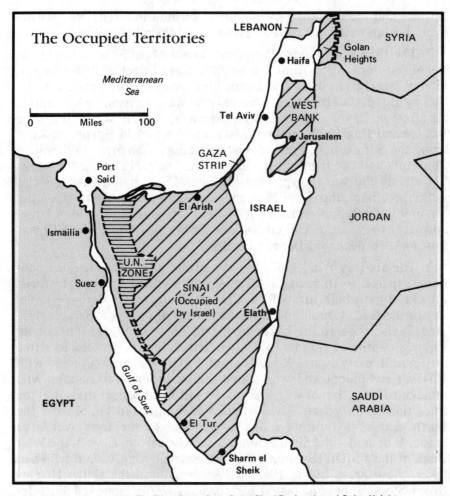

The occupied territories 1978: The West Bank, Gaza Strip, Sinai Peninsula and Golan Heights.

A close look at the map of Israel before 1967 indicates why Israel is reluctant to give back the West Bank and Gaza Strip. These areas give Israel what is known as defensible borders.

4. **The Yom Kippur War, 1973.** The fourth Arab-Israeli War began on October 6, 1973 (Yom Kippur, the holiest day of the year to Jews), when Egypt attacked Israel by surprise across the Suez Canal. The war lasted almost a month, with Egypt gaining a small amount of land in the Sinai. Syrian troops attacked Israel on the Golan Heights but were beaten back. Several other Arab countries sent troops to fight. The Soviet Union increased its arms shipments to the Arabs, hoping to avoid another victory by Israel. To counter the Soviets, the United States sent help to Israel. Oil-rich Arab nations pressured the United States not to help Israel and began an oil embargo (a refusal to sell oil). Once again, the UN arranged a cease-fire to end the fighting. In

1973 the UN also passed Resolution 338, calling for "negotiations . . . between the parties concerned . . . aimed at establishing . . . peace in the Middle East."

Developments Since 1973

1. In 1977, Egyptian President **Anwar Sadat** visited Israel to begin peace talks. He was the only Arab leader to ever visit Israel. Later in the year, Israeli Prime Minister **Menachem Begin** visited Egypt.

2. In 1979, at Camp David near Washington, D.C., an Egyptian-Israeli Peace Treaty was signed by Sadat and Begin. President Jimmy Carter of the United States brought the two leaders together. The peace treaty provided that: (1) Egypt and Israel would recognize each other and exchange ambassadors; (2) the state of war that existed between them from 1948 to 1979 was over; (3) Israel would return the Sinai Peninsula to Egypt, in stages between 1979 and 1982. A UN peacekeeping force would be restablished on the border; and (4) negotiations would begin on the status of the Palestinian Arabs.

3. Many Arab nations were angry at Egypt's actions and broke off relations. In 1981 Muslim extremists assassinated Sadat, and **Hosni Mubarak** became the new Egyptian president.

4. In 1982 Israel invaded Lebanon in response to repeated terrorist attacks by the Palestine Liberation Organization (PLO) and the inability of the Lebanese government to control PLO actions. By 1984, the PLO forces had left Lebanon. The Israeli action in Lebanon stirred much controversy among Israelis, and after the 1984 Israeli elections, its army was pulled back from Lebanon except for a small "security zone" in southern Lebanon. While Israel was in Lebanon, it became an ally of a Lebanese Christian militia (a small army). This militia massacred thousands of Palestinians in Sabra and Shatila, two refugee camps in Beirut. Although Israel was not involved in this tragedy, it came under criticism.

5. Also in 1982, Israel, in compliance with the peace treaty with Egypt, withdrew completely from the Sinai Peninsula.

6. In 1987 an uprising by Palestinians in the West Bank and Gaza Strip began. This uprising, called the **Intifada,** was a protest against continued Israeli occupation of the land it had won in war. Many Palestinians supported the PLO and its leader, **Yasir Arafat,** and their goal to establish a Palestinian state on the West Bank. However, the PLO was branded as a terrorist group by Israel, because it was one of several Arab organizations that had carried out murderous actions against civilians in the Middle East and elsewhere in the world. Consequently, the Israeli government refused to negotiate with the PLO over the status of the occupied territories. Within Israel, the question of what to do with the occupied territories has created discussion and divisiveness. Many Israelis want to keep the territories because they

view a Palestinian state as a military threat and they claim that a Palestinian state already exists in Jordan. Others want to meet some of the Palestinian demands. As the 1990s began, the status of the occupied territories was still unresolved and the Intifada continued.

Arab Views of the Conflict

1. The creation of Israel in 1948 was wrong and was another sign of Western imperialism in the Middle East.

2. Israel was established on land that belonged to Arabs.

3. Arabs never accepted the UN Partition Plan of 1947.

4. The majority of people in the Middle East are Arabs. Israeli society and culture represent a threat to Arab values.

5. Israel's creation stemmed from European guilt about what happened to Jews during the Holocaust. It is wrong to take out this guilt on the Arabs. A Jewish state should have been created somewhere, but not in the Middle East.

6. Palestinians deserve a land of their own, as promised in the Balfour Declaration as well as during the British mandate period.

7. The UN has condemned Israeli actions in the occupied territories.

8. Jerusalem is a holy city to Muslims, as it contains the Dome of the Rock and the El Aksa Mosque and is the third holiest city after Mecca and Medina. Jerusalem should be under Muslim authority, not occupied by Israel.

9. Arab sovereignty in Palestine, prior to 1948, was more recent than Jewish sovereignty.

10. Israel seeks to expand beyond its borders.

11. Israel must give back land it gained in wars, as a condition for any peace negotiations.

12. The Intifada shows the wrongfulness of Israeli occupation and the need for a Palestinian state.

Israeli Views of the Conflict

1. Israel is located on land that was the original homeland of the Jewish people and that was promised to them in the Bible.

2. Arabs sold land to Jews prior to 1948; other Arabs fled from the land in the 1948–1949 war.

3. The UN Partition Plan was approved by a majority of the world's nations.

4. As a small nation of 4 million people, Israel does not represent a threat to the 100 million Arabs in 15 nations in the region. Arabs who still live in Israel have a high standard of living and live in the only democracy in the Middle East.

5. A Jewish state is needed as a safe place and refuge, because of the centuries of anti-Semitism in Europe and in Arab lands.

6. Jordan exists as a state for Palestinians. It was created, illegally,

by the British in 1922 from 77 percent of the land that Britain held as a mandate from the League of Nations. There is no need or obligation to create a second Palestinian state. Most Jordanians today are Palestinians.

7. UN votes condemning Israel are signs of Arab ill-feeling and reflect Arab pressure on oil-poor countries to vote with the Arabs or face oil embargoes.

8. Jerusalem was the capital of Jewish kingdoms in ancient times and is a holy city to Jews, containing the Western Wall and the sites of the first two temples. These areas were restricted to Jews when Jordan ruled Jerusalem from 1948 to 1967. Today, the Israeli government permits the Muslim holy sites to be watched over by members of the Israeli Muslim community.

9. Jewish sovereignty in Palestine was earlier in history than that of the Arabs.

10. If Israel had not been attacked so often by the Arabs, it would not have any land other than that given to it under the 1947 Partition Plan. Israel has never intentionally tried to take away land from any Arab nation, while it has been the Arabs who have tried to take away and destroy Israeli land.

11. Israel is willing to negotiate with the Arabs and return land if the Arabs end the war they have waged since 1948. With the exception of Egypt (since 1979), no Arab nation recognizes Israel's right to exist. Israel has shown that it is willing to exchange land for peace (for example, the return of the Sinai to Egypt).

12. The Intifada is just another phase of the attempt by Arabs since 1948 to destroy Israel. The Intifada would end if the Arabs were to recognize Israel's right to exist.

Other Elements at the Start of the 1990s

1. The United States and the Soviet Union have put pressure on the parties to resolve their differences peacefully.

2. Both Israel and the Arab nations have increased their arms spending.

3. Iraq's threats of nuclear and gas attacks against Israel have caused concern about the possibility of a fifth Arab-Israeli war.

4. The Arabs are worried about the settlement in Israel and the occupied territories of Russian Jews, now allowed more freedom to emigrate from the Soviet Union.

5. The PLO has renounced terrorism and talks about an international peace conference, which the United States supports. However, it has been delayed by disagreements over Palestinian representation.

Other Political Developments in the Middle East, 1979–1990

Iran-Islamic Fundamentalism and the War with Iraq. The Shah of Iran, **Mohammed Reza Pahlavi,** introduced many Western and modern practices to his country during the 1960s and 1970s. However, many religious leaders felt that traditional Islamic customs were threatened by Western ideas. These leaders were Islamic **fundamentalists** who wanted to keep Islam pure and fundamental, without any "contamination" from the outside world. They opposed the shah and were also upset with the dictatorial manner in which he ruled. Riots and demonstrations against the shah forced him to leave Iran in 1979. In his place the country was run by an Islamic Revolutionary Council, led by **Ayatollah Ruholla Khomeini.** This Iranian Revolution, also known as the Islamic Revolution, caused concern in other Muslim nations in the Middle East. The Ayatollah's government was anti-Western and held 52 Americans as hostages from 1979 to 1981. Although Khomeini died in 1989, the new rulers of Iran have followed similar foreign and domestic policies.

In 1980, war between Iran and Iraq broke out when Iraq, under its leader **Saddam Hussein,** attacked Iran. Known as both the **Iran-Iraq War** and the **Gulf War,** this confict had several causes. These included: *political* causes—each nation wanted to dominate the Persian Gulf area; frequent criticism by Hussein and Khomeini of each other; border disputes existed; *social* causes—Iraq feared the "export" of the Iranian Revolution; there were great religious differences between the Sunni Muslims of Iraq and the Shi'ite Muslims of Iran; and *economic* causes—the oil fields of the Persian Gulf area are very valuable; the Gulf itself is the most important route for transporting oil from the Middle East. The fighting ended in 1988 under a UN-supervised agreement, but it caused hundreds of thousands of casualties and hurt the economies of both nations. The war ended as a stalemate.

Lebanon—Civil War and Syrian Occupation. The civil war that has been going on in Lebanon since 1975 can be explained by examining its political and religious history. When the French mandate in Lebanon ended in 1943, a government was created that was supposed to strike a balance between Lebanese Christians and Muslims. Since the Christians were then the majority group, it was decided that most of the top government positions (such as president, armed forces commander) would go to Christians. From the 1940s to the 1970s, Lebanon prospered economically and was peaceful. However, Muslims became the majority group, and they wanted changes in the political structure to give them more power. It was also in this period that Palestinian refugees, including PLO leaders, settled in Lebanon as a result of the Arab-Israeli wars. From these settlements, many Palestinians made terrorist raids into Israel. Frequently, Israeli forces attacked these settlements in retaliation. Lebanese Christians, represented by the **Phalange** Party, were against the Palestinian presence in Lebanon.

In 1975 Muslims and Christians began to fight each other. In addition, different Muslim groups began to fight one another and different Christian groups also began to fight one another. Each of the groups formed its own private army, or **militia.** In 1976, Syria, under **President Hafez el-Assad** sent in troops as requested by the **Arab League** (an organization of Arab nations in the Middle East). Although Syria's purpose was to restore order, at various times the Syrians have supported different militias in Lebanon. By 1990 there were 40,000 Syrian soldiers in Lebanon, and President Assad began to drop hints of incorporating Lebanon into a "greater Syria."

Other Middle Eastern nations, such as Iran and Libya, have also supported one or more of the warring groups. Some of these groups, such as the Islamic Jihad, have carried out terrorist activities against foreigners and other Lebanese in order to focus world attention on their political goals. These terrorist activities have included taking citizens of France, the United States, Germany, and Russia as hostages and sometimes killing them, hijacking a TWA airliner, and killing American and French soldiers in a suicide bomb attack. As the 1990s began, there was no single government in Lebanon acceptable to all its people and able to bring stability to the nation. The civil war resulted in separate **enclaves** (closed-in areas) in Beirut and elsewhere, under the control of whichever militia proved to be the strongest. The Lebanese economy has been ruined by the war.

War in Afghanistan (1979–1989). In 1979, a Marxist pro-Soviet government came to power in Afghanistan. It faced opposition by the majority of Afghan people, who began an armed struggle against it. The Soviet Union invaded Afghanistan, claiming that it was reacting to a request by the Afghan government. However, many observers believed that the real reasons for the Soviet actions were to gain access to oil and gas deposits in Afghanistan and possibly to reach through Iran into the Persian Gulf. The Soviets also may have been afraid of the impact of Islamic fundamentalism in Afghanistan and Iran on the Muslim communities in the Soviet Union. The Soviet military action was condemned by nations around the globe and caused controversy in the Soviet Union itself. The Afghan fighters, the **Mujahadeen,** were supplied by the United States and were able to deny the Russians a victory. In 1989 the Russians retreated from Afghanistan with severe military and political losses.

Libya and State-Supported Terrorism. Even since **Colonel Muammar Qaddafi** came to power in 1969, Libya has supported terrorist groups. These groups have carried out actions mainly against Israeli and United States interests. In 1986, American bombers raided Libya in retaliation for violence directed against Americans in Europe and the Middle East.

Pan-Arabism. This term refers to the idea of all Arab nations uniting and standing together on political and economic issues. The movement reached a high point while **President Nasser** ruled Egypt. However, since his death in 1970, and due to several disputes among the Arab nations, the movement has died down. The movement was tied to the idea of Arab socialism (government control of industry and the attempt to improve living conditions for all Arabs).

QUESTIONS

Matching. Match the society in column 1 with the achievement of that society in column 2.

Column 1	Column 2
____ 1. Egyptians	A. code of justice
____ 2. Sumerians	B. cuneiform, city-states
____ 3. Babylonians	C. alphabet, maritime activity
____ 4. Phoenicians	D. iron weapons
____ 5. Hittites	E. hieroglyphics

Timeline. For each event below, select the number for the time period in which the event occurred.

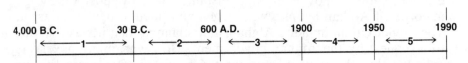

1. Partition of Palestine

2. Conquests of Alexander the great; Hellenistic influence

3. Balfour declaration

4. Roman destruction of "the second temple"

5. End of the British Mandate in Palestine

6. End of Ottoman sovereignty in Palestine

7. The "June (Six-Day) War"

8. Two nations that had previously been at war sign a treaty of peace

9. Iraqi invasion of Kuwait

10. Intifada

Issues. Each of the statements below refers to one of the three agreements indicated by a letter. For each statement, choose the correct letter.

A. Balfour Declaration

B. Egyptian-Israeli Peace Treaty

C. Partition of Palestine

1. Israeli sovereignty recognized by an Arab nation.

2. Occurred just before the first Arab-Israeli War.

3. This occurred before all the others.

4. Occurred after the most recent Arab-Israeli War.

5. Issued before the British Mandate went into effect.

6. Occurred after all the others.

7. Decision by the United Nations at the end of the British Mandate.

8. The Yom Kippur War (The October War) occurred six years prior to this agreement.

9. Occurred as a result of face-to-face meetings between nations that once were enemies.

ESSAYS

1. Historical events have both causes and consequences. For each of the following, describe one cause and one consequence:
   A. Partition of Palestine (1947)
   B. Arab oil embargo (1973–74)
   C. Lebanon civil war (1975–present)
   D. Overthrow of the Shah of Iran (1979)
   E. Egyptian-Israeli Peace Treaty (1979)
   F. Iran-Iraq War (1980–88)
   G. Intifada (1987–present)
   H. Iraqi invasion of Kuwait (1990)

2. The dispute between Arabs and Israelis has led to several wars since 1948.
   A. Discuss two arguments offered by Arabs on this dispute.
   B. Discuss two arguments offered by Israelis on this dispute.

UNIT TWO
SOUTH AND SOUTHEAST ASIA

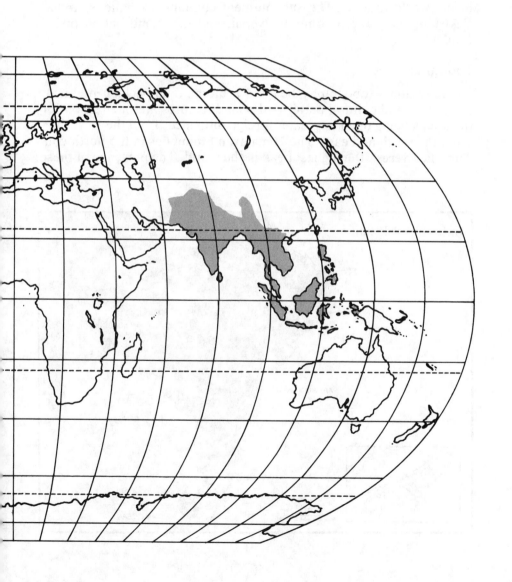

I. Physical Geography (The Physical Setting of South Asia)

Overview

The region known as South Asia is also called the Indian or Asian **subcontinent.** It is a very large area, bigger in size and population than all of Western Europe. Consequently, it could be called a continent by itself except for the fact that it is attached to the Asian mainland. The subcontinent is slightly less than half the size of the United States. India, called "Bharat" in that country, is the seventh largest nation in the world in area. The subcontinent contains six nations: India, Pakistan, Bangladesh, Bhutan, Nepal, and the island nation of Sri Lanka.

Topography

The region's topography has had a dramatic impact on political, economic, and cultural patterns. Its land features are one reason for the area's being open to greater foreign influences from the west than from the north and east. The **Himalayan Mountains** in the north contain **Mt. Everest,** the highest peak in the world. The presence of these

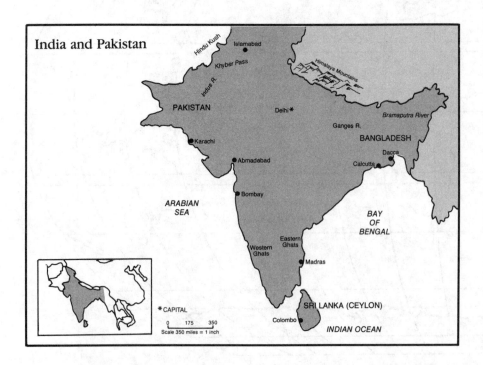

India and Pakistan

mountains has acted as a barrier to contact with peoples to the north and northeast of the region, separating the subcontinent from the rest of Asia. In the northwest, openings in the mountains, such as the **Khyber Pass,** have resulted in the movement of peoples, goods, and ideas. This movement, an example of **cultural diffusion,** has generally been from west to east and has included the Aryans (2000 B.C.), Alexander the Great (327 B.C.), Muslims (1000 A.D.), and Afghan refugees (1980s). As a result, a traveler to the subcontinent today would find a mixture of many ethnic groups, religions, and languages.

South of the Himalaya Mountains lies the **Indo-Gangetic Plain,** also known as the **Hindustan Plain.** This is a very fertile area and home to more than half of India's population. Farther south is the **Deccan Plateau,** lying between the **Eastern** and **Western Ghats.** Many mineral resources are found here. Moving farther south, one finds good farm land near the coasts.

The **Thar Desert,** the main desert in the region, is in the western part of the subcontinent. Its relative flatness and dryness have been barriers to settlement.

Water Bodies

The subcontinent, which is actually a peninsula jutting out from the Asian mainland, is surrounded by the Arabian Sea, the Indian Ocean, and the Bay of Bengal. The three chief river systems begin in the Himalayas: the **Indus River** flows through Pakistan and into the Arabian Sea; the **Ganges** and **Brahmaputra** rivers flow through India, converge in Bangladesh, and empty out into the Bay of Bengal. The Indus River Valley was the site of the earliest known civilization in the subcontinent, which was located at Mohenjo-daro and Harappa in about 3000 B.C. Much flooding occurs in the soil-rich delta region of Bangladesh, due in part to the onrushing waters of the Ganges and Brahmaputra rivers. The heavy monsoon rains and occasional tidal waves are additional factors causing destruction in the delta.

Impact of the Monsoon

The **Monsoon** rains occur from June to September, bringing to the subcontinent 90 percent of its annual rainfall. They can be a blessing, bringing crop surpluses or a curse, bringing famine, flooding, and drought, depending on their timing and the amount of rain that falls. The monsoon's direction is generally northeasterly, coming across the Arabian Sea and affecting mainly north-central India and Bangladesh.

51

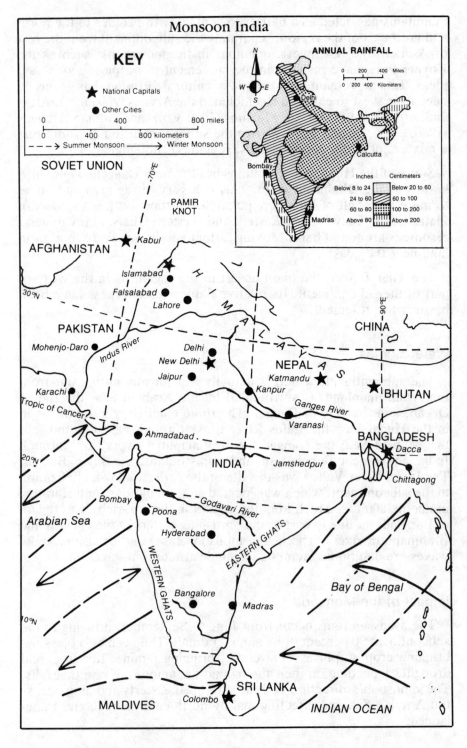

Monsoon India

KEY

★ National Capitals

● Other Cities

0 — 400 — 800 miles

0 — 400 — 800 kilometers

- - -> Summer Monsoon ——> Winter Monsoon

ANNUAL RAINFALL

N
W-E
S

0 — 200 — 400 Miles
0 — 200 — 400 Kilometers

Delhi
Bombay
Calcutta
Madras

Inches	Centimeters
Below 8 to 24	Below 20 to 60
24 to 60	60 to 100
60 to 80	100 to 200
Above 80	Above 200

SOVIET UNION

PAMIR KNOT

AFGHANISTAN
★ Kabul

30°N

★ Islamabad
Falsalabad ●
Lahore ●

HIMALAYAS

CHINA

90°E

PAKISTAN

Mohenjo-Daro ●

Indus River

Delhi ●
New Delhi ★
Jaipur ●

Kanpur ●

NEPAL
Katmandu ★

BHUTAN ★

Karachi ●
Tropic of Cancer

Ganges River
Varanasi ●

BANGLADESH

20°N

Ahmadabad ●

INDIA

Jamshedpur ●

Dacca ★
Chittagong ●

Bombay ●
Poona ●

Godavari River

Hyderabad ●

EASTERN GHATS

Arabian Sea

WESTERN GHATS

Bay of Bengal

Bangalore ●
Madras ●

10°N

0°N

SRI LANKA

MALDIVES
Colombo ★

INDIAN OCEAN

70°E

QUESTIONS

Fact or Opinion. If the statement is a fact, write F. If the statement is an opinion, write O.

1. India has been more influenced from the west than from the east.

2. A good monsoon is proof of God's blessings upon the Indian subcontinent.

3. A drought will occur if there is a poor monsoon and little water in reserve in India's dams.

4. The largest nations in physical size on the subcontinent are India and Pakistan.

Modified True-False. Read each statement carefully. If it is true, write TRUE. If it is not true, then write a word or words in place of the underlined word or words that would make the statement true.

1. A drought would occur if the monsoons give little rain.

2. The Ganges and Brahmaputra Rivers originate in the Hindu Kush mountains.

3. The Khyber Pass is in the western part of Nepal.

4. The body of water lying to India's west is the Bay of Bengal.

5. The Himalayan Mountains have prevented much cultural diffusion between India and China.

ESSAY

The monsoons can be either a "blessing" or a "curse" for the people of South Asia.

1. Why can the monsoons be a "blessing"? Give two reasons.

2. Why can the monsoons be a "curse"? Give two reasons.

II. Economic Geography (Economic Development of South Asia)

Agriculture

Over the last ten years, food production in India has increased. Self-sufficiency has been achieved, at least temporarily, despite some "bad monsoon" years. Consequently, imports from nations such as

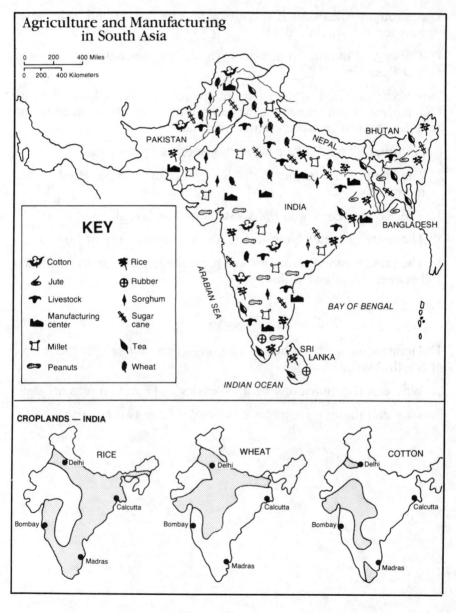

Agriculture and Manufacturing in South Asia

0   200   400 Miles
0   200   400 Kilometers

PAKISTAN

NEPAL

BHUTAN

INDIA

BANGLADESH

ARABIAN SEA

BAY OF BENGAL

SRI LANKA

INDIAN OCEAN

KEY

🐾 Cotton   🌾 Rice

🍃 Jute   ⊕ Rubber

➤ Livestock   ♦ Sorghum

🏭 Manufacturing   🎋 Sugar cane
center

⊓ Millet   ▮ Tea

🥜 Peanuts   ♠ Wheat

CROPLANDS — INDIA

RICE
Delhi
Calcutta
Bombay
Madras

WHEAT
Delhi
Calcutta
Bombay
Madras

COTTON
Delhi
Calcutta
Bombay
Madras

the United States have declined. Crop production focuses mainly on rice, wheat, cotton, tea, jute, and sugar cane.

Much of this agricultural development has resulted from the **Green Revolution,** that is, the use of modern science and technology to improve agricultural productivity. Examples of modern **technology** include laboratory-produced fertilizers, insecticides, and improved seeds, which are high-yielding and drought-resistant, such as IR-8. Scientists involved in these efforts are known as agronomists. A leading figure in this work has been the American agronomist Dr. Norman Borlaugh (winner of a Nobel Peace prize in 1970). Critics, however, have noted some negative aspects of the Green Revolution:

1. Resistance among farmers to new planting and landholding patterns.

2. Higher financial costs when using new technology and machinery (more readily used by "agribusiness," or large landholders, rather than small farmers).

3. Need for better nationwide infrastructure, such as storage facilities, dams, and highways.

4. The taste of the food produced is different from traditional crops.

AGRICULTURAL PRODUCTION IN INDIA 1972-1984

Commodity	1972	1975	1974	1984
	Thousands of metric tons			
Wheat	26.4	25.8	22.0	45.1
Rice	57.9	70.5	60.0	59.8
Barley	2.5	2.9	2.3	1.8
Corn	6.2	5.5	5.0	8.0
Potatoes	4.8	6.1	4.6	10.1
Cassava	5.9	6.3	6.3	—
Bananas	3.1	—	3.2	4.5
Peanuts	3.9	6.6	5.2	7.3
Sugar (raw)	3.3	5.3	4.3	5.5
Jute	0.8	0.8	1.0	1.6
	Millions			
Cattle	176.9	180.3	179.9	182
Sheep	43.3	40.0	40.2	42
Buffaloes	55.0	—	60.0	63
Goats	69.0	—	69.0	78
Poultry	118.0	—	118.4	150

Sources: *Encyclopedia Britannica; United States Statistical Yearbook.*

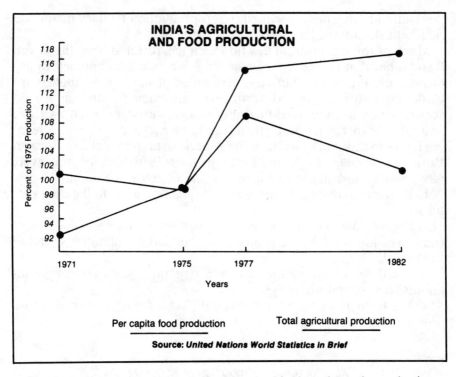

India's food production has increased greatly. As this chart shows the production in 1982 was about 117% of what it was in 1975.

Industrial Production

India has some of the world's largest steel mills and is a major producer of bauxite. Other major industrial products include textiles, machinery, cement, and scientific instruments. Recently, Indian scientists have made advances in nuclear energy and in developing space satellites. India is the most industrially advanced nation in the subcontinent, having one of the world's ten highest GNP's. Nevertheless, as is true of all industrialized societies around the globe, India must find ways of coping with the environmental consequences of industrialization. The tragic accident involving the Union Carbide Company at Bhopal in 1984 and the increasing effect of air pollution on the Taj Mahal, for example, have been of great concern to India.

Economic Conditions: Decision-Making and Planning

During the British colonial period, basic economic decisions were made by the British, primarily for their own benefit. Since independence, India has adopted elements both of a free enterprise/capitalist system and a socialist system. This combination is called a

mixed economy. Although the government controls certain parts of the economy, it tries to develop strategies to benefit all parts. These strategies can be seen in the **Five-Year Plans.** Disputes have arisen among economic planners, however, in choosing priorities and goals. Key choices involve funds for items such as heavy industry, exportable goods, small-scale cottage industries, and village development schemes. Decision-makers must keep in mind two facts about India's population:

1. More than 80 percent of the people live in villages.
2. Population growth can limit economic gains.

Although the standard of living in India and its neighboring countries has generally improved since the departure of the British, severe

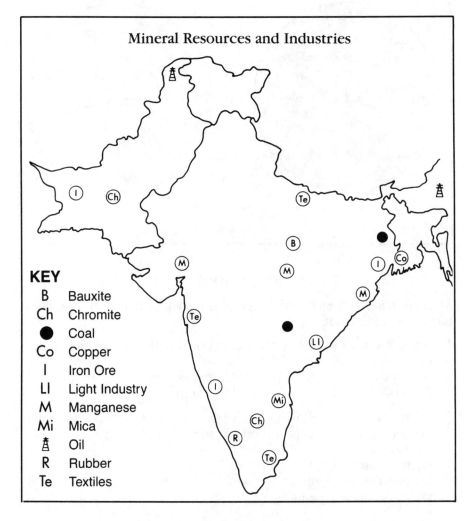

Mineral Resources and Industries

KEY

B	Bauxite
Ch	Chromite
●	Coal
Co	Copper
I	Iron Ore
Ll	Light Industry
M	Manganese
Mi	Mica
♨	Oil
R	Rubber
Te	Textiles

poverty and malnutrition still exist in many areas. These features are evident in such large cities as Calcutta as well as in the villages.

The attempts by nations such as India to sharply raise the standard of living for all citizens, as well as promote economic growth, has necessitated borrowing money from overseas and importing needed goods. Consequently, India continues to face a large foreign debt and a trade imbalance (that is, the value of imports exceeds that of exports).

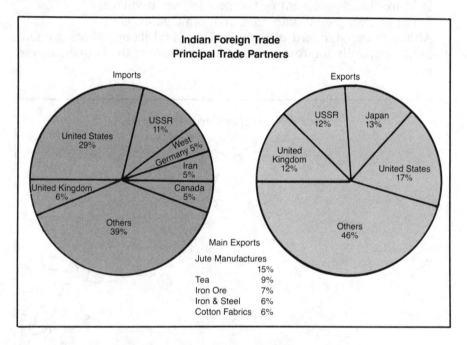

Indian Foreign Trade
Principal Trade Partners

Imports

United States 29%
USSR 11%
West Germany 5%
Iran 5%
United Kingdom 6%
Canada 5%
Others 39%

Exports

USSR 12%
Japan 13%
United Kingdom 12%
United States 17%
Others 46%

Main Exports

Jute Manufactures	15%
Tea	9%
Iron Ore	7%
Iron & Steel	6%
Cotton Fabrics	6%

QUESTIONS

Multiple Choice. Select the letter of the answer that correctly completes each statement.

1. An agronomist would be most concerned with news of an increase in
   A. cars
   B. food
   C. population
   D. tractors

2. Which of the following has the greatest effect on limiting/decreasing per capita food consumption in India?
   A. monsoons
   B. inadequate funds
   C. population increase
   D. government spending

3. To say that India is self-sufficient in agriculture means that it
   A. needs foreign aid
   B. can pay back other nations for food shipments
   C. grows enough food for its people
   D. can avoid famines

4. Norman Borlaugh would be most pleased with India's added production of
   A. space satellites
   B. steel
   C. fertilizer
   D. airplanes

5. In the 1980s, which condition was probably most responsible for stimulating economic growth in India?
   A. a small urban population
   B. an increasing infant mortality rate
   C. a diversity of languages
   D. an increased investment of capital

ESSAYS

1. The "Green Revolution" has been important in South Asia's agricultural development.
   A. Define the term "green revolution."
   B. Describe two features necessary to make this "revolution" successful.
   C. Describe two negative aspects of the "green revolution."

2. Briefly define each of the following:
   A. mixed economy
   B. trade imbalance
   C. agribusiness
   D. infrastructure

III. Human and Cultural Geography

Overview

The most important human feature of South Asia, and in particular that of India, is the size of the population. With over 800 million people, India ranks as the second largest nation on earth and is the world's most populous democracy. Pakistan and Bangladesh, after Indonesia, are the second and third largest Muslim nations in the world. The study of population patterns in these and other nations is what **demography** is all about. The ways in which a population views itself and practices certain life styles, along with the human values it holds to be important, may be thought of as its **culture.**

Demography

India's population is three times that of the United States; yet India is only about one-third the physical size of the United States. Consequently, India has a higher **population density** (population density is determined by dividing a nation's population by its area). This greater amount of crowding can be seen in such large cities as Bombay, Calcutta, Madras, and New Delhi. However, most of India's people live in rural areas. Over 80 percent of the population lives in the hundreds of thousands of villages. To "know the village," therefore, is to know India. (See below for more data about villages.)

1. **Growth rates.** A nation's annual population growth rate tells us about how fast the nation's population grows each year. The rate is expressed as a percentage and is determined by subtracting the number of deaths per thousand in a given year from the number of births per thousand in the same year. For example, India's birth rate in 1985 was 33.3 per thousand; subtract from this figure the death rate of 12.5 per thousand to arrive at a growth rate of 20.8 per thousand, or 2.08 percent. (The growth rate in the United States at the same time was less than .7 percent.) The growth-rate figure for India is very high and can crucially add to already existing problems of housing, food, and employment. Indian government officials are very concerned about the high growth rate and try, therefore, to determine ways of reducing it. Their problems stem from the fact that the high growth

Population Growth in India

1948—345 million
1957—392 million
1961—439 million
1967—501 million
1971—548 million
1977—615 million   Growth rate: 2.1% a year
1985—768 million (estimated)

SOURCES: *Encyclopaedia Britannica;* United Nations *Statistical Yearbook.*

rate is caused by a birth rate that is *increasing* and a death rate that is *decreasing*. What are the reasons for these patterns?

2. **Birth rate.** The reasons for a high birth rate in India are generally the same as those for high rates in Pakistan, Bangladesh, and other developing nations that are predominantly rural and agricultural. An agrarian society requires much manual labor, and therefore families tend to have many children to help work the land. Additional factors contributing to a high birth rate include: arranged marriages at an early age; a high infant-mortality rate; children seen as a form of "social security" for their parents in old age; desire for sons to pass on the family name and caste; the low status of women; religious motivations; and joint/extended family patterns.

3. **Death rate.** The reasons for a decreasing death rate in India are generally the same as those for decreasing death rates throughout the world. These include: increase in food production, better hygienic and sanitary conditions, and the introduction of modern medicine. (A dramatic and welcome example of the latter was the recently declared eradication of smallpox in India. This disease had long been a leading cause of death among Indians.) The result of a lower death rate means an increase in life expectancy. This has special significance for India, in light of the fact that 36.8 percent of its current population is under 14 years of age.

4. **Attempts to lower the growth rate.** The Indian government has been moderately successful in some regions with the introduction of family-planning programs. These include birth-control clinics, monetary incentives for sterilization, and "Madison Avenue" advertising campaigns preaching the advantages of having a small family. (The few instances of government-mandated birth-control tactics have met with controversy and were considered undemocratic.) Additional national strategies involve improving literacy and education rates, improving employment opportunities for women, and implementation of the Hindu Marriage Act. (This act requires a minimum age of 18 for men and of 15 for women to marry.) As India becomes more industrialized and urbanized, its birth rate may decline. Such reduction would follow a pattern that has occurred in other nations in the 20th century, such as in Japan, the United States, and West Germany.

Languages of South Asia

A great diversity of languages is found in India. Sixteen languages are recognized. Of these, the one spoken by the largest number of Indians is **Hindi.** However, it is spoken by less than half of the population, and mainly in the north. Southern Indians have local languages, such as **Tamil,** and have objected to any imposition of a uniform national language. Disputes over language have harmful political effects, and in many cases they have fostered stronger ties to people's locality than to their national government. Other principal languages in South Asia include **Bengali** (Bangladash), **Urdu** (Pakistan), and **Sinhalese** (in Sri Lanka). English is understood by small numbers of people, mainly in urban areas, throughout all nations in South Asia. Among educated people it is a unifying focus. However, many people are wary of using it as an official language because of its link to the age of imperialism.

PRINCIPAL LANGUAGES OF INDIA AND PAKISTAN	
People Speaking (in millions)	Language
170	Hindi
90	Bengali
58	Urdu
55	Telugu
42	Tamil
40	Marathi
38	Punjabi
30	Kannada
30	Gugerati
20	Malayalam
20	Oriya
15	Rajasthani
10	Assamese
8	Kashmiri

The Village

The village is central in understanding India's social structure, as villages contain such a high portion of the population. A council of elders in each village, called the **panchayat,** usually makes rules for the people about local issues, such as sanitation, streets, and family disputes. Families arrange marriages so that young people will marry within their own social group or caste. This practice is called **endogamy.** Another village practice is seen in sons' assuming the occupations held by their fathers. This custom, along with the **jajmani** system, has created self-sufficient communities. (Under the jajmani system, an economic pattern was followed whereby a jajman—a landowner—and members of a caste group would inherit the service relationships and mutual obligations that their immediate ancestors had.)

These customs, along with other traditional practices such as the limited, designated household roles for women, may undergo change as the villages become less isolated from the outside world. This isolation, historically, was the result of poor transportation and communication links. However, the increase in paved roads, electricity, schools, and the introduction of radio and television are making villagers more aware of the world around them and of modern 20th-century cultural patterns. The social changes in village life, being brought about by these forces, are proceeding slowly. It is uncertain as to which traditional cultural patterns will remain the same, which will be modified, and which will be changed completely.

Hinduism: The Main Religion in India

As with all the world's great religions, Hinduism is a system of beliefs that provides answers to some of the perennial questions humans have asked. These questions concern the origins and meaning of life and proper conduct towards others.

Over 80 percent of the people of India consider themselves Hindus. Even though there are differences in some beliefs and practices among Hindus, certain basic ideas are accepted.

1. Each human being occupies a place on the **wheel of life (mandala)**. A person's place on the mandala is determined by the law of **karma**. According to this law, what happened to a person's soul in a previous life **(incarnation)** will affect the person's current status. The soul undergoes a process of **rebirth, or reincarnation (samsara)**. Whether reincarnation results in the soul's moving "up" or "down" depends on how a person performed his or her **dharma (obligation and behavior based on family and caste)**.

2. The goal of a Hindu is to achieve **moksha (release of the soul from the cycle of birth and rebirth on the mandala)**.

3. There are many gods and goddesses in Hinduism. However, it could be said that each of these deities is but one form or manifestation of a single God. From its origin in about 3000 B.C. until now, the three chief Hindu deities have been **Brahma** (associated with creation), **Vishnu** (associated with preservation), and **Shiva** (associated with destruction). The most popularly worshiped today are Vishnu and Shiva, either in their own form or in the different male and female forms they take. Two examples of these forms are: Vishnu, often worshiped in the form of Rama or Krishna; Shiva, sometimes worshiped as an ascetic doing **yoga** (a form of meditation) or in the form of Kali or Durga.

4. There is no one specific holy text or bible in Hinduism. Rather, there are several writings that are looked to for guidance and inspiration. The *Vedas* were written somewhere between 1500 B.C. and 800 B.C., and they contain hymns dealing with creation and reverence for nature. The **Upanishads** were written about 500 B.C., and they include discussions about the soul and proper ways of behavior. The **Ramayana,** a very popular long epic poem written between 400 B.C. and 100 B.C., is about Prince Rama (an incarnation of Vishnu) and his wife Sita. The story is performed and read throughout India and Indian

communities all over the world. It is viewed as a guide for dharma, love, and devotion. The **Mahabharata,** which contains the **Bhagavad Gita,** is one of the longest and best-known poems in the world. It describes the confict between related families and kingdoms, involving exile, wars, and conquest. It is revered for its pronouncements on morality and proper behavior.

5. The **caste** system evolved as a hierarchy or ranking of social groups based on heredity and occupation. There have been four major groupings, more accurately referred to as **varnas** than as castes: **Brahmans** (priests), **Kashatriyas** (soldiers), **Vaishyas** (merchants), and **Shudras** (laborers). The **Untouchables** were considered to be outside of and beneath the caste system. In the 20th century, a Hindu is more likely to describe himself or herself as belonging to a **jati** (sub-caste) rather than simply to one of the larger varna groupings. A varna may contain dozens of jatis. With the growth in educational opportunities and of newer and more technological occupations, especially in urban areas, the link between varna and occupation is disappearing. For example, someone whose ancestry has been in a jati within Shudras may become educated and hold down a job as a computer engineer. Additional things to remember about the caste system are:

1. Ritual purity and avoidance of pollution, endogamy, and observance of religious taboos are the elements that keep one attached to his or her jati.

2. The Indian constitution prohibits discrimination against a person because of his or her jati. Nevertheless, in many villages, tensions between people of different jatis still exists.

3. A jati lower in social ranking may rise in status by adopting more pure ideals, such as becoming vegetarian. This process is called **sanskritization.** Another example would be for a lower-ranking jati to refrain from making leather items from a cow. Because of cow reverence in India among Hindus, working with leather is considered a polluting activity.

Islam as a Major Religion in South Asia

Islam is the major religion of Pakistan and Bangladesh, the next two most populous nations in South Asia after India. The Islamic community in India, although in the minority, is very large. Muslims in India number over 80 million, constituting about 11 percent of the total population. This figure is larger than that of any Muslim nation in the Middle East and would be sufficient to rank among the four largest Islamic populations in the world if the Muslims in India were to make up a nation. Islam came to South Asia from its birthplace in the Middle East and has had a profound impact. For example, even though India is primarily a Hindu nation, its most famous building, the Taj Mahal, was built by a Muslim ruler in the 17th century. (For a discussion of Islam, see Unit One on the Middle East. For more information on Islam in South Asia, refer to the next section on history and politics.)

The history of Hindu-Muslim relations in South Asia has been at times peaceful and at times violent. The term **communalism** describes those instances when serious tensions have arisen between the two groups. Respect by each group for the other begins with an appreciation of basic beliefs, practices, and differences, as well as shared concepts. A checklist of some of these follows:

	Hinduism	**Islam**
Holy sites	Benares (Varanasi) Ganges River	Mecca, Medina, Jerusalem (No holy rivers)
Buildings	Carved images of deities, ornate and decorative	Carved images of Allah and Mohammed are not permitted; writings from the Koran
Holy books	Vedas, Upanishads, Ramayana, Mahabharata	Koran
Dietary taboos	Beef	Pork
Obligations	Dharma	Five Pillars
Deity beliefs	Belief in different gods is acceptable	Monotheistic
Life after death	Reincarnation, moksha, depending on karma	Heaven for true believers and those who act righteously
Divisions	Stratification/hierarchy based on caste	Equality of all before Allah; schism between Sunni and Shiite sects
Attitude on life	Ahimsa—doctrine of nonviolence	Jihad—concept of holy wars
Political attitudes	Democratic; separation between civil and religious authority	Theocratic—Koran as basis for laws in society

Buddhism in South Asia

Buddhism grew out of Hinduism as a result of the teachings of the **Buddha,** born as **Siddhartha Gautama.** Gautama was born as a high-caste Hindu in 560 B.C. However, he and his disciples wished to keep some ideas (the mandala) of Hinduism while seeking to change other ideas (end the caste system). Buddhism became popular in India during the rule of Ashoka (250 B.C.). However, its influence gradually diminished. This was because some of its ideas were accepted by Hindus and became part of the Hindu religion and also because of the destructive impact of Muslim invasions after 800 A.D. It is estimated that there are about one million Buddhists today in India. However, the population of Sri Lanka is mostly Buddhist. Buddhism became much more popular in Southeast Asia and in East Asia. (See these sections for more information on Buddhism.)

Sikhism

Sikhs form about 2 percent of India's population and are concentrated in the northwestern region known as the Punjab. The religion was founded around 1500 by the guru (teacher) **Nanak,** born as a Hindu but raised with Islamic ideas. The Sikh (disciple) faith has aspects of both Hinduism and Islam. However, it has no caste system. Sikhs have a reputation as successful business people and good soldiers. Sikhs vow never to cut their hair or beards and to carry a dagger or saber with them at all times. Their attempt to break away from India and form a separate state has led to conflicts with the Indian government in this century. (See the next section on history and politics.)

Jainism

Jains, who make up less than 1 percent of India's population, follow the beliefs set down by the guru Mahavira in about 500 B.C. He was born a Hindu, as were Gautama and Nanak, and also rejected certain Hindu doctrines while accepting others.

The main Jain doctrine is that all of nature is alive. This belief led to the refusal to kill any living thing and to a strict notion of non-violence, the ideal of **ahimsa.** This idea was gradually incorporated into Hinduism.

Christians, Jews, and Parsees are also found in India. Their total numbers are very few, making up no more than 3 percent of the population.

66

QUESTIONS

Multiple Choice. Select the letter of the answer that correctly completes each statement.

1. In India, the traditional role of women has changed during the 20th century mainly because of the
   A. impact of increased urbanization
   B. growth of political unrest
   C. use of passive resistance
   D. effects of religious persecution

2. Demographers are most concerned with studying trends in
   A. religion   C. dress
   B. culture   D. population

3. The most widely-spoken language in India is
   A. Tamil   C. Bengali
   B. Hindi   D. Urdu

4. The practice of endogamy results in married couples who
   A. will have many children
   B. have come from village communities
   C. have had their marriage arranged by their families
   D. come from different castes

5. Which does NOT belong with the others?
   A. Krishna   C. Shiva
   B. Vishnu   D. Mandala

6. The duties and obligations of a caste member are known as his
   A. dharma   C. moksha
   B. karma   D. reincarnation

7. The Bhagavad Gita is the name of a famous
   A. battle   C. poem
   B. family   D. city

ESSAYS

1. Explain three basic teachings or ideas of Hinduism.

2. Explain two ways in which Hinduism differs from Islam.

3. Population growth has been an important issue in India.
   A. Explain two reasons for the increasing birth rate in India.
   B. Describe two ways in which the government has tried to limit the birth rate.

IV. History and Political Geography (Historical Setting of South Asia)

The Historical Setting (3500 B.C.–1200 A.D.)

Early Civilizations. Among the earliest peoples to settle in South Asia were the **Dravidians.** It is thought that in about 2500 B.C., along the Indus River in what is now Pakistan, two major cities grew—Mohenjo-Daro and Harappa. These settlements were several hundred miles apart and were similar to other early river-valley civilizations in the world. Between 1500 B.C. and 500 B.C., the Dravidians were conquered by a people from Central Asia, the **Aryans.** Aryan settlements grew in what is currently Pakistan, India, and Bangladesh. The blend of Aryan and Dravidian cultures led to some of the major developments in South Asian culture, such as the Sanskrit language and the Hindu religion. The years from 1500 B.C. to 1200 A.D. can be described as the Hindu period.

As was true of the Aryans, the next significant group of invaders came to the subcontinent from the northwest. Under the leadership of Alexander the Great in 327 B.C., Greeks came through the Khyber Pass and other openings in the western Hindu Kush Mountains. The Greek impact was limited and short-lived, affecting mostly the north, and had its greatest effect on Indian art. For example, images of Buddha began to take on certain Greco-Roman features.

Early Empires. Two dynastic empires soon emerged in South Asia; these were the **Mauryas** (325 B.C.) and the **Guptas** (350 A.D.).

Chandragupta Maurya founded the **Maurya dynasty,** took many of the areas formerly held by Alexander the Great, and established an empire in northern India. His grandson, **Ashoka** (250 A.D.), became one of the greatest Indian rulers in history. He did not seek to extend his empire and permitted different religions to exist. He was very much influenced by Buddhism. (Remember that Buddhism arose from the teachings of the first Buddha, Siddhartha Gautama, who was born in 560 B.C.). Although Ashoka failed in his attempt to spread Buddhism in India, many Buddhist beliefs became incorporated into Hinduism. The Maurya empire crumbled after the death of Ashoka.

The **Guptas** controlled much of northern India for approximately 200 years, between 350 A.D. and 550 A.D. During this period, notable achievements were made in such fields as mathematics (the idea of zero and a decimal system), literature, surgery, art, architecture, and religion (the expansion of Hinduism). As a result, this period under the Gupta emperors became known as India's "Golden Age." Eventually, however, the Gupta empire was unable to withstand attacks by outsiders, such as the Mongols and Turks, and became disunited. Disunity in the subcontinent was to remain until the period of Muslim rule.

The Islamic Period (1200–1760)

The Delhi Sultanate, (1206–1526). The 34 different kings who ruled during the history of this kingdom, or sultanate, held power in northern and central India. However, the earliest Muslim takeover in the subcontinent began in the 8th century with the conquest of part of what is now Pakistan. Muslim invaders, such as Mahmud of Ghazni, continued to come from the west (Afghanistan), to spread Islam, and gain more territory. Their successors established the Delhi sultanate. During the last years of the sultanate, the south of India was exposed to European contact and settlement. Vasco da Gama of Portugal landed in 1498 in Calicut. Soon thereafter, Spanish, French, Dutch, and English traders began to appear and established trading posts.

The Mughal (Mogul) Dynasty, (1526–1760). This dynasty emerged as a result of military victories by **Babur** over the Delhi sultan. Babur was a Turkish-Mongol prince, a Muslim, and a descendant of Genghis Khan. Babur's grandson, **Akbar,** became a very popular ruler, particularly because he won the respect of his Hindu subjects. His rule (1555–1605) was also known for political stability and cultural achievements.

One of Akbar's successors was **Shah Jahan** (1628–1658). He continued many of Akbar's policies and was responsible for building the Taj Mahal. This great building was a memorial to his wife, Mumtaz Mahal.

Another Mughal ruler was **Aurangzeb** (1658–1707), who was a harsh and unpopular leader. A very strict Muslim who wanted to spread Islam, he carried out policies that angered Hindus, Sikhs, and other groups. This was one factor leading to the breakdown of the Mughal empire. Other factors included corrupt administration, wasteful spending of money, and excessive military campaigns. Although the empire did not end until 1857, the Mughal rulers after Aurangzeb had very little influence in India. The weakness and disunity of the Mughals was one reason England was able to gain control in India.

The British Raj (Rule) (1760–1947)

The British involvement in India, an example of imperialism, grew from economic contact to direct political control. Britain was able to out-maneuver its European rivals, build alliances with some Indian rulers of small areas, and inflict military defeat on other rulers.

The British East India Company. Granted a charter from Queen Elizabeth I in 1600, the British East India Company received permission from the Mughals to trade in India as early as 1613. From this time until 1858, the company exercised powers usually associated with a government. It had, for example, its own private army. One of its employees, **Robert Clive,** led military forces to victories over both

French and native Indian armies. As a result of the most important of these victories, at Plassey in 1757, the British became the dominant economic and unofficial political power in the subcontinent.

The Sepoy Mutiny and Direct Rule by Britain. The Sepoy Mutiny of 1857 was fought against the British for both religious and political reasons. It began when Indians in the British army (sepoys) suspected that the grease used on bullet cartridges came from cows and pigs. If so, to bite into these cartridges would have violated Hindu and Muslim beliefs. These suspicions led to a rebellion that gradually spread beyond the military and became an anti-Western movement. (In fact, some Indian historians view the Sepoy Mutiny as a war of independence.) Eventually it was severely crushed. Nevertheless, the East India Company was abolished and replaced as a governing body by the British crown. In 1876, Queen Victoria was proclaimed Empress of India. What was now called the Crown Colony of India actually included present-day Pakistan, India, and Bangladesh.

Rule by Britain brought some benefits to the colonized people, such as improved transportation and communication, health services, education, and political unity. However, colonial rule was more beneficial for the British, allowing them to exploit Indian resources and provide employment for many English people. In addition, Indians felt that their cultural values, beliefs, and practices were threatened because they clashed with those of the British. British ethnocentrism stirred bad feelings.

Growth of an Indian Nationalist Movement. The movement for Indian independence grew from distrust of British economic, cultural, and political practices. In addition, Indians felt it was wrong for Britain to preach democratic ideals while denying Indians democratic rights, such as the right of self-determination. The Sepoy Mutiny could be viewed as the first major step in an Indian nationalist movement. Other important developments included:

1. In 1885 the **Indian National Congress** was founded, initially to promote a gradual relaxation of British economic and political control. It eventually became known as the **Congress Party.** In the 20th century, leading political figures associated with the Congress Party were **Mohandas Gandhi, Jawaharlal Nehru,** and **Indira Gandhi.**

2. In 1906 the **Muslim League** was created by those Muslims who feared that the Congress Party was becoming too strongly dominated by Hindus. One of its founders was **Mohammed Ali Jinnah.**

3. From 1914 to 1918 British participation in World War I adversely affected Britain in the colony of India. Indian soldiers fought in Europe and gained military distinction. However, they soon began to question for whose interests they were really fighting. Also, they

came to realize that the terrible tragedies associated with the war cast doubt on the British claim of the superiority of European culture and civilization.

4. In 1919 the **Amritsar Massacre** occurred when British troops fired on unarmed Indians attending a political rally. The death of hundreds of people in this town in the Punjab infuriated Indians.

5. In 1921 the **Montagu-Chelmsford Reforms** provided for a limited amount of self-government. This included a two-house legislature with limited powers that would have more members elected by Indians than appointed by the British.

6. In 1935 the **Government of India Act** extended the policy of limited self-government by letting Indian provinces have more control over their own affairs. It was intended to set the groundwork for India to become a self-governing dominion within the British empire, like Canada.

7. **Gandhi's nonviolent movement.** Known as **Mahatma** ("the great soul"), Mohandas K. Gandhi organized boycotts and other nonviolent activities, such as a march to the sea to protest a salt tax, in an attempt to shame the British and achieve swaraj (self-rule). Gandhi also went on frequent hunger strikes. His nonviolent actions stemmed from the Hindu ideas of "ahimsa." His tactics were described as examples of passive resistance and civil disobedience.

World War II, Partition and Independence. With the end of World War II in 1945, Britain moved to seek a peaceful transition for Indian independence. Britain was exhausted after the war and did not want to spend the money and use the personnel needed to maintain the colony. It also wanted to adhere to the principles of the United Nations charter concerning self-determination for all people. However, even though the British had hoped to leave behind them one united country, there was much tension between Hindus and Muslims. The Congress party, led by Jawaharlal Nehru, and the Muslim League, led by Mohammed Ali Jinnah, were unable to resolve all their differences. These differences led to much bloodshed and threatened to bring on a civil war if no agreement was reached on a partition plan. Eventually, on August 15, 1947, independence came with the creation of two independent nations, India and Pakistan, formed by a partition of the subcontinent.

Independence Period (1947 to the Present)

Political Structure in India. India has existed since independence as the world's largest democracy. It has a parliamentary form of government similar to that of Britain but different from that of the United States.

71

Important Leaders

India has had several important political leaders.

1. **Jawaharlal Nehru,** the first prime minister (1947–1964). Nehru brought some stability to the new nation and tried to achieve a sense of "unity in diversity." He hoped to build a spirit of nationalism, in spite of the many differences among India's population, including religion, language, and varying loyalties to local states and regions.

2. **Indira Gandhi,** prime minister (1966–1977, 1980–1984). Mrs. Gandhi, the daughter of Nehru, held power longer than any Indian leader. Although popular when she first took office, she gradually began to govern with an "iron fist" in order to pursue her policies concerning economics, birth control, and other issues. Her proclamation of a "state of emergency" in the 1970s was seen as harming India's democracy and led to her downfall in the 1977 elections. From 1977 to 1980, her successors, Morarji Desai and then Charan Singh, proved unable to achieve their goals. Mrs. Gandhi returned to power in 1980, faced with severe internal problems such as persistent poverty and the desire by Sikhs to have their own nation in the Punjab region. Her strong actions against Sikh militants provoked a harsh reaction and led to her assassination by two Sikhs in 1984.

3. **Rajiv Gandhi,** prime minister (1984–1989). The son of Indira Gandhi, Rajiv Gandhi tried to obtain foreign help for India in meetings with American President Reagan and Soviet Premier Gorbachev. Although he began his term of office amidst much sympathy due to his mother's death, Rajiv proved to be a weak and unpopular leader. He made little progress in solving domestic problems (poverty, Sikh dissension). His administration was criticized for being corrupt. An Indian politician in an opposition party claimed that the mood of the people was "one of extreme disenchantment." Consequently, in the elections of November 1989, Mr. Gandhi and his Congress Party were voted out of office.

4. **Vishwanath Pratap Singh,** prime minister (1989–). V. P. Singh's Janata Dal Party won 141 of the 525 seats up for election in the Lok Sabha in 1989. Other parties support the Janata Dal and joined with it to form a coalition (a combining of different political parties to run a government). The coalition is called the National Front and is headed by V. P. Singh, India's eighth prime minister. Singh was very active in promoting economic policies between 1984 and 1986 that helped Indian industries and the middle class. However, he will have to find ways of maintaining this economic boom, while helping the lower classes at the same time.

Political Structure in Pakistan and Bangladesh

Although Pakistan today can be described as a parliamentary democracy with a constitution, its first years after partition were very

A Comparison of Two Democracies

	The United States	**India**
Basic form	Federal republic; one central government and 50 state governments	Federal republic; one central government and 17 state governments
Legislature	A bicameral system: Congress consisting of the Senate and House of Representatives	A bicameral system: Parliament composed of the Council of States (Rajya Sabha) and House of the People (Lok Sabha)
Executive	A President indirectly elected by the public (presidential form)	A Prime Minister, elected by the legislature (parliamentary form; the Prime Minister usually is head of the majority party in the Parliament)
Governing document	Constitution of 1787, with subsequent amendments	Constitution of 1950 with subsequent amendments
	Both documents describe the political structure, protect civil rights and liberties, and were influenced by British legal traditions.	
Political parties	Two main parties: Democrat and Republican	Several parties: Congress, Janata Dal, Dharatiya

unstable. Under British rule, the Muslims had very little experience in politics. Therefore, it is not surprising to find frequent instances of divisiveness and "strong-man" rule in Pakistan since independence in 1947.

Mohammed Ali Jinnah's death in 1948 was a severe blow to the young nation. The ineffective political struggles for power by civilians ended when the military suspended the constitution in 1958 and declared martial law. General **Mohammed Ayub Khan** ruled the country until 1969. Another example of dictatorial rule by the military occurred in 1977, when **General Mohammed Zia** took power away from the civilian-elected prime minister, **Zulfikar Ali Bhutto.** General Zia's rule ended with his death in a plane crash in August 1988. In that year, voters put into power the **Pakistan People's Party** and its leader, **Benazir Bhutto.** As the daughter of a former prime minister, Ms.

Bhutto became the second woman to head a government in the sub-continent and the only woman ever to govern a Muslim nation. Still in power today, Bhutto has had trouble resolving severe problems involving poverty, corruption, education, and Islamic fundamentalism.

Bangladesh came into existence in 1971. Previously it had been the part of Pakistan known as East Pakistan. It was separated from the western part of Pakistan by 1,000 miles. Political, religious, and economic tensions led to a rebellion by East Pakistan in 1971. A war broke out in which India sided with the East Pakistanis. By December, the rebellion was a success and the nation of Bangladesh was declared.

Bangladesh's first prime minister, **Sheik Mujibur Rahman,** led the struggle for independence. His inability to deal with food riots and a growing population as well as a growing perception of corruption were some of the reasons for his assassination. Since then, the country has had several coups. The current leader is Lt. General **Hussain Mohammed Ershad.**

Current Political Issues in South Asia

Separatist (secessionist) movements are the most dangerous political issues facing India and Sri Lanka in the 1990s. Different groups in both nations have grievances against the national governments and want to break away.

In India's Punjab state, Sikhs want to form their own nation—Khalistan. Resentment against the central government in New Delhi was fueled in 1984 when Mrs. Gandhi sent troops to attack Sikh militant separatists in the Golden Temple at Amritsar. In the northern state of Kashmir, India is concerned about growing unrest by the Muslim majority there. Kashmir is the larger part of an area that was taken over by India after the 1947 partition. However, Pakistan challenges India's claims to the state, especially as Muslims are in the majority. Early in 1990, efforts by the Jammu and Kashmir Liberation Front to secede from India led to riots and violence. India claims that Pakistan has been behind these activities. India has also been bothered by anti-government activity by tribal groups, such as the Assamese in the northeast.

In Sri Lanka, the Tamil people, who are of Indian origin, want to have their own state. The Sri Lankan government has had difficulty in putting down terrorist actions by Tamils against members of the majority Sinhalese community. Although some Sri Lankans think that people in South India are helping the terrorists, the Colombo government nevertheless has welcomed the presence of Indian troops to help keep the peace.

Communalism (ethnic tension between Hindus and Muslims) has been a frequent source of irritation in India. Part of this tension stems from the partition of the subcontinent in 1947. Much bloodshed broke out between the two groups, as some Muslims in India wished to migrate to Pakistan, while some Hindus in Pakistan wished to migrate to India. Religious differences between the two groups has been another source of friction.

Wars have been fought three times between India and Pakistan. While the two nations are now at peace, it remains to be seen whether they can permanently overcome problems over borders, distrust, communalism, and nuclear arms.

India has tried to follow a policy of **nonalignment,** hoping to establish itself as a leader of Third World nations. This policy has come into question, however, as India has fought a war with China over a border dispute (1962) and has been more friendly towards the Soviet Union than towards the United States. It was not as alarmed as Pakistan when Soviet soldiers were fighting rebels in Afghanistan from 1979 to 1989.

The history of South Asia has been carved by its native inhabitants as well as by outsiders. The British dream of having the colony of India become one united nation upon independence did not materialize. The internal (national) and external (international) problems facing South Asian nations will take time to overcome. It should be remembered, nevertheless, that they have done much to improve themselves since independence.

QUESTIONS

Matching. Match the people in column 1 with the correct description in Column 2.

	Column 1		Column 2
____	1. Ashoka	A.	India's first Prime Minister
____	2. Indira Gandhi	B.	Pakistan's first Prime Minister
____	3. Mahatma Gandhi	C.	Leader killed by Sikh militants
____	4. Mohammad Ali Jinnah	D.	Spread Buddhism in India
____	5. Shah Jahan	E.	Builder of Taj Majal
____	6. Jawaharlal Nehru	F.	Non-violent protester of British policies

Multiple Choice. Select the letter of the answer that correctly completes each statement.

1. The partition of the Indian subcontinent into India and Pakistan after World War II was based largely on
   A. political and religious factors
   B. economic concerns
   C. military strategies
   D. health and medical problems

2. The Muslim League was primarily responsible for creating the nation of
   A. Nepal
   B. Sri Lanka
   C. Bangladesh
   D. Pakistan

3. Which of the following was most upset with the political goals of the Indian National Congress?
   A. Nehru
   B. Jinnah
   C. M. Gandhi
   D. I. Gandhi

ESSAY

At various times in the 20th century, the Indian subcontinent has been faced with severe political issues. For each of the following, explain what the problem was, and give either one reason for it or one result of it:

1. Amritsar Massacre

2. communalism

3. partition

4. civil war in Sri Lanka

5. Sikh militance

6. status of Kashmir

I. Physical Geography (the Physical Setting of Southeast Asia)

Overview

The region known as Southeast Asia consists of ten nations. Six are on the Asian mainland: Kampuchea (Cambodia), Laos, Malaysia, Myanmar (Burma), Thailand, and Vietnam. The other four are island nations: Brunei, Indonesia, the Philippines, and Singapore. In the past, parts of the region have been known by other names, such as the Spice Islands, the East Indies, and Indochina. The land portions of this region total about half the area of the United States.

Topography

Most of mainland Southeast Asia is located on two peninsulas—the Indochina Peninsula and the Malay Peninsula. The island nations of Indonesia and the Philippines form **archipelagoes.** The soil found on these islands, much of it from volcanic ash, is very rich. Mountain chains on the mainland divide the land area into river valleys, in which most of the population lives. Many tropical jungles and swamps exist here. Geography has tended to isolate some peoples from others and is partially responsible for the great diversity of cultures found in Southeast Asia.

Water Bodies

The two oceans that sandwich the region, the Indian and Pacific, have acted as "highways," bringing foreigners from South Asia, East

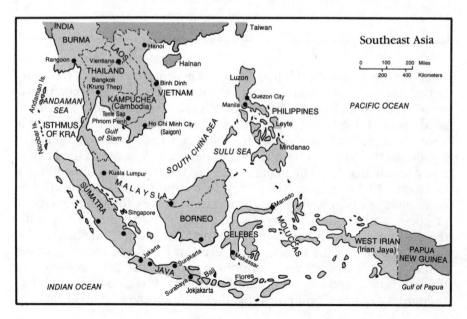

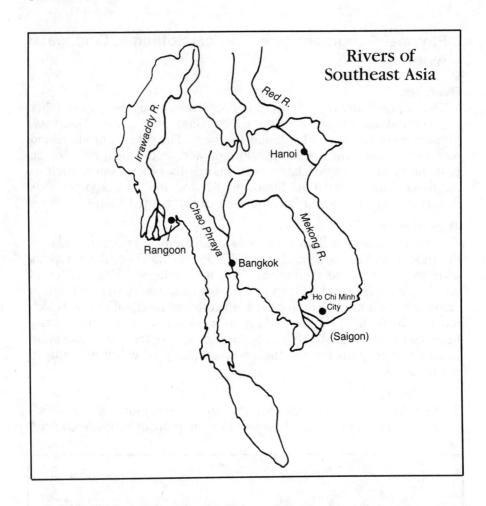

Rivers of
Southeast Asia

Asia, Europe, and the United States. This foreign contact has continued for over 500 years and has contributed to the "patchwork
quilt" of cultures found in the ten Southeast Asian nations. The **Strait
of Malacca,** lying between Indonesia, Malaysia, and Singapore, is a
vital strategic and economic link between the Indian and Pacific
oceans, in the way that the Panama Canal is a link between the Pacific
and Atlantic oceans. The major rivers are the **Irawaddy, Chao Phraya**
(Menam), **Mekong,** and **Red.** They flow southward, forming fertile
river valleys and providing transportation routes for the movement
of goods and people. The rivers and straits in the area, along with
the major seas, including the Java Sea and the South China Sea, make
up half the size of the region. As a result, it is easy to see why water
bodies have had such an enormous effect on the diet, commerce,
transportation, and history of Southeast Asia. It is also estimated that
Indonesia and the Philippines together contain over 20,000 islands.

Climate

The climate is tropical, characterized by much humidity and rainfall. These features are similar to those found in the Caribbean Sea area in the West Indies, Haiti, the Dominican Republic and Puerto Rico. However, there is very heavy rainfall in Southeast Asia, especially in the summer. The winds that cause this heavy rainfall are referred to as the summer monsoons. As in South Asia, the monsoons can make the difference between a good or a bad harvest.

II. Economic Geography (Economic Development of Southeast Asia)

Agriculture

Due to the amount of rainfall and kind of soil, rice is the major crop grown in Southeast Asia. For many years, in fact, Myanmar was the world's largest exporter of rice. From the rich forest lands come teak and ebony. Farming is the occupation of well over half the people of the region. Although famine has never been a problem, nations of the region still look for ways to increase food production. Increases can come from using more modern farming methods as well as from the Green Revolution. Much hope also rests with the Mekong River development project. This project includes the construction of several dams along the Mekong River. It is expected that these dams will control floods, provide water for irrigation, and be a source of electricity.

Industrial Production

The region is rich in natural resources. Chief among these are tin, iron ore, and petroleum. Rubber is also the basis of a major industry. Nevertheless, Southeast Asian nations lack sufficient technology, money, and a skilled, educated labor force to exploit the many natural resources.

ASEAN

The **Association of Southeast Asian Nations,** which is made up of Malaysia, Thailand, the Philippines, Indonesia, and Singapore, was formed in 1967 to promote cooperative economic advancement. It seeks to increase exports and gain more help from nations such as Japan.

Economic Decision-Making

Different economic systems are found in the countries of Southeast Asia. Capitalist features predominate in Singapore, Malaysia, and the Philippines. Greater centralized control of the economy is found in Indonesia, Kampuchea, and Vietnam.

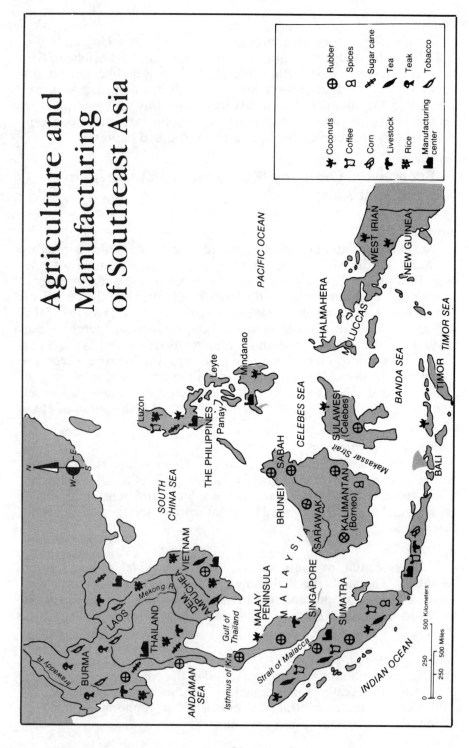

Agriculture and Manufacturing of Southeast Asia

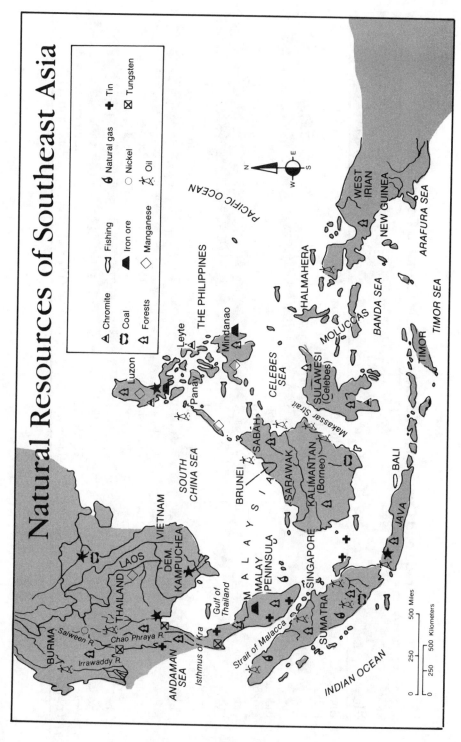

Natural Resources of Southeast Asia

Legend:
- ◮ Chromite
- ◖ Coal
- ⚏ Forests
- ⎰ Fishing
- ◣ Iron ore
- ◇ Manganese
- ✚ Tin
- ⧖ Natural gas
- ○ Nickel
- ⚒ Oil
- ⊠ Tungsten

PACIFIC OCEAN

WEST IRIAN

NEW GUINEA

ARAFURA SEA

HALMAHERA

MOLUCCAS

BANDA SEA

TIMOR SEA

THE PHILIPPINES

Mindanao

Leyte

Luzon

Panay

CELEBES SEA

SULAWESI (Celebes)

TIMOR

Makassar Strait

SOUTH CHINA SEA

SABAH

BRUNEI

SARAWAK

KALIMANTAN (Borneo)

BALI

JAVA

VIETNAM

LAOS

DEM. KAMPUCHEA

THAILAND

M A L A Y S I A

MALAY PENINSULA

SINGAPORE

SUMATRA

Gulf of Thailand

Isthmus of Kra

Strait of Malacca

BURMA

Salween R.

Chao Phraya R.

Irrawaddy R.

ANDAMAN SEA

INDIAN OCEAN

500 Miles
250
500 Kilometers
250
0

Trade and Commerce in Southeast Asia (Selected Countries)

Country	% of Trade To U.S.	From U.S.	Leading Trade Partners Exports (%)	Imports (%)	Major Exports Product (%)
Burma (1982)	1	5	Indonesia (15) Singapore (12)	Japan (39) Singapore (11)	Rice (37) Teak (26)
Kampuchea (1982)	3	10	Hong Kong (18) Vietnam (55)	Japan (18) Thailand (17)	Rubber (93)
Indonesia (1982)	16	14	Japan (50) USA (16)	Japan (25) USA (14)	Oil (70) Natural gas (13)
Laos (1981)	11	5	Japan (34) USA (11)	Thailand (34) Singapore (17)	Timber (77) Coffee (14)
Malaysia (1983)	13	3	Japan (20) Singapore (23)	Japan (25) Australia (16)	Petroleum (24) Lumber (11)
Philippines (1981)	30	23	USA (30) Japan (22)	Japan (25) USA (23)	Sugar (10) Textiles (11)
Singapore (1983)	18	15	Malaysia (18) USA (18)	Japan (18) USA (15)	Petroleum products (27) Machinery (32)
Thailand (1982)	12	13	Japan (14) Netherlands (13)	Japan (23) West Germany (14)	Rice (14) Tapioca (12)
Vietnam (1980)	—		USSR (12) Japan (31)	Japan (16) USSR (18)	Manufactured goods (73) Handicrafts (19)

Source: *Encyclopaedia Britannica*

QUESTIONS

Multiple Choice. Select the letter of the answer that correctly completes each statement.

1. Geographically, the nations of Southeast Asia are
   A. part of mainland Asia
   B. island nations
   C. mostly archipelagos
   D. both island and mainland nations

2. A leading rubber-producing nation is
   A. Singapore
   B. Malaysia
   C. Indonesia
   D. Thailand

3. What do Indonesia and the Philippines have in common? They both
   A. border China
   B. are island nations
   C. have gone to war over trade routes
   D. have peninsulas

4. The word Indochina refers to a
   A. river
   B. nation
   C. region
   D. mountain

5. Which would not be considered an island nation?
   A. Malaysia
   B. Indonesia
   C. Laos
   D. the Philippines

6. In Southeast Asia, the continued importance of the monsoon cycle shows that this region is
   A. becoming a major exporter of oil
   B. developing heavy industry
   C. opposed to the use of nuclear power
   D. dependent on traditional farming methods

ESSAY

Read the following statements carefully. Give two reasons to explain each of the following:

1. Southeast Asia is more of a supplier of raw materials than a manufacturer of finished goods.
2. Southeast Asia has been known by many names throughout the course of history.

III. Human and Cultural Geography

Overview

The most striking feature of Southeast Asia's population is its variety. This variety can be seen in the different languages, religions, and ethnic groups. Therefore, the region can be described as a "patchwork quilt" of peoples. With a total population of slightly over 400 million, the ten nations have more people than in all of North America. Indonesia, with 185 million people, is the fifth largest nation in the world.

Demography

Although the majority of people live in the villages and the mountains, there are several large cities in Southeast Asia. The population density is uneven. The Indonesian island of Java, for example, has over 1500 people per square mile, while the nation of Indonesia has 225 people per square mile. Most other areas have less than 125 people per square mile.

Language

The many languages spoken in Southeast Asia are primarily a reflection of the area's history. Several of these can be traced to nations from outside that have had great influence here. French is spoken in Kampuchea, Laos, and Vietnam; Spanish in the Philippines; English in the Philippines, Myanmar, Malaysia, and Singapore; and Dutch in Indonesia. Migration of people from India and China have brought Tamil and Chinese to parts of mainland Southeast Asia. Languages native to the region are Thai, Vietnamese, Burmese, Lao, Malay, Pilipino and Tagalog.

Religion

A diversity of religions exists, basically for the same historical reasons that a variety of languages exists. **Animism,** a form of nature worship, is native to the region. The five major "outside" faiths and their centers of popularity can be seen in the accompanying map. The number of Muslims in Indonesia make it the largest Islamic nation in the world. However, the religion with the greatest number of followers in the mainland nations is **Buddhism.** Buddhism began in India. Some of the main ideas about Buddhism are:

1. **Siddhartha Gautama** became the **Buddha** or the "Enlightened One."

2. The **Four Noble Truths** are from Gautama's teachings: Suffering is part of life; Selfish desires cause suffering; To end suffering, one must give up these desires.

To end these desires, one must follow the Eightfold Path. This consists of a series of words and acts, such as right speech, right occupation, right thought, and right conduct; following the "middle way" between extremes, such as denial or indulgence.

3. The goal of Buddhists is to reach enlightenment and then **nirvana.** Nirvana results in a release from the mandalas (wheel of life) and extinction of the soul.

4. Two major schools, or sects, of Buddhism are found in Southeast Asia. The **Hinayana** ("Little Vehicle") Buddhists are found in Burma and follow a more strict and traditional form of practice. The **Mahayana** ("Greater Vehicle") practitioners are more liberal and have adopted certain ideas such as that of the **bodhissatva.** (A bodhissatva is someone who has achieved buddhahood but has given up this status to return to earth and be of help to human beings.)

Ethnic Groups

There are a great variety of ethnic groups in Southeast Asia. These include both those native to the region and those that have ancestral ties to foreign areas. Among the ethnic groups native to Southeast Asia are the Khmers (Kampuchea), Chams (Vietnam), and Malays (Indonesia, Malaysia, Philippines). "Outside" groups include Europeans, Indians, and Chinese. Of these, the Chinese are the most numerous. Referred to as the hua-chiao ("overseas Chinese"), they have usually settled in urban areas and have had a major economic impact in several nations, such as Singapore. However, they have also been the target of prejudice on occasion, especially in Indonesia and Malaysia. The various ethnic groups have slowly made progress in learning to live with each other and with adapting traditional customs to modernization and to Westernization.

QUESTIONS

Multiple Choice. Select the letter of the answer that correctly completes each statement.

1. The "hua-chiao" are Chinese who
   A. control Singapore
   B. live outside of China
   C. live in coastal areas of Southeast Asia
   D. fought the Indonesian government

2. The word "buddha" can be translated as meaning the
   A. middle way   C. eightfold path
   B. enlightened one   D. the noble truth

3. The most populous nation in Southeast Asia is
   A. Indonesia   C. Vietnam
   B. Kampuchea   D. Myanmar

4. Mahayana Buddhism differs from Hinayana Buddhism in its emphasis on the concept of
   A. nirvana   C. enlightenment
   B. the bodhissatva   D. the four noble truths

ESSAYS

1. The region of Southeast Asia, in terms of its people and culture, has been described as a "patchwork quilt." Discuss the validity of this description by giving four specific examples.

2. Buddhism has played a major role in shaping the history and culture of Southeast Asia.
   A. Explain two basic teachings or ideas of Buddhism.
   B. Name one person associated with the development of Buddhism.
   C. Discuss the impact of this person on the religion.
   D. Describe one impact of Buddhism on Southeast Asia.

IV. History and Political Geography (Historical Setting of Southeast Asia)

The Historical Setting (1500 B.C.–1500 A.D.)
Early Civilizations. Little is known about the earliest inhabitants of Southeast Asia. They were most likely dark-skinned people, who

grew rice and worked with bronze. Migrations from the Indian sub-continent and China added to the native populations. (To this day, China refers to the entire region as "nanyang," lands of the southern ocean.) The Indian cultural diffusion included its ancient language, **Sanskrit,** as well as the spread of Hinduism, Buddhism, and Islam. Chinese influence was seen in the adoption of the Confucian cultural patterns and in the racial similarities between ethnic Malays and Chinese. China also controlled Vietnam for almost 1,000 years, up until 939 A.D. In other parts of Southeast Asia, several kingdoms emerged and grew into large empires.

The **Funan empire,** 100 A.D., was located in Kampuchea and South-east Vietnam. It controlled trade routes with India and China. The **Khmer empire,** 800 A.D., located in Kampuchea, based its wealth on agriculture and was known for the impressive capital at Angkor. The temple at Angkor (Angkor Wat) is an example of cultural diffusion from India; its sculpture shows both Hindu and Buddhist influences. The **Srivijaya empire,** 800 A.D., located in Indonesia, became powerful by securing the Strait of Malacca as a key link in the trade between India and China. It was known for a magnificent Buddhist structure, Borobodur, on the island of Java.

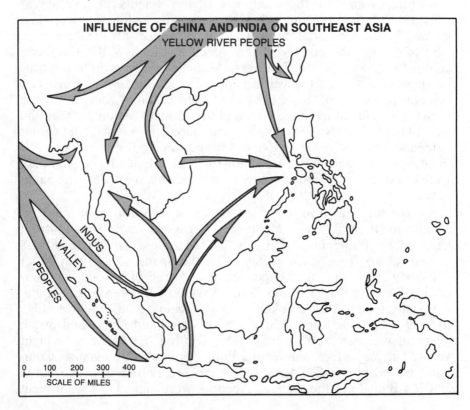

INFLUENCE OF CHINA AND INDIA ON SOUTHEAST ASIA
YELLOW RIVER PEOPLES
INDUS VALLEY PEOPLES
0 100 200 300 400
SCALE OF MILES

The Colonial Period (1500 A.D.–1963 A.D.)

When the Portugese took control of the Strait of Malacca in 1511 and the Spanish landed at Cebu Island (part of the present-day Philippines) in 1521, the period of European colonialism began. Eventually, four other nations—England, France, Holland, and the United States—established colonies in Southeast Asia. With the exception of the present-day nation of Thailand, every part of the region was colonized at one point in its history. By 1963, when the British left Malaysia and Singapore, nearly all of the region had become independent nations. (Technically, the colonial period did not end until 1983; in that year, England gave up its protectorate in Brunei.)

What were the main reasons for colonialism? European nations were interested in the spices from the region. The aim of Christopher Columbus in 1492 was to reach the "spice islands" in the "Indies." In later years, European interest in the area was focused on its mineral deposits, its agricultural products (see the sections on physical and economic geography), and political control of territory.

Nationalistic, anti-colonial movements began in Southeast Asia in the 19th century and gained strength after World War II. The war was of importance for these nationalistic movements for several reasons: (1) Between 1942 and 1945, the European colonial powers lost much of their territorial control to the Japanese; (2) the Japanese, who took over the colonies, were hated as much as the European colonial powers, and the Southeast Asian people rose up to fight for independence; (3) at the war's end, some of the former European colonial powers took back control of their colonies, but they were weary and drained from the war, and they sought to comply with the aims of the United Nations charter, and therefore were willing to grant independence; (4) other colonial powers who took back control of their former colonies were unwilling to grant independence, and they were confronted by native leaders who had fought against the Japanese.

A peaceful transition to independence occurred in these nations: Myanmar (then Burma), Malaysia, Singapore, and Brunei—from England; the Philippines—from the United States. (The United States gained control from Spain in 1898, after the Spanish-American War.)

Bloody transitions to independence occurred in Indonesia, Cambodia, Laos, and North and South Vietnam. Indonesia, under the nationalist leader **Ahmed Sukarno,** fought against the Dutch from 1945 to 1949. Cambodia (now Kampuchea), Laos, and North and South Vietnam were created in 1954, after fighting the French for eight years. The major forces defeating France were the Vietnamese Communists, led by **Ho Chi Minh.** After the French defeat in the battle at Dien Bien Phu, the Geneva Accords were signed. They brought the war to an end and provided for French withdrawal from Indochina.

In the early 1960s fighting broke out in South Vietnam, as the North attempted to establish one unified nation of Vietnam. Fighting against the South Vietnamese government were the Viet Cong (South Vietnamese Communists) and ultimately the army of North Vietnam. The Viet Cong and North Vietnamese received material assistance from China and the Soviet Union. The South received help from the United States in the form of material as well as over 500,000 combat troops. In 1973, President Richard Nixon withdrew American forces in the hope that both North and South Vietnam could work out their differences peacefully. The South Vietnamese government, under President Nguyen Van Thieu, grew weak and very unpopular. Fighting resumed, resulting in a North Vietnamese takeover in 1975 and the proclamation in 1976 of a united country. Hanoi became the country's capital, while Saigon, the former capital of South Vietnam, had its name changed to Ho Chi Minh City.

Independence Period (1963–the Present)

The political structures that have evolved since independence reflect the varied backgrounds of the nations in Southeast Asia. Therefore, it is not surprising to find different forms of government.

Key Issues Since Independence

Local vs. central control is a problem in Myanmar, where local tribal groups in rural remote areas (Karens) refuse to obey decisions of the national government in Yangon (Rangoon).

Civil War and invasion have plagued Cambodia since **Prince Norodom Sihanouk** was overthrown in 1970. The military rulers who took over were unable to defeat the **Khmer Rouge,** a Communist force backed by Vietnam. By 1976, the Khmer Rouge, under its leader **Pol Pot,** controlled the nation and changed the official name to Kampuchea. The Pol Pot government proved to be harsh and genocidal, killing thousands of people. It tried to impose a drastic social and economic restructure of society between 1975 and 1978. The Pol Pot government angered Vietnam, who had long wished to take over the territory. (Historically the people of Kampuchea and Vietnam had been enemies.) With Soviet encouragement and material aid, Vietnam conquered Kampuchea in 1978 and installed a government headed by a native figure, **Hun Sen.** This government has since faced a rebellion by Khmer Rouge forces. China has given its support to the Khmer Rouge, mostly from its wish to halt Vietnamese and Soviet influence in Southeast Asia. The United States has also indicated support for the Khmer Rouge, with certain limitations. In late 1989 Vietnam claimed to have withdrawn all troops from Kampuchea. In 1990, the

Nation	Form of Government	Current Leader*
Brunei	Monarchy	Sultan Muda Waddaulah
Indonesia	Military Government	President General Suharto
Kampuchea (Cambodia)	Communist Dictatorship	Prime Minister Hun Sen
Laos	Communist Dictatorship	Chairman Kaysone Phomvihan
Malaysia	Constitutional Monarchy	Prime Minister Mahathir bin Mohamad
Myanmar (Burma)	Military Dictatorship	General Saw Maung
Philippines	Federal Republic	President Corazon Aquino
Singapore	Parliamentary Government	Prime Minister Lee Kuan Yew
Thailand	Constitutional Monarchy	Prime Minister Prem Tinsulanonda
Vietnam	Communist State	Chairman of Communist Party, Nguyen Van Linh

* Given the instability in Southeast Asian politics, these leaders may hold office only for a short time. They were their nations leaders at the start of the 1990s.

United Nations tried to get all concerned parties to agree to its administering "free and fair elections."

Instability and corruption are features in many parts of Southeast Asia. However, they erupted into a striking change of government in the Philippines in 1986. **Ferdinand Marcos,** who had ruled with strong military backing since 1965, was an unpopular ruler who enriched himself and did little to help the masses of people. Widespread demonstrations, a controversial election, and declining military support enabled **Corazon Aquino** to come to power in 1986, as Marcos fled into exile. Mrs. Aquino has been moderately successful in her role, but faces several problems in controlling hostility from Communist and Muslim groups, conquering poverty, and dealing with Filipinos who were supporters of Marcos. Mrs. Aquino refused to let Marcos be buried in the Philippines after his death in 1990 and was able to put down a subsequent revolt by some army forces only by getting help from the United States.

Among other tensions which have existed in the region in the post-independence period:

1. Indonesia has had disagreements with Malaysia. It also had riots that caused the death of many Chinese in 1965 in the midst of a strong anti-Communist policy.

2. Chinese and Vietnamese antagonism surfaced in 1979 with a short-lived border war.

3. Thailand has been worried about the spread of communism from Indochina, as well as the problem of coping with refugees from the fighting in Kampuchea.

4. Singapore, mostly inhabited by Chinese, strives to maintain good relations with its two large Malay-dominated neighbors—Indonesia and Malaysia.

QUESTIONS

Multiple Choice. Select the letter of the answer that correctly completes each statement.

1. In the 20th century, most nations of Southeast Asia have been characterized by
   A. struggles for independence
   B. a high standard of living
   C. political stability
   D. tolerance of ethnic minorities

2. Which of the following pairs of colonial power and colony is correct?
   A. England-Thailand
   B. Holland-Indonesia
   C. Spain-Malaysia
   D. France-Singapore

3. Former French Indochina was divided in 1954 into how many parts?
   A. two
   B. three
   C. four
   D. five

4. This division came about at a meeting in
   A. Bangkok
   B. Ho Chi Minh City
   C. Paris
   D. Phnom Penh

5. As a result of the Spanish-American War of 1898, the United States came into control of
   A. Vietnam
   B. the Philippines
   C. Laos
   D. Malaysia

ESSAY

Since World War II, several Southeast Asian nations have faced various political problems. Among these nations have been the following:

Vietnam
Kampuchea (Cambodia)
The Philippines

For each of these nations, do the following:

1. State the capital city.

2. Describe one political problem faced by the nation.

3. Name one person or group connected with this problem.

4. Discuss the role played by this person or group.

5. Explain whether or not the problem exists until this day.

UNIT
THREE
EAST ASIA

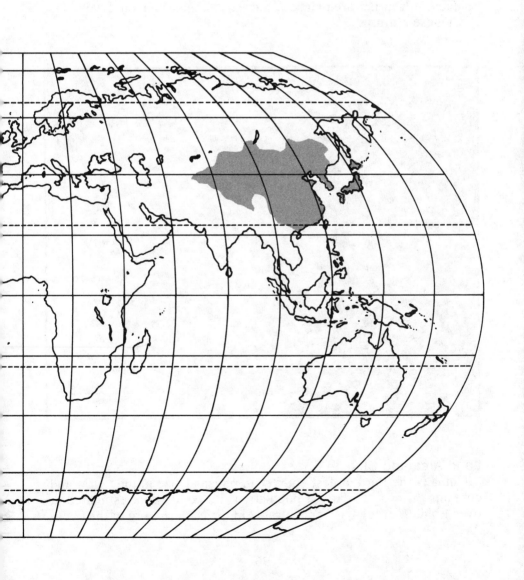

I. Physical Geography (The Physical Setting of China)

Overview

Until the age of exploration in the 1500s, China was largely isolated from other regions of the world by the ocean, the deserts, and the mountains along its borders. For the most part, Chinese civilization developed independent of external influences and in a unique Chinese fashion. As a result, the Chinese developed a strong ethnocentric attitude, believing that their civilization was superior to all others and that China was the **Middle Kingdom,** the center of the universe. This attitude was reinforced by the fact that most cultures China came into contact with in the area (Japan, Korea, Vietnam) adapted elements of Chinese culture.

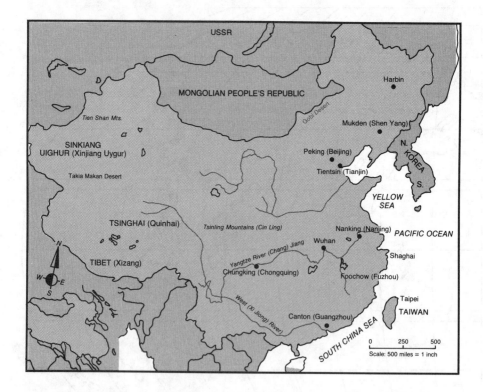

Land Area and Climate

China is the third largest country in physical size in the world and contains the world's largest population. Its population, estimated at over 1 billion in 1990, is concentrated in the eastern third of the country.

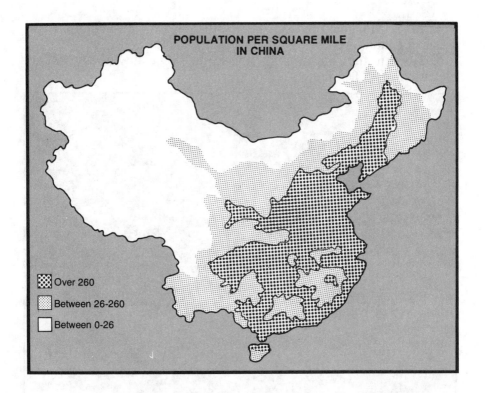

POPULATION PER SQUARE MILE IN CHINA

Over 260
Between 26-260
Between 0-26

The land area of China is over 3 million square miles. Its long, irregular coastline provides China with many excellent harbors. **Latitude, altitude, wind patterns,** and **distance from the sea** determine the varied climates of China. In general, the farther north a region lies, the cooler it will be; the farther west a region lies, the drier it will be because it is farther from the source of the summer **monsoon.** Chinese farmers depend on the summer monsoon rains for their crops, but the monsoons are not dependable. Sometimes the rains fail and the crops suffer drought. Sometimes the rains are excessively heavy and the crops suffer floods.

China has five major geographic and climatic regions:

1. **Southern China,** which is warm and moist year-round, is a major-rice-growing region and contains the southern hills region and the Xi and Chang (Yangtze) river valleys.

2. **North China,** a cold, relatively dry region, is a major wheat-growing region and contains the Huanghe (Yellow) River Valley and the North China Plain.

3. **Manchuria** lies in northeastern China and contains vast mineral resources and a large region of lowland plains.

4. **Inner Mongolia and Xinjiang** (Sinkiang), in north-central and western China, are largely desert and dry steppe.

5. **Tibet,** in the southwest, is a vast, cold plateau with an average elevation of 15,000 feet.

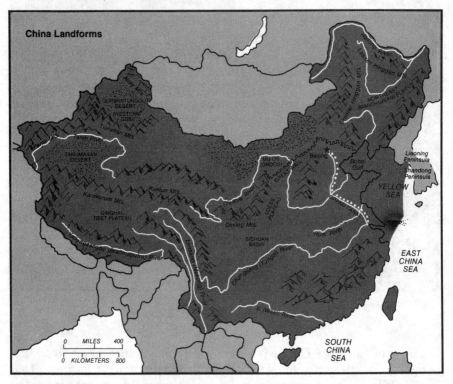

Mountains and Deserts

The **Gobi Desert** stretches across most of north-central China (Inner Mongolia). Some of the world's highest mountains are located in and adjacent to the borders of China. To the northwest are the **Altai** and **Tien Shan** and to the southwest, the **Himalayas,** the highest mountains in the world. The **Qinling** (Tsinling), in central-eastern China, separate the dry, cold northern region from the wet, warm southern region and serve as a cultural dividing line in China.

The difficult terrain (hills, plateaus, mountains, and deserts) has resulted in sparse population in both north and west China. However, the eastern third of China, known as **China Proper,** is very heavily populated, containing about 90 percent of China's people.

The River Valleys

The heaviest concentrations of population in China Proper are in the great river valleys of China—the **Huanghe** (Hwang-ho or Yellow), the **Chang** (Yangtze), and the **Xi** (Hsi or West).

98

The northernmost of the three, the **Huanghe,** is the major farming region of China. It flows through the great loess (fertile yellow soil) region of northern China and picks up and carries a vast amount of topsoil, which is deposited in the bed of the river and on the flood plains of the North China Plain. The river carries so much silt that the riverbed has been built up to an elevation higher than the surrounding plains and must be controlled by dikes. When the dikes fail, the river floods, destroying crops and homes and killing people. For this reason, the river has become known as "China's sorrow" and the North China Plain, the "famine region of China."

The **Chang** (Yangtze), China's longest river, flows through some of China's most productive farmland. The rich deposits of topsoil from floods encourage farming, and many of China's most important industrial cities, such as Nanjing (Nanking), Wuhan, Hankow, Chongqing (Chungking), and Shanghai, are located along it.

The **Xi** (Hsi or West) River, in the far south of China, is an important source of irrigation, and at its mouth lies the city of Guangzhou (Canton) and nearby, the British colony of Hong Kong.

QUESTIONS

Multiple Choice. Select the letter of the answer that correctly completes each statement.

1. The major rice-growing area in China is in the
   A. south
   B. north
   C. west
   D. southwest

2. Which is the main reason for the heavy population concentration in China's eastern region?
   A. The capital is located in the east.
   B. Most of China's fertile farmland is in the east.
   C. Most of China's oil resources are located in the Yangtze River Valley.
   D. Overland trade with China's neighbors declined.

3. The Yellow River is also known as
   A. the Yangtze
   B. the Yalu
   C. the Hsi
   D. the Huanghe

Fact or Opinion. Write F if the statement is a fact. If it is an opinion, write O.

1. The best place to live now in China would be near the Taklamakan Desert in Sinkiang Province.

2. All Chinese have rice as a basic part of their diet.

3. Over 90 percent of the Chinese people live on one-third of the land.

4. If China adopted American agricultural techniques, China's agricultural production would increase by 50 percent.

ESSAY

Geography has been an important factor in shaping China. Explain three ways in which China's geography has influenced its people and/or history. (Use three different geographical features in your answer.)

II. Economic Geography (Economic Development of China)

Resource Potential

China has adequate supplies of coal, iron ore, petroleum, natural gas, tin, antimony, tungsten, uranium, and many other minerals. It also has enormous hydroelectric-power potential, and China has constructed some dams and hydroelectric power plants. Most of China's petroleum reserves are located in the sparsely populated western regions, but pipelines transport crude oil to refineries and the densely inhabited eastern areas. Enough oil is produced for export. Most of the exported oil goes to Japan. China has major deposits of iron ore and coal in Manchuria, which have made possible the development of a sizable steel industry and have also made Manchuria a center of other types of heavy industry, such as locomotive production.

However, agriculture is still China's major source of income. The majority of the Chinese people are still engaged in agriculture, and the capital for investment in developing industries must come from the sale of agricultural products. Since only one-third of China's land is arable, peasants must overproduce to feed the vast Chinese population and also have products to sell abroad. The intensive agricul-

Resources and Industries of China

Natural Resources

Coal	Lead	
Copper	Petroleum	
Tin	Tungsten	
Gold	Iron	

Industries

Agricultural Machinery	Chemicals	Steel
Aircraft	Engineering Tools	Textiles
Aluminum	Railroad Cars	
Cement	Shipbuilding	

ture employed by the Chinese farmers (hand labor, terracing, irrigation, etc.) and the new incentives under the "responsibility system" have increased production, but the growing population demands ever more goods and services. To modernize China, its agricultural economy must be transformed into an industrial economy. To achieve this goal, the Chinese are using technology to overcome the scarcity of both food and consumer goods.

Changes in the Economic System Under Mao Zedong

For generations, China was an agrarian nation. The majority of the people were tenant farmers who rented their land from the landed gentry, who made up 10 percent of the population but owned 70 percent of the land. Rent and taxes kept the vast majority of tenant farmers impoverished. They lived on a subsistence level, providing their families with the necessities of life—food, clothing, and shel-

101

Agricultural Products of China

Cattle		Hemp, Jute	(M)	Millet		Sheep		Tea	
Corn		Hogs	(K)	Kaoling		Silk (S)		Tobacco	
Cotton			(P)	Potatoes		Soybeans		Wheat	
Fish			(R)	Rice					

ter—unless the monsoons failed them, and then many of them starved. The peasants were constantly faced with the threat of famine, starvation, and exploitation by the landlords and the government.

After the establishment of the People's Republic in 1949, Mao made drastic changes in China's economy. Foreign-owned industries were almost immediately nationalized, and Chinese-owned industries were also gradually nationalized. Banks, transportation, and mining also came under government control. Production goals and methods to meet those goals were set by Communist leaders through five-year plans. The Communists carried out land reform, and the peasants were given small plots of land of their own. Under Mao's leadership, the Communists were determined to industrialize China. The capital for investment had to come from the sale of agricultural products. However, since the peasants on their small plots simply were not producing enough to provide that capital, the Communist government began to take control of the land and agricultural production.

Cooperative farms were formed where individual farmers still owned the land but shared the ownership of machinery, tools, and work animals, and the farmers worked the land collectively. However, cooperatives also did not provide the desired increase in production.

The next step was the **collective farm,** where the land, the tools, machinery, and animals belonged to the collective (the state) and decisions on production were made by government officials. Individuals were paid wages, and the goods produced and the profit from that production now belonged to the state. Individuals were still allowed to own their homes, and they still enjoyed a private family life.

During the Second Five Year Plan (1958–1962), called **The Great Leap Forward,** all the country's resources were to be directed toward greater industrialization. **Communes**—huge state-owned farms which were economic, political, and social units—were formed. The commune managed local schools, hospitals, power plants, radio stations. Agricultural planning was done by Communist Party members, as was the planning for the industry the commune was engaged in. Ownership of private property ended. The communes had communal dining halls, nurseries, and dormitories. The plan called for increasing grain production by 100 percent in one year. Instead, it decreased by 20 percent in two years. Drought, peasant resistance, and inefficient central planning caused the failure of the Great Leap. As a result, the government divided the communes into production brigades to set goals and production teams to perform the labor. Most of the decisions were made by the commune members themselves. The government gave them quotas, but they decided how to meet those quotas and what to do with any surplus. Although production increased, it did not meet the needs of the growing Chinese population.

Economic Development Under Deng Xiaoping

Deng Xiaoping has been the most powerful figure in China since the death of Mao in 1976. In 1978 he began a program known as the **"Four Modernizations"** in agriculture, industry, defense, and science and technology, which made significant changes in China. Deng believed there should be less government control and planning. To carry out this program, Deng introduced elements of capitalism (free enterprise) and as a result China now has a **mixed economy** rather than a strict command economy.

Beginning in 1979, the communes were dismantled and the "responsibility system" was started, under which the land still belongs to the state but individual families lease plots of land. The peasants decide what to raise on the land and how to raise it. They contract with the state for a certain amount of their produce. Anything produced above that amount belongs to the peasant, who can choose what to do with the surplus. Free markets were established to sell the extra produce. Production has increased considerably. Estimates are that the average peasant's income has more than doubled and production has grown by over 7 percent per year.

The responsibility system was extended to state-owned industries in 1984. Managers are now allowed to make production decisions. They must still meet quotas set by the state but can decide what to do with surplus production. The factories and the machinery belong to the state, and the state still controls raw materials, but managers are free to obtain raw materials themselves. The industries pay a tax on the profit of sales of surplus goods, but the rest of the income can be used for reinvestment or to reward workers.

Some private enterprise has also been encouraged. The government offered tax breaks and low-interest loans to people to organize small businesses, such as fast food, beauty shops, brick-making, carpentry, and so on. The number of workers who can be employed in these private enterprises is limited by the government.

The production of consumer goods has also been stressed. There has been a push to raise the standard of living of the average Chinese, and there has been much greater production of radios, bicycles, cameras, TVs, and other consumer goods. Other major economic changes have been the encouragement of foreign investment in Chinese industries and allowing foreign industries to locate in China.

New Educational and Cultural Policies

As part of the Four Modernizations program, the government tried to improve education. The closing of schools during the Cultural Revolution and the persecution of teachers caused a major weakness in scientific and technical skills in China. To bridge this gap the government began to allow Chinese students to study abroad, and there were several thousand foreign advisers and many foreign students studying in China.

There was less emphasis on the use of art to further socialist ideals. During the Cultural Revolution, artistic expression was severely restricted. Under Deng, Western television and music were allowed into China.

Many leaders of the Chinese Communist Party believed Deng went too far in allowing capitalism into the Chinese economy. They feared corruption and the exploitation of workers. They also feared that the party would lose social and political control. The new freedom in education and culture was also seen by many government leaders as dangerous. But Deng and his supporters felt it was essential in order to advance science and technology. Indeed, the student "democracy" movement of May and June 1989 indicated that those who foresaw danger were right, and Western influences were blamed for the student rebellion that began in Beijing. Deng ordered a military crackdown on the democracy movement.

Conditions Posing Problems in Achieving Goals

In spite of the many hindrances to development in China, progress has been made and the majority of the Chinese people enjoy a higher standard of living than before the Communist Revolution. Nonetheless, several factors make it difficult for the Communists to achieve their economic goals.

Since China's economy still has an agricultural base, most of the capital for investment still must come from agriculture. Secondly, economic development has been uneven since regional differences present problems for development. Southeast China has excellent conditions for agriculture and has made economic gains. However, the North China Plain suffers recurring floods and drought, and much of the western regions are desert. Northeastern China (Manchuria), with its major iron and coal resources, has seen major industrial development. Uneven regional economic development creates another problem. As the regions are inhabited by diverse ethnic groups, so the economic development, or lack of it, serves to prolong ethnic differences and conflicts. Moreover, attempting to provide at least an elementary education for the Chinese people has put enormous strains on the economic resources of the state. China's large population and level of education are both important factors in determining the level of development in the country and, for the time being, serve to hinder that development.

QUESTIONS

Multiple Choice. Select the letter of the answer that correctly completes each statement.

1. The "Great Leap Forward" was expected to produce gains in China's
   A. imports
   B. birth rate
   C. army
   D. gross national product

2. An example of government-organized collectivist and group ideology was seen in China's
   A. foreign relations
   B. military
   C. commune system
   D. maritime trade

3. Manchuria has become important as a center of
   A. heavy industry
   B. rice cultivation
   C. ship building
   D. mining for gold

4. Arable land can be described as land that is
   A. dry
   B. composed of loess
   C. affected by earthquakes
   D. fertile

ESSAY

China's economy underwent changes under both Mao Zedong and Deng Xiaoping. For each of these leaders, do the following:

1. Describe two economic changes that occurred.

2. Explain the reasons for these changes.

III. Human and Cultural Geography

Confucianism

   Confucian thought, the foundation of Chinese civilization, influenced social organization, political structure, and the educational system. **Confucius,** or **Kung Fu-tzu** (551 B.C.–479 B.C.), lived during a time of great turmoil in China, marked by constant civil war. Confucius believed he knew how to bring about peace and harmony. His teachings became the basis of Chinese society during the Han dynasty (202 B.C.–220 A.D.).

   Confucius was not concerned with religion and did not teach about a divine being or salvation. He taught **ethics** (good and bad conduct) or moral precepts. A conservative, he believed the Chinese should follow ancient ways that had worked well in the past. Confucius taught that one should *not* do to others what one would *not* want done to oneself, stressing actions *not* to be taken against others.

   Confucius believed there was a basic order to the universe and that people must live in society to fulfill their potential. To achieve a peaceful and harmonious relationship in society, Confucius taught five basic relationships. Each person, according to Confucius, had a place in society, and if each person accepted the duties and obligations of his or her role, society would function properly. In each relationship there is a superior and an inferior. The superior shows love for and responsibility for the inferior. The inferior owes loyalty and obedience to the superior.

Five Relationships:
1. **Ruler and subject**
2. **Father and son**
3. **Husbands and wives**
4. **Older brother and younger brother**
5. **Friend and friend.** This is the only relationship not based on a superior/inferior foundation. Friends were to respect and honor each other.

Confucianists believed that the ruler held the **mandate of heaven** (the right to rule granted by the will of heaven). If he was a just ruler and cared for his subjects, he would continue to hold the **mandate.** But if he was not, the people had the right to rebel and overthrow the ruler. The success of their rebellion would be proof that the ruler had lost the **mandate.**

The Four Chinese Social Classes
1. **Scholars,** who made up a very small portion of society, held the highest position in Chinese society. They were the only ones eligible to take the civil service examinations and serve in government.
2. **Peasants,** who made up the largest portion of society, were the second highest class because they were the primary producers, providing the grains and textiles necessary for food and clothing.
3. **Artisans,** or craftspeople, were skilled workers who made up the third group. They were secondary producers.
4. **Merchants,** the lowest socially, though often the wealthiest, made their profits from the labor of others.

The nobility were above the class system. Soldiers and a group called "chien-min" (barbers, entertainers) were below the system.

Taoism (Daoism)
Taoism, a Chinese philosophy traditionally attributed to **Lao-tzu** ("old master"), originated in the 6th century B.C., about the same time as Confucianism. Taoism teaches the necessity of the individual's having a sense of nature, understanding his or her part in it and adapting to it.

The Taoists believed there was a natural order to existence and that people should do as little as possible to change that natural order. By accepting things as they are, people could live in harmony with the natural laws. Taoists opposed the existence of a large bureaucratic government and many governmental laws. Individuals should seek to find their own nature and place in the natural world and act according to instinct, since human instincts are good, and it is learning and custom that have taught them to be bad. Once people rid themselves of the burden of unnatural laws and customs, they could find the **tao** (or way) of the universe.

Like Confucianism, Taoism did not immediately become widely accepted. However, over the years it underwent major changes. It borrowed heavily from old Chinese folk religions and became a religion with a priesthood, ceremonies, and elaborate rituals. Some Taoists practiced alchemy (trying to change inferior metals to gold), some practiced magic, and others did ritual exercises.

Legalism

The Legalist philosophy originated in the same period as Confucianism and Taoism. The Legalists assumed that human nature was evil and that people must be restricted by laws, and through harsh punishment, forced to obey those laws. They taught that a strong central government was essential to maintain peace and order and that the ruler should have unquestioned authority. They also believed that only two occupations should be allowed: farmer (to provide sustenance) and soldier (to support the ruler).

Buddhism

Buddhism originated in India in the 6th century B.C. and was carried to China by Indian merchants during the 1st century A.D. (See Southeast Asia for a discussion of Buddhism.)

The first Chinese converts were from the upper class. The complex philosophy and elaborate rituals appealed to them. Buddhism was greatly changed by the Chinese, who translated difficult Buddhist concepts into traditional Confucian ethics. They stressed the obligations of children to parents. They interpreted **nirvana** not as a place empty of human thought and desire but as a continuation of life on earth, without the usual suffering. In the period of disorder after the fall of the Han dynasty, many Chinese began to accept Buddhist beliefs. Buddhist temples and monasteries became centers of education, and monasteries became economically and socially powerful.

The Chinese saw no contradiction in being a Buddhist-Confucianist-Taoist-Legalist. Buddhism offered optimism and hope for a better existence; Confucianism offered order and harmony and strong family relationships; Taoism offered rituals and ceremonies; and Legalism offered control. So a Chinese could be all these things.

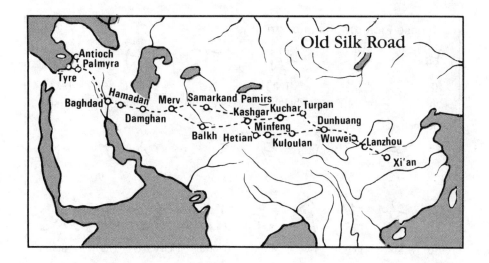

Chinese Contributions

Historically, China was one of the world's leading civilizations in technological development. The Chinese contributed much to the Western world: silk, tea, porcelain (china), paper, block printing, gunpowder, the mariner's compass, and many plants and plant products. Most of these early Chinese inventions and products were diffused to the West (Europe) between 200 B.C. and 1800 A.D. by one of two routes—the **Old Silk Road,** which led from China through Central Asia into the Middle East and from there to Europe, or by the southern sea route, from China to India and onward to the Middle East and again from there to Europe.

Chinese Influence Upon Other Peoples in East Asia

The original Chinese writing was a system of **pictographs.** Each symbol was a recognizable picture of an object. Eventually the Chinese developed a system of **ideographs**—symbols used for expressing ideas. The writing system includes more than 50,000 symbols. This elaborate system of writing spread to Korea, Japan, and Vietnam.

Buddhism was adapted to the Chinese civilization and Chinese Buddhism spread from China to Korea, Japan, and Vietnam. The Zen Buddhism practiced in Japan is said to have originated in China and diffused to Japan by way of Korea.

The Confucian tradition of ancient China also influenced the cultures of Korea, Japan, and Vietnam. Confucian influence can be seen in their family systems, ethical systems, and class systems, which are adaptations from the Chinese. Confucianism can also be seen in the dominance of the idea that there should be harmony between the

109

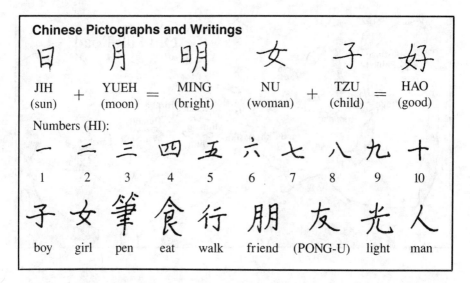

Chinese Pictographs and Writings

日　＋　月　＝　明　　女　＋　子　＝　好
JIH　　YUEH　　MING　　NU　　TZU　　HAO
(sun)　(moon)　(bright)　(woman)　(child)　(good)

Numbers (HI):

一　二　三　四　五　六　七　八　九　十
1　2　3　4　5　6　7　8　9　10

子　女　筆　食　行　朋　友　光　人
boy　girl　pen　eat　walk　friend　(PONG-U)　light　man

individual and nature and in the importance given to the peasant in all three societies. Japanese and Korean art also reflect Confucian influence.

China's Population

A large population requires large amounts of resources for subsistence and therefore makes development difficult. China has a huge population (about 1.1 billion) and a limited amount of arable land. The people themselves are perhaps China's most important resource and the cheapest factor in production, but their numbers are one of its greatest problems. To counteract this population problem, the Chinese government encourages a "one-child policy." This policy is relatively ineffective in the countryside but has had success in urban areas. China's goal is not just to decrease the birth rate but to actually decrease the size of the population. The government also encourages late marriage.

QUESTIONS

Multiple Choice. Select the letter of the answer that correctly completes each statement.

1. On which Asian nation did Chinese culture have the greatest impact?
   A. India
   B. Thailand
   C. Japan
   D. Pakistan

2. A goal common to Confucianism, Taoism and Buddhism is to
   A. establish peace and harmony
   B. provide the basis for democratic government
   C. return the power of emperors
   D. promote individual artistic activity

3. The Chinese writing system makes use of
   A. letters
   B. ideographs
   C. phonetics
   D. an alphabet

4. The "Five Relationships" were part of the philosophy of
   A. Mencius
   B. Confucius
   C. Sun Yat-sen
   D. Mao Zedong

5. Of the world's total population, China contains about
   A. one-half
   B. one-third
   C. one-fourth
   D. one-fifth

ESSAYS

1. Chinese culture has been influenced by each of these philosophies:

   Taoism
   Buddhism
   Confucianism
   Legalism

   Select any three of these and do the following:
   A. Explain one idea of this philosophy that is not found in the other two.
   B. Describe one way in which this philosophy has affected Chinese culture.

2. China faces a serious "population explosion."
   A. Describe two reasons for this "explosion."
   B. Explain why China is so concerned about the increasing growth rate of the population.
   C. Describe two ways in which the Chinese government is attempting to limit the population growth.

IV. History and Political Geography (Historical Setting of China)

Historical Development

Until 1912, Chinese history was divided into periods of dynastic rule, characterized by periods of stability and strong central government followed by periods of civil war and chaos. According to Chinese tradition, the ruler was responsible for setting a moral example and caring for his subjects. If he failed, the people had the right of rebellion. Dynasties were usually strong when first established, but weakness and corruption became common as time went on. When natural disasters such as flood and drought created famine or when China was invaded, it was a sign from heaven (the emperor, the "son of heaven," ruled through the will of heaven) and rebellion would break out. After a period of civil war and chaos, a winner would emerge, whose success indicated that the new ruler had gained the mandate of heaven and a new dynasty would begin.

Changes in the Dynastic Order Result in Changes in Chinese Civilization

Chinese civilization originated in the Yellow River Valley about 4,000 years ago. According to legend, the **Xia (Hsia) dynasty** ruled for about 500 years, from about 2000–1500 B.C. During this period the Chinese developed a written language and agriculture. By the time of the **Shang dynasty** (1523–1028 B.C.), most Chinese were farmers, but there were also skilled crafts people, who produced bronze jewelry and weapons.

The **Zhou (Chou) dynasty** (1028–256 B.C.), the longest in Chinese history followed the Shang. The Zhou kings ruled over a feudal system. The last 400 years of their rule was a period of conflict and led to the development of such philosophies as Confucianism, Taoism, and Legalism. It is known as the time of **Warring States** and also known as the time of a **Hundred Schools of Thought.** Despite the turmoil, China made great strides during this time. Iron tools and the iron-tipped plow were introduced, fine bronzes were produced, irrigation canals were dug, and agriculture was improved.

The conflict was ended by **Qin Shi Huang (Ch'in Shih-Huang-ti),** the first emperor of China, who established the **Qin (Ch'in)** dynasty (221–206 B.C.), the shortest dynasty in Chinese history. The first Chinese empire was organized along Legalist lines. Qin Shi Huang required that books supporting other philosophies be destroyed. He sent hundreds of thousands of laborers to work on the **Great Wall,** which ran approximately 2,000 miles across northern China. The different laws of the different feudal states were replaced with imperial law; roads were built for armies to move on; canals were dug; Chinese

112

script (writing) was made standard, and weights and measures were standardized.

The centralized state begun during the Qin dynasty was continued during the **Han dynasty (206 B.C.–220 A.D.).** The Han rulers united the Chinese people and extended both the territory and the influence of the empire into central Asia and Tibet. Parts of Korea and Vietnam came under Chinese influence as **tribute** states. The structure of government, which continued to exist in China until 1912, was established. China was divided into administrative units, with governors responsible to the emperor. Legalist rule was relaxed, and Confucianism became the official state philosophy. **A civil service examination** system was established. To serve in government, an individual had to be trained in the Confucian classics and pass a series of civil service exams based on Confucianism. Education became important and scholars became highly respected. Major cultural achievements were made during the Han dynasty. The Chinese learned to make paper, invented a calendar, improved pottery-making, and began the production of ceramics.

The fall of the Han dynasty began another period of conflict, but China was united again by the **Tang dynasty** (618–907). Tang rulers expanded their control to include nearly all of modern-day China. The arts flourished. China's greatest poets lived during the Tang dynasty. Chinese Buddhists invented movable block printing about 800 years before Gutenberg in Europe. Porcelain was first made. Because of the great achievements of the Tang dynasty, it is often referred to as **China's Golden Age.**

The next great dynasty, the **Song (Sung)** lasted from 960 to 1279, and this period is also considered a **golden age.** Chinese culture and trade continued to flourish. The Chinese invented the compass, improved ceramic techniques, developed gunpowder, began the use of paper money in trade, and produced some of China's greatest landscape paintings. The Song were defeated by the Mongols in 1279, and so began the **Yuan dynasty,** one of the only two foreign dynasties to rule China. The Mongols ruled China from 1279 to 1368. Mongol rule was established by **Kublai Khan,** but the size of the Mongol empire made it difficult to rule. The Mongols left Chinese officials in office in the provinces, and China was ruled through its own political institutions. However, the Chinese resented foreign rule and rebellions broke out.

In 1368 the Mongols were replaced by the **Ming dynasty** (1368–1644). The Ming dynasty is most famous for the production of fine porcelain and for the sea voyages carried out during the Ming rule. China sent ships to South and Southeast Asia and carried out extensive trade with areas as far away as the Red Sea and East Africa.

Beautiful palaces were constructed in Peking, including the Imperial City with the residence of the emperor, the Forbidden City, at its center. The Portuguese were the first Europeans to arrive and founded a colony at Macao in 1557.

To repel Mongol invasions, the Ming called on the Manchu, a people to the northeast, for assistance. However, the Manchus conquered China and established the second foreign-ruled dynasty, the **Qing (Ch'ing)** (1644–1912).

The Manchus ruled an empire where they were greatly outnumbered by the Chinese people they ruled. To facilitate their rule, they distanced themselves from the Chinese. Chinese were forbidden to emigrate to Manchuria in the northeast, Manchus and Chinese were not allowed to intermarry, and the Manchus retained their own language. Most of the key positions in government and the military were held by Manchus.

China's Relationships with the West

Westerners became interested in opening relations with China for a number of reasons. Western missionaries wished to convert the Chinese to Christianity. Western traders were interested in obtaining Chinese silks, tea, ceramics, spices, and other luxury goods and in selling Western goods to the Chinese. In the 19th century during the period of European imperialism, the Europeans sought to conquer Chinese territory and exploit its resources.

Chinese interest in Christianity and foreign trade was limited, however. The government, in an effort to limit foreign influence, restricted the activities of the missionaries. The Chinese were willing to sell goods to the Europeans but believed that the Europeans had nothing of interest or necessity to sell to them. European trade with China was restricted to the port of Canton (Guangzhou) in 1757, and severe restrictions were placed on that trade. Foreign relations with the Chinese could only be conducted through the tributary system. The Chinese considered themselves superior to all other nations, and all non-Chinese were considered "barbarians."

The West Carves Up China in the 19th Century

The Chinese enjoyed a favorable balance of trade with the Europeans for many years. However, in opium, the Europeans finally found a product that turned the balance of trade in their favor. By 1839 the British were making enormous profits from the opium trade, and the Chinese government took steps to end the trade. British opium was confiscated and destroyed, and the British were informed they could no longer trade with China. In 1840 the British sent warships to China and the **Opium War** began. In 1842 the Chinese were defeated because of the superior technology of the West.

The treaty ending the war, the **Treaty of Nanking** (Nanjing) (1842), was the first of the **unequal treaties** forced upon China. The Chinese were forced to open five ports to trade; **Hong Kong** was ceded to the British; China was to pay a $21 million indemnity to Britain; foreign merchants were to be allowed to reside in the treaty ports; and the Chinese were not allowed to set tariffs (taxes on imports) in the treaty ports. Other nations, including the United States, Germany, Russia, and France, quickly followed suit, and China was forced to agree to more demands. Western diplomats were allowed to live in Peking (Beijing), Christian missionaries were able to establish churches, foreign powers were granted **concessions** in Chinese ports, and foreigners gained the right of **extraterritoriality.**

Furthermore, China was carved into **"spheres of influence,"** areas of China where only one imperialist Western power was allowed to dominate, with exclusive rights to trade. In 1894 China and Japan went to war over their interests in Korea, a Chinese tributary state. The Japanese, who had instituted rapid industrialization and militarization in the 1850s to prevent Western nations from carving up Japan, defeated China. China was forced to cede Taiwan and the Pescadores Islands to Japan, and Chinese influence in Korea was ended. Within a few years, Japan annexed Korea. China was being whittled away, but the Chinese, because of their lack of technological progress, were powerless to stop it. To prevent its exclusion from the China trade, in 1899 the United States encouraged Western nations to adopt the **Open Door policy:** all nations would have equal trading rights in China and would recognize the territorial integrity of China.

Chinese Response to Foreign Imperialism

Although the scholar-bureaucrats of China were resistant to change, some attempts at reform were made. The tributary system was replaced by a government office to deal with foreign representatives as diplomatic equals. Those in the government who favored reform wished to adopt Western technology without making any major changes in China's government or society. These reformers believed that the Chinese had been defeated only because of the superior armaments of the West. Western experts were employed to create and train a modern army and navy. A small effort was also made at industrialization. Coal mines were opened, arsenals and dockyards were built, and railroads and telegraph lines were constructed.

The real power in China between 1861 and 1908 was the **Empress Dowager Tzu-hsi** (Cixi), who ruled as regent for her son and then her nephew. In 1898 **Kuang Hsu** (Guang-xu) took control of the government from his aunt and issued daily edicts calling for reforms. This period was called the **Hundred Days Reform.** Kuang Hsu's edicts called for changes in government, in education, foreign policy, agriculture, technology, and the military. These reforms threatened the interests of Confucian scholars, government officials, Tzu-hsi, and also foreign interests in China. Tzu-hsi regained control of the government within three months and ended the reform movement. In 1900, anti-foreigner Chinese, called "Boxers," with the secret support of the Empress Dowager, attacked the foreign delegations in Peking, hoping to expel the foreigners (Westerners) from China. The Boxers were defeated by combined foreign forces after 55 days.

Overthrow of the Emperor, 1911–1912

Revolts against the Manchu Qing (Ch'ing) dynasty began in the late 1700s. However, most of the rebellions were limited and easy to suppress. One of the strongest uprisings against the Manchu was the **Taiping Rebellion,** which spread across southern and central China from 1850 to 1864.

A successful rebellion against the Manchus began on October 10, 1911. The revolutionaries declared a republic and elected **Sun Yat-sen** as the provisional president. His program for China was known as the "Three Principles of the People," and the party to carry it out was the **Kuomintang,** the National People's Party, or the **Nationalist Party.**

Three Principles of the People

1. **Nationalism** meant both restoring the pride of the Chinese people and Chinese rule; and removing the foreigners, their concessions, and their spheres of influence.

2. **Democracy** meant popular sovereignty but was to be approached in three stages: first, a military government to remove the Manchu dynasty and defeat the Westerners; second, rule of the Kuomintang; and third, constitutional government, with popularly elected executive, judicial, and legislative branches.

3. **Livelihood** meant a program of land reform, the redistribution of land to the peasants, and the elimination of the system of tenant farming. The government was to control transportation, communication, and heavy industry.

The Manchus turned to **Yuan Shih-kai** (a former general in the Manchu army) to defeat the revolution. Instead, Yuan reached an agreement with the revolutionaries and used his power to force the abdication of the Manchu emperor. In return, Sun Yat-sen resigned as president of the republic and was replaced by Yuan. Yuan became a military dictator and eliminated the democratic reforms instituted by Sun and the Kuomintang. Sun and his followers tried to overthrow him, but Sun was forced into exile. Yuan died in 1916, and Sun returned to China. However, warlords who had been building up their own power in the provinces began to struggle against each other to gain control of the country. China fell into a decade of total chaos, with warlords fighting each other.

The Nationalist Period

Sun Yat-sen died in 1925, and after a brief power struggle, **Chiang Kai-shek** emerged as the new leader of the Kuomintang. In 1926, Nationalist forces, led by Chiang Kai-shek, began a military expedition to overthrow the warlords and gain control of Peking, called the "Northern Expedition." It was interrupted in 1927 when Chiang, fearing that the Communists in the Kuomintang were about to seize control, turned on them. Some were executed and many arrested and imprisoned. When the Communist threat had been eliminated, the expedition continued and Peking was captured in 1928. The Nationalists were recognized as the official government of China, even though the north, west, and much of the south were still in the hands of warlords. Chiang made attempts at reform, but his major efforts were to consolidate his power over the warlords and the Communists and to prevent Japanese aggression in China.

Appeal of Marxism

Marxism appealed to many Chinese for a number of reasons. The Communists predicted the end of imperialism worldwide and called for a government made up of peasants, the proletariat, and the scholars, appealing to nearly all levels of Chinese society.

Marxism promised a program of land reform to end tenant farming. Through government ownership of the means of production and the equal distribution of wealth, poverty in the cities would be eliminated. The Russian (Bolshevik) Revolution in 1917 had overthrown a corrupt, despotic government much like their own, and it appeared that the Communist government there was making strides towards equal distribution of wealth and industrialization. Marxism promised the development of industrialization in China to make it possible for China to compete with the West. Moreover, Marxism seemed to be the exact opposite of the old Confucian order that had kept so many people poverty-stricken and without political power. Finally the Communists had a charismatic leader, **Mao Zedong** (Mao Tse-tung).

Japanese Invasions

In 1931 the Japanese invaded the Chinese province of Manchuria. Chiang Kai-shek's forces were not powerful enough to resist those of the Japanese. The last emperor of the Qing (Ch'ing, Manchu) dynasty of China was installed as a puppet ruler, with the Japanese maintaining real control, and they began to develop iron and steel industries in Manchuria.

In July of 1937, the Japanese invaded the Chinese mainland and World War II in Asia began. Japan captured approximately the eastern third of China, but the Nationalists and their armies stubbornly held out from their new capital at Chungking.

The damage done to China during World War II was tremendous. Chinese cities were reduced to rubble, peasants' crops were destroyed, industries were destroyed, millions of Chinese were dislocated, and many Chinese died. When the war ended in 1945, the Nationalists were war-weary, for they had been fighting since 1911.

Long March of the Communist Forces

After Chiang's purge of the Communists in 1927, **Mao Zedong (Mao Tse-tung),** one of the founders of the Chinese Communist Party in 1921, escaped to southeastern China. Mao built up a following among the peasants and organized a guerrilla force called the Red Army.

In 1931, the same year Japan conquered Manchuria, Chiang decided to eliminate the Communists. Finally, in 1934 Chiang's Nationalist Army had the Communists surrounded and blockaded. However, Mao organized his followers, broke through the Nationalist lines, and the Communists began the "Long March." Approximately 100,000 Communists began a 5,000 to 6,000-mile march across some of the most rugged terrain in China. Twenty thousand of them reached northern China in 1935.

With the Japanese attack in 1937, both the Communists and Nationalists found themselves resisting further Japanese aggression. From 1940 on, however, as the Nationalists fought the Japanese, the Communists extended their influence in China. Mao concentrated on building up the Red Army and extending its control. In the areas of China under Communist control, economic and social reforms were introduced. Land rentals were reduced and education programs were begun.

The Communist Victory

When World War II ended, both the Nationalists and Communists tried to regain control of the areas in eastern China that had been under Japanese control.

In 1947 the Communists and Nationalists battled for control of Manchuria. After the Communists won, they began to push the Nationalists southward. In 1949 the Nationalists could no longer hold the country, and they fled to **Taiwan,** an island off the coast of mainland China. They established a government called the Republic of China, with Chiang Kai-shek as president, and claimed that the mainland, actually part of their country, was in rebellion.

On October 1, 1949, the Communists established the **People's Republic of China,** with Mao Zedong as the chairman of the Chinese Communist Party and **Chou En-lai** (Zhou Enlai) as premier. The capital was established at Peiping, and the city was renamed Peking.

Why the Nationalists Lost the Civil War

One of the most important reasons the Nationalists lost the war was that the Communists were supported by the peasants. When the Nationalists ruled, they did little to relieve the burden of the Chinese peasants (80 percent of the population). Mao and the Communists promised an extensive program of land reform and reduced land rents in the areas under their control.

The Communist forces did little actual fighting against the Japanese during World War II. They used the war instead to spread their influence throughout northern and central China. When the war ended, the Communist forces were strong, fresh, and ready. The Nationalist Army, on the other hand, was war-weary and demoralized. The Communist leaders who survived the Long March had suffered with their people and were seen as popular folk heroes. They were hardened and disciplined. Moreover, the leaders of the Communists—Mao Zedong, Chu Teh (Zhu De), and Zhou En-lai—knew how to appeal to the Chinese people who were tired of inflation, war, and corruption and blamed Chiang and the Nationalists.

Goals of the People's Republic of China in 1949

The three major goals of the Communists in 1949 were to reestablish China's world prominence, to push economic development, and to improve life for the Chinese people. To reestablish their prominence, the Chinese had to control China again and remove the foreign imperialists. Industries owned and operated by foreigners were nationalized, Christianity was banned, and Christian missionaries were expelled from China. The Communists brought under Chinese control border areas that had at one time been part of the Chinese empire or tributary states. Such areas included Sinkiang (Xinjiang), Manchuria, Inner Mongolia, and Tibet (Xizang).

To achieve world prominence, the Communists realized that China must be capable of competing with the Western powers both economically and militarily. Consequently, their early economic goal was to industrialize China as rapidly as possible. They stressed industrial production at the expense of agriculture and employed five-year plans.

To achieve their goals, the Communists had to transform Chinese society and win the loyalty of the Chinese people. To suppress Confucianism and turn the Chinese into supporters of the Communist state, the Communists were determined to replace family loyalty with loyalty to the state and party. The Communists used the education system to do this. The legal system was used to improve the position of women. New marriage laws prevented families from forcing girls to accept arranged marriages. Divorce laws gave women equal rights. Women were employed in all occupations. The Communists also un-

119

dertook mass campaigns to improve health and sanitation. Rural "doctors" were trained in the combined use of traditional Chinese medicine and Western medical practices.

A thought-reform movement was established to eradicate the influence of traditional Chinese ideas and replace them with socialist ideology and the cult of "Maoism." Former owners of industries, the intelligentsia, business people, and others were subjected to stringent retraining sessions and indoctrinated in socialist ideology. Mao's "Red Book"—*The Thought of Mao Zedong*—became required reading in schools, in factory study sessions, peasant study sessions, etc.

The Cultural Revolution

In the late 1950s, Mao's almost complete control of events in China was challenged for the first time. Conservative party leaders questioned Mao's revolutionary domestic and foreign policies. Mao's opponents were called reactionaries or counterrevolutionaries and were led by **Liu Shaoqi** (Liu Hsao Ch'i). In 1965 their differences became an actual power struggle. Because the conflict was over economic, educational, scientific, political, and social programs, it became known as the "Cultural Revolution."

Mao closed the schools and sent high school and college students into the streets to rout out reactionaries. The students, who were known as **Red Guards,** attacked, intimidated, and humiliated Mao's opponents and anyone they suspected of being reactionary or influenced by Western ideas. They plunged China into chaos. Factories closed, industrial production fell, and transportation facilities were disrupted. Estimates of the number of people who died ran into the hundreds of thousands. The chaos eventually led to a military crackdown, and by 1969 the Cultural Revolution was over. Mao appeared to have won the struggle.

Policies Pursued Since Mao's Death

Following the Cultural Revolution, a power struggle emerged between the moderates led by Zhou Enlai (Chou En-lai), premier of the People's Republic since 1949, and the radicals, led by Jiang Qing (Chiang Ch'ing), Mao's wife.

After Mao's death in 1976, Jiang Qing and three of her strongest allies, who became known as the "Gang of Four," tried to take power. However, they were arrested, charged with plotting to seize power, and crimes against the people and the party during the Cultural Revolution. In 1980 they were tried. All four were found guilty, and Jiang was given the death penalty (which was commuted to life imprisonment in 1983). One of the purposes of the trial was to punish the Gang of Four for the way they treated members of the Chinese leadership during the Cultural Revolution. Another was to decrease the esteem in which Mao was held by the Chinese people. Deng

Xiaoping, the real ruler of China since Mao's death, felt it was necessary to remove the cult of Mao to effectively carry out his policies. Mao's support for the Gang of Four was revealed during the trial, and it showed the Chinese people that Mao's policies in his old age were in error.

United States-China Relations, 1949 to the Present

In 1949 the United States refused to recognize the People's Republic of China as the legitimate government of China. Instead, it recognized the Nationalist Chinese government on Taiwan, under the leadership of Chiang Kai-shek. In 1950 the Communists seized United States' consular buildings in China, and all direct diplomatic ties were broken off.

The Korean War broke out in June 1950 when North Korean troops invaded South Korea. United Nations' forces were rushed to Korea to support the South Koreans. By autumn of 1950 the United Nations' and South Korean forces had pushed north to the Yalu River, the boundary between North Korea and China. Fearing an invasion of Manchuria, Mao sent Chinese forces across the Yalu, and fighting raged until 1953, when an armistice was finally signed reestablishing the Korean border along the 38th parallel.

As a result of the Korean War, the United States recognized Nationalist China (Taiwan) as the legitimate government of all China and resisted all attempts to seat representatives of the Chinese Communist government in the United Nations. The United States' Taiwan policy was considered by Mao as another humiliating blow from a Western imperialist power.

In October 1971 the United States ended its objection to seating the People's Republic in the UN, arguing instead that both Chinas should be seated. However, Communist China was seated and Nationalist China was expelled from the world organization in 1971. The People's Republic of China was given a permanent seat on the UN Security Council (previously held by Taiwan).

Another region in Asia that caused friction between the United States and Communist China was Vietnam. When the Communists began to make inroads in South Vietnam through the activities of guerrillas known as Viet Cong, the United States increased its military aid and sent military advisers. In 1965 the United States began to send combat forces to Vietnam. The Viet Cong were assisted and reinforced by the North Vietnamese, who in turn received aid from the Soviet Union and Communist China. China strenuously objected to the American role in Vietnam and its invasions of Cambodia and Laos.

In 1971 there was an improvement in relations between the United States and Communist China when an American ping-pong team was

121

invited to China. This was the first time in over twenty years that an American group had been invited to China. In 1972 President **Richard Nixon** made a state trip to China, and the two nations agreed to reciprocal contact and exchange, and they also agreed to expand trade. In 1973 missions of the two nations were established, and in January 1979, full diplomatic relations were established.

Taiwan continues to be a problem for the United States and China. The United States recognizes Taiwan as an independent nation, while Communist China still considers it a province of China.

Trade relations between the United States and China have considerably expanded. The United States became China's second largest trading partner, after Japan. Diplomatic and trade relations were strained, however, by the Tienanmen Square massacre of students in June 1989.

Relations Between the People's Republic and the Third World

Communist China sees itself as the example of revolutionary change for the former colonies of Western powers and also as the leader of the Third World nations. It has supported Marxist revolutions in Third World nations, provided technical and financial assistance, and set up cultural exchanges with nations in Africa and Asia.

Sino-Soviet Relations

The Sino-Soviet Treaty of Friendship of 1950 seemed to indicate that a long-lasting supportive relationship between China and the Soviet Union had begun. The Soviet Union agreed to assist China against aggressive attacks and provide economic and military assistance. By 1960, however, the Soviet Union had cut off its assistance.

Reasons for the split between China and the USSR included:

1. **Krushchev's attacks on Stalin.** Mao was a great admirer of Stalin.

2. **Peaceful coexistence.** Krushchev believed that through peaceful coexistence, the world's people would see the superiority of the Communist system, and communism would spread worldwide. Mao believed war and revolution were necessary.

3. **Leadership.** The Soviet Union considered itself the leader of the world Communist movement. Mao disputed its claim to leadership.

4. **Soviet support for India.** In 1962 when Indian and Chinese forces clashed over territory, the Soviet Union assisted India.

5. **Border disputes.** The Soviets hold territory which China claims in Central Asia and northeastern China. There have been occasional outbreaks of fighting between troops stationed on the borders.

6. **Afghanistan.** China objected to the Soviet invasion in 1979.

Mikhail Gorbachev's trip to China in May 1989 was intended to normalize relations, but his visit was upstaged by the student rebellion in Tienanmen Square.

China's New Status in the Pacific

Chinese diplomatic relations with Japan were reestablished following President Nixon's trip to China in 1972. Since then, the two countries have signed trade agreements and Japan has become China's largest trading partner. Japan imports China's agricultural products and petroleum, and China imports Japanese machinery and technology. Japan has given China millions of dollars in loans for development.

In 1984 Great Britain and China reached an agreement to return the island of Hong Kong to Chinese control in 1997. Hong Kong's economy will continue to be based on private enterprise for at least 50 years, until 2047. Its social and legal systems will remain, and it will be allowed a great deal of control over its own affairs. China will be in charge of defense and foreign affairs.

QUESTIONS

Multiple Choice. Select the letter of the answer that correctly completes each statement.

1. The "unequal treaties" were the result of a war fought against
   A. Japan
   B. England
   C. Russia
   D. Vietnam

2. Which of the following required a high degree of knowledge and education?
   A. the tribute system
   B. the civil service
   C. the foreign service
   D. the military

3. The Chinese considered foreigners to be barbarians. This attitude was an example of
   A. ethnocentrism
   B. cultural diffusion
   C. empathy
   D. interdependence

4. During the 19th century, Western nations were able to gain control over parts of China mainly because
   A. the Chinese had a strong tradition of nonviolence
   B. China lacked the military technology needed to stop these ventures
   C. China was promised aid for its industries
   D. the Chinese lacked a strong cultural identity

5. During the Communist Revolution in China, many farmers supported the Communists because the Communists promised
   A. land reform
   B. a peace treaty with Japan
   C. a federal republic
   D. aid from the industrial nations

ESSAYS

1. Select any four of the following leaders and discuss how each one played an important role in China's history in this century.

> Sun Yat-sen
> Chiang Kai-shek
> Mao Zedong
> Chou En-lai
> Deng Xiaoping

2. Many events have had profound significance in China's history. Among these have been the following:

> Opium Wars (1840s)
> Taiping Rebellion (1864)
> Civil War (1927–1949)
> "Cultural Revolution" (1966–1970)
> Tienanmen Square Massacre (1989)

Select any four of these and do the following for each one:
A. Explain one reason why it occurred.
B. Explain one result of this event for China.

I. Physical Geography (the Physical Setting of Japan)

Location and Size

Japan is an island nation (archipelago) lying off the east coast of the Asian mainland in the northern Pacific Ocean, separated from the mainland by the Sea of Japan and the Korean Strait. Because it has no land borders with the rest of Asia, Japan has been able to maintain its insular (separate) quality, develop a sense of identity, and borrow

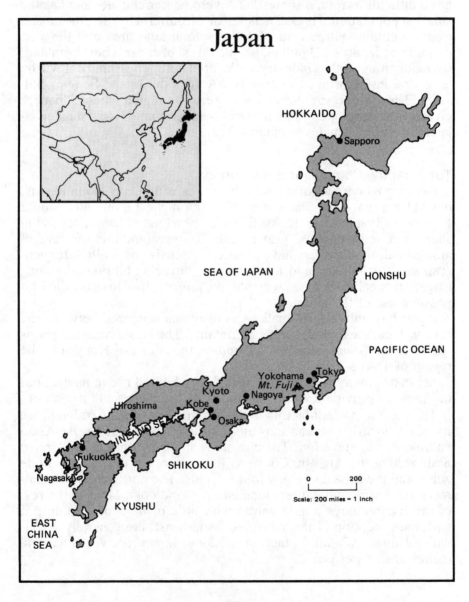

125

selectively from the cultures of the nations near it. Through the processes of cultural borrowing, adaptation, and assimilation, Japan has created a uniquely Japanese society. Korea (a "land bridge" to Japan) served as a cultural bridge between Japan and China.

Japan's land area is approximately 143,000 square miles, and it has a coastline of over 16,000 miles, with many excellent harbors. The four main islands of Japan are **Hokkaido, Honshu, Shikoku,** and **Kyushu.** Hokkaido, the northernmost and second largest of the islands, has a difficult terrain, a somewhat severe winter climate, and has the smallest population. Hokkaido is Japan's frontier. Honshu, the largest island, contains 60 percent of Japan's total land area and the vast majority of Japan's 123 million people. Most of Japan's best farmland, its major cities, and its industry are located here. The island of Kyushu is second in importance to Honshu. Across the Inland Sea lies Shikoku. These three southern islands were the region where Japanese civilization developed. Japan also contains some 3,400 smaller islands, many of which are uninhabited.

Topography, Climate, and Resources

Because 85 percent of the total land area of Japan is mountainous, only 11 percent of the land is arable. The highest mountain, Mount Fuji, or Fujiyama (over 12,000 feet), is an extinct volcano, conical in shape and snow-covered year round. To overcome this shortage of arable land, the Japanese have practiced intensive agriculture for generations—reclaiming land from the sea, terracing hillsides, building irrigation canal systems, and employing human labor to make the best possible use of the land.

Japan has only a few small areas of plains squeezed between the seacoast and the foothills of the mountains. The most important plains region is the **Kanto,** which is located on the island of Honshu in the region of Tokyo-Yokohama.

Japan has many rivers. They are of very limited use in navigation, but they do provide a source of hydroelectric power and irrigation.

The most important factors in determining the climate of Japan are its island location (ocean currents), latitude, nearness to the Asian continent, and elevation. The climate is similar to that of the United States along the Atlantic Coast, as it lies in much the same latitude zone, and the Japanese enjoy four seasons. The northern Japan summers are warm, and winters long, snowy, and cold. Most of the rest of the Japan enjoys a mild winter with little or no snow. Summers, with the exception of the subtropical southeast, are generally warm, with adequate rainfall. In fact, nearly all of Japan receives at least 40 inches of rain per year.

Japan lies at the northern edge of monsoon Asia. In summer, the moist, cool winds bring rains to the southeastern coasts of Japan. The winter monsoon drops heavy snowfall on the northwestern slopes of Honshu and Hokkaido. September and October in Japan can be a dangerous time as it is the season of typhoons (tropical wind storms much like hurricanes), which can cause severe damage to buildings, crops, and people and very often result in tsunami (seismic sea waves), which do even more damage.

Japan's resource base, like its arable land, is severely limited. Deposits of iron ore and petroleum are limited. Deposits of coal are extensive, but the coal is low-grade. The Japanese must import the raw materials needed for industrial production.

Japan lies in what is often referred to as the fire rim of the Pacific or the "ring of fire," an earthquake and volcano zone. More than

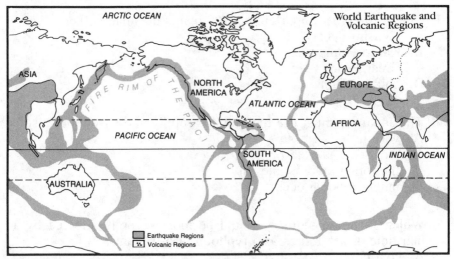

Japan is located in a volcano and earthquake prone area know as the "Fire Rim of the Pacific"

half of the world's active volcanoes lie in this zone. Most of Japan's volcanoes are inactive, though there is an occasional eruption. Earthquakes occur much more frequently. An average of four earthquakes a day strike Japan. Most are slight tremors, but every few years a major quake strikes Japan.

The sea plays an enormous role in the lives of the Japanese. They depend on it as a source of livelihood, of food, transportation, and in recent years for commerce. For many years the sea also served as an effective barrier to invasion by other countries.

QUESTIONS

Multiple Choice. Select the letter of the answer that correctly completes each statement.

1. Which statement best characterizes Japan?
   A. part of the Asian mainland
   B. the longest archipelago in the world
   C. an island nation
   D. flat topography

2. Which part of Japan is larger than the other three?
   A. Kyushu
   B. Honshu
   C. Shikoku
   D. Hokkaido

3. One of the most important coastal plains in Japan is the
   A. Kyushu Plain
   B. Kanto Plain
   C. Great Plain
   D. Shikari Plain

4. The Japanese must use their land carefully and wisely because
   A. very little is arable
   B. most of it is desert
   C. the topography is uneven
   D. much flooding occurs

5. Which Japanese industry would be most severely affected by a maritime disaster such as a typhoon or a tsunami?
   A. coal mining
   B. electronics
   C. cameras
   D. fishing

ESSAYS

1. As an island nation, Japan has been greatly influenced by its nearness to water. Discuss two ways in which Japan has been affected by its being surrounded by water.

2. Japan has a shortage of arable land. Describe three ways in which Japan has overcome this situation.

II. Economic Geography (Economic Development of Japan)

Economic Recovery after World War II

At the close of World War II, Japan lay in ruins. More than 3 million people had been killed; 10 million were homeless. One-fourth of Japan's industry and manufacturing facilities had been destroyed. Communications and transportation lines had been badly damaged. Nearly all of the maritime fleet had been destroyed, and harbor and port facilities were in ruins. The Japanese empire had been reduced to the four main islands, and as a result it had lost its source of raw materials.

The leaders of the occupation (see Section IV: United States Occupation of Japan, 1945–1952) realized that to build a democratic nation, there would also have to be economic reform. A program of land reform to increase food production by providing greater incentives to farmers, who now owned the land, was the most successful and long-lasting program. A second step in economic reform was to destroy the **zaibatsu** (monopolies). However, since the financial resources of the zaibatsu could help rebuild Japan, the effort to break them up was dropped. The zaibatsu still exist in Japan today (Mitsui, Mitsubishi, Fuji, Sumitomo). A third effort at economic reform was to organize and encourage the organization of labor unions.

Characteristics of the Japanese Economy

There has been tremendous growth in the Japanese economy since 1950. Today its GNP is over $2,500 billion, second only to the United States. Per capita income in 1986 was over $21,000, and the unemployment rate is less than 3 percent.

Japan is the world's leading shipbuilding nation. It is a leader in producing textiles, cameras, microscopes, and electronic goods. By the 1980s it had become one of the leading producers of cars and trucks. It exports steel and machinery. It is second only to the United States in the manufacture of computers. In 1986 its trade surplus was over $80 billion.

How did the Japanese make such incredible economic gains after the almost total destruction of World War II?

Japan's economic recovery was aided by:

1. **Its people.** The Japanese people were disciplined and hard-working. The labor force was highly skilled, receptive to on-the-job training, and well-educated. For many years they accepted low wages, which gave Japanese industry a competitive edge in the world market.

2. **Technology.** When industry was rebuilt after the war, the latest in technology was used, allowing the Japanese to use more efficient methods than countries with older factories and giving it a competitive edge.

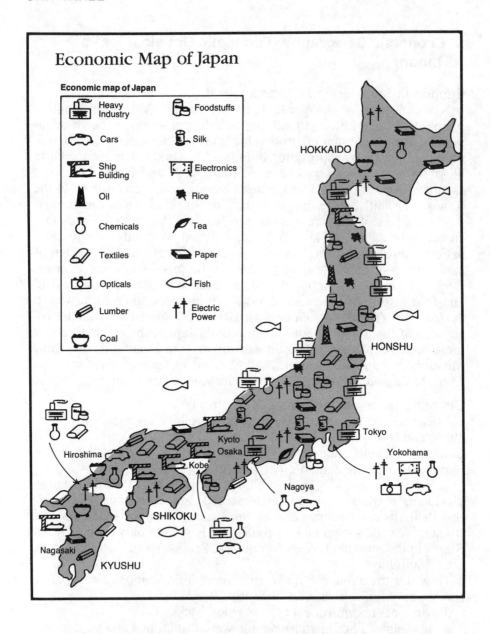

Economic Map of Japan

Economic map of Japan

3. **United States' assistance.** The United States provided Japan with millions of dollars of aid, assistance, and loans to rebuild its economy because it wanted a strong democratic ally in Asia.

4. **Restrictions on the military.** Japan does not have the enormous cost of maintaining military forces. Instead, the United States is committed to defending Japan. Japan spends less than 1 percent of its GNP on the military, while the United States spends over 7 percent.

5. **Government assistance.** Business in Japan is assisted by the government through low-interest loans, subsidies for new businesses, favorable trade agreements with other nations, and tariffs to protect Japanese industries.

Continuing Needs and Problems Facing the Japanese Economy

Japan's scarcity of raw materials and oil has affected its pattern of economic development. Japan must import almost all of the mineral ores it needs for industry, such as copper, iron ore, lead, coal, zinc, and all its petroleum. Until the 1970s most petroleum came from the Middle East. When OPEC embargoed oil in 1973, Japanese industry suffered from energy shortages and unemployment rose. Since then, the Japanese have found a new source of oil in China. Japan's economic life depends on the ability to import raw materials and its capacity to maintain and expand its exports to pay for those raw materials.

Although arable land in Japan is scarce, by making use of the advanced farming technology of the "Green Revolution," Japanese farmers provide about 70 percent of the nation's food supply. Most of the rest of its food supply comes from the United States, China, Australia, and Canada.

Japan Must Import to Live

Wool	100%	Wheat	91.7%
Cotton	100%	Sugar	86%
Crude Oil	99.7%	Coal	65%
Iron Ore	99.3%	Lumber	47%
Soy Beans	96.4%		

United States-Japanese Economic Interactions

Since the 1970s the balance of trade between the United States and Japan has run heavily in favor of Japan. The U.S. buys about 24 percent of Japanese exports. The United States feels that the Japanese government's restrictions on the import of foreign goods is largely responsible and that Japanese tariffs keep American goods from selling in Japan. Japanese investments are welcomed in the United States, but the Japanese government restricts foreign investments in Japan. The United States government has accused Japan of employing unfair trade practices.

Japan needs to maintain its high level of exports to pay for imported raw materials, and the United States needs to increase its exports to Japan to decrease its trade deficit. Consequently, the United States has asked Japan to voluntarily decrease some exports to America, to open their markets to more American goods, and to allow American companies to operate in Japan on an equal basis with Japanese companies. The United States has threatened to increase tariffs and place import quotas on Japanese goods unless Japan ends its unfair trade practices. Japan has promised to increase its defense spending, relax trade barriers, and export less. Some concessions have been made, but the Japanese do not really wish to allow the Americans free access to the Japanese market.

Japan's Role in the Global Economic Picture
While Japan may be dependent on other countries for resources, economic strength gives it power in international relations. While it has not played an international political role consistent with its economic strength, its influence has been felt through its trade policies. In the 1980s Japan participated in a series of economic summits with the world's leading non-Communist economic powers. The Japanese have promised to increase foreign access to Japan's domestic markets at these economic summits, but so far no major changes have been made. Also in recent years, there has been a large increase in Japanese economic investment in the United States.

QUESTIONS

Multiple Choice. Select the letter of the answer that correctly completes each statement.

1. Japan has overcome its shortage of mineral resources by relying on
   A. Shinto spirits
   B. allies
   C. imports
   D. the United Nations

2. "Yen" is a word most often used when talking about
   A. transistors
   B. money
   C. sushi
   D. architecture

3. Japan is considered an "economic giant" for all of the following reasons EXCEPT for the fact that
   A. most of the labor force is engaged in agriculture
   B. Japan makes use of scientific management and innovation
   C. its industry utilizes standardization
   D. most of its labor force is engaged in industrial production

4. Japanese-American interdependence is characterized most by
   A. America's wish for Japan's goods and Japan's need for American markets
   B. America's need for foreign investment and Japan's need for American surplus goods
   C. America's dependence on agricultural imports and Japan's need for electronics
   D. America's need for nuclear arms and Japan's ability to supply material for that need

ESSAY

The following statements are about Japan's economy:

1. Japan is more of a producer of finished goods than a supplier of raw materials

2. Japan is considered the "Great Britain of the Orient"

3. Japan's G.N.P. has grown enormously since World War II

4. Japan must import in order to survive

Choose any three of these statements. Discuss the validity of each one by giving at least two reasons or explanations.

III. Human and Cultural Geography

The Japanese People

The early inhabitants of Japan migrated from northern Asia, Korea, China, and Southeast Asia over hundreds of years. These peoples gradually intermingled and intermarried and became the Japanese people we know today. The Japanese people are ethnically **homogeneous** (alike), and the only really distinct group of people who remained were the **Ainu** (the original inhabitants of Japan), who were pushed northward, finally to the island of Hokkaido, by the people we call Japanese.

The Japanese tend to think of themselves as a racially pure people. As a result, they seldom accept foreigners as full members of their society. Japan's strong sense of cultural unity is a result of Japan's

133

relative isolation from foreign influence for many centuries and its cultural homogeneity for at least 1,000 years.

Shinto, the "Way of the Gods"

Shinto, the native religion of Japan, began as a simple form of nature worship. The Shintoist believed that all natural things—trees, rocks, storms, ocean waves—contained *kami* (the spirits of the gods). Later on, Shinto came to include hero and ancestor worship.

Shinto taught no moral precepts, no ethical code. It taught that the Japanese should be thankful for and reverent to all aspects of nature; grateful for life, birth, fertility. Shinto teaches that physical, not moral, purity is of the utmost importance.

Because Shinto teaches no concept of a single god and no moral precepts, it has been relatively easy for the Japanese to accept other religious teachings. Buddhism and Shinto have existed side by side for over 1,000 years.

Buddhism

Buddhism was introduced from Korea in 552 A.D. At first, it was only popular among the nobility and upper classes. Buddhist teachings were too complicated and its outlook too pessimistic to appeal to the common people. During the Kamakura period, Buddhism in Japan underwent basic changes, however, and its teachings were made easier to understand and accept. Consequently, Buddhism began to be accepted by the lower classes, who combined Shinto and Buddhism. Happy events such as birth and marriage were observed with Shinto ceremonies and funerals with Buddhist rites.

One of the Buddhist sects, which became especially popular with the samurai (warriors), is **Zen.** Zen teaches that each person must seek enlightenment individually through meditation and that no others can help an individual achieve enlightenment. The meditation requires great self-discipline and the ability to conquer oneself. The self-discipline learned in Zen was later applied to the code of the warrior, Bushido. The simplicity taught by Zen is revealed in Japanese painting, poetry, and the tea ceremony.

Chinese Influence

The first contacts between the Japanese and Chinese took place through Korea. Chinese civilization was much more advanced than that of the Japanese, and some powerful Japanese determined that it should be introduced in Japan. By the 10th century, Japan had been transformed, but it was not just an imitation or copy of China. Chinese culture was adapted to suit Japanese needs.

During the rule of **Prince Shotoku** in the late 500s and early 600s, Japanese students were sent to China to study religion, philosophy, art, architecture, and government administration. The greatest flowering of Chinese culture in Japan occurred during the Nara period (710–794). The Yamato rulers established a central government based on that of the Chinese, and officials were appointed to govern administrative units, but no civil service was established. Japanese officials were chosen, instead, because of their connections and families. The Chinese emperor ruled by the mandate of heaven, but the Japanese emperor held the throne because he was considered divine.

The Chinese writing system was adopted, but it presented problems. So eventually the Japanese developed a writing system of their own based on the Chinese. It is a mixture of Chinese characters for words and symbols that stand for sounds. The phonetic (for sound) symbols are called kana; there are 50 of them.

In 708, the Japanese built their first permanent capital city, Nara, modeled after the Chinese capital. Later in the 8th century, a new capital city was built at Heian (now Kyoto), which remained the imperial capital until 1868.

During the Heian period (794–1185), contact with China was decreased. Japan stopped sending students and envoys to China to study. They believed that they had advanced to the point where they could develop their own arts and culture without Chinese influence. Japanese art and literature blossomed. The world's first novel, *The Tale of Genji,* describing Heian court life, was written by Lady Murasaki about 1000 A.D. Painting, sculpture, poetry, architecture, and landscape gardening flourished. The literacy rate increased considerably. During their long period of isolation, the Japanese developed a strong feeling of their own uniqueness.

Cultural Developments During the Feudal Period

Zen Buddhism was introduced to Japan at about the same time the first shogunate was established. Zen influenced the development of chanoyu (tea ceremony), ikebana (flower arranging), and landscape gardening. Literature and poetry flourished. Haiku poetry was developed and refined during shogunal rule. Japanese **Noh** drama, **Bunraku** (puppet plays), and **Kabuki** drama developed. Landscape painting achieved remarkable refinement. Japanese arts reflected cultural refinement (haiku, landscape painting, tea ceremony). Their art also reflected the times, with drama often depicting their present way of life as well as the conflict of the changing times.

Population Characteristics of Japan Today

Japan's population in 1988 was estimated at about 123 million. The country itself is slightly smaller than California. With a population density of about 850 people per square mile, Japan is one of the most

Haiku is the simplest form of poetry. It consists of one verse with seventeen syllables, spaced over three lines in a 5-7-5 pattern. A good haiku sets a mood, then flashes a sudden understanding of life—all in three lines.

The Pond

The ancient pond
A frog leaps in
The sound of water

BASHO

A Remembrance

Show that we two
looked at together—this yew
Is it fallen anew?

BASHO

Mist

Above the veil
of mist, from time to time
there lifts a sail . . .

GAKOKU

The Crow

On a leafless branch
a crow has settled:
autumn nightfall.

BASHO

crowded nations in the world, and living space for urban Japanese is incredibly limited. About 86 percent of the Japanese people are employed in manufacturing, mining, and service industries. The other 14 percent are engaged in agriculture. The birth rate has decreased in recent years, but because of improved health care and increased life expectancy, the population continues to grow slowly. By the year 2030, Japan's population is expected to stabilize, or cease to grow.

The Japanese population is one of the most homogeneous in the world. Over 99 percent of the people are ethnic Japanese. The largest minority group are the Koreans. Only one major language, Japanese, is spoken in the country, and over 80 percent of the people belong to the same religious grouping—a blend of Shinto and Buddhism.

Education System

The importance of education in Japan is unmatched in any other country. Entrance to the top-ranking universities is highly competitive. Only one of six applicants is accepted. As a result, the pressure on a Japanese student to achieve is incredible.

Education is compulsory through junior high school. Entrance exams must be passed to enter high school and university. Some of the better schools even have entrance exams for kindergarten. Since good jobs and the right education are so closely linked, the competition in schools is fierce.

The school day, the school week, and the school year are longer in Japan than in the United States. Discipline is strict, and all the students are expected to study a foreign language. Most students receive outside tutoring and/or attend "cram" schools, even during vacations. Teachers are considered responsible for students' behavior both inside and outside the school.

Urban Issues and Problems

Many of Japan's cities are clustered together in a megalopolis (one city blends into the edges of another). Because of the size of Japan's urban areas and its industries, Japan has one of the highest rates of pollution in the world. Smog is a serious problem. Rivers and coastal waters are being polluted by industrial wastes. The increasing use of insecticides and chemical fertilizers by farmers adds to the pollution problem.

Japan's cities are terribly overcrowded. There is a severe housing shortage. Transportation, while among the best in the world, is inadequate to meet the needs of the enormous urban populations.

Evolving Role of Women

Since the end of World War II, the roles and status of women have changed. Much of this is due to the constitution, which gave women equal rights. They were allowed to vote, to own property, to hold political office, and to seek divorce. They must receive an education, and more and more of them go on to receive a university education. Nearly 40 percent of the Japanese work force is female, though the majority of them have low-status, service-oriented jobs. Many of them earn less money than men doing the same job. The man's authority as head of the family has decreased somewhat. In addition, about six of ten working women are married. They share not only economic responsibility but authority as well. Arranged marriages are still common, however.

Treatment of Minorities

There are only a few non-Japanese people in the country. About 12,000 **Ainu,** the original inhabitants of Japan, live on the northern island of Hokkaido. Most of them have been integrated into rural life on Hokkaido.

The second major group of non-Japanese people are the Koreans, most of whom came during World War II to work in wartime industries. Koreans are discriminated against in employment, housing, and social life. They were not allowed to become Japanese citizens until 1985.

A third minority group are the burakumin people, descendants of people who did jobs considered unclean by the Japanese, such as butchering. They used to live separately in small villages and were considered outcasts. Today they live in segregated slums in the cities and are discriminated against in housing, employment, education, and social life. There may be as many as 3 million burakumin.

Social and Work Relations

The Japanese share an intense loyalty to groups, such as the family or the company. Group loyalty means putting the interests of the group before one's own interests, being willing to accept the decisions of the group, and avoiding situations that might shame the group. This loyalty concept extends to the workplace. Employers assure their workers of lifetime employment and expect loyal service in return. Japanese employees take great pride in their company and do not change jobs often because it would be disloyal to the company.

The Japanese do not like emotional confrontations and blunt speech, which might hurt feelings or cause one to lose "face" (pride). They reach decisions in business as they do in government, by consensus, they negotiate until everyone agrees on a decision. Consensus may take a long time, but for the Japanese it means that everyone is satisfied with a decision.

Most probably the great emphasis on conformity grew out of the problem of accommodating too many people on too little land. People had to learn to cooperate and restrain themselves because the Japanese have had to live uncomfortably close to each other physically. Only harmony in human relationships would make such close physical proximity bearable.

Impact of Japan's Aesthetic Ideas

The Japanese still maintain their identity through traditional values and activities. They have a strong love of nature, which is expressed in activities such as hiking and skiing and in landscape gardens and flower arranging. The Japanese still use haiku as a creative medium. Millions of Japanese write haiku, and there are national poetry contests each year. Most Japanese are skilled in at least one of the traditional arts: music, dance, drama, painting, calligraphy.

QUESTIONS

Multiple Choice. Select the letter of the answer that correctly completes each statement.

1. The most populated part of Japan is
   A. Honshu
   B. Kyushu
   C. Hokkaido
   D. Shikoku

2. Even though Japan has few natural resources, it has a high standard of living mainly because it has
   A. developed technology that can be exchanged for the resources it needs
   B. printed more money whenever living standards have started to decline
   C. imported manufactured goods
   D. produced goods and services without obtaining resources

3. Which statement best describes Japan today?
   A. Japan has become an urban society that has adopted Western values in nearly every aspect of life.
   B. Japan has continued to rely on China and Korea for its cultural values and technological development.
   C. Japan has remained primarily an agrarian society with an emphasis on maintaining traditional values.
   D. Japan has adopted modern technological advances while maintaining aspects of the traditional culture.

4. Birth and marriage ceremonies are celebrated with rituals associated with
   A. Zen
   B. Bushido
   C. Shintoism
   D. Buddhism

5. Nara, Kyoto and Tokyo are cities which have all been
   A. centers of heavy industry
   B. conquered by the Chinese
   C. capitals of Japan
   D. populated by the Ainu

6. Haiku is a form of
   A. painting
   B. poetry
   C. furniture
   D. architecture

ESSAY

Read carefully the following statements about Japan.

1. Japanese culture has been greatly influenced by China.

2. Japan's population is generally homogeneous.

For each of these statements, discuss the validity with reference to three specific reasons or facts.

IV. History and Political Geography (Historical Setting of Japan)

Early History

One of the major sources of information on early Japanese history is contained in the chronicles of Chinese and Korean visitors to Japan as early as the 3rd century A.D. Another source of information is found in archeological discoveries, indicating that Stone Age people lived in Japan perhaps as long as 200,000 years ago. The third major source of information is contained in the myths, legends, and traditions of the Japanese, which were first written down in the 8th century A.D. in the **Kojiki** (Record of Ancient Matters) in 712 and the **Nihongi** (Chronicles of Japan) in 720.

The **Jomon** culture in Japan dates from about 3000 to 300 B.C. The people of this culture maintained themselves by hunting and gathering and represent Mesolithic culture in Japan. From 300 B.C. to 300 A.D. a new wave of migrants from the mainland introduced wet-rice cultivation, bronze working, and finally iron-working. This new culture was called **Yayoi.**

The **Tomb** period (300–650 A.D.), so-called because of burial mounds or tombs created during this period, was the most advanced culture of prehistoric Japan. During the Tomb period, references to Japan show up in Chinese chronicles and indicate that Japan was organized along clan lines. Towards the end of the Tomb period, the Yamato clan gained ascendancy and became the most powerful of the warring clans in Japan.

The Yamato clan leaders were the first emperors of Japan. In 645 A.D. nobles who favored the adoption of Chinese culture began a program known as the **Taika Reforms** (Great Reforms) that made political, social, and economic changes. They proclaimed the Yamato ruler emperor of all Japan, abolished private ownership of land, and declared that all territory was the property of the imperial government. To justify and solidify this claim, they called for the writing of an official history of Japan. According to the official histories (**Kojiki** and **Nihongi**), the rulers of Yamato were descended from Amaterasu, the sun goddess, who was descended from Izanagi and Izanami, the creators of Japan. Since the emperor is considered divine, the Japanese have never questioned the imperial family's right to the throne.

Often the emperor has been a ruler in name only, and a strong noble or warrior (samurai) family or, in modern times, military leaders have ruled Japan. The emperor's most significant role has been as high priest of the Shinto religion and intermediary between the people and the gods. Japanese history is divided by the names of the families who ruled Japan and who used the emperor to legitimize their authority, but they never attempted to take the throne.

Important Dates in Japanese History

300 B.C.–250 A.D.	Legendary period
3000–300 B.C.	Jomon Culture
250 B.C.–250 A.D.	Yayoi Culture
250–645 A.D.	Tomb Culture
552 A.D.	Introduction of Buddhism to Japan
604 A.D.	Shotoku Taishi's *Seventeen Article Constitution*
645 A.D.	Taika Reform
702 A.D.	Taiho Code
710–784 A.D.	Nara period
794–1185 A.D.	Heian period
858–1156 A.D.	Fujiwara period
1192–1333	Kamakura (or Minamoto Shogunate) period
1274, 1281	Mongol invasions
1338–1567	Ashikaga (Shogunate) period
1549	Arrival of Francis Xavier and Christianity
1603–1868	Tokugawa (Shogunate) period
1868–1912	The Meiji restoration

The Feudal Period (1185–1600)

During Japan's feudal period, power rested in the hands of a military ruler rather than in those of the emperor. **Feudalism** was a political, economic, and social system based on land rights and individualized bonds of loyalty.

In the period from 794 to 1185, called the **Heian** period, a single family, the **Fujiwara,** came to dominate the imperial court and government. During this period the power of the central government declined, allowing clans in the countryside to claim land belonging to the emperor. As a result, the economic strength of the imperial government decreased, as did its ability to protect the outlying regions of the empire. The noble families in the countryside became more powerful, as peasants who could not protect themselves from roving bands of robbers and the Ainu gave up their land, which became part of the noble's estate. In return, the peasant was entitled to the protection of the noble and his **samurai** (warriors on horseback). The **daimyo** (the more powerful lords) built palaces, collected taxes from the peasants, and increased the size of their military. The military and the peasants built up a loyalty system to the daimyo who protected and employed them. The daimyo and the samurai became the real rulers of Japan. A feudal system similar to Europe's during the Middle Ages was the result. The daimyo controlled their own land, collected taxes, created armies, built castle headquarters, and through the peasants encouraged economic self-sufficiency. This feudal system lasted for approximately 500 years.

As the power of the Fujiwara declined, two daimyo families, the Taira and the Minamoto, struggled for power. The **Minamoto,** under the leadership of Yoritomo, won this struggle. Yoritomo forced the emperor to grant him the title of "shogun" (military ruler or general), and the daimyo and samurai gained control of Japanese government, which would last until the Tokogawa Shogunate. The shoguns were the real heads of government until the Meiji Restoration in 1867. The imperial family was used to legitimize the power of the shoguns by the granting of the shogun title.

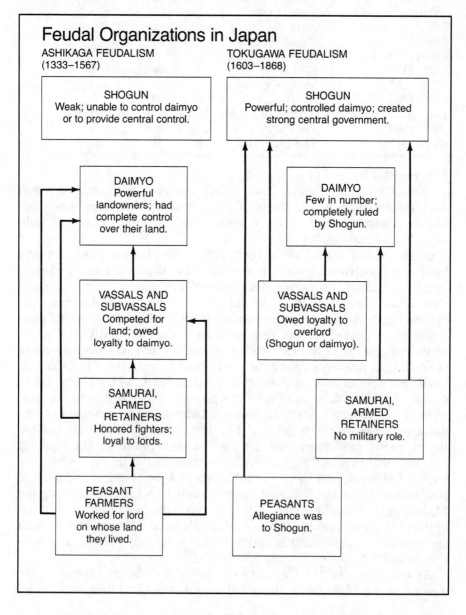

Feudal Organizations in Japan

ASHIKAGA FEUDALISM (1333–1567)

SHOGUN
Weak; unable to control daimyo or to provide central control.

DAIMYO
Powerful landowners; had complete control over their land.

VASSALS AND SUBVASSALS
Competed for land; owed loyalty to daimyo.

SAMURAI, ARMED RETAINERS
Honored fighters; loyal to lords.

PEASANT FARMERS
Worked for lord on whose land they lived.

TOKUGAWA FEUDALISM (1603–1868)

SHOGUN
Powerful; controlled daimyo; created strong central government.

DAIMYO
Few in number; completely ruled by Shogun.

VASSALS AND SUBVASSALS
Owed loyalty to overlord (Shogun or daimyo).

SAMURAI, ARMED RETAINERS
No military role.

PEASANTS
Allegiance was to Shogun.

Bushido

During the feudal period a warrior code developed, which drew on the military discipline of the samurai, Confucian ethics, Shinto, and Zen Buddhism. Bushido (the way of the warrior) was a code of conduct that stressed the importance of superior-inferior relationships and the unswerving loyalty of the samurai to their lords and through them, to the lord's superiors, including the emperor. Family loyalty was important, though it was expected that a loyal samurai would sacrifice his family for the good of his lord. The samurai subordinated individual desires for the good of the group or society. Self-discipline and self-control were stressed, as was complete indifference to death. It was considered glorious to die in battle and absolutely unacceptable to surrender. To avoid surrender or capture, a samurai was expected to commit harakiri or seppuku (ritual suicide involving disembowelment). Samurai also committed suicide in this way to atone for behavior unworthy of a samurai, for example, disloyalty to his feudal lord, if that disloyalty was discovered. According to the code of bushido, a samurai must be brave, honorable, loyal to lord and emperor, and able to subordinate his emotions.

Mongol Invasion

In 1270 Kublai Khan demanded that the Japanese pay tribute, but the Minamoto shogun refused. The Khan sent a Mongol force of 40,000 to Kyushu in 1274. The Japanese samurai were no match for the Mongol force, but they received assistance in the form of a typhoon, which destroyed much of the Mongol fleet. The Mongols were forced to abandon their invasion. To the Japanese, the typhoons were divine winds, kamikaze (kami–gods; kaze–winds) sent by the gods to protect Japan. A similar storm destroyed much of the Mongol fleet when they attempted a second invasion in 1281.

The Tokugawa Shogunate

During the Ashikaga Shogunate (1338–1568), there was much civil strife and little central control. By the late 15th century, Japan fell into the hands of local warlords. Three of the most important were Nobunaga, Hideyoshi, and Ieyasu. Nobunaga began to reunify Japan. He conquered other local warlords and eventually brought about twenty provinces under his control.

Nobunaga was followed by Hideyoshi, who within a few years had gained control of all Japan. After his death, the struggle for control was won by Ieyasu, who gained the title of shogun and created Japan's last shogunate, the **Tokugawa.**

A strong bureaucratic central government was established, with the new capital at Edo (Tokyo), from which the Tokugawa ruled over a 250-year period of peace and stability. They did this by imposing

143

controls designed to preserve the social and economic order as it existed in 1600. These controls included:

1. **The system of sankin-kotai** (alternate attendance). Each of the daimyo was required to spend every other year in Edo, and his family was required to reside in Edo at all times as hostages.

2. **The class system of the nation became a caste system.** Membership in a class was made hereditary, and the classes were ranked according to their value to society. At the top of the system were the **samurai;** the second class were the **peasants;** the third class were the skilled workers, the **craftspeople;** and the fourth class were the **merchants.**

3. **Japan was isolated.** Portuguese traders came in the 16th century and were followed by Christian missionaries. Fearing the foreign influences that came with Christianity, the Tokugawa persecuted Christians and eventually crushed the religion. The Tokugawa feared all foreign influence, and all foreign traders, except a small contingent of Dutch and Chinese who were confined to a small island in Nagasaki harbor, were expelled from the country. Japanese were forbidden to go abroad, and Japanese in other countries were forbidden to return.

Although the Tokugawa controls were designed to prevent change in Japan, change did take place. The 250 years of imposed peace and isolation led to an increase in internal commerce, the development of cities, and the strengthening of the economic power of merchants. Most of the samurai, with no wars to fight, fell on hard times and often married daughters of merchants to improve their fortunes. Many of the samurai became scholars and teachers, and the literacy rate increased considerably. During their long period of isolation, the Japanese developed a strong feeling of their own uniqueness.

Americans Arrive in Japan

On July 14, 1853, **Commodore Matthew Perry,** in command of four United States ships, sailed into Tokyo Bay. The Japanese had never seen steamships before and were astonished at the fire power of the American warships. Perry carried with him a letter from American President Millard Fillmore, demanding that Japan open its ports to American trade and ships and government guarantee of fair treatment of American sailors (shipwrecked sailors were badly treated).

The Japanese were opposed to the American demands, but the government of the shogun realized that the Japanese could not defend themselves against American technology. In 1854 the shogun's government signed a treaty opening two Japanese ports to American ships to take on supplies, and an American consulate was opened. Within four years, the United States had been granted full trade rights in several other ports, extraterritoriality, and limitations on the Japanese right to impose tariffs on American goods. Soon the European powers were demanding the same rights. The Japanese believed that Japan would be cut up into spheres of influence, as China had been, unless they took steps to prevent it.

Meiji Restoration (1868–1912)

Many Japanese blamed the shogunate for failing to defend Japan against foreign interference and believed that the Tokugawa could not resist the foreigners. In 1868 samurai forces overthrew the shogunate and restored the emperor's rule. This so-called Meiji Restoration brought to the throne Emperor Matshuhito, who was only 15 years old.

Changes by 1912

The Japanese who led the overthrow of the shogun and the restoration of the emperor believed that the only way to remove the threat of the Western powers was a rapid program of modernization to enable Japan to compete with the West. Japan already had a high literacy rate, a high degree of urbanization, a large pool of skilled labor, and channels for mass training of citizens. What stood in the way of full-scale modernization was the feudal system, which the leaders of the restoration set about to destroy.

The daimyo (feudal lords) were persuaded to give up their estates, and Japan was divided into prefectures under the direct control of the government in Tokyo (the new name for Edo). Class divisions and restrictions were abolished, and equality of all people was declared. The samurai lost all their special privileges, and universal military service was adopted. An education system was established.

The leaders of the restoration created a highly centralized bureaucratic government, which was an **oligarchy** (a small group controlling the government and allowing little opposition). In 1889 the Japanese were presented with a written constitution, a "gift from the emperor." The new constitution established a two-house legislature, called the Diet. This was a severely limited democracy, and the small elite group who took control of the government in 1868 remained in control. However, the Western powers recognized Japan's efforts to provide at least a limited democracy, and by 1899 the Western powers gave up the special privileges they had gained in the "unequal treaties."

A program of rapid modernization was begun. The government constructed railroads, highways, and telegraph lines and also built industries—textile mills, armaments factories, shipbuilding facilities—and opened mines. Later, these industries were sold to private enterprise, thereby sponsoring the development of the **zaibatsu** (Japanese industrial monopolies that controlled all aspects of an industry). Japanese students were sent to Western nations to study, and Western advisers were employed. Western experts were hired to assist the Japanese in developing a modern army and navy. By the close of the 19th century, the foundations of a truly modern state had been laid.

Japanese Expansion Prior to World War II

Japanese aggressions against weaker neighbors were a result of its need to acquire raw materials for its industrialization and were modeled after imperialist actions of the Western powers in the late 19th and early 20th centuries. By the late 19th century, Japan's rulers were concerned that Korea, "a dagger pointed at the heart of Japan," would fall into the hands of an imperialist Western power because the Manchu dynasty in China could not defend it. This led to the **Sino-Japanese War** (Sino-Chinese) of 1894 to 1895 which was won by Japan. The **Treaty of Shimonoseki** granted Japan control of Taiwan, the Pescadores, and China's Liaotung Peninsula, plus an indemnity of several hundred million dollars and trade concessions in China. Korea was declared to be independent of China, and Japan began to seek control of the region.

Japan's chief rival in Korea was Russia, and the Japanese launched an attack in 1904 against the Russian fleet based at Port Arthur, beginning the **Russo-Japanese War.** The Russians were driven out of Korea and southern Manchuria, and Japan captured Port Arthur. In 1905 American President Theodore Roosevelt negotiated peace between the two belligerents. The **Treaty of Portsmouth** gave Russia's lease on Port Arthur and its concessions in southern Manchuria to Japan. By 1910 Korea had been annexed by Japan.

World War I gave Japan the opportunity to further expand its interests in Asia. Declaring itself at war with Germany and an ally of Great Britain, Japan seized German-held territories in China. It also gained control of German-held islands in the northern Pacific—the Marshall, the Caroline, and the Marianas.

In 1915, the Japanese secretly presented the Chinese with the **"Twenty-One Demands,"** which called for political, economic, and military concessions. However, China made these demands public. The United States objected, as did many Japanese who opposed their governments' imperialist policies, and Japan dropped the demands. By the end of World War I, Japan had become the dominant military and economic power in Asia.

Japan's success led to a program known as the **"Greater East Asia Co-Prosperity Sphere,"** in which Japan tried to persuade all East Asian nations that economic cooperation with Japan was to everyone's best interest. Japan would provide technical services and manufactured products, and other nations would provide raw materials and agricultural products. It was little more than the application of the old mercantilist colonial policy by Japan in East Asia.

The 1920s saw a period of social, political, and economic unrest in Japan. There was conflict between the modernized, younger elements of society and the tradition-bound society of the countryside and the older generation. A rapid population increase (in fact, population doubled from 1868 to 1925) resulted in a high unemployment rate. Most of Japan's farmers had been reduced to tenant status.

The worldwide depression of the 1930s hurt Japan's foreign trade. Extreme nationalist groups in Japan believed that their problems could be solved through military expansion, and they encouraged the nationalist fervor of the Japanese. Japanese expansion began in Manchuria. It had rich deposits of coal and iron ore, fertile agricultural plains, raw materials, and space for Japan's excess population. In 1931 Japanese military forces invaded Manchuria, and Japan established a puppet state called **Manchukuo.** The League of Nations objected to the invasion but Japan merely withdrew from the League.

In 1937 Japan invaded China, and World War II in Asia began. World War II in Europe broke out in 1939, and in 1940 Japan, Germany, and Italy signed the **Tripartite Pact,** more commonly called the **Rome-Berlin-Tokyo Axis.** In 1941 Japan invaded Southeast Asia to gain control of vital oil, tin, and rubber resources. The United States placed an embargo on trade with Japan.

For several months in 1941 the United States and Japan were engaged in talks to resolve their differences. On December 7, 1941, Japan launched an invasion of the Dutch East Indies and an attack on the American naval base at Pearl Harbor, Hawaii. The following day the United States declared war on Japan.

Within a few months, Japanese forces had extended their control over a region stretching from Japan to Australia on the south and to the borders of India on the west. The American victory at the Battle of Midway in 1942 was the turning point of the war, and the United States began a campaign of "island hopping" (conquering important Japanese-held islands while by-passing others and leaving the Japanese forces cut off from communication and supplies) to push its way toward the Japanese homeland. President Harry Truman, in the summer of 1945, ordered the use of the first atomic bomb, which was dropped on the city of Hiroshima on August 6, 1945. After a second atomic bomb was dropped on Nagasaki on August 9, Japanese Emperor Hirohito announced Japan's surrender. For the first time in its history, Japan was conquered, and was about to be occupied, by a foreign power.

United States Occupation of Japan, 1945–1952

United States' occupation of Japan led to the diffusion of some American ideas and practices into Japanese culture. United States armed forces, under the leadership of **General Douglas MacArthur, the Supreme Commander of the Allied Powers (SCAP),** occupied Japan from 1945 to 1952. Japan was stripped of its military conquests, and its territory was restricted to the four main islands. The armed forces were disbanded and weapons factories were closed. Government and military leaders accused of war crimes were brought to trial, and those who had played a role in Japan's military expansion were removed from positions of power. Nationalistic organizations were banned. MacArthur had a new constitution written for Japan, which went into effect in 1947. It is one of the world's most democratic documents.

The American occupation of Japan also brought a number of economic and social reforms. The zaibatsu (the industrial monopolies) were broken up; a land-reform program required landlords to sell land cheaply to their tenants; all titles of nobility were abolished; the legal authority of the head of the family over other family members was abolished, and compulsory education was extended for three more years.

The Impact of the Atomic Bombs of 1945

Japan, the only nation in the world ever to have experienced the use of nuclear weapons, is opposed to their development and stockpiling. Major demonstrations have occurred in Japan protesting American storage of missiles and the arrival of American nuclear submarines. Similarly, the Japanese protest the testing of nuclear weapons by all nations.

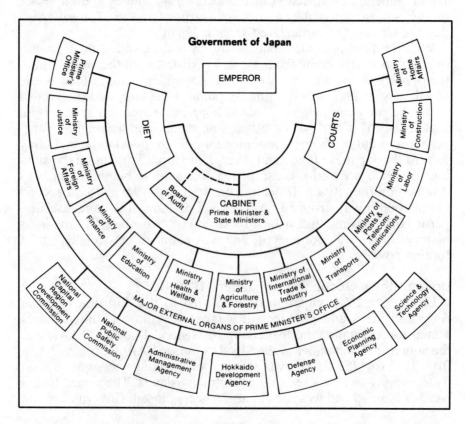

To allay Japanese fears, the United States-Japanese Mutual Security Pact was revised in 1960 to include a clause stating that the United States could not bring nuclear weapons into Japan without the knowledge of the Japanese government, nor could it use its forces based in Japan in military action without the approval of the Japanese government. Japan has developed the peaceful use of nuclear power, but many Japanese also protest the opening of nuclear power plants.

Democratic System of Government

The 1947 constitution created a parliamentary system with a two-house parliament called the **National Diet.** The lower house, the House of Representatives, is the more important. The prime minister is elected by the House and is responsible to it. The prime minister and his cabinet can be removed by a "no-confidence" vote, in which case new elections will be held for the House of Representatives, and the new House then elects a new prime minister. The constitution lists the rights of the Japanese people, which are much like the rights contained in the American Bill of Rights but also include equal rights of women, collective bargaining, equal education, etc. The right to vote was granted to all citizens over the age of twenty. One of the most well-known provisions of the constitution is Article IX, which renounces the use of war and the "maintenance of land, sea and air forces, as well as other war potential." It does allow the maintenance of defense forces or forces necessary to maintain internal peace.

According to the constitution the emperor is the symbolic head of state and a symbol of the unity of the Japanese people. His is a ceremonial, not a governing, role. The present emperor, Akihito, came to the throne in 1989 upon the death of his father, Hirohito.

Politics in Japan since World War II has been dominated by the **Liberal Democratic Party** (LDP). The LDP is closely allied with big business and receives much of its support from rural villages, towns, and small cities. The LDP's major opposition comes from the Socialists, the Democratic Socialists, and the Communists. Supporters of these parties tend to be concentrated in the major urban areas. Their major disagreements with the LDP have been over Japanese-United States relations. Trade unions tend to support these parties.

National politics centers on factions of the LDP within the parliament, with each faction having a leader in the Diet. Legislation is usually passed by **consensus,** with compromises having been worked out before a bill is actually presented for passage. The LDP has managed to hold political control by forming coalitions with other minority parties when necessary.

Present Military Status of Japan

In spite of the provisions of Article IX of the constitution, Japan does maintain self-defense forces for the defense of the Japanese islands. These self-defense forces originated in 1950 when the American occupation forces were withdrawn from Japan. They were limited to 250,000 men, and service was voluntary.

Treaty of Mutual Cooperation and Security Between the United States and Japan

According to the terms of the mutual security treaty between the United States and Japan, the United States agrees to take the major responsibility for defending Japan against aggressors. Many Japanese oppose this treaty because they fear Japan could be drawn into a United States war against its will, and the presence of American forces in Japan might even provoke an attack on Japan. Japan's military forces have been steadily built up since 1954, but the government maintains that they are only for purposes of self-defense. In recent years Japan has been pressured by the United States to spend more on its own defense. The Japanese people remain opposed to more spending.

Japan's Role in World Organizations

Japan's role in the United Nations has been affected by the Soviet bloc's distrust of Japanese-American defense arrangements. Relations between the Soviet Union and Japan have sometimes been strained by the presence of American bases in Japan and the close military alliance of the United States with Japan. A dispute over the southern portion of the Kurile Islands and the uneasiness the Soviets feel over Japan's close military alliance with the United States caused the Soviet union to block Japan's admission to the United Nations from 1952 to 1956. In 1956 the two nations resumed diplomatic relations, and Japan was admitted to the world organization in 1956.

ECONOMIC AND SOCIAL PROFILES OF SELECTED COUNTRIES—EAST ASIA

	Population Millions (est.) 1976 1985		Per Capita Income 1983	GNP (billions of dollars) 1983	Urban Population % 1976 1984		Literacy Rate % 1976 1985		Doubling Population Time
Japan	113	120	10,120	1215	76	76	99	100	not available
Korea (South)	36	41.2	1950	79	48	64	88.5	93	44 years
Korea (North)	16	20	790	16.2	44	62	NA	NA	30 years
China (Peoples Republic)	852	1043	296	302	13	21	40	68	60 years
Taiwan (Republic of China)	16.3	19.1	3040	58.0	67	71	86	89	40 years

As this table shows, Japan has a higher per capita income, gross national product, urban population, and literacy rate than its East Asian neighbors. These factors influence all of Japan's relations with its neighbors.

Japanese Relationships with Other Asian Nations

Many of the nations of Southeast Asia have found it difficult to throw off the image of Japan as the militaristic/imperialist nation that invaded, conquered, and exploited their territories during World War II. Some of the nations feel Japan is still exploiting them economically through trade. To create good will in Southeast Asia, Japan paid war reparations to the countries that suffered from Japanese aggression. Japan has also provided economic and technical assistance to developing nations and has contributed large amounts to the Asian Development Bank. Japanese industries have been developed in many areas.

In 1972 the People's Republic of China and Japan signed an agreement. Japan recognized the People's Republic as the official government of China and cut its diplomatic ties with Taiwan. This led to a treaty ending World War II between China and Japan and also to trade agreements.

Increasingly, other Asian nations (South Korea, Taiwan, Singapore, China) are competing with Japan in the world market in such areas as textiles, cameras, electronics, even cars. But Japan is still, by far, the leading industrial and economic power in Asia.

QUESTIONS

Multiple Choice. Select the letter of the answer that correctly completes each statement.

1. After World War II, Japan was occupied by and aided in its recovery by
   A. China
   B. Russia
   C. Korea
   D. the United States

2. The Tokugawa Shogunate was best known for its policy of
   A. isolation
   B. interdependence
   C. education
   D. imperialism

3. The Meiji Restoration was significant for its
   A. military conquest of Korea
   B. enlightened approach to modernization
   C. victory over Russia
   D. return to a policy of feudalism

151

4. The Kojiki and Nihongi are books dealing with Japan's
   A. economy
   B. politics
   C. history
   D. military

5. Since the early 1970s, Japan's foreign policy has become more independent of United States policies because
   A. Japan opposes the U.S. policy of ending the Cold War with Russia
   B. Japan has grown as an economic superpower
   C. the U.S. has failed to honor its commitments to Japan
   D. Japan is so strong militarily that it no longer needs the U.S. to protect it

6. The Diet serves as Japan's
   A. royal family
   B. legislature
   C. economic control board
   D. army

ESSAY

Explain how Japan's relations with the United States have been affected by any three of the following:

1. Commodore Perry's trip, 1853

2. Pearl Harbor Attack, 1941

3. Hiroshima and Nagasaki bombings, 1945

4. The MacArthur occupation, 1946–1952

UNIT
FOUR
AFRICA

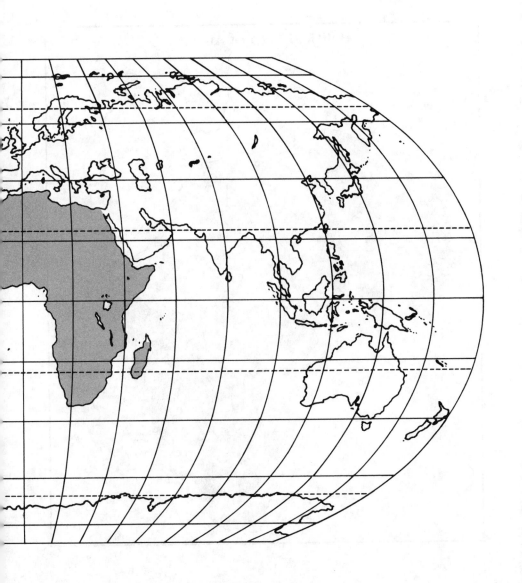

I. Physical Geography (The Physical Setting of Africa)

Overview

The geography and climate of Africa have played an important role in its historical, economic, and cultural development. For many years Africa was known as the "Dark Continent." The smooth coastline with few natural harbors, the falls and rapids near the mouths of rivers which made interior navigation difficult, and the deserts isolated Africa south of the Sahara. It was not until modern times that Westerners began to learn of the early civilizations in Africa and its many diverse cultures.

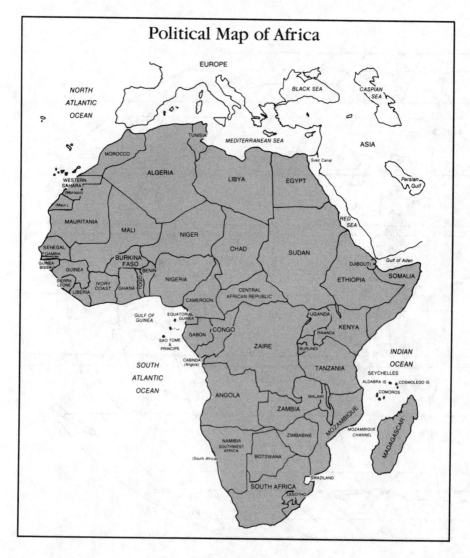

Political Map of Africa

Size and Location

The African continent is the second largest continent in the world. Stretching nearly 5,000 miles north to south and 4,500 miles east to west, the continent contains 11,700,000 square miles of territory. The total land area is approximately three times the size of the continental United States. Africa contains 20 percent of the world's land surface, but only 12 percent of the total world population.

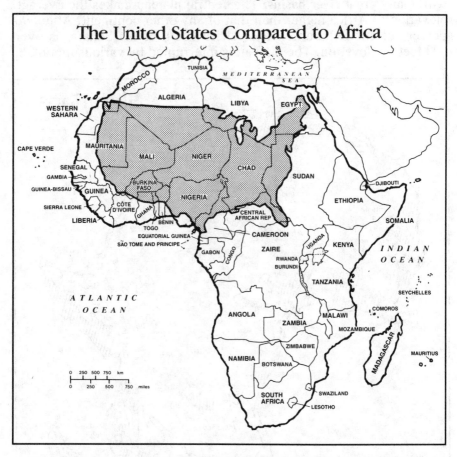

The United States Compared to Africa

The African continent is nearly divided in half by the equator, and it stretches from approximately 38° north latitude to about 35° south latitude. Because of this, the central portion of Africa lies within the tropics.

The Mediterranean Sea lies to the north and has served as a link between Africa and European culture. To the west is the Atlantic Ocean, and to the east lies the Indian Ocean, which served as a trade route between Africa and India, Southeast Asia, and China. On the east coast is the Red Sea, which served as a trade route between

Africa and Arabia, and a route for cultural diffusion, especially the diffusion of Islam. In the northeast is the Suez Canal, which is a major route for the transport of crude oil between the Persian Gulf nations and Europe.

Mountains

Much of Africa is a great **plateau** or a series of plateaus interspersed with many great **river basins.** The central plateau makes the average elevation of Africa higher than that of any other continent. About 90 percent of sub-Saharan Africa (Africa south of the Sahara) is over 500 feet in elevation. The plateau is interrupted by various mountain

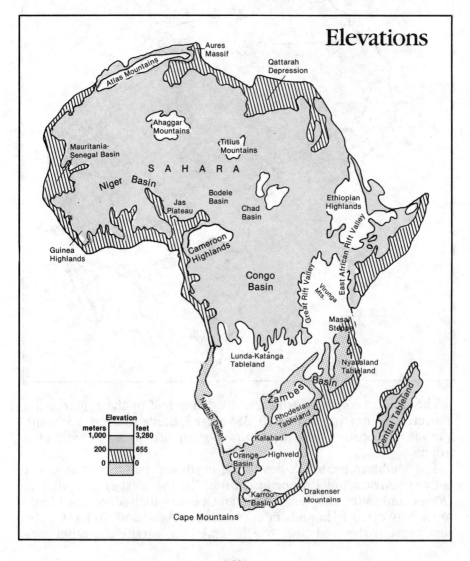

Elevations

ranges. The **Atlas Mountains** are located in the northwest. The **Ethiopian Highlands** in the northeast contain Lake Tana, the source of the Blue Nile. In the central region are the **Ruwenzori** (Mountains of the Moon) **Mountains.** Africa's highest mountain is **Mt. Kilimanjaro** (19,340 feet), and **Mt. Kenya** (17,040 feet) is the second highest. The **Drakensberg Mountains** are found in South Africa. The **Tibesti Mountains,** the **Ahaggar Mountains,** and the **Tassili-N-Ajjer** are in the Sahara Desert.

Great Rift Valley

In the east the plateau is sliced by the **Great Rift Valley,** a great trough or canyon, created by upheavals and disturbances in the earth's surface millions of years ago. The Eastern Rift Valley is about 4,000 miles long, while the Western Rift is about 1,000 miles long. The sides of the rift are as much as 100 miles apart and the depth of the valley from hundreds of feet to a mile. The rift influenced migration in East Africa, forcing people to move in a north-south direction.

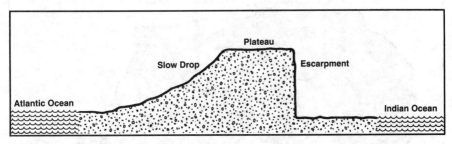

Rivers

The great central plateau region drops sharply near the coast, creating a series of waterfalls and rapids on most of Africa's great rivers. As a result, Africa has a narrow coastal plain and interior navigation is difficult. However, many of the rivers are navigable once the falls and rapids have been traversed. For example, the Congo (Zaire) River is navigable from the Atlantic Ocean for only 85 miles, but beyond the falls and rapids it becomes a major transportation route for Central Africa, with nearly 8,000 miles of navigable waters. The falls and rapids mean that Africa has great **hydroelectric power** potential. Much of this potential, however, goes untapped because of a lack of capital and also because there is little call for electricity in the villages.

The **Nile River,** at over 4,100 miles long, is the longest river in the world. The **White Nile,** which has its source in Lake Victoria, joins the **Blue Nile,** which has its source in Lake Tana in Ethiopia, at Khartoum in Sudan. The river flows north and empties into the Mediterranean Sea at Alexandria in Egypt, where it forms the **Nile delta,** an important agricultural area. Egypt is desert except for a strip, approximately ten miles wide, along the Nile. The predictable Nile flood provides a fresh deposit of alluvial soil each year and makes irrigation, transportation, and communication possible. In Sudan aquatic vegetation creates a region known as the Sudd, where the vegetation is so thick that travel becomes difficult and channels must be cut through the vegetation. **Lake Nasser,** created by the construction of the **Aswan High Dam,** is located in Egypt on the Nile.

The second longest river in Africa is the **Congo (Zaire).** With its tributaries it drains an area of 1.4 million square miles. The **Zambezi River** contains Victoria Falls. Below the falls, a dam and man-made lake (**Lake Kariba**) have been created to provide hydroelectric power. The **Niger River** rises in the Guinea Highlands, flows northeast

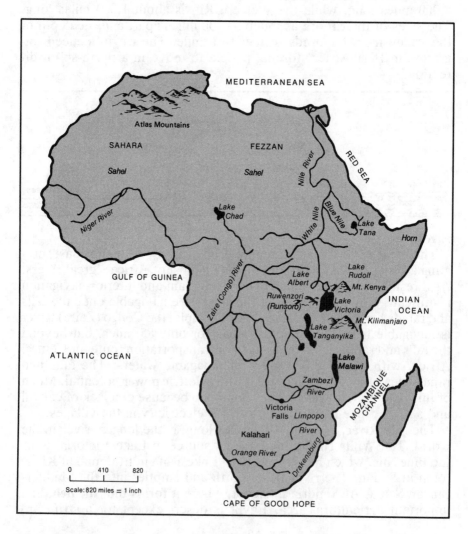

through Mali, turns to the southeast and joins the Benue in Central Nigeria, then flows south to empty into the Gulf of Guinea in Nigeria, where it forms the **Niger delta.** The Niger, like the Nile, flows through a desert region, and many of the early West African kingdoms or civilizations developed along the Niger.

The Deserts

The **Sahara,** the largest desert in the world, covering 3.5 million square miles, was not a total barrier to migration and trade. Arab traders set up camel caravan routes in the west, while the Nile River and coastal waters in the north and east provided routes of trade and cultural diffusion.

The Sahara was not always a vast wasteland. Archeological discoveries indicate that at one time it was a well-watered grassland and that streams, lakes, and animals abounded. Climate changes, resulting from the Ice Age, are largely responsible for the changes.

Today the Sahara is largely uninhabited, with heavier population settlements in the areas where **oases** (places in the desert where there is enough ground water to make cultivation possible) or rivers are found, such as the Nile River Valley. The Niger River in the western Sahara made the development of the early kingdoms of Ghana, Mali, and Songhai possible.

The Sahara is inhabited mainly by two groups—nomadic peoples (those who move from place to place searching for grazing land for their animals) and semi-nomadic peoples and by people who have settled in the oases and are engaged in agriculture, raising date palms, vegetables, and grains. In recent years mineral deposits, such as petroleum, natural gas, iron, phosphates, manganese, and copper, have been discovered in the desert.

The southern edge of the Sahara is bordered by a region known as the **Sahel.** It is a region of steppe, a marginal zone between the deserts to the north and the savanna to the south. The Sahel has long been inhabited by animal grazers and farmers. As long as the number of inhabitants remained relatively small, the Sahel supported human population. However, as the numbers of both people and animals have increased, the strain on the land and its water resources has increased. As a result, the process of **desertification** (the process by which arable land becomes a desert) is taking place and the Sahara is inching slowly southward into the Sahel.

Other major desert regions in Africa include the **Namib,** the **Kalahari,** and the deserts of southeastern Ethiopia and Somalia. The Kalahari has been inhabited by the Bushmen (Khoisan peoples) for hundreds of years.

161

The Sahel

The Lakes

East Africa and the area of the Great Rift are often referred to as the "lakes region" since many of Africa's great lakes are located there. **Lake Victoria,** the largest lake in Africa, the world's second largest fresh water body and the world's third largest lake, is located between the two rift valleys and is very shallow. **Lake Tanganyika** in the Western Rift Valley, one of the deepest lakes in the world, reaching a depth of about 4,800 feet, is the second largest lake in Africa and the seventh largest in the world. The third largest lake in Africa is **Lake Malawi** (Nyasa). **Lake Chad** is located on the southern edge of the Sahara and in the Sahel, making it a very important source of water. Unfortunately, the lake is prone to evaporation and varies in size and volume throughout the year. Africa's lakes are an important source of fish, one of the major sources of protein in Africa.

162

Climate and Vegetation Zones

The three most important factors in determining the climate of Africa are latitude, altitude, and wind patterns. Since the equator divides Africa nearly in half, climatic zones are similar in the north and south.

Extending north and south of the equator in Central or Equatorial Africa and in West Africa is a **rain forest** region, which makes up about 15 percent of Africa. It is characterized by high humidity, daily rainfall (60 to 80 inches average per year) and high temperatures (90°) year round. Vegetation is basically on three levels. The ground cover consists of ferns and creeping plants. There is a second level of middle-growth trees and a third layer of tall trees, forming what is known as a canopy and preventing sunlight from reaching the rain forest floor.

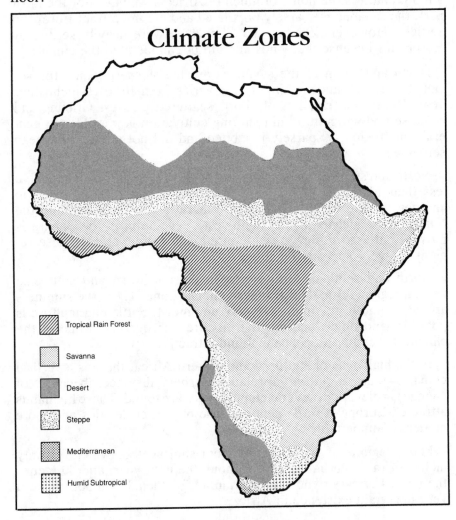

Climate Zones

Tropical Rain Forest

Savanna

Desert

Steppe

Mediterranean

Humid Subtropical

The rain forest region is inhabited by some settled farmers, by some people who practice shifting cultivation, and by hunting-and-gathering groups such as the Pygmies. It is sparsely populated in Central (Equatorial) Africa and heavily populated in the coastal regions of Nigeria, Benin, Togo, and Ghana. The characteristics of the rain-forest region discouraged European settlement.

North and south of the rain forest are the **savanna** zones, which cover about 40 percent of Africa. In the north the region is called the **Sudan,** and in the south, the **Veldt.** The savanna is characterized by a distinct wet season and a dry season. Rainfall varies from 20 to 60 inches per year. Vegetation consists of tall grasses, brush, and scattered trees. It is useful for grazing livestock and for shifting cultivation, and it is the home of much of Africa's wildlife. For the most part, the savanna is sparsely populated and did not attract European settlers. However, Zambia and Zimbabwe were heavily settled by Europeans because the winds and altitude moderated the climate.

North and south of the savannas are the **steppe** regions, the so-called marginal lands. Rainfall here varies from 10 to 20 inches per year. Vegetation consists of short, scattered grasses. Grazing and some settled agriculture and shifting cultivation is possible. In general, this region is sparsely inhabited and did not attract European settlement.

North and south of the steppes are the **desert** regions, which receive less than 10 inches of rain per year. The desert regions make up another 40 percent of Africa. The **Sahara** lies to the north and the **Namib** and **Kalahari** in the southwest. Vegetation in the Sahara is mostly scattered desert grasses, often called cram-cram. These regions are very sparsely inhabited.

North and south of the deserts, in the northwest and southeast coastal regions, is a **Mediterranean** climate zone. There the summers are warm and dry; winters are cool and moist. Settled agriculture is possible, and olives and citrus fruits are raised. This is one of the climate zones that Europeans found attractive.

In the highlands of southern and eastern Africa, there is a **vertical** climate—that is, within a relatively short distance, because of changes in elevation, several climate types are found. These highlands attracted European settlement because of the fertile soils and more moderate temperatures.

Many regions of Africa suffer from shortages of water. Twenty inches of rain may fall one year, none the next year, and 40 inches the next. Farmers, who rely on rainfall for their livelihood, have a very uncertain existence in Africa.

QUESTIONS

Multiple Choice. Select the letter of the answer that correctly completes each statement.

1. Kiliminjaro is a
   A. mountain peak
   B. river
   C. lake
   D. desert

2. What part of Africa are the rift valleys in?
   A. northern
   B. southern
   C. eastern
   D. western

3. Which type of terrain is least common in Africa?
   A. savanna
   B. desert
   C. mountain
   D. rain forest

4. Which is the most valid description of Africa's topography?
   A. a relatively tilted plateau
   B. all rivers are navigable for their entire lengths
   C. mountain ranges extending east and west
   D. savanna areas are unfit for human habitation

5. Desertification most seriously affects those nations near the
   A. veldt
   B. sudan
   C. sahel
   D. oceans

Matching. Match each river with the large body of water into which it empties. An answer may be repeated.

Column 1	Column 2
_____ 1. Congo	A. Atlantic Ocean
_____ 2. Zambezi	B. Pacific Ocean
_____ 3. Nile	C. Indian Ocean
_____ 4. Niger	D. Mediterranean Sea
	E. Red Sea

ESSAY

Below are two stereotypes about Africa.

1. Africa is a country.

2. Africa is all "jungleland" as depicted in *Tarzan* movies.

Explain what is wrong with these statements by presenting specific information.

II. Economic Geography (Economic Development of Africa)

Resources

The soils of Africa are generally poor, oxidized, and hard. Much of the soil contains laterite, which is not useful for agriculture. The soil of the tropical rain forest appears to be rich but is not. It is **leached;** the heavy rainfall forces the minerals so deep into the ground that plant roots cannot reach them, and the heavy vegetation is actually supported by the decay of humus on the forest floor. When the rain forest is cut down, heavy erosion occurs and **desertification** begins.

Africa is rich in mineral resources. In the countries of the Sahara and Nigeria, petroleum is an important source of revenue. Zaire, Zambia, and Zimbabwe have enormous copper deposits. South Africa is a leading producer of gold and the world's major source of diamonds. The continent produces about 80 percent of the world's diamond supply. Other important minerals found in Africa include bauxite, uranium, tungsten, cobalt, tin, and zinc.

Barriers to African Development

Because of geographic, climatic, and economic factors, Africans have had to make major adjustments to suit the environment. In the process, distinct hunting, farming, herding, and fishing societies have developed in various regions of Africa. These groups have long traded with one another, making them interdependent.

Many factors combined to slow development in Africa and to limit the Africans' ability to live in certain regions and provide enough food. One factor is that about 75 percent of the region south of the Sahara is short of water. This is a result of the unpredictability of rainfall, the few great river systems for a continent of this size, and the concentration of lakes in the rift valleys. A lack of capital has made it difficult for many African nations to construct major irrigation projects.

The Africans have made limited use of available natural resources. Historically, the major reason was that resources were located far

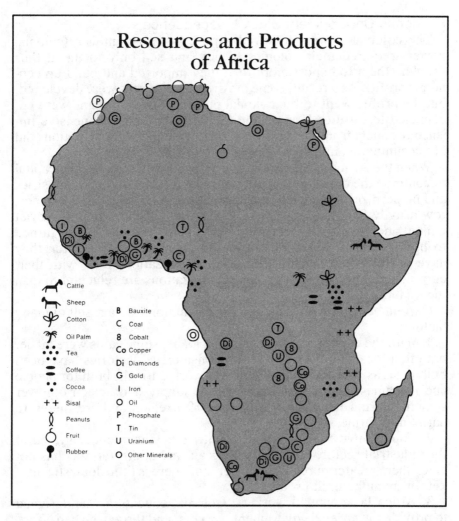

Resources and Products of Africa

from market centers. Today, they lack the technology to develop these resources, and they also lack the capital for investment in mining and processing industries. Since the resources are located far from market centers, the lack of capital makes it difficult to construct transportation facilities and to maintain existing ones. Moreover, rivers are not navigable all the way to the trade centers because of falls and rapids, and certain climate zones (desert, rain forest) also make it difficult to construct transportation routes.

In sub-Saharan Africa the tsetse fly, which attacks livestock, made the use of horses and oxen impossible, so the Africans developed farming techniques that relied on human labor. Reliance on traditional methods of agriculture and a lack of agricultural equipment makes the exploitation of soils, trees, and minerals difficult.

Economic Development Since Independence

The colonial powers followed a policy of **mercantilism** (colonial powers required their colonies to buy and sell only to them, thus enabling them to export more than they imported and build up economic profit). As a result, some of Africa's resources were developed, but the profits went to the colonial powers. Since Africans were encouraged to raise **cash crops** and forced to buy more expensive finished products from the "mother" country, most African nations did not accumulate any **capital** reserves.

When the African nations became independent, they needed capital to continue the development of their resources and to build industries and modernize. As a result, African nations have been forced to borrow heavily from the **superpowers** (the United States and the Soviet Union) and from their former colonial rulers. They have also turned to international organizations such as the **World Bank.** However, they have borrowed so heavily from such organizations that, with their current economic problems, these organizations are reluctant to loan them more.

Current economic problems of African nations are a result of many factors:

1. With the capital from international loans, some gains were made, but often local conditions were not considered. Factories have been built in areas where the climate makes work difficult, both for people and machines. Dams that were built to supply hydroelectric power sometimes ruin the **ecological balance** of a region and are therefore harmful to farmers.

2. Capital investment in most countries has been concentrated in the industrial sector. Since most Africans are still rural, this has not given them greater purchasing power, and there is little domestic market for manufactured products.

3. Africa lacks skilled workers. Colonial education was designed to provide lower-level government workers, and those who can afford higher education today are more interested in law, medicine, etc.—education that provides prestige or entry into politics and government.

4. Transportation and communications systems in Africa are still inadequate. Roads are difficult to build and maintain in the tropical climates. It is difficult to transport resources to the sites of manufacturing plants.

5. To achieve progress, people must work together, and this is difficult in nations where ethnic rivalries are prevalent.

6. Much of the money from international loans and foreign aid has been squandered in schemes designed to promote national pride (such as huge government buildings, statues, etc.) or simply confiscated by corrupt leaders.

7. World economic conditions have also effected Africa. During the 1970s, many African nations were forced to pay high prices for petroleum. During the 1980s, countries like Nigeria, which export oil, suffered from low oil prices. Prices for many of Africa's cash crops have dropped in the world market.

The heavy debt burden and the export of cash crops creates an economic dependency for trade, capital, and food, which is deeply resented by many African peoples and interpreted as **neo-colonialism** (establishing colonial-type political and economic control in independent developing nations). Many countries in Africa have **nationalized** (placed under state control) industries, and the presence of **multinational corporations** (companies with branches in several nations) has been encouraged, even though many Africans resent the foreign ownership and fear a loss of control.

Various attempts at economic development have included the introduction of socialism or mixed economic activities. When **Julius Nyerere** became president of Tanzania with Tanzania's independence in the 1960s, he introduced a socialist system called **ujamaa** (familyhood, sharing). In 1967 a program of nationalizing industries and plantations and creating **cooperative farms** began. Villages in the rural areas were formed into cooperatives, schools and clinics were established, and new farm machinery and techniques were introduced. In the 1970s the rising cost of petroleum products hurt Tanzania, and there were some problems with ujamaa. Hit by drought in 1980 to 1984, Tanzania had to appeal for international aid. Nyerere was replaced in 1985.

Nigeria has a mixed economy—major industries and oil production are nationalized, while small industries and agriculture remain in private hands. Multinational corporations are required to serve local needs as well as their own interests. Nigeria has experienced success in industrial and petroleum output, but agricultural production still lags, and food must be imported. Many other nations have a mixed economy,such as Kenya, Angola, Zambia, Uganda, Algeria, and Egypt.

The trend has been to invest in the urban, industrialized areas and to neglect the rural sector of the economy, and most Africans still live at or near the poverty level. So many Africans have moved to the cities in search of work that the cities are overcrowded and shantytowns have sprouted up on their outskirts. The unemployment rate is high since there are not enough jobs for all of the Africans who have migrated to the cities. City services have proven inadequate to handle the needs of the rapidly expanding population, and pollution and unsanitary conditions are a problem. There is also a notable difference between the "haves" (the rising middle class) and the "have nots" (unemployed rural immigrants), which emphasizes the inequality that still exists in Africa.

Agriculture

Over 70 percent of the African people are still engaged in agriculture. Most African farmers are **subsistence farmers,** raising just enough to support their families. Many of these farmers use a method known as **bush-fallow** (the same crop is planted until the land loses its fertility and then the land is allowed to lie fallow until the fertility is naturally renewed). In order to gain capital, many governments have encouraged the raising of cash crops, such as coffee, peanuts, cotton, cocoa, and palm products for export. Major food products include maize, cassava, and yams. Because of the demand for cash crops, African farmers do not raise enough food for themselves, and many food products must be imported. In addition, food production is unable to keep up because the population is increasing so rapidly. But there are other reasons:

1. **Deforestation and erosion.** Most Africans still use wood as a source of fuel, and forests are being destroyed. The loss of forest cover leads to soil erosion and loss of topsoil.

2. **Lack of government encouragement and assistance.** Many African governments are interested in the export of cash crops and accumulation of capital and have failed to provide programs to encourage greater food production.

3. **Desertification.** Overgrazing and overcultivation in the marginal lands (particularly in the Sahel) has increased the rate at which the desert is advancing into what was once agricultural land.

4. **Scarcity of water and erratic rainfall.** African farmers, without government assistance, simply cannot afford the high cost of sinking wells and building irrigation systems.

5. **Failure to fertilize the land.** Many Africans use natural fertilizer for fuel. Most farmers cannot afford artificial fertilizers, and African soils are not naturally rich.

6. **Civil wars.** Civil wars in some countries (notably Ethiopia, Sudan, Mozambique, Chad) have resulted in a great decrease in food production and contributed to famine in those countries.

7. **Drought in the 1970s and 1980s.** Over twenty countries in Africa suffered drought in the 1970s and 1980s. The drought was particularly severe in the countries of the Sahel (though drought has effected Tanzania, Mozambique, Kenya, Somalia, and others). Food production dropped and millions of people died.

The birth rate in Africa remains high because people in rural areas have little access to education and health services. Rural Africans have many children because children can assist in the fields, provide social security (eventual care for their elders), and assure continuance of the family lineage. At the same time, better medical care has decreased the death rate and increased life expectancy.

The "Green Revolution," with its hybrid seed and new fertilizers and methods, promises great hope. However, African farmers need government encouragement and assistance to benefit from the Green Revolution. They must be convinced that the new technology is better than traditional methods, and they need financial assistance to purchase the expensive new seeds and fertilizers.

QUESTIONS

Multiple Choice. Select the letter of the answer that correctly completes each statement.

1. South Africa is one of the world's greatest sources of
   A. oil
   B. gold
   C. iron
   D. timber

2. Which factor of production do poorer African nations need from the World Bank?
   A. labor
   B. capital
   C. land
   D. management

3. An increase in cash crops would directly increase a nation's
   A. imports
   B. exports
   C. population
   D. territory

4. A family that grows only enough food to feed itself is engaged in farming that is known as
   A. single-crop
   B. cash-crop
   C. subsistence
   D. modernized

ESSAYS

1. Many African nations face barriers to economic development. Discuss four of these, including two that are natural and two that are non-natural (human).

2. Food production is inadequate in many parts of Africa. Give two reasons for this situation, and two suggestions for improving food production.

III. Human and Cultural Geography

The People of Africa

A 1988 estimate of Africa's population puts it at 615 million, approximately 12 percent of the world's population. The people of Africa may be more diverse than the people of any other continent. They differ from one another both culturally and physically for two main reasons. First, Africans have intermingled and intermarried with others for generations. Second, because of geography many of the Africans developed in relative isolation. In fact, there are over 2,000 distinct cultural or ethnic groups.

Anthropologists seem to agree that most of the people of sub-Saharan Africa reveal physical characteristics of the Negroid race. Physical characteristics vary from group to group, however. Skin color ranges from very dark to light, hair texture varies, and the world's tallest as well as the shortest peoples are found in Africa. The people of North Africa reflect Caucasian characteristics. Many Europeans have settled in South Africa, Kenya, and Zimbabwe. East Africa and the Republic of South Africa also have many Asian peoples.

African Languages

Somewhere between 800 and 1,000 different languages are spoken on the African continent. The **Bantu** languages of sub-Saharan Africa are the most widely spoken. **Swahili,** a mixture of Arabic and Bantu, is spoken in East Africa. The **Khoisan** (click) languages are spoken by the Bushmen and Hottentots. **Hausa** is common in West Africa, and **Arabic** is common in North Africa. In addition, many European languages are spoken and reflect the colonial heritage. For example, in many of the newly independent African countries, English and French were the colonial European languages widely spoken. Today they are used as official languages.

Religion in Africa

Most Africans still believe in their traditional religions, although about 15 percent are Christians and about 26 percent are Muslims.

Traditional Beliefs

Traditional African religions were as varied as the ethnic groups that created them, and there are over 2,000 ethnic groups on the African continent. In spite of this, there are certain beliefs that most of the traditional African religions have in common. These include belief in ancestral spirits, belief in continuity of the clan and ethnic group, and belief that the land is held in ancestral trust. Traditional religions developed a philosophy of the individual's relation to the natural world and of the individual's place in that world. It helped to provide each clan and ethnic group with an identity.

In traditional Africa the individual was a member of a family, which was a part of a clan, which in turn was part of an ethnic group or tribe. It is common belief that the African is part of a continual chain that includes dead ancestors, living relatives and as-yet-unborn relatives, and that a person's spirit lives as long as he or she is remembered by future generations.

Also common in sub-Saharan traditional religious belief is the idea that ancestral spirits are involved in the lives of the present generation. It is believed that the ancestral spirits watch over the living. The spirits of ancestors are helpful as long as they are respected, but when they are not, they will bring harm to their descendants. As a result, prayers, ceremonial rites, and even sacrifices are necessary to show respect for ancestors.

According to tradition, the land was held in trust by the ancestors and could not be owned. The African only had the right to use it. The land belonged to the family, the clan, the ethnic group, and the right to work or use it was handed down from generation to generation.

Also common in traditional African religion was belief in a supreme God, who created the world and then withdrew, and in lesser gods whose spirits inhabit natural things (animism). These spirits determine everything that happens; they control life and death, good and evil. Most Africans do not worship rivers, trees, animals, etc.; instead, they worship the spirits they represent.

Among some traditional African groups, there was also a belief that the chiefs or kings were divine. In others, the chief was considered the custodian of the land, and he could assign the right to use it.

Islam in Africa

Islam, the religion of the prophet Mohammed, originated in the deserts of the Arabian peninsula in the 7th century. Shortly thereafter, Muslim conquerors swept across North Africa in search of converts to Islam and also arable land. They offered the conquered peoples three choices: fight, convert, or pay tribute. Conversion to Islam was the easiest and most practical response. Many of the teachings of Islam were similar to those of traditional African beliefs and were liberal enough to allow an African to become a Muslim and still retain many traditional beliefs and customs (See the unit on the Middle East for a discussion of Islam.)

Islam spread to West Africa as a result of the trade carried along the trans-Saharan trade routes by the Arabs. In time, Islam spread to the kingdoms of Ghana, Mali, and Songhai, which became theocracies (where religious leaders are also government leaders). Muslims established universities, religious centers of learning and research that enriched the lives of the people of West African kingdoms.

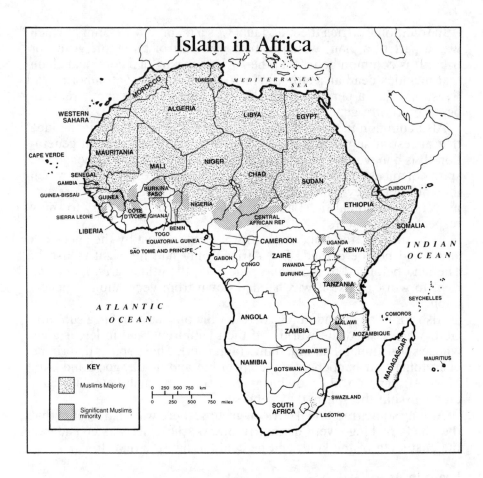

Islam in Africa

In the eastern coastal regions of Africa, Islam was spread by Arab traders who controlled the trade between Africa and the Far East and who settled in coastal cities and towns.

In a region of great ethnic diversity, Islam has provided a focus for unity, and in some of the North and West African countries, it was used as a rallying point for independence movements. The Arabic language also provided unity and in many areas, the first written language. Koranic (Koran, the holy book of Islam) studies led to a new class of educated leaders. Islamic law, which exists along with traditional African law, and laws established during the colonial period in most of North Africa provided a uniform system of justice, while Muslim traders increased the amount of trade and market activity.

Fundamentalist Islamic movements in some African countries have created tension and violence in the 20th century. The assassination of the Egyptian president, Anwar Sadat, in 1981 is one example. The political unrest in Sudan as a result of an attempt to institute Islamic law in the 1980s is another.

174

Christianity in Africa

The Coptic Christian Church was established in Egypt in the 1st century A.D. as a result of Greek influence. Coptic Christianity was brought to the Sudan or Nubia by Egyptian missionaries and made its way to Axum in the 4th century, where it was adopted as the official religion.

In the 1400s and 1500s, Portuguese and Spanish explorers who came to Africa were accompanied by Christian missionaries. Numerous missions were established along the west coast, but not many Africans converted to Christianity. In the late 19th century, missionaries followed the explorers into the interior of Africa, where they established schools to teach the doctrines of Christianity. By the end of the 19th century, Europeans had carved Africa into colonial empires, and Christianity came to be associated with colonial regimes. Nevertheless, millions of Africans converted to Christianity, both for spiritual and practical reasons. As with Islam, there were certain similarities between Christianity and traditional African beliefs, such as the African belief in a supreme God and the Christian belief in a single God, that enabled many Africans to adopt Christianity. Moreover, Africans soon learned that training at the mission schools was necessary if they wanted to take part in the economic activities and administration of government under their colonial rulers. Many of them used their knowledge of scientific theory, human rights, and self-determination learned in the mission schools to become leaders of independence movements in their nations. There have been movements to establish independent African Christian Churches and to make Christianity more African in form. Many Africans believe that Christianity can be adapted to African life and tradition without sacrificing its major teachings.

Role and Expression of Traditional African Art

Two of the dominant and most famous of the traditional African art forms are sculpture and masks. African sculpture served ritual purposes and was often designed with the intent of social control. African sculpture includes figurines, fetishes (objects thought to have magical powers to bring good or evil and protect the owner from evil forces), and stools. A piece of sculpture was not designed to be looked at and enjoyed as a beautiful creation. Instead, it was designed for use in ceremonies, to represent spirits of ancestors or gods, or even to house spirits of unborn babies. Some, usually those of animals, were carved to represent admirable qualities, such as strength, speed, or endurance. Some represented fertility. Since these sculptures were often representations, it was not considered proper for them to be too realistic. As a result, African art was often abstract or exaggerated. The most favored material for sculpture was wood, but bronze, brass, gold, clay, ivory, and soapstone were also used.

African masks, which can be considered a form of sculpture, were worn in ceremonies of ritual dance. The mask, which was often worn with a costume, was part of a spiritual disguise. Often the masks were hidden except when the ceremonies took place. When used in ceremonial rites, worn by rapidly whirling and swaying dancers, the masks became powerful representations of the spirits and gods.

African dance is generally symbolic and has strong ties to traditional religions. Dance was used at initiation ceremonies, funerals, and before going into conflict with other groups. There are dances for a good harvest, a successful hunt, and so on. There are dances to thank, appease, and make requests from the spirits. Dance is also performed for entertainment. Dance is most often accompanied by music. Instruments include drums, gourd rattles, horns, flutes, stringed instruments, and xylophones, depending on the region. African music is polyrhythmic, consisting of as many as five rhythms being played at the same time.

African Cultural and Social Institutions

The **diffusion** of Western ideas and institutions resulted in significant changes in African lifestyles and world views of Africans.

Perhaps the most significant change taking place in Africa is the development of many major **urban** areas. With its rapidly growing population, there isn't enough arable land to support the people, causing many young Africans to migrate to urban areas in search of jobs. Here their lives undergo dramatic change.

In traditional Africa and still in the rural areas today, an African is a member of an **extended family,** a **clan,** a **lineage,** and an **ethnic group.** As members of an extended family and clan, Africans have social security and are assured of support. In the cities, the extended family becomes a luxury young people can no longer enjoy. Also, in urban life arranged marriages become less and less common. Moreover, since urban Africans no longer depend on the land, the old ethnic authority structure is breaking down. The influence and authority of chiefs or elders is no longer so strong and is seldom felt in the cities.

In much of traditional Africa, and again, still in some of the rural areas today, **polygamy** was practiced. In urban areas this is no longer practical for most Africans, and more and more Africans practice **monogamy.** However, some urban dwellers, who can afford to, still practice polygamy.

African women have traditionally played an important role in society. Among many ethnic groups, **division of labor** meant that men were hunters and or warriors, and among most herders, men were responsible for the herds. This left women to tend the fields, and they were often responsible for marketing the produce. Several ethnic groups practiced **matrilineal descent,** in which inheritance is carried through the mother's family line. Urban African females are active today in politics, law, medicine, and other professions. In rural areas the traditional female role is still strong, though more and more men engage in the cultivating of the fields.

The majority of Africans still live in rural areas and depend on the land for subsistence. The rural areas retain traditional values, attitudes, and practices. There is strong loyalty to the ethnic group and the traditional authority system. The influence of the council of elders is strong, and there is a strong community spirit. Women are largely engaged in traditional roles, and the birth rate is high.

These traditional values and the traditional morality are often in conflict with the changing attitudes of the urban dwellers. The conflict is compounded by the increasing role played by the **media** and education. Through the mass media and the education process, Africans gain knowledge of Western ideas of mass democracy, socialism, majority rule, and minority rights, and they wish to adopt these concepts. **Industrialization** and **modernization** are bringing new technology to Africa, which in turn requires some change in traditional roles and relationships. Women who are wage earners are no longer willing to accept subordinate roles, for example.

Although there have been major changes in the lifestyles of many Africans, tradition still has a strong hold in Africa. Many urban Africans return to the rural areas for ceremonies such as marriage, birth, death, and circumcision. In urban areas, members of ethnic groups often band together to provide support.

QUESTIONS

Multiple Choice. Select the letter of the answer that correctly completes each statement.

1. The most widely spoke language in Africa is
   A. Swahili
   B. Bantu
   C. Arabian
   D. Hausa

2. Which of these groups has African society been organized around for thousands of years?
   A. occupational
   B. ethnic
   C. economic
   D. national

3. The spread of Islam throughout Africa is an example of
   A. national security
   B. socialism
   C. self-determination
   D. cultural diffusion

4. Animistic beliefs emphasize
   A. warriors
   B. spirits
   C. land
   D. chiefs

5. The influence of traditional African cultures is best seen today in Western
   A. art forms
   B. technological advances
   C. family patterns
   D. political ideas

6. Racial and family patterns have been studied mostly by
   A. economists
   B. biologists
   C. anthropologists
   D. archeologists

Fact or Opinion. If the statement is a fact, write F. If it is an opinion, write O.

1. All Africans belong to the same race.

2. Matrilineal patterns are the best ways for African families to follow.

3. Population density in the Sahel is low.

4. European languages are spoken in Africa.

5. Islam will become the major religion in central Africa by 2001.

ESSAY

There is a great human diversity in Africa. Discuss the validity of this statement with regard to these items:

1. religion

2. race

3. language

Give specific information in your answers.

IV. History and Political Geography (Historical Setting of Africa)

Discovering Africa's Past

Recent archeological finds in eastern Africa indicate that humans originated in Africa. Evidence indicates that there were humanlike creatures in Africa as much as 5 million years ago, and that humans may have developed there 1,750,000 years ago. Basic technology first occurred in Africa. Africa enjoyed a long and rich history before the era of European exploration, conquest, and colonization.

Sources of African History. Our knowledge of early African history is gained in many ways.

1. **Archeological evidence** is one important source of information. Archeologists working in digs have discovered many **fossils** (remains of living things) and **artifacts** (remains of things made by humans) which tell us much about life in Africa millions of years ago. Radiocarbon dating, which determines the age of organic matter by measuring its carbon 14 emission, is used to date the fossils.

2. African **oral tradition** is another important source of information. African oral tradition consists of myths, legends, fables, and histories passed orally from generation to generation. The myths and legends of the Africans are vital clues to the African past. They tell us much about the African perception of themselves (identity), their respect for ancestors, and their relationship to the natural world. The oral tradition has provided continuity of culture and customs in much of sub-Saharan Africa and has enabled many African Americans to trace their lineage.

3. A third important source of knowledge is provided by the **writings of the Arab traders and scholars** who traveled in Africa and chronicled their visits as early as the 8th century.

4. A fourth important source of knowledge consists of studies done by **anthropologists,** or the scientists who study the origin and development of humans and their culture. Some anthropologists, such as the members of the **Leakey family** (Louis, Mary, and Richard), work on archeological digs to unearth finds relating to early humans. In 1959, Dr. Mary Leakey and her husband Dr. Louis Leakey found a skull from a humanlike creature that lived about 1,750,000 years ago.

The Beginnings of Agriculture and Iron Age Technology

It appears that agriculture was practiced in the Nile delta as early as 4000 B.C. At the same time, some experts believe that the cultivation of sorghum and millet began in West Africa.

The development of agriculture made permanent settlements possible and led to the development of villages, governments, specialization, and increased population. The development of Iron Age technology and the production of iron tools and weapons made possible the increase of food production needed for the growing population.

Iron Age technology began in Africa in the kingdom of Kush in East Africa about 500 B.C. The technology of iron production may have been brought to Kush from a Middle Eastern people known as Assyrians. The technology of iron-making first appeared in West Africa among the Nok peoples of northern Nigeria about 300 B.C. It is believed that Iron Age technology spread southward throughout Africa with the Bantu migrations about 100 A.D.

Various groups of Africans traded with one another. Eventually market towns emerged. There was trade with places as distant as India, Rome, Southeast Asia, and China. The trade with Southeast Asia had a long-lasting effect in that the cultivation of certain Southeast Asian crops (rice, yams, bananas) was brought to Africa.

Early African Civilizations

Early civilizations other than the Egyptian civilization, which arose along the Nile River, developed in Africa. Two major civilizations that developed in northeastern Africa were Kush and Axum.

Kush civilization developed as early as 2000 B.C. At times, Kush was a province of Egypt. Consequently, Egyptian civilization influenced Kush. For example, in the Kush capital of Napata, there was a religious center dedicated to an Egyptian god. About 700 B.C. Kush invaded and conquered Upper Egypt, and eventually the Kush kings ruled as pharaohs over an empire stretching from the Mediterranean to modern Ethiopia. The Kushites were driven out of Egypt by the Assyrians in about 600 B.C., and the Kush capital was moved from Napata to Meroë in about 540 B.C. The reasons for this move were probably economic. The wealth of Kush was based on the trade of much sought-after African goods, such as ivory, gold, and ebony, with areas to the north and east. As Kush declined it was eventually succeeded by Axum in about 350 A.D.

Axum originated in the coastal region of modern-day Ethiopia about 300 B.C. and evolved into the modern Ethiopian state. The Axumites were Semitic, and they developed a written language of their own. The wealth of Axum was based on the control of Northeast African and Red Sea trade routes, which brought them into contact with both the Mediterranean and Arabian worlds. The capital of Axum, Adulis, was a cosmopolitan area with peoples from Greece, Egypt, Rome, Persia, and India. Iron was traded to other Africans, and the goods received in exchange (ivory, gold, slaves, etc.) were in turn traded with Greece, Egypt, Arabia, and other countries.

Axum extended its control over Meroë in about 350 A.D. and also conquered areas on the Arabian peninsula. Axum adopted Coptic Christianity in about 100 A.D. Persia invaded the Arabian provinces of Axum in the late 500s, gaining control of some of Axum's more important trade routes, and the power of Axum began to decline. Muslim invasions in the 600s and 700s also lessened the trading power of Axum, but the kingdom continued and eventually extended its borders to those of present-day Ethiopia.

In West Africa the kingdoms of **Ghana, Mali,** and **Songhai** developed along the Niger. All three kingdoms were powerful for several reasons. First, they **controlled the trans-Saharan trade routes in West Africa.** Second, they were located between the salt mines to the north and the gold mines to the south. Third, **they had developed agriculture.** Fourth, they had **strong central governments.** Fifth, they all **used iron,** and sixth, they all had **large armies.**

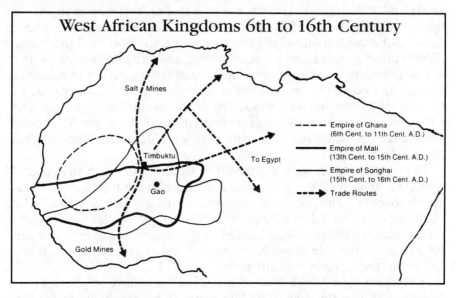

West African Kingdoms 6th to 16th Century

Salt Mines

Timbuktu

To Egypt

Gao

Gold Mines

Empire of Ghana (6th Cent. to 11th Cent. A.D.)

Empire of Mali (13th Cent. to 15th Cent. A.D.)

Empire of Songhai (15th Cent. to 16th Cent. A.D.)

Trade Routes

Ghana developed in about 300 A.D. The people to the north wanted gold, and the people to the south who had the gold needed salt from the people in the north. Their trade routes passed through Ghana, and the king taxed the trade in both directions and became very wealthy. He also claimed title to all gold in the kingdom and controlled the amount of gold on the market. The tax money was used to support the government and army. Iron tools made the farmers of Ghana more efficient, and iron weapons made it possible for them to subdue enemies and expand territory. In the 11th century, Ghana was attacked by Muslims. The warfare disrupted the trade routes and interfered with agricultural production, and Ghana went into a state of decline. By 1235 it no longer existed.

Mali originated in 1200, replacing the kingdom of Ghana. Its power was based on the use of iron, its wealthy farming region, its control of the trans-Saharan trade routes, and the salt and gold mines. Like Ghana, Mali taxed all goods transported through the kingdom and became extremely prosperous. Income from taxes was used to support the government and military and to build enormous mosques and palaces. Timbuktu became an important center of Arab learning. Mali was a Muslim kingdom, and its most famous ruler, Mansa Musa, on his pilgrimage to Mecca scattered so much gold in North Africa that it took years for the gold market to recover. In the early 1400s people from the north and south attacked, and people within the kingdom revolted. Mali went into a state of decline, from which it did not recover.

Songhai, a Muslim kingdom, began to expand into an empire in the 1400s under Sunni Ali. The empire of Songhai was greater in extent than either Ghana or Mali (at its height it contained an area about equal to the continental United States) and also controlled the trans-Saharan trade routes and sources of gold and salt. Both imports and exports were taxed. Cities grew up around commercial and religious centers and one of them, Timbuktu, became a center of learning. In the late 1500s Songhai was invaded by armies from Morocco equipped with guns and cannons. The spears and arrows of the larger Moroccan army were no match for them, and they were defeated. The Songhai empire disappeared.

The kingdom of **Kongo** originated in Central Africa in the coastal region in the late 1300s. Trade and agriculture were the basis of Kongo's economy. The king was considered divine and absolute. The Portuguese appeared in Kongo in 1482 and were interested in obtaining slaves. The divisions caused by disagreements over European influence and the sale of the Kongolese as slaves caused serious problems, and the kingdom disintegrated.

In southeastern Africa a kingdom called **Zimbabwe** originated perhaps as early as the 500s A.D. The people of Zimbabwe engaged in agriculture, iron-making, and trade. They constructed massive stone walls and buildings of stone without the use of mortar. Trade was carried on with regions as far away as India and China. It is not known what happened to the people of Zimbabwe.

Slavery and the Slave Trade in Africa

Slavery has existed in the world since the development of civilization. It existed in ancient Greece, Rome, and China and Africa long before the arrival of the Europeans. However, slavery in Africa was quite different from the slavery that developed later, especially in the Americas. Slaves were captives taken in warfare or criminals and debtors. Slavery was not necessarily hereditary, and it was not seen as total ownership of another human being. Slaves had certain rights and might even be allowed to purchase freedom and own property.

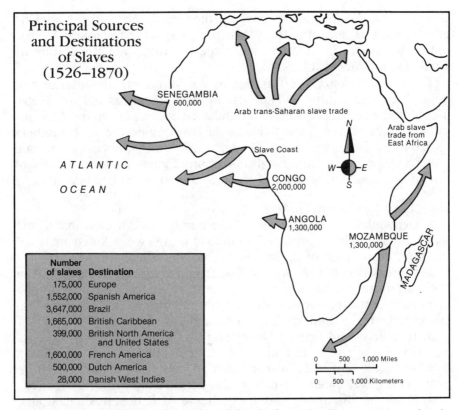

Principal Sources
and Destinations
of Slaves
(1526–1870)

SENEGAMBIA
600,000

Arab trans-Saharan slave trade

Arab slave
trade from
East Africa

Slave Coast

ATLANTIC

OCEAN

CONGO
2,000,000

ANGOLA
1,300,000

MOZAMBQUE
1,300,000

MADAGASCAR

Number of slaves	Destination
175,000	Europe
1,552,000	Spanish America
3,647,000	Brazil
1,665,000	British Caribbean
399,000	British North America and United States
1,600,000	French America
500,000	Dutch America
28,000	Danish West Indies

| 0 | 500 | 1,000 Miles |
| 0 | 500 | 1,000 Kilometers |

The slave trade also existed in Africa before the Europeans arrived. Arabs captured slaves or took them in exchange for other goods and sold them in India, Egypt, Persia, and other places.

The first African slaves to be transported to Europe were taken by the Portuguese in the 1400s. There was no great need for slaves in Europe, however, and they did not become an important item of trade until after the development of plantation agriculture in the Caribbean and North America. In order to raise sugar and tobacco on large plantations, many workers were needed. The native peoples of America did not survive the labor. Indentured servants eventually gained their freedom. Africans accustomed to hard labor in the tropics seemed a suitable replacement, and the slave trade increased greatly by the mid 1500s. The Europeans were involved in the highly destructive slave trade from the 1500s to the 1800s, and their primary interest in Africa was in acquiring slaves.

A "triangular trade" developed. Cheap European goods, usually cloth and trinkets, were shipped from Europe to Africa (the outward passage) where they were traded for African captives. The Africans were transported to the Americas (the middle passage) where they were traded for sugar and tobacco. These were transported back to

Europe (the inward passage) where they could be sold for considerable profit. The profits from this triangular trade in large part provided the capital investment that made the Industrial Revolution in England and America possible.

For the most part, the Europeans did not go into the interior and take their own captives. They established stockades (slave "factories") in the coastal regions and purchased captives from the Africans or from Arab slave raiders. However, to provide the vast numbers of captives the slave traders demanded, it became necessary to raid other villages and groups, and this required guns. As a result, one of the most important articles of trade to the Africans became guns.

Effects of the Slave Trade

1. **Depopulation.** An estimate of the number of Africans lost to the slave trade might approach 50 million. Many were killed in tribal warfare. Many died of disease in overpacked slave ships.

2. **Increased tribal warfare.** Villages and crops were destroyed in the warfare to provide captives for the slave trade. Bitterness among Africans themselves developed that still effect relations between ethnic groups in the modern African nations.

3. **Insecurity and fear.** Africans fearing the slave raids sometimes abandoned their villages and moved farther into the interior. Others lived in a constant state of fear, more interested in avoiding capture than in the development of their own society. Arts and crafts declined.

4. **Economic disruption and decay.** Some African states abandoned their traditional ways of making a living and took part in the slave trade. While the slave trade lasted, they were wealthy and powerful, but when the slave trade ended, their economies were ruined and the states disappeared. Benin is an example.

5. **The trans-Saharan trade was destroyed.** Because of the huge profits in the slave trade, the trans-Saharan routes of trade lost importance and the kingdoms in the interior of West Africa declined.

6. **Racism.** To justify the slave trade, those involved nurtured the belief that black Africans, because of their color, were inferior. This belief was accepted by Europeans and Americans who knew nothing of Africa and its cultures. The resulting prejudice and bias was later used to excuse the imperialist expansion of European nations into African territories.

The Era of Discovery and Chartered Companies

In the late 15th century, the European nations became rivals for the rich trade of the Indies and other parts of Asia. European monarchs granted monopolies on trade to chartered companies such as the British East Africa Company, Dutch East Indies Company, and French East India Company. The trading companies established trading posts and stopovers (way stations) along the coast of Africa, which were located on the route to Asia. Until the 19th century, the European presence was limited to the coastal areas and the trade in gold, ivory, and slaves.

European Imperialism*

In the late 19th century, the Europeans began to explore the interior of Africa and to expand their control. This imperialist expansion was made possible by the technological superiority of the Europeans. As the Europeans expanded in Africa, they dominated the Africans as well as their territory. They used the excuse of "the white man's burden," a legacy of the slave trade, to justify this expansion, claiming that it was their duty to bring civilization, progress, and Christianity to the less developed regions of the world. In reality, their major goals were to accumulate profit and power. This period of European imperialism was influenced by industrial capitalism and the increasing demands for raw materials for European factories and for markets for European manufactured goods. The Europeans needed African resources—mineral, land, forest products. They also desired greater power and prestige. The more territory they controlled, the more powerful and important they became, and European nations became rivals for African territory.

The Africans resisted the intrusion of Europeans and felt they were defending themselves against invasion. The Zulu fought the British and Boers in South Africa. The Sudanese fought the British. The Mandingo fought the French in West Africa. The Germans were forced to fight in East Africa. The Africans fought conventionally and also used guerrilla tactics, but their weapons were no match for those of the Europeans. Some of the African peoples used passive resistance. The Bushmen and Hottentots in South Africa simply disappeared into the bush.

In 1875, European holdings in Africa were fairly small, but by 1914 all of Africa except Ethiopia and Liberia were under European control. The "scramble for Africa" began after King Leopold of Belgium announced he was taking control of the vast Congo Free State in central Africa in 1879. In 1885 at the Berlin Conference, the European nations reached agreement on how Africa should be divided into colonial territories.

Some Africans served as mercenaries in the European armies or worked with the colonial governments. The British used a colonial policy known as **"indirect rule."** They left tribal leaders in charge, but the Africans were actually puppet rulers who followed directions from the British colonial administrators.

* See this topic also, in the unit on Western Europe.

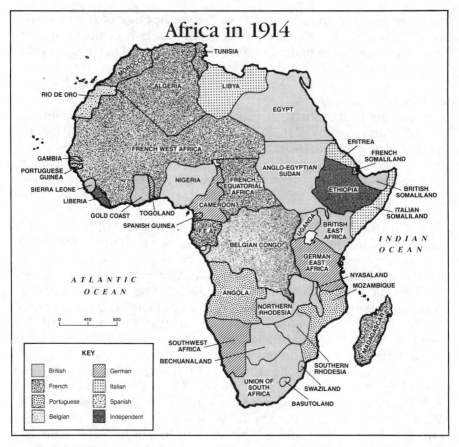

Africa in 1914

The French practiced a policy of **assimilation.** Their hope was to make the Africans "French" by changing their culture and traditions. The French ruled more directly than the British and removed the traditional rulers.

The Belgians used a policy of **paternalism,** treating the indigenous peoples as children who needed to be cared and provided for.

The Portuguese at first believed the Africans needed to be taught discipline and obedience. In the 20th century, however, this attitude changed, and they adopted a policy of **assimilation** intended to eventually make the Africans citizens of Portugal.

German rule in Africa was different in different colonies. In some they used **forced labor.** In others they tried the **"indirect rule"** approach.

Effects of European Rule on Africa

1. **Establishment of boundaries.** When the Europeans divided Africa, they drew up boundaries that had nothing to do with physical features or ethnic boundaries. As a result, ethnic groups found their

territories divided among more than one colony; some were within boundaries with traditional enemies. Because the colonies were granted independence based on the European-drawn boundaries, the problems created by dividing ethnic territories or expecting enemies to coexist remain in modern Africa.

2. **Changes in agriculture.** To provide raw materials for their industries, the Europeans encouraged the development of plantations and the cultivation of cash crops such as cocoa, cotton, coffee, peanuts, and palm oil. Many Africans concentrated on the cultivation of these cash crops, and food crops to feed themselves had to be imported. In areas of heavy European settlement, such as South Africa and the Kenya Highlands, the best farmland was reserved for Europeans.

3. **Transition from barter to money economy.** Taxes such as the head tax or the hut tax had to be paid in cash. To pay the tax, many Africans were forced to work for Europeans. They had to move to the city, sometimes with their families, sometimes leaving the family in the countryside to work the land, thereby destabilizing the family system. In addition, the money economy created greater disparities in wealth. Some Africans accumulated capital, while others did not. As a result, social tension was created between the "haves" and the "have nots."

4. **Changes in the landholding system.** Europeans introduced the idea of individual ownership of land. This weakened tribal ties and also meant that for some, there was no land, thus destroying the Africans' traditional way of making a living.

5. **Exploitation of resources.** The Europeans needed raw materials for their factories, so they developed the resources of Africa by opening mines and plantations. The benefits of this development went to the Europeans, not the Africans.

6. **Improved transportation and communications.** In order to exploit the resources of Africa, the Europeans had to build railroads and communications systems. These improvements benefited the Africans by assisting in the development of national unity and opening remote regions of the interior to economic development. However, they also accelerated the migration of African labor to areas where work could be found, further weakening tribal and family ties.

7. **New legal and judicial systems.** The European nations introduced their own ideas of law and justice in the colonies. Secular law and religious law were separated, while traditional law was changed or abolished, again weakening group ties and eroding traditional authority systems.

8. **Education.** Although education was not freely available to all Africans, some education was provided. Through European education, Africans learned of democracy and natural human rights and again began to reject traditional authority systems. Traditional Af-

rican culture was downgraded and European culture upheld as the example of how things should be. Educated Africans became the core of the nationalist movements in Africa and led the struggle for political independence from colonial domination.

9. **Preventive medicine and improved nutrition.** Because of Western medicines and medical practices, the infant mortality rate and overall death rate dropped dramatically. As a result, Africa has the most rapidly increasing population growth rate (about 3 percent) of any of the continents.

African Nationalism and Pan-Africanism

The nationalist movements in Africa varied from region to region and colony to colony. However, for Africans of all colonies, nationalism meant that they wanted to rule themselves and to decide what form that rule would take.

During World War II, many Africans served in the armies of their colonial rulers in Asia, Europe, and Africa. Many others moved to the cities to work in wartime industries for comparatively high wages. In the cities they acquired new skills, learned about life in other parts of the world, joined labor unions and political organizations, and came into contact with the ideas of young nationalists. They began to see that a unified nation might be built and began to transfer their loyalties from traditional groups and authority to these new groups and the idea of a modern nation state.

When the war ended, many of the colonies in Asia achieved independence. Successful independence movements in Asia encouraged the Africans to seek their own independence. Some African nationalists employed the nonviolent methods of Mahatma Gandhi and used passive resistance. Others employed guerrilla tactics. The Europeans, struggling to repair their own economies, industries, and societies, could not afford a prolonged struggle in Africa. They began to prepare their colonies for independence.

In 1957 the Gold Coast gained its independence from Great Britain. It changed its name to Ghana. Guinea gained its independence from France the following year. By 1977 there were more than 40 independent nations in Africa. The era of African colonialism was over.

A major problem for many of the newly independent African nations caused by the colonial legacy has been to deal with rivalries among the many ethnic groups inhabiting their nations. The new African nations must try to unite people with diverse languages, religions, and customs. Many African leaders have met this challenge by outlawing all but one political party and creating single party states. Most leaders do not see this as undemocratic, because membership in the one party is open to all and they feel that a single party will ensure a more stable government.

INDEPENDENCE COMES TO AFRICA*		
Country	Year of Independence	From
SOUTH AFRICA	1931	BRITAIN
SUDAN	1956	BRITAIN & EGYPT
GHANA	1957	BRITAIN
GUINEA	1958	FRANCE
CAMEROON	1960	FRANCE
CENTRAL AFRICA EMPIRE	1960	FRANCE
CHAD	1960	FRANCE
CONGO (PEOPLE'S REPUBLIC OF)	1960	FRANCE
THE CONGO (DEMOCRATIC REPUBLIC OF—ZAIRE)	1960	BELGIUM
DAHOMEY (BENIN)	1960	FRANCE
GABON	1960	FRANCE
IVORY COAST	1960	FRANCE
MALAGASY REPUBLIC (MADAGASCAR)	1960	FRANCE
MALI	1960	FRANCE
MAURITANIA	1960	FRANCE
NIGER	1960	FRANCE
NIGERIA	1960	BRITAIN
SENEGAL	1960	FRANCE
SOMALIA	1960	ITALY & BRITAIN
TOGO	1960	FRANCE
UPPER VOLTA	1960	FRANCE
SIERRA LEONE	1961	BRITAIN
BURUNDI	1962	BELGIUM
RWANDA	1962	BELGIUM
UGANDA	1962	BRITAIN
KENYA	1963	BRITAIN
MALAWI	1964	BRITAIN
TANZANIA**	1964	BRITAIN
ZAMBIA	1964	BRITAIN
GAMBIA	1965	BRITAIN
RHODESIA	1965	BRITAIN
BOTSWANA	1966	BRITAIN
LESOTHO	1966	BRITAIN
EQUATORIAL GUINEA	1968	SPAIN
SWAZILAND	1968	BRITAIN
GUINEA-BISSAU	1974	PORTUGAL
MOZAMBIQUE	1975	PORTUGAL
ANGOLA	1975	PORTUGAL
CAPE VERDE ISLANDS	1975	PORTUGAL
COMORO ISLANDS	1975	FRANCE
SÃO TOMÉ E PRINCIPÉ	1975	PORTUGAL
DJIBOUTI	1977	FRANCE

*Liberia and Ethiopia already independent.
**Tanzania was formed by the union of Tanganyika and Zanzibar. Tanganyika gained independence in 1961 and Zanzibar in 1963.

Some African nations have approached the problem by not holding elections. In others, elections are so corrupt that they are meaningless.

In many African nations the military has staged a *coup d'état* (overthrow of the government). Sometimes the coup was to overthrow leaders who were thought to be bad, ineffective, or corrupt. Sometimes it was in an effort to improve economic conditions or to subdue rival political factions that had built up their own military. Sometimes it was simply the desire of military leaders for more power.

In about 1960 there was a call for **pan-Africanism,** a joining together of African nations to improve conditions for all African peoples. The goals of pan-Africanism are to improve economic, political, and social conditions for all Africans. Nationalist feelings in the various African nations have been a stumbling block to pan-Africanism, however.

In 1963 the **Organization of African Unity** was created to try to foster cooperation and unity in order to achieve progress. It has had success in solving some problems but has no real authority to force its decisions on any nation.

South Africa

The Dutch established a supply station at the Cape of Good Hope in 1652. Before long, Dutch settlers began to arrive, and the supply station became Cape Colony. (The Dutch settlers and their descendants are known as **Afrikaaners.** The Dutch farmers were known as **Boers.**) The Hottentots and Bushmen were pushed north as the settlers took more land for farms. The farmers (Boers) employed black slave labor.

In the late 1700s the British came to establish their own supply stations, and in 1806 they seized the Cape Colony. In 1836 several thousand Boers began the "great trek" northeastward to escape British rule and preserve their Afrikaaner culture. They were resisted by the Zulu (Bantus), who were defeated at the Battle of Blood River in 1838. By the 1850s the Boers had established two republics in the interior: the Transvaal and the Orange Free State. However, when diamonds were discovered in the Orange Free State in 1871 and gold in the Transvaal in 1886, British miners and businesspeople began to arrive.

Hostilities between the Afrikaaners and the British increased until the Boer War of 1899 to 1902, in which Afrikaaners were defeated. In 1910 the British united the two Boer republics, Cape Colony and Natal into the Union of South Africa, which became a self-governing country of the British Empire in 1934.

African and Asian (mostly from the British colony in India) workers were recruited for work in the mines and associated industries. Many Afrikaaners believed in the superiority of the white race and its culture, and the British did little to prevent this attitude or the resulting discrimination and segregation.

In 1948 the Afrikaaner Nationalist Party gained control of the government and began the policy of **apartheid** (Afrikaans word meaning "separateness"). This policy rigidly defined four racial groups: white, black, Asian, and coloured. Under this policy each group was to have its own living areas and develop its own political institutions. Black Africans had to carry passbooks containing information on where they lived and worked and where they could travel. Intermarriage was forbidden, separate education was provided, strikes by black

POPULATION OF SOUTH AFRICA

Official Category	Number of People (millions)	% of Total Population
Black	23.9	67.7
White	4.8	18.3
Colored	3	10.6
Asian	1	3.4

Source: 1985 & 1986 Book of the Year

workers were outlawed, jobs were restricted to racial groups, separate facilities had to be maintained, and blacks could not own land outside reservations. Blacks had no vote and no representation in government. They were denied basic human rights. The Bantu Authorities Act of 1951 established ten Bantustans (homelands) for the blacks. Until 1985 a policy of forced relocation of unemployed blacks to the homelands was followed. The blacks were to be allowed "separate but equal" development on these homelands. They were to become independent countries with their own governments and economies.

In 1912 the **African National Congress** (ANC), an organization to unite the South African blacks, to end segregation, and to work for the right to take part in government, was created. The ANC was originally a nonviolent organization. They used strikes and employed many of the same methods used by Mahatma Gandhi. After the **Sharpeville Massacre** in 1960, the ANC turned to the use of sabotage. They blew up power lines and refineries to undermine confidence in the government, disrupt the economy, and bring international attention to their plight. The government banned the ANC and arrested its leaders, including **Nelson Mandela.**

Beginning with the Soweto riots in 1976, activity against the policy of apartheid increased in South Africa. As more and more nations condemned the policy, some restrictions were relaxed. Petty apartheid (separate facilities) was largely dropped, though some beaches remain restricted. Blacks were allowed to form labor unions, but they still had no voice in government.

As protests and violence escalated, international pressure on South Africa to change their policies increased. The government, under the leadership of **P. W. Botha,** repealed the pass laws and the Mixed Marriages Act. Many black prisoners were released.

In 1986 the United States Congress passed sanctions against South Africa. Most American companies sold their interests and left South Africa. The British Commonwealth nations also voted for sanctions. In 1974 South Africa lost its voting privileges in the United Nations.

South Africa is economically dependent on the black workers and will probably be forced to take further action to end the restrictive policies of apartheid. In February 1990, the new president, **F. W. deKlerk,** released Nelson Mandela, who had been in prison since

1964. It was hoped the two leaders could negotiate to win political rights for blacks.

Kenya

In the late 19th century, Kenya came under the control of the British government as part of the East Africa Protectorate. Before long, British settlers came.

The nationalist movement in Kenya began in the early 20th century. **Jomo Kenyatta,** the leader of the nationalist movement, became president of the **Kenya African Union** in 1947. Its major goals were to regain control of the land lost to the Europeans, to halt exploitation of Africans by Europeans, and to gain basic civil rights for Africans.

An organization known as the **Mau Mau** was created in 1952, which used terrorist and guerrilla activities to free Kenya. The British declared a state of emergency and placed thousands in detention camps.

In 1956, the British began gradual reforms and Africans were allowed some participation in government. However, Africans demanded independence and in 1963 Kenya was granted independence. In 1964, Kenya became a republic in the British Commonwealth of Nations and Jomo Kenyatta its first president.

There were many problems in Kenya as a result of differences among the many ethnic groups (the Kikuyu, the Luo, the Masai, the Kalenjin, etc.). Kenyatta, a Kikuyu, urged his people to forget their ethnic loyalties and accept a principle he called **harambee** (pulling together). Kenyatta died in 1978 and was succeeded by **Daniel Arap Moi.**

Because the major political parties in Kenya represented the major ethnic groups and helped prolong the ethnic rivalries, Kenya was declared a one-party state in 1982. The only legal political party is **KANU (Kenya African National Union).** Moi has been reelected twice, but the last election, in 1988, was controversial, for secret ballots were not used. Kenya has been accused by international organizations of abusing human rights in recent years. Kenya has also had border disputes with Somalia.

The government began a program to **"Africanize"** Kenyan life and economics. Asians were required to obtain work permits and could not be employed unless there were no Kenyans suitable for the job or they had special talents. Many Asians emigrated to Great Britain. In 1968 Britain limited immigration, and the remaining Asians have suffered economically and socially. As part of the program to "Africanize" Kenya, European ownership of land has also been reduced.

Most of Kenya's people make a living in agriculture, although fertile land is scarce. Kenya has one of the most rapidly increasing populations in the world. The per capita income is about $230. Major exports are cash crops such as coffee, tea, and sisal. Industrial development is limited, and the unemployment rate is high. The country has two official languages, English and **Swahili,** and many ethnic languages are spoken by the groups inhabiting the country.

Nigeria

Over 200 different ethnic groups live in Nigeria, but the four largest and most politically dominant are the **Hausa** and **Fulani** in the north, the **Ibo** in the southeast, and the **Yoruba** in the southwest.

In the mid-19th century, the British began their expansion into Nigeria. By 1914 all of Nigeria was a British colony. After World War I a nationalist movement arose. The British gradually allowed more African participation in government until in 1954 a constitution creating a federal union, ensuring the power of the three major regions—the east, the west, and the north—was accepted. Independence was finally granted in 1960.

Almost immediately, regional differences became obvious. The northern region, with the largest population, controlled the federal government. In 1966 there was a coup led by Ibo military officers, and General Ironsi took control of the government. Later in 1966 violence broke out against Ibo living in the north, and General Ironsi was killed by Hausa soldiers and replaced by Yakuba Gowon, a northerner. General Ojukwu, the leader of the Ibo region, declared eastern Nigeria independent as the Republic of **Biafra.**

Civil war broke out about two months later. Biafra was unable to hold back the Nigerian troops or to feed its people. An estimated one million Biafrans died as a result of military action or starvation. Early in 1970 Biafra surrendered.

Military coups have been frequent since 1970. The country is now ruled by a military government. It has been divided into 19 states, and each state has a military governor.

Nigeria made a rapid recovery from the civil war, largely because of oil revenues. However, mismanagement and overspending of funds led to an economic decline in the early 1980s. In 1987 the government announced plans for economic austerity, began to encourage a birth-control program, and promised a return to civilian government by 1992. Besides petroleum, exports include cash crops such as rubber, palm products, and timber. The per capita income is about $500.

Africa in the Global Context

For the most part, African nations since independence have chosen to remain **nonaligned** (choosing to be neither pro-Soviet nor pro-United States). African leaders also feared **neo-colonialism.** For this reason, many were reluctant to maintain strong relationships with their former colonial rulers or with any industrialized Western nation. Others were economically so weak that they had to allow colonial banks and industries to remain in place. In addition, many nations which maintained fierce independence from foreign involvement immediately following independence have been forced by economic and political crises to accept the presence of **multinational corporations.**

International Organizations. Many African nations have joined a number of international organizations to promote African unity, improve economics, and strengthen their influence in world markets and world events.

1. **The United Nations.** The African nations now have the most powerful voting bloc in the United Nations General Assembly, with about 50 members, and can influence **UN** decisions and policies. African nations have received much aid and assistance through various UN agencies.

2. **The World Bank.** The Bank, a specialized agency associated with the UN, provides loans and technical assistance to developing nations.

3. **The International Monetary Fund.** The **IMF,** another specialized agency of the UN, provides loans to members with balance-of-payments problems and provides technical assistance.

4. **The Commonwealth of Nations.** Many of the former colonies of Great Britain belong. It was organized to promote economic cooperation and to coordinate scientific, military, and educational affairs.

5. **The Lome Convention.** In 1975 a number of African, Caribbean, and Pacific nations voted to associate themselves with the **European Economic Community** to gain economic benefits through trade and tariff agreements.

6. **Organization of Petroleum Exporting Countries. OPEC,** designed to control world oil prices by coordinating and controlling production, has four African member states: Algeria, Gabon, Libya, Nigeria.

7. **Organization of African Unity.** The **OAU** was founded in 1963 to promote unity, solidarity, and cooperation among African states. It has little power beyond talking and trying to encourage cooperation. It has enjoyed some success in settling boundary disputes and developing energy sources.

Foreign Intervention. In certain instances African countries or groups within those countries have been forced to ask for, or unable to prevent, foreign **intervention** in their internal affairs.

1. **The Congo (Zaire) in the 1960s.** After the **Belgian Congo** became independent in June 1960, the Province of **Katanga,** under the leadership of **Moise Tshombe, seceded** and declared its independence. Belgium sent troops to end the rebellions. The prime minister (Patrice Lumumba) of the Congo appealed for Soviet aid, and the Soviets sent weapons, transport equipment, technicians, and advisers. Soviet influence alarmed some Congolese and most Western nations, who encouraged the president of the Congo (Kasavubu) to dismiss Lu-

mumba. An army leader, Joseph Mobutu, ordered the Soviets to leave the country, and in 1961 Lumumba was assassinated. Meanwhile, the Katanga rebellion continued, with Tshombe employing European and South African **mercenaries** to resist a United Nations peacekeeping force that had been sent into the region. An agreement to end the secessionist movement was finally reached, and UN troops left the Congo in 1964. Tshombe was elected president, but in 1965 he was overthrown in a military coup led by Mobutu. In 1971 Mobutu changed the name of the country to **Zaire.** Foreign investors have been invited back into the country (most fled during the terrorism of the rebellions), but continued conflict in the country has discouraged them.

2. **French military involvement in Chad.** Chad gained independence from France in 1960. Chad has a sparse population (being located mostly in the regions of the Sahara and the Sahel). The population is divided between the Christian south and the Muslim north, and tribal differences are also a problem. In 1960 a southerner, **Francois Tombalbaye,** became president. A rebellion broke out in the northern and eastern sections in 1965 and resulted in civil war. In 1975 a military coup overthrew Tombalbaye's government, but another southerner took control of the government. The conflict between the north and south continued, with France supporting the southern government. Northern forces called on Libya for assistance, and Muammar Qaddafi sent Libyan troops. In 1981 foreign troops were withdrawn, but in 1982 civil war broke out again. Libyan forces entered the war in support of the north, and French and Zairian forces entered the war in support of the south. In 1984 France and Libya agreed to remove their forces, but Libyan troops remained in the north in violation of the agreement. In 1987 the government launched an attack against the northern and Libyan forces and regained control of all but a small strip of land where Libya has an air base.

3. **Superpower rivalry in Ethiopia and Angola.** Except for a short time during World War II when it was occupied by Italian forces, Ethiopia was one of the only two African nations that maintained their independence. **Emperor Haille Selassie** ruled Ethiopia from 1916 to 1974. The United States provided the emperor with aid and assistance partly because of the country's strategic location on the Red Sea. In 1974 he was overthrown, and the army began making socialist reforms—land was taken from landowners and turned over to peasant associations. In 1976 a military agreement was reached with the Soviet Union and United States military advisers were expelled. Ethiopia and Somalia have had border disputes since Somalia became independent in 1960. Because the Soviet Union was supporting Ethiopia, Somalia turned over a military base to the United States.

Angola received its independence in 1975. After independence, three rival groups fought for control and there was a civil war. The MPLA (Popular Movement for the Liberation of Angola) was supported by the Soviet Union and Cuba; the FNLA (National Front for the Liberation of Angola) was supported by the United States, France, and Zaire; and UNITA (National Union for the Total Independence of Angola) was supported by Portugal, China, South Africa, and white Angolans. By 1976 MPLA had achieved victory. The MPLA established a Marxist state with Soviet backing and Cuban support troops. The United States continued to provide assistance to UNITA rebels, based now in neighboring Zaire, so conflict continues. An agreement, arranged by President Mobutu of Zaire in 1989, was designed to phase out the Cuban support troops in Angola by 1992.

United States/African Relationships

As part of its policy to contain the spread of communism in the 1960s, the United States began to provide aid and assistance to many African nations.

Americans (government and private citizens) have provided assistance (medical, food, volunteers) to drought-stricken and famine-ridden regions of Africa. Starting in the 1960s, the Peace Corps has helped to develop rural Africa—teaching agricultural techniques, establishing schools, and carrying out many other programs.

The American government has provided millions of dollars in military loans and grants. American multinational corporations have established branches in many African nations, providing employment and infusing some money into the local economy. The United States maintains military bases in Kenya, Somalia, and Liberia.

In the past, black African nations have had difficulty reconciling American ideals on human rights with the reality of racial prejudice and inequality in the United States. However, the civil rights gains of the 1960s and the recent change in American policy from **"constructive engagement"** to **divestment and sanctions** against the government of South Africa have done much to improve this situation.

QUESTIONS

Multiple Choice. Select the letter of the answer that correctly completes each statement.

1. During the 19th century, the African continent was affected most by
   A. the French Revolution
   B. the Crusades
   C. European imperialism
   D. the introduction of socialism

2. Which statement is most accurate about the African slave trade from the 15th through the 19th centuries?
   A. The slave trade was limited to East Africa.
   B. The slave traders brought ivory and timber to Africa.
   C. The slave trade involved African, Arab, and European slave traders.
   D. Most slaves were transported from Africa to Europe.

3. Which statement is accurate concerning the policy of apartheid in the republic of South Africa?
   A. It has been encouraged by other nations.
   B. It is a result of attempts to improve the conditions of blacks living in homeland areas.
   C. It has its roots in European imperialism in Africa.
   D. It has resulted in separate but equal treatment for whites and blacks.

4. Which nation was once controlled by a white minority government?
   A. Nigeria   C. Zimbabwe
   B. Zambia   D. Ghana

5. Important archeological finds concerning humans have been made by the Leakey family in the vicinity of
   A. the Niger River   C. Victoria Falls
   B. Olduvai Gorge   D. the Horn of Africa

6. Which policy is the Organization of African Unity most interested in developing?
   A. apartheid   C. pan-Africanism
   B. Africanization   D. Westernization

7. The Nigerian Civil War was primarily due to
   A. tribal conflicts   C. failure of cash crops
   B. water use   D. language differences

ESSAYS

1. Many important civilizations and kingdoms arose in Africa prior to the coming of the Europeans. Select four of these civilizations or kingdoms. For each one do the following:
   A. Give its name and general geographical location.
   B. Describe one significant accomplishment.

2. The new nations that have emerged since World War II have faced many problems. Describe two of these problems, giving both the reasons for these problems and suggestions for their resolution. Give specific references to nations and leaders.

UNIT FIVE
LATIN
AMERICA

I. Physical Geography (The Physical Setting of Latin America)

A Definition of Latin America

Latin America refers to the area in the Western Hemisphere that is south and southeast of the United States. Within this area there are nations and other lands that are not really part of the Latin American group of countries or cultures. They are the English-speaking Caribbean basin nations, such as Barbados, Belize, and Jamaica, and the Dutch-speaking islands of Curaçao and Aruba. There are also a number of Native American cultures that have survived within certain Latin American nations. Besides geographical locations, there are other characteristics that help to define the meaning of Latin America.

The national languages of Latin American nations are generally Romance languages—Spanish, Portuguese, and French. Some Native American languages, such as Guarani, Quechua, and Amayra, are also spoken. In Haiti, the use of Creole is widespread, and English is used in Puerto Rico (see the chart below).

South America	Central America	Caribbean
Brazil (Port.)	Mexico (Sp.)	Cuba (Sp.)
Argentina (Sp.)	Guatemala (Sp.)	Dominican Republic
Uruguay (Sp.)	El Salvador (Sp.)	(Sp.)
Paraguay (Sp.)	Honduras (Sp.)	Haiti (Fr.) (Creole)
Bolivia (Sp.)	Nicaragua (Sp.)	Puerto Rico (Eng.)
Chile (Sp.)	Costa Rica (Sp.)	(Sp.)
Peru (Sp.)	Panama (Sp.)	Martinique (Fr.)
Ecuador (Sp.)		Guadeloupe (Fr.)
Colombia (Sp.)		
Venezuela (Sp.)		
French Guayana (Fr.)		
(national languages are in parentheses)		

The nations of Latin America all have a colonial heritage that is either Spanish, Portuguese, or French, and Roman Catholicism is the major religion. The term "Latin America" is used to describe the nations, peoples, cultures, and the **diversity** of this vast and complex area.

The process of **cultural diffusion** continues to play an important role in shaping society in Latin America. Recent immigration from Asia and the Middle East has had a significant impact.

LATIN AMERICA

⊛ National Capitals
• Other Capitals
• Other Cities

0   500   1,000 miles
0   500   1,000   1,500 kilometers

Political Geography

Latin America can be divided into three geopolitical regions. South America, Middle (Meso) America (Mexico and Central America), and the Caribbean Sea islands that are classified as Latin American. There are a total of 24 nations and dependent lands.

Climate of Latin America

Currents of Latin America

Physical Geography

Latin America, which is one-sixth of the earth's land surface, is approximately 8 million square miles. From the northern border of Mexico to the southern tip of Chile, it is 6,000 miles. The nations of Latin America range in size from Brazil, the world's fifth largest country (larger than the continental United States), to the small Caribbean islands of Martinique and Guadeloupe.

Latin America lies between latitudes 33° north and 56° south. The geographical location of most of Latin America within the tropics and subtropics in large measure determines its climate, rainfall, and vegetation. Other geographical factors also influence the climate, rainfall, and agriculture and help determine the political, economic, and social patterns of Latin America.

Mountains, Plateaus, and Highlands

The mountain ranges and high plateaus have influenced the economic, social, and political life in much of Latin America. Paralleling the Pacific Ocean, there are a number of large mountain chains in the Americas. In Mexico, the **Sierra Madres** (Occidental and Oriental) run north and south. Between these two mountain ranges is a vast central plateau, where more than half of the nation's population lives. The **Sierra Madre del Sur** run through Central America. In South America the **Andes Mountains** run along much of the continent's western coast. The Andes rank second only to the Himalayas as the world's highest mountain range. They have served to isolate cultures and delayed cultural diffusion.

The **Atacama Desert,** the strip of land on the Pacific Coast in Peru and Chile, is a result of the Andes' acting as a barrier to block rainfall. To the east of the Andes lies the high plateau region (antiplano).

The **Guiana Highlands** and **Brazilian Highlands** are the two other regions in South America that in otherwise tropical areas have helped offset the difficult climatic conditions of the surrounding lowland area.

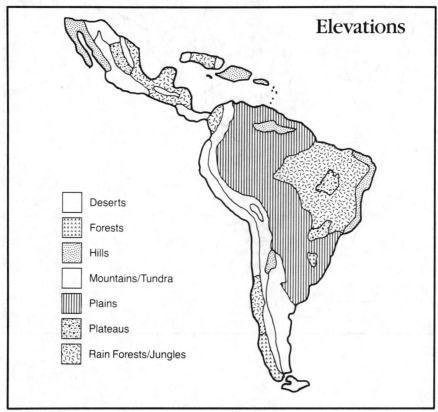

Elevations

Deserts
Forests
Hills
Mountains/Tundra
Plains
Plateaus
Rain Forests/Jungles

South America
Land Forms

GREATER ANTILLES   Guadeloupe   LESSER
West Indies   ANTILLES
CARIBBEAN   SEA   Martinique   Barbados
Curacao   Trinidad
and Tobago

LLANOS
Orinoco R.
Caroni R.
Angel
Falls
PAXARAUMA MTS.
GUIANA
HIGHLANDS   Ilha de Morajo   EQUATOR   0°

Galapagos
Islands   Rio Negro   Amazon   River
Napo R.

Nevo
Hauscapri   Purus R.   AMAZON LOWLANDS   Cabo do
Sao Roque
SELVA   Madeiro   SERRA DO
PIAUI
Ucali R.   Cuapore R.   PLANALTO DO
MATO GROSSO   BRAZILIAN
Berni R.   Mamore R.   HIGHLANDS   15°

GRAN
CHACO   Pilcamayo R.   DO ESPINHACO

TROPIC OF CAPRICORN   Salado R.   Iguasso R.
ATACAMA DESERT   Parana R.   Iguasso Falls
Uruguay R.
PACIFIC   A T L A N T I C
OCEAN   O C E A N

Cerro
Aconoagua   PAMPAS   Rio de la Plata

Colorado R.

Chubat
PATAGONIAN
PLATEAU   45°

Falkland Is.
Strait of Magellan
Tierra del Fuego
Cape Horn

0   300   600   900 Kilometers   N
0   300   600 Miles

Water Bodies

The **Amazon River,** the world's second longest river and its tributaries, which reach into Colombia, Venezuela, Ecuador, Peru, and Bolivia, has until recently been the only transportation network in the Amazon basin. The **Río de la Plata,** which is a large estuary fed by the Uruguay and Parana rivers, is the water transportation network that serves Argentina, Bolivia, southern Brazil, Uruguay, and Paraguay.

In Venezuela, the **Orinoco River** runs for about 1,500 miles until it empties into the Atlantic Ocean. The Orinoco basin's agriculture production and ranching industry rely on this river system.

Latin America has very few large lakes. **Lake Maracaibo** in northwest Venezuela is within the petroleum-producing region. **Lake Titicaca,** one of the world's highest lakes, borders on Bolivia and Peru and serves primarily as a source of fish for the largely Native American population. In Mexico, **Lake Chapala** is a large lake which still serves as a source of fresh-water fish. Lake Texcoco, once a major lake, has all but disappeared due to drainage to facilitate the growth of Mexico City.

QUESTIONS

Multiple Choice. Select the letter of the answer that correctly completes each statement.

1. The major religion in most of Latin America is
   A. Roman Catholicism
   B. Protestantism
   C. Islam
   D. Buddhism

2. Most nations of Latin America have a colonial heritage that is
   A. Spanish
   B. Portuguese
   C. French
   D. British

3. The nation with the largest land area in Latin America is
   A. Brazil
   B. Argentina
   C. Mexico
   D. Peru

4. Most of Latin America lies within the climatic zone known as the
   A. tropics
   B. subtropics
   C. Arctic circle
   D. humid continental

5. The term Latin America refers to the three geopolitical regions: South America; Meso (Middle) America; and the
   A. Caribbean Sea Islands
   B. Sahel region
   C. Indian subcontinent
   D. East Indies Islands

   Matching. Match the geographical items in Column 2 with the correct countries or regions in Column 1.

Column 1	Column 2
_____ 1. Brazil	A. Rio de la Plata
_____ 2. Mexico	B. Atacama Desert
_____ 3. Argentina	C. Sierra Madre del Sur
_____ 4. Chile	D. Amazon River
_____ 5. Central America	E. Lake Chapala

ESSAYS

1. Why can Latin America be described as an area of cultural diffusion and diversity?
2. How does the physical geography of Latin America determine its climate, rainfall and vegetation?

II. Economic Geography (Economic Development of Latin America)

Economic Development in Latin America

Latin America has had a history of economic dependence dating from the colonial period. During the colonial period, because of the mercantilist policies of Spain and Portugal, the future Latin American nations were primarily exporters of raw materials and importers of manufactured goods. The Dutch, French, and most notably the British dominated trade with Latin America in the 1800s.

The economies of the newly independent Latin American nations continued to have a "colonial" character. Latin America was heavily dependent on imported consumer goods, food, and machinery and on the export of raw materials as payment for these imports. The dependence on one or two commodities made many smaller Latin American countries vulnerable to economic pressure. Even large countries like Brazil (coffee and sugar) and Argentina (cowhides, wheat) were dependent on the prices that their major exports earned.

In the second half of the 19th century, first Germany and then the United States began to trade with and invest in Latin America. This was a challenge to Britain's economic dominance of the region. The Latin American countries continued to export agricultural products and raw materials. Coffee, tobacco, sugar, copper, and nitrates paid for the increased imports of luxury goods, machinery, and other manufactured products.

Before World War I, the European nations accounted for 60 percent of the **foreign investment** in Latin America. United States' trade and investment grew substantially between the wars. North American **capital investment** concentrated on mines and railroads, which stimulated the import of American machinery. Although German and British trade and investment resumed after World War I, the United States' dominance, particularly in the Caribbean, Mexico, and northern South America, continued. During these years, the Latin American nations faced increased competition to sell their raw materials in Europe because of new sources of these raw materials in Asia and elsewhere.

Since World War II, Latin American trade has undergone rapid changes in volume and direction. By the end of the 1960s, the region's economic giants—Brazil, Mexico, Argentina, and oil-rich Venezuela—accounted for 56 percent of the total value of Latin American trade. These nations began to produce more manufactured goods. By the late 1980s, Brazil had become the world's eighth largest economy. Mexico, Venezuela, Peru, Argentina, and other nations to a lesser extent became more industrialized because of foreign investment and loans. Foreign capital was also used by the Latin American nations to develop their **infrastructures** and establish **credit** to buy needed **technology.** However, in the 1970s the foreign debt of the Latin American nations increased enormously, and in the late 1980s it began to have a negative impact on their economies.

Industry

Industrial development started in the late 19th century. In Argentina, Brazil, and Mexico, the first manufacturing involved small workshops and factories that produced textiles and food products. There was also some production of machine tools and spare parts for the operation of sugar-refining mills, railroads, and other service needs. Before World War I industrial growth took place in the larger Latin American nations. Factories producing textiles, food products, and other light consumer goods expanded their output. In the 1930s there were also attempts to develop heavy industry. For example, in Brazil, steel production began.

World War II encouraged the growth of industry because it became difficult to import manufactured goods. Existing factories were used to capacity, and new plants were added. After the war, Latin American governments promoted industrialization, which was financed largely by American capital. Various methods used to promote in-industrialization were **protective tariffs,** preferential **exchange rates** for fuels and industrial raw materials, government construction of **infra-structure** projects (transportation and power facilities), and govern-ment investment in some heavy industries such as steel and petro-leum.

In Argentina, Chile, and Venezuela, consumer-goods industries were first encouraged. Heavy industry for such products as steel and chemicals came later. In Mexico and Brazil, the governments sought to promote consumer and capital goods at the same time. By the late 1960s, in Argentina, Brazil and Mexico, industry produced about 30 percent of the **gross national product** (GNP). Steel output increased enormously, and automobile production in these nations rose to a combined total of over 1 million cars.

By the 1980s Brazil was in the top ten nations in terms of industrial production, producing airplanes, computers, automobiles, and mili-tary goods that competed in global markets. Mexico City was a great center of industrial production, while Venezuela developed an im-portant petroleum industry.

The stress on industrialization has had mixed results. On the pos-itive side, many new jobs for the increasing population are created; national pride increases because of reduced dependence on **foreign imports;** manufacturing centers develop and spur the growth of cities; and an industrial class of manufacturers and factory workers grow. Moreover, new wealth is created, which stimulates overall economic growth, and national financial institutions grow. However, there have also been negative aspects to industrialization. The stress on manu-facturing has led to a neglect of agricultural exports, which tradi-tionally accounted for much of the foreign exchange earned. Industry has not been able to employ all the rural workers who have left ag-riculture. Moreover, some industries are not competitive, are too costly to run profitably, and have been a drain on the national budget. Pollution, urban squalor, and crime have often been by-products of industrial growth.

The money borrowed to finance this industrialization has created crises in Brazil, Mexico, Venezuela, Argentina, Peru, and smaller economies that cannot repay their growing foreign public and private debt. This **debt** crisis has seriously effected growth rates, destroyed national currencies due to spiraling inflation, and led to political in-stability.

Agriculture

Since the pre-Columbian period, agriculture has been the most im-portant part of the economy in the Latin American nations. More than one-half of the population is employed in agriculture in almost all Latin American countries. However, in proportion to the population employed, agriculture produces a small percentage of the **gross national product.** The region produces large crops of coffee, bananas, cacao, sugar, and cotton, but their **export value** often does not justify the amount of labor and investment. Agriculture supplies both food and raw materials for the region, and most Latin American countries depend heavily on the export of agricultural products to earn foreign currency. Latin America suffers from cultural and physical obstacles that hold back the development of more modern agriculture. Often, lands have been overused until the effects of erosion, mineral depletion, and **single-crop usage** soon make the land increasingly incapable of producing. Climate and topography have played important roles in reducing the fertility of arable lands. For example, in pre-Columbian times, Native Americans in the Andes region used a **terrace farming system** to lessen the effects of erosion, but during the colonial period this system was abandoned.

The arrival of the Europeans changed the landholding system. Large landed estates, **latifundia,** were created, which were inefficiently operated. Absentee landlords still control huge tracts of land. In contrast, millions of Latin American families are subsistence farmers, growing a handful of **food staple** crops such as corn, beans, potatoes, plantains, manioc, and rice. The growing demand for **land reform** has been strongly resisted by the traditional landed elite.

Commercial agriculture, however, is increasing throughout Latin America. Crops for export began to be grown in the colonial period, especially in Brazil and the Caribbean, where sugar and cacao became important. In the 1800s coffee, wheat, wool, and beef made the agricultural exports of Brazil, Argentina, and Uruguay increasingly important. In the 20th century the development of refrigerated transportation made bananas and other fruits valuable exports. However, the heavy reliance on **one-crop economies** in Central American nations, such as Honduras, has had a negative effect on commercial agriculture. By contrast, in Brazil, where **agriculture diversification** is possible, export crops such as soya have earned needed foreign currency.

Latin America needs to increase its agricultural production to meet its fast rate of population growth. In the Andean region and elsewhere, farmers have turned to the growing of coca leaves, marijuana, and poppy plants to escape the endless cycle of poverty. Without land reform, agricultural productivity will continue to be held back by culture and physical problems.

Mineral and Energy Sources

During the conquest of Latin America, the Europeans searched for precious metals, especially gold and silver. Much of the mineral

209

Agricultural Products
of Latin America

wealth, primarily gold and silver objects taken from the more advanced pre-Columbian peoples, was shipped to Europe. From the 1500s to the 1700s, new deposits of gold, silver, and diamonds were found in Mexico, Peru, Bolivia, and Brazil. Although other mineral deposits—for example, iron ore, lead, tin, copper, and zinc—were discovered, they were not used to any great extent.

In the late 19th century, mining activities were extended to new areas. Increased foreign investment from western Europe and the United States provided **capital, technology,** and **management.** In the 20th century, in Peru, Chile, Bolivia, Mexico, Brazil, and elsewhere, mining production increased and contributed significantly to the gross national products of these nations. Certain nations became increasingly dependent on their mineral wealth. For example, Bolivia (tin), Chile (copper), Peru (bismuth), and Brazil (manganese and iron ore) became major centers of the world production of these metals. Today, prospects for mining production should continue to increase in many Latin American countries.

Energy resources are less abundant in Latin America. Mexico is the leading producer of oil; Petroleos Mexicanos (Pemex) controls the distribution from Mexico's oil fields. Newly discovered fields in the Gulf of Mexico have increased Mexico's known reserves.

In South America, Venezuela is the leading producer of petroleum. In 1970, Venezuela produced approximately 70 percent of Latin America's petroleum. Argentina, Brazil, Columbia, Peru, Ecuador, and Chile are all petroleum-producing nations, but most of the oil

MINERALS AND WHERE THEY ARE PRODUCED

Mineral	Where Found
Silver	Mexico (number one in the world), Argentina, Colombia, Peru, Bolivia, Costa Rica, Educador
Tin	Bolivia
Copper	Chile (Atacama Desert), Argentina, Bolivia, Colombia, Cuba
Nitrates (fertilizer)	Chile (Atacama Desert), world's leading producer
Oil	Venezuela, Mexico, Colombia, Argentina, Trinidad, Peru
Iron ore	Venezuela, Peru, Chile, Brazil, Argentina, Guatemala
Aluminum (bauxite)	Surinam (first in the world), Guyana (second), Jamaica
Iodine	Chile
Manganese	Brazil, Cuba
Antimony	Bolivia, Mexico, Peru
Platinum	Colombia (third in the world)
Diamonds	Brazil (second in the world)
Uranium	Brazil

produced by these nations is used to meet their own energy needs. Recent finds by Peru and Ecuador in their Amazon lands have raised hopes of exporting oil; however, in comparison with other regions, particularly the Middle East, the proven reserves are very limited. The lack of large oil reserves could handicap the long-term development of Latin America's industrial base.

The Quest for Development in Latin America

Few areas of Latin America have the proper combination of industrial capacity, capital for investment, raw materials, energy resources and technology needed for developing their economies. Brazil comes the closest to having all of these necessary factors. However, even Brazil, which has increased its industrial capacity, encountered enormous problems in the 1980s. The desire to satisfy the demand for consumer goods while providing manufactured goods and agricultural products for export led to a substantial increase of foreign investment capital. Today, Brazil's foreign debt, the highest in Latin America, is over $100 billion. Despite a favorable balance of trade, Brazil can hardly meet its **debt interest payments.** Hyperinflation (extremely rapid rise in prices for goods and services), urban problems such as poor housing and increasing crime, and a declining standard of living have affected the nation's political stability.

In other less well endowed nations, modernization and industrialization have resulted in many new and difficult problems. Mexico, Argentina, Peru, Colombia, and Venezuela face enormous economic uncertainties. Economic problems have led to increasing **migration** from rural to urban areas, and the search for **economic opportunity** has led people to migrate to other nations.

Multinational corporations have been established in Latin America. These corporations seek to profit from the cheap labor, available raw materials, and the need for investment capital for industrialization. Often they have a competitive advantage over national industries. Multinational corporations show the growing **interdependence** of the more industrialized and less-developed regions of the world. In Latin America the export of much-needed capital as profit instead of reinvestment by these multinational corporations is a serious problem.

Some Latin American nations have sought to work together in regional projects in order to better develop their economies. Brazil and Paraguay are jointly building the Itaipu Dam to harness the energy of the Paraná River system for electrical power. There have been several attempts at regional economic cooperation by Andean nations, some Caribbean countries, and by Brazil and Argentina.

Many countries that are lacking in natural resources have turned to **tourism.** This is particularly true of the Caribbean island nations of the Dominican Republic and Haiti. Even the more **diversified** economies of Mexico and Brazil have come to depend on tourism as a source of needed foreign currency.

Latin America in the Global Context

Today, Latin American nations have ever more global trading relationships. For example, Japan's economic investment and trade with Latin America has recently expanded. The more industrialized nations, such as, Brazil, export such manufactured products as automobiles, military equipment, and commercial aircraft as well as agricultural products to Africa and the Middle East. The petroleum industries of Latin America, most notably that of Venezuela, are increasingly a part of the global oil network. United States' economic relations with Latin America remain strong. However, global interdependence has led to more **diversified economic relationships.**

QUESTIONS

Multiple Choice. Select the letter of the answer that correctly completes each statement.

1. The nation that dominated trade in Latin America during the 1800s was
   A. Great Britian
   B. France
   C. Germany
   D. the United States

2. By the 1980s the Latin American nation that was among the top ten nations in terms of industrial production was
   A. Brazil
   B. Mexico
   C. Argentina
   D. Peru

3. Large landed estates in Latin America are called
   A. latifundia
   B. terraced farms
   C. subsistence farms
   D. minifundia

4. Increased foreign investment from Western Europe, the United States and Japan has provided Latin American nations with all of the following EXCEPT
   A. capital
   B. technology
   C. management
   D. raw materials

5. Brazil's foreign debt problem has caused all of the following EXCEPT
   A. hyperinflation
   B. high debt interest payments
   C. a rising standard of living
   D. a favorable balance of trade

   Matching. Match the correct minerals, agricultural problems and energy resources in Column 2 with the correct countries or regions in Column 1.

Column 1	Column 2
____ 1. Argentina, Uruguay	A. Bananas
____ 2. Central America	B. Beef Cattle
____ 3. Brazil, Cuba	C. Fish
____ 4. Peru	D. Sugar cane
____ 5. Bolivia	E. Tin

ESSAYS

1. Why do many areas of Latin America suffer from cultural and physical obstacles that hold back the development of more modern agriculture?

2. Why has foreign capital investment become a problem for many Latin American nations?

214

III. Human and Cultural Geography

Demographic Characteristics of Latin America: The People Today

A Latin American may be a person with a mixed racial, ethnic, and cultural composition. Native American, European, African, and Asian peoples have blended together in many Latin American countries to form heterogeneous populations. This is particularly true in the nations of Latin America such as Brazil, Mexico, and Venezuela, where rapid **urbanization** has led to a blurring of racial lines. However, there are countries in Latin America where major groups of homogeneous ethnic and racial populations exist. For example, in Argentina, Uruguay, and Costa Rica, a large percentage of the population has a primarily European heritage, whereas in parts of the Andean region and in Guatemala, many Bolivians, Peruvians, Ecuadorians, and Guatemalans would be classified **demographically** as Native American.

The high demographic growth rate of Latin America has led to expanding populations, particularly in nations with large urban centers. In Brazil, Mexico, Peru, and elsewhere, the growth of urban areas has not only led to demographic changes but also has changed traditional patterns of economic activity. In addition, the pressures of urbanization have altered **environmental conditions.** For example, in the cities of São Paulo and Mexico City, the enormous increase in population and concentration of industry and automobiles have caused severe pollution and large areas of urban squalor. In the Amazon region, there has been an enormous deforestation due to the burning of rain forests, logging, and mining. This is in part a direct result of demographic changes.

Latin America does not have as large a population as Asia, Africa, and Europe. Nevertheless, the trend towards urbanization, accompanied by increased mining, ranching, and other uses of previously unused land, has led to major environmental damage that has serious long-term global consequences.

Demographic Pressures

In the 1970s the annual population increases in Mexico, Costa Rica, the Dominican Republic, Colombia, Venezuela, and Paraguay were over 3 percent. This profound *demographic growth* in Latin America is a result of a number of factors. One factor is a persistent tradition that values high birth rates. Another factor is the Roman Catholic Church's stand against abortion and contraception. In addition, improvements in public health services have led to a higher survival rate after birth. Furthermore, the decline in the death rate, especially the infant mortality rate, has been a factor in increasing populations.

The massive migrations of people from rural areas to the cities has led to the rapid growth of urban centers. This migration is the result of depressed rural conditions and the belief that work and a better life can be found in the cities.

By 1970 approximately 54 percent of the population of Latin America was classified as urban. The urban population has been increasing at a rate of 3 to 4 percent every five years, and this growth is expected to continue to the end of the century.

The largest cities of Latin America have experienced the greatest population increase. In a number of cities, the annual population increase has been 7 percent, which means that the city's population will double in about a decade. This rapid growth has led to the growth of **squatter settlements,** called "barridas" or "favelas." They are inhabited by people who do not have access to enough **productive** work and many goods and services.

The rapid urban growth has placed severe strains on urban **infrastructures** and led to mounting problems. Shortages, congestion, pollution, overcrowding, and a growing crime rate are common in São Paulo, Rio de Janeiro, Mexico City, Lima, Bogotá, and elsewhere. In some Latin American cities, large numbers of poor urban youths are unemployed.

In some Latin American nations, increased immigration from Europe, the Middle East, and Asia has led to other demographic changes. In Argentina and Brazil, massive immigration from Italy, Germany, Spain, Portugal, and elsewhere in Europe has resulted in a **Europeanization** of the urban populations. Immigration has had an effect not only on the industrial and agricultural sectors of the economies of Brazil, Argentina, Venezuela, Paraguay, and Uruguay but also on their cultures and their **ethnic diversity.** For example, in Brazil, a large community of Japanese immigrants has contributed to the development of an agricultural sector in São Paulo.

Social Factors

In Latin America, the family has traditionally represented **stability** and **security.** Political and economic uncertainties have contributed to the importance of family ties and connections. There has also been a tradition of male dominance in Latin American societies that has shaped male-female and family relationships into the 20th century.

In recent years, demographic growth, urbanization, and increased participation of women in the labor force have led to some changes in the traditional roles of men and women. There are increasing numbers of women who head families in large urban areas in Latin America. Most countries have granted **suffrage** to women. Nevertheless, obstacles to **full equality** still remain deeply ingrained in male-dominated societies, where **machismo** is the accepted social behavior.

The differences between urban and rural life styles have led to a breakdown of some family traditions. In the large Latin American cities, families face the same problems as in other societies. When both parents work or there is only one parent, it is difficult to raise children in traditional ways. Abandoned children are a problem in some Latin American countries, such as Brazil, Peru, and Colombia. There is also a rise in urban crime committed by young people.

Urban centers have been favored over rural areas in terms of development. As a result, the economic and social problems of rural areas have been largely ignored. This neglect is a major cause of the migration of rural people to the cities. However, the cities are not able to provide adequate housing and social services for the new city dwellers.

The migration of poor rural laborers has also had an effect on the remaining Native American populations. Certain tribes were able to preserve their culture because until recently they were isolated. In Brazil, for example, the building of highways in the Amazon basin, the setting of fires to claim land for cattle raising, and increased mining using **technology** that is destructive to the land and water has destroyed some Native American tribes. The invasion of lands set aside for tribal reservations by poor rural farmers and miners has led to increased violations of the Native Americans' **human rights.**

The continuing inequalities and differences between urban and rural areas reflect the power of the city over the countryside. The uneven distribution of economic development has led to increasing differences between social classes. The gap between rich and poor has increased in the Latin American nations. Urban areas have increasingly become the centers of wealth and power. Industrial production and financial affairs are concentrated in the cities.

The growth of industry has led to the rise of a group of urban **elites,** the factory owners, financial leaders, bankers, and merchants who have gained much political influence because of their economic power. The unwillingness of the urban elites to more evenly distribute their profits has often placed them on the side of the landed elite, the military, and the Roman Catholic Church, and against change.

Latin American Contributions to a Global Culture

The people of Latin America have made important contributions to world culture in the fields of arts, music, dance, and literature. The cultural achievements of the Native Americans prior to the arrival of European and African influences have not been very well preserved. The accomplishments of these pre-Columbian societies are mostly known through monuments, such as temples and other buildings. However, pottery, jewelry, statues, dance, music, and certain handicrafts that have survived clearly show the creativity and skill

217

of these peoples. Unfortunately, the Spaniards destroyed much that existed of these peoples' writings.

The Europeans brought their own styles of art and music to the Americas during the colonial period. However, along with the dominant imported European culture, other cultures existed that had connections with Africa and the pre-Columbian heritage. Modern Latin American culture is a blend of Native American, African, and European cultures. Latin Americans have blended these together to form a rich, vibrant, changeable, but uniquely Latin American culture that varies from country to country.

QUESTIONS

Multiple Choice. Select the letter of the answer that correctly completes each statement.

1. Demographic growth in Latin America is the result of all of the following factors EXCEPT
   A. Roman Catholic Church's stand against abortion
   B. improvements in public health services
   C. a persistant tradition that values high birth rates
   D. the trend towards urbanization in many countries.

2. A group of Latin American nations whose population is of primarily European heritage is
   A. Argentina, Costa Rica, Uruguay
   B. Guatemala, Nicaragua, Ecuador
   C. Mexico, Cuba, Bolivia
   D. Colombia, Venezuela, Peru

3. Rapid urban growth in Latin America has resulted in
   A. a decline in the crime rate in large cities
   B. a low percentage of unemployed urban youth
   C. the elimination of marginal populations
   D. the growth of squatter settlements

4. Full equality for women in Latin America has been difficult to obtain because
   A. urbanization has led to a decrease in women's right
   B. women in Latin American are interested only in suffrage
   C. machismo is the accepted social behavior
   D. in most families both parents usually work

5. The invasion of lands set aside for tribal reservations by poor rural farmers and miners is a violation of Native American
   A. human rights
   B. ethnic diversity
   C. demographic growth
   D. urbanization patterns

Matching. Match the correct definition in Column 2 with the correct vocabulary word in Column 1.

Column 1	Column 2
____ 1. elite	A. the movement to cities
____ 2. marginal population	B. the different parts of a whole
____ 3. technology	C. practical application of knowledge
____ 4. composition	D. people without access to goods and services
____ 5. urbanization	E. leading member of society

ESSAYS

1. Describe the problems that rapid urbanization has caused in many Latin American nations?
2. How have the people of Latin America contributed to the development of a global culture?

IV. History and Political Geography (Historical Setting of Latin America)

Early History

Most probably, the first people came to North and South America thousands of years ago during the Ice Age, over a land bridge across the Bering Strait. These *nomadic* hunters from Asia moved into North America and over thousands of years spread throughout the Americas.

In Latin America, a number of Native American civilizations flourished independent of and isolated from developments in Africa, Asia, and Europe until Columbus' voyage in 1492. These pre-Columbian civilizations were as brilliant as the ancient civilizations of other continents. However, certain differences hindered further development. The horse, mule, camel, and other work animals were not present in the Americas when these civilizations prospered. The wheel and iron tools and weapons also were not in use.

The Mayan Civilization

The Mayan civilization developed in what today is the Yucatán Peninsula of Mexico and Central America. By the 2nd century B.C., groups of Mayan clans were living in cultural communities. By the time of the **classic period** of their history (300–900 A.D.), a large number of rival city-states existed. They were ruled by nobles and a priestly class. Warriors, farmers, merchants, and slaves made up the vast majority of the highly rigid, **stratified** Mayan **social structure.**

The Mayans made great accomplishments in science, especially in astronomy and mathematics. The Mayan calendar was very accurate, and Mayan buildings rival those of other ancient peoples. Religion dominated Mayan life.

The reason for the decline of Mayan civilization is still a mystery. By 900 A.D. the Mayans had moved north to the Yucatán Peninsula and south to the Guatamalan highlands. Although new settlements were established after 1000 A.D., they did not reach the level of the earlier cities.

The Aztec Empire

The Aztecs were a warrior people with a rigid social structure, who rose to the leadership of an alliance of city-states in the 1400s. The Aztec capital was Tenochtitlán, an island city in Lake Texcoco, the site of present-day Mexico City. The Aztec empire was ruled by a warrior king, who was supported by a warrior class and a priestly class who controlled the Aztec religious ceremonies. The Aztecs had, as did other Meso-American peoples, a **polytheistic** religion. Of particular importance was their god of war, **Huitzilopochtli,** who could only be worshiped properly through human sacrifice and the offering of blood.

War was the policy of the Aztec empire towards all peoples who did not accept a **tributary** status, which included the supplying of slaves for sacrifice. Although the Aztec empire was expanding in the early 1500s, the Aztecs could not conquer all of their enemies in central Mexico. Cortés relied heavily on the military support of the Aztecs' enemies, particularly the **Tlaxcalans,** in his conquest of the empire in the 1520s. Trade played an important role in the Aztec empire. Farming was also of great importance. Corn, beans, squash, and peppers were the main staples. Land ownership was controlled by the government. Land was given to families headed by male warriors and could be handed down.

The Aztecs were a **literate** people who spoke a language called Na'nhautl. The Aztecs were skilled at making parchment paper and in gold and silver metallurgy. To measure time, they adopted the Mayan calendar. They were skilled engineers and architects.

The Incas

The Incas ruled a highly regimented empire that included much of the Andean region of South America, stretching from southern Colombia through Equador, Bolivia, Peru, into northern Chile and northwestern Argentina. Beginning in the 1200s A.D., the Incas began to expand and conquer other peoples, including other advanced civilizations such as the Tihuanaco and the **Chimu.** The acceptance of

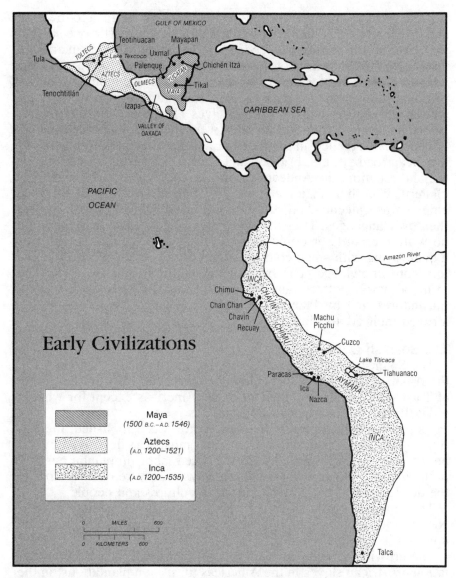

Early Civilizations

GULF OF MEXICO

Tula
TOLTECS
Teotihuacan
Lake Texcoco
AZTECS
Tenochtitlán
OLMECS
Izapa
VALLEY OF
OAXACA

Mayapan
Uxmal
Palenque
YUCATÁN
MAYA
Chichén Itzá
Tikal

CARIBBEAN SEA

PACIFIC
OCEAN

Amazon River

Chimu
Chan Chan
Chavin
Recuay

INCA
CHAVIN
CHIMU

Machu
Picchu

Cuzco

Lake Titicaca
Tiahuanaco

Paracas
Ica
Nazca

AYMARA

INCA

Talca

▨	Maya (1500 B.C.–A.D. 1546)
▦	Aztecs (A.D. 1200–1521)
▒	Inca (A.D. 1200–1535)

0   MILES   600

0   KILOMETERS   600

Incan rule meant that a conquered people could retain their own rulers.

Religion played a crucial role in Inca life. The term "Inca" refers to the ruler of the empire and his extended family, which numbered in the thousands. The Inca was believed to be a descendent of the sun god, Inti, and was worshiped like a living god. The Incas sought through their worship to influence their gods to help them, and a large group of priests regulated the ceremonial life of the empire. Offerings of food, animals, and at times human sacrifice were made to the gods.

221

Land was not privately owned. It was given by the Inca to the tribe and distributed. The land was subdivided into four parts: one section was given to the farmers; a second was set aside for the sun and the crops given to the priests of the temples; a third went to the emperor, who used the crops for the government officials, the military, and his personal household use; and the last section was farmed for those who could not provide for themselves. Potatoes, cotton, maize, beans, squash, cotton, and tomatos were the principal crops.

The Incas excelled in engineering and architecture. Remnants of the Incan road system, bridges, and building construction can still be found throughout the Andean region. Cuzco, located in the highlands of Peru, was their major capital. The official language of the Inca empire was Quechua, but the Incas allowed subject peoples to use their own languages. They had no written language and therefore kept no written records or books. Instead they used a **quipu,** which was a main string with small colored strings attached and tied into knots to record knowledge. The Incas were skillful artisans who excelled in metal work, pottery, and textiles. In the 1530s the Spanish conquistadores, led by Pizzarro, ended the reign of the Incas and destroyed their civilization.

The Spanish Colonial Empire

The Spanish and Portuguese were the first to make vast claims in the Americas and carve out colonial empires. In 1494, in the **Treaty of Tordesillas,** Spain obtained all of the Americas except for what is today Brazil, which went to Portugal.

As the Spanish empire in the New World was established, the Native American civilizations were for the most part destroyed by superior military forces and diseases. Forced labor on plantations and in the mines, the **encomienda** and **mita** systems were other factors in the destruction of the Native American cultures and people.

The Spaniards brought the characteristics of their society to their New World empire. Spain imposed a political, religious, and linguistic unity on its colonial empire.

The growing scarcity of Native American labor led to the importation of African slaves in the Americas for use on plantations, in the mines, and for other purposes. Efforts by the Roman Catholic Church to protect the Native Americans from abuses of their **human rights** were largely ignored in a colonial economy, which operated on the principles of the mercantilist system. **Bishop Bartolomé de Las Casas** sought to enlist the Spanish crown in the protection of the Native Americans, but his efforts failed. The **latifundio** and **hacienda** (large, self-sufficient plantations) forms of land ownership predominated.

The Spanish colonial organization was based on a hierarchical structure, which placed the Spanish at the top of colonial society.

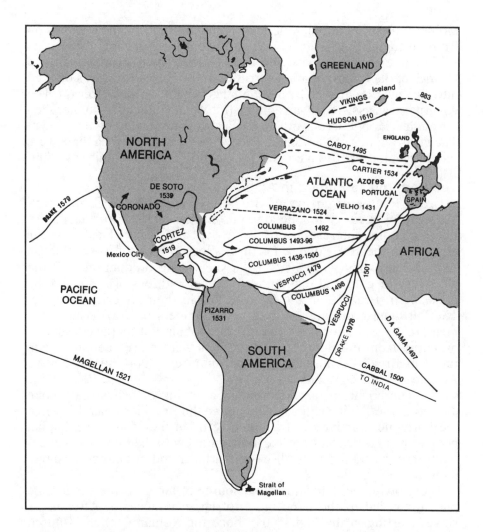

This privileged class of Spanish elite, **peninsulars** (Spanish-born nobles), and **creoles** (their American-born sons), dominated the colonial economy and owned vast areas of land. Next were the **mestizos** (Caucasian and Native American ancestry), followed by **mulattos** (Caucasian and African ancestry), African slaves, and the Native Americans.

The Spanish Roman Catholic Church helped in the subjugation and control of the Native American population and the ordering of colonial society. Both the regular hierarchy and the religious orders (the Jesuits, Franciscans, and Dominicans) took responsibility for the education of the Native American populations. The Jesuit order played a particularly important **mission** role in protecting the Native American populations. Jesuit interference with the Spanish colonists' exploitation of the Native American population led to their expulsion from Portuguese America (1759) and Spanish America (1767).

The Spanish empire was controlled by the crown through the royal **Council of the Indies.** Spanish territory in the New World was divided into **viceroyalties** headed by appointed governors, called **viceroys.** The governor was assisted by an administrative and judicial tribunal called the **audiencia.** Numerous other officials were appointed by the crown. The viceroyalties of **New Spain, Peru, New Granada** and **La Plata** were the four major territorial units of the Spanish colonial empire by 1800.

The Portuguese Empire in America

Credit for the discovery of Brazil is given to Pedro Cabral, who claimed the territory for the king of Portugal in 1500. Portugal's primary colonial interests were in Africa and Asia. This situation changed in the 1600s due to Portugal's loss of most of its colonies in Asia, the growing value of Brazil's sugar-cane production, and the discovery of gold and diamonds. Portugal had less of a dominating presence in Brazil than the Spanish had in their American empire. The Portuguese did not settle in large numbers in Brazil, and since men greatly outnumbered women, the population increase resulted primarily from intermarriage. Class lines were more economic than racial in Brazil because of this intermixture of Portuguese, Native Americans, and Africans.

The Tupi-Guarani, an Amerindian grouping of tribes that spoke **dialects** of the Tupian language, inhabited the Brazilian coastline when the Portuguese arrived to trade and settle in the 1500s. The Tupian peoples were fierce and warlike, but contact with the Europeans eventually proved fatal due to disease, warfare, and attempted enslavement for labor.

The growing need for a reliable source of labor on the sugar-cane plantations led to the importation of large numbers of Africans as slaves starting in the mid-1500s. Since the Roman Catholic Church did not play as wide a role in Brazil as in Spanish territory, the African slaves were able to retain some of their **religious** and **cultural beliefs.** These blended with Christian and Native American concepts and emerged as Candomble, an Africanized ritualistic and formalized cult that existed underneath the façade of the Roman Catholic Church.

The Portugese penetrated deeply into the interior of the South American continent. **Bandeiras,** quasi Euro-Amerindian military expeditions, in search of Indian slaves and precious mineral wealth, pushed Portuguese claims to the Andes Mountains.

The Dutch, French, and English in Latin America

In the second half of the 16th century, the Dutch, French, and English sought to establish colonies in the Americas. They took pos-

Colonial Empires of the New World

ATLANTIC OCEAN

VICEROYALTY OF NEW SPAIN

GUIANA

VICEROYALTY OF NEW GRANADA

PACIFIC OCEAN

Colonial Empires of
the New World
1776

||||| Spanish

■ French

AAA Portuguese

⠂⠂⠂ Dutch

VICEROYALTY OF PERU

VICEROYALTY OF BRAZIL

VICEROYALTY
OF
LA PLATA

0   500   1000

session of territory primarily in the Caribbean region and along the northeastern coast of South America.

Starting in the 1580s the Dutch attempted to gain control of northeastern Brazil. The profitable sugar industry was a target of growing Dutch sea power, financial strength, and technical and business expertise. The Dutch presence in the sugar-producing areas south of the Amazon River lasted until the 1640s, when a reestablishment of Portugal's independence from Spain enabled the Portuguese to drive out the Dutch. The Dutch were able to hold onto Dutch Guiana, present-day Surinam, and they retained the Netherlands Antilles: the islands of Curaçao, Aruba, Bonaire, St. Eustatius, Saba, and part of St. Martin.

During the 1500s, besides laying claims to parts of North America, the French sought to establish a presence in the Caribbean and South America. Attempts to gain a foothold in Brazil were defeated by the Portuguese in the mid-1500s. Settlements in Cayenne in French Guiana began in 1604. Control of this territory shifted back and forth among the French, Dutch, Portuguese, and British. Martinique and Guadaloupe in the French West Indies were settled and colonized beginning in 1635 and became valuable sugar producers. Haiti was ceded by Spain to France in 1697. The western region of the island of Hispaniola became France's most prosperous colony in the Americas. The establishment of a **plantation economy,** based on slave labor and restrictive **mercantilist** trade policies, was promoted by the French crown.

Besides the settlements along the eastern coast of North America, the British were also able to establish themselves throughout the Caribbean. Jamaica, Barbados, and Trinidad-Tobaggo were their princiciple possessions in what became the British West Indies in the late 1600s. Large numbers of African slaves, as elsewhere in the Caribbean, were brought in to provide labor for the sugar-cane plantations in the British West Indies. The first English settlements of South America, in present-day Guyana, began in the 1600s.

The English, French, and Dutch colonies in the Caribbean basin all developed a highly profitable **sugar-plantation economy,** utilizing imported African slave labor. The colonies were controlled by trading policies that favored the "mother" country. The European colonial powers exploited the resources of the Caribbean islands to further their own economic development.

Establishment of Political Independence in Latin America

The 1700s were a period of great political, social, and economic change for the European powers. Britain's thirteen colonies in America won their independence as a result of the American Revolution. In the late 1700s the French Revolution shook the stability of Europe. The writings of the **Enlightenment,** expressed in the works of Locke, Rousseau, Voltaire, Montesquieu, and others, led to the spread of revolutionary ideas in Europe and the Americas. In the 1700s Spain sought to reform its American empire. New viceroyalties were created, and an **intendancy system** was introduced to increase revenues and improve the colonial administration. A Spanish officer appointed by the crown, an intendente, had complete control in matters of justice, war, fiscal problems and general public administration over a given area.

The Napleonic era that followed the French Revolution caused dislocations that eventually led to a period of Latin American revolutions from 1808 to 1826. Despite the distance and isolation of Spain's colonies from Europe, the political ideas of the Enlightenment and the American and French revolutions affected the people in the Spanish colonies. The English, Dutch, French, and Americans increasingly traded with Spain's American empire, thereby decreasing the loyalty and dependence of the colonies on Spain. Moreover, some of the **creole** elite in the Spanish colonies, such as the Venezuelan **Francisco Miranda**, promoted the independence of Spanish America.

Napoleon's armies invaded Spain and Portugal in 1806 to 1807. The capture and exile of the Spanish royal family to France and the placement of Joseph Bonaparte on the Spanish throne broke the bond that united Spanish America to Spain. A movement that began as a rejection of French control ended as a series for **wars of independence** against Spain.

The liberators, **Simón Bolívar** and **José San Martín,** and their supporters, raised armies to drive the Spanish out of South America. In Mexico, the leadership of Fathers **Hidalgo** and **Morelos** and other revolutionaries led to the eventual success of **Agustín de Iturbide**, who established Mexican independence in 1821. Creole nationalism was too strong to overcome, and with the help of the mestizo population, the Spanish were driven out.

Case Studies on Independence: Haiti

The movement towards Haitian independence was sparked by the French Revolution. Throughout the 1790s, the former slaves, first led by **Toussaint L'Ouverture,** increasingly sought to drive out the white slaveowners. Despite a major attempt to restore French authority by Napoleon in 1802, independence was inevitable. In 1804, **Jean-Jacques Dessalines,** an ex-slave, was able to drive out the French, and Haiti became the second nation in the Western Hemisphere to win complete independence.

Case Studies in Independence: Mexico

In 1810, **Miguel Hidalgo,** a priest, joined with other creole plotters, most notably Ignacio de Allende, and issued the famous **Grito de Dolores.** This symbol raised the cry of rebellion against the Spanish government in New Spain. The first phase of the struggle for independence ended with the royalists' defeating the insurgents and executing many of the leaders of the rebellion. Despite this setback, one of Hidalgo's lieutenants, **José Morelos,** called together a congress, who wrote a constitution and declared independence. Morelos was captured and executed in 1815. However, independence was finally secured in 1821 when **Agustín de Iturbide,** a creole military officer who had helped defeat the earlier rebellions, negotiated with Vincente

LATIN AMERICAN INDEPENDENCE MOVEMENT TO 1828

Country	Year of Independence	Leaders in Independence Movement
Haiti	1803–1804	Toussaint l'Ouverture
Mexico	1821	Father Miguel Hidalgo
		José Morelos
		Agustín de Iturbide
Colombia	1819	Simón Bolívar
Venezuela	1821	Francisco de Miranda
		Simón Bolívar
Ecuador	1822	José de Sucre
		Simón Bolívar
Argentina	1816	José de San Martín
Chile	1818	José de San Martín
		Bernardo O'Higgins
Peru	1824	José de Sucre
		Simón Bolívar
Bolivia	1825	Simón Bolívar
Uruguay	1814, 1828	José Artigas
Brazil	1822	José Benifacio
		Emperor Dom Pedro
Paraguay	1811	Fulgencio Yegros
Central American Republics	1812–1825	José Delgado
		José del Valle

Guerrero, by then the principle insurgent leader, to form the **Plan of Iguala,** which called for independence under a monarchy. Iturbide forced the Spanish out and briefly ruled Mexico as emperor.

Case Studies: Argentina, Chile, and the Role of José de San Martín

In 1810, a revolutionary regime in Buenos Aires declared independence. José de San Martín, the real architect of independence, had liberated the future Argentina by 1816. He crossed the Andes Mountains with an army in 1817 and helped **Bernardo O'Higgins** drive the Spanish army out of Chile the following year. San Martín was also involved in the liberation of Peru, but he left the final military struggle in that country after an historic meeting with **Simón Bolívar,** "the Liberator."

Case Studies: The Andean Region and the Role of Simón Bolívar, "the Liberator"

Simón Bolívar, by birth a member of the creole landowning elite, supported the growing independence movement. Between 1810 and 1821 "the Liberator" was involved in wars to free the future nations of Venezuela, Colombia, Ecuador, Bolivia, and Peru. He was made the first constitutional president of **Gran Colombia** in 1821. With the help of **Francisco Santander** and **Antonio José de Sucre,** Bolívar defeated the Spanish royalist forces by 1826, and they withdrew from Peru.

Case Studies: Brazil

Napoleon's invasion of Portugal resulted in the royal family's leaving for Brazil. **Joao VI** became king of Portugal, Brazil, and the Algarve in 1816. However, in 1821 political events in Portugal caused Joao to return there. He left behind his son, **Pedro I,** as regent of Brazil. In 1822, Pedro issued his famous "I am staying" statement after the Portuguese parliament ordered him to return to Portugal. Later that year, independence was declared. In contrast to Spanish America, Brazilian independence was achieved peacefully. Pedro I was declared emperor of Brazil in 1822.

Case Studies: The Caribbean

The one area where Spain retained its colonies was in the Caribbean. Cuba and Puerto Rico remained possessions of Spain until the Spanish-American War in 1898. The economies of these two Greater Antilles islands were dominated by the sugar-plantation owners, and slavery was the main source of labor, particularly in Cuba.

In the British, French, and Dutch Caribbean colonies, with the exception of Haiti, independence has been attained more recently, if at all. Many of the British-held islands achieved independence in the post-World War II period. Some islands have remained attached to Great Britain. The French-speaking islands were made overseas departments which gave them the privilege of representation in the nation's politics and the right of French citizenship. However, the real political power remained in France.

Early Attempts at Unification Fail

The initial attempts at unification of the newly independent states did not last, mainly because nationalistic feelings in the Latin American countries led to political fragmentation. The political union of present-day Colombia, Venezuela, Ecuador, and Panama in **Gran Colombia** was established in 1819 through the efforts of Simón Bolívar, Francisco Santander, and others. At the Congress of Cucuta in 1821, a constitution was adopted. Bolívar and Santander were elected the first president and vice-president for all of Colombia. Santander remained to direct the government after Bolívar went off to liberate Peru. The central government promoted a program of liberal reform. However, attempts by the landed elites to safeguard their local authority and autonomy in Venezuela and Ecuador, led in, 1826 to an open revolt which broke out in Venezuela. The return of Bolívar temporarily brought unity and peace. However, a brief war soon began between Peru and Gran Colombia in 1828, and this caused the local landed elites to renew their struggle for a political entity that would be more easily influenced and run in their interests. In 1830, first Venezuela and then Ecuador formally seceded. The remaining part of Gran Colombia became the Republic of New Granada.

The Federation of Central America was created when the five provinces—Guatamala, El Salvador, Honduras, Nicaragua, and Costa Rica—declared independence in 1821 and joined the Mexican empire under Iturbide. They drafted a constitution and adopted a republican form of government. The new government immediately had political difficulties, and in 1823 the five provinces left the federation and became independent states. By the 1840s the federation had ceased to exist.

Sources of Stability and Power: The Landed Elite, the Military, and the Roman Catholic Church

The failure of unification in South America and in Central America was a result of the concentration of power in the hands of the creole landed elite in the independent nations of Latin America. The large landowners gained enormous power in their local areas and were unwilling to surrender it to a strong central government. The creole aristocracy, who owned large estates called **latifundio,** replaced the Spanish officials and peninsulars. They were unwilling to share political power, and the large landowners became a conservative force that sought to maintain stability and their traditional local powers.

The role of the military also proved to be a continuing problem in Latin America. In the early years, military leaders were called on to maintain law and order and act as a stabilizing influence. In some countries, the military was the only organized force that could prevent chaos after the wars of national independence.

The rebellions that frequently broke out in the Spanish-speaking republics in the 1800s led the armed forces of many nations to control their countries for long periods. The rise of the **military dictator, the caudillo,** became a tradition in many countries. José Antonio Paez of Venezuela and Andres Santa Cruz of Bolivia are early examples of caudillos in their nations. Venezuela suffered 50 revolutions, and Bolivia 60 revolutions by 1900.

Military figures continued to gain and hold onto power in the 20th century. The military continues to see itself as the preserver of stability and tradition. Today, a military **coup d'etat** is justified to prevent the possibility of a Communist takeover and social disintegration. This was the case in Chile when General Augusto Pinochet seized power in 1973.

After the wars of independence, the Roman Catholic Church remained a key institution throughout Latin America. Until recently, the Church often supported the landed elite and military in their efforts to preserve tradition and social order and showed little concern for social problems. However, in recent years the role of the Church in some Latin American nations has changed, as the clergy has taken a more active role in causes concerning human rights. Some members of the clergy have supported the ideas of the **liberation theology,** a church of the people, and even rebellions against the government in power. The struggle within the Church between conservatives who believe that the clergy should continue its traditional historic role and radicals who want the clergy to play a more social and political role continues.

Political Evolution Since Independence

In Latin America, a concept of **citizenship** was slow to develop after independence. There also were difficulties in attempting to institute a **republican** form of government. Political participation was open primarily to the wealthy members of society. The landed elite consolidated their hold on the executive and legislative branches of government. In theory, some **democratic traditions** were established in many Latin American countries in the 19th century. For example, constitutions were written; elected legislative bodies were provided for, and judicial systems were created. However, in practice, the caudillo acted as a **dictator** and often ignored the democratic features of governing.

Case Study: Argentina (1820s to Today)

The landed elite, primarily cattle ranchers, were the real source of power in Argentina. Argentinian **nationalism** developed during the rule of the caudillo tyrant **Juan Manuel de Rosas,** Rosas ignored the constitution and often used his military power to persecute and terrorize his enemies. Although the provinces of Argentina remained loosely associated under Rosa's **federalist** control, by the time of his overthrow in 1852, he had, to a large measure, forged national unity. However, the establishment of **democratic traditions** did not come until later in the 1800s.

In the 1940s, a military officer, **Juan D. Perón,** rose to power. Peron was a **populist caudillo** who used the democratic process to promote a program that favored the middle and labor sectors of society. Perón was elected president twice. Juan Perón and his first wife **Eva Peron** relied on the support of the workers. His program, **Justicialismo,** sought a balance between society's opposing forces. Perón was overthrown in 1955 by the military, with the support of the traditional elite who found his programs threatening. However, Perónism continued to be a political force. In 1972 Perón was reelected but died shortly thereafter. His new wife, Isabel, succeeded him but soon was overthrown by a military coup d'etat. A period of harsh military rule followed. In the 1980s democratic elections were allowed but the future of **democracy** in Argentina is still undecided.

The Case of Mexico

In the late 1820s, a military caudillo, **Antonio Santa Anna,** rose to power. He dominated Mexican politics to the mid-1850s and supported a conservative and **centralist** concept of government. Unfortunately, Santa Anna resorted to dictatorial rule and corrupt policies that had disastrous consequences. Mexico, under Santa Anna's leadership, fell victim to United States' expansionism. The successful rebellion led by Americans in Texas in the 1830s and the Mexican War in the 1840s led to a loss of over 40 percent of Mexico's territory.

After Santa Anna's exile in 1855, **Benito Juárez** tried to rule Mexico under more **democratic ideals.** In the mid-1870s, **Porfirio Díaz,** a soldier and protegé of Juárez, was elected president and held political power until the revolution of 1911. During Díaz' rule, Mexico was transformed into a politically stable and economically progressive nation, but at the expense of political freedom and democratic government. Foreign investment was encouraged in railroads, oil, and mining. Diaz' political power was based on the use of a repressive police force, the **rurales,** to control his opponents. The peasants continued to live under terrible conditions, and the urban labor movement was suppressed. Díaz was supported by the elite **hacienda** owners, the Roman Catholic Church, and the military.

Political Revolutions

In the 20th century, several revolutions have led to important changes in some nations of Latin America. Their long-term effects are not yet clear. However, traditional institutions are faced with increasing **social and economic** problems brought on by demographic change.

Case Study: Mexico Since 1911

The Mexican Revolution of 1911 led to important changes in that nation. After the fall of Díaz, military leaders succeeded each other as president and created a constitutional government based on a one-party political system. The Roman Catholic Church lost much of its influence and power. The Mexican labor movement was allowed to develop and became an important force. The labor unions competed with the new developing industrial **oligarchy** to influence the government.

Mexico became more **nationalistic,** and the **nationalization** of the petroleum industry in the 1930s by Lazaro Cardinas symbolized the nation's change of direction. In the years after 1940, the leaders of the ruling political party, the **PRI,** sought to create political stability by allowing a middle class to develop and by encouraging economic change. However, the PRI has continued to hold power despite growing political opposition.

Case Study: The Cuban Revolution 1959–

Cuba remained a Spanish colony until 1898 when independence was established as part of the treaty that settled the Spanish-American War. The United States' influence in Cuba continued after its military occupation ended in 1902. Between 1933 and 1959 **Fulgencio Batista** dominated, and although he provided political stability, economic problems led to increased suffering. A rebellion supported by young professionals, students, urban workers, and some farmers was led by **Fidel Castro.** By 1959, Castro's military forces had defeated Batista's army and seized power.

Castro brought about great political, social, and economic changes. He turned to the Communist nations, especially the Soviet Union, for economic support and protection from the United States. By 1965, Castro's socialist state was officially ruled by the Cuban Communist Party and guided by the principles of Marxism-Leninism.

Castro sought to export the Cuban Revolution by supporting guerrilla movements in Bolivia, Colombia, Nicaragua, El Salvador, and elsewhere. This forced the United States to pay greater attention to the social and economic problems in Latin America. Starting in the 1960s, the United States began to work to politically and economically isolate Cuba.

Case Study: The Sandinista Revolution in Nicaragua

United States' interest in Nicaragua dates from the late 1840s when the American government contested British supremacy in Central America. The United States began a military occupation of the nation in 1912, which lasted until 1933. In the mid-1930s, the National Guard, trained by United States' military officers, took responsibility for maintaining order. The National Guard was the instrument for the rise of the **Somoza** dictatorship, which ruled Nicaragua from 1936 through most of the 1970s. Although there was economic progress under Somoza in agricultural production, and then in the industrial sector, there was little real distribution of income.

The assassination of **Pedro Chamorro,** the publisher of an opposition newspaper in 1978, sparked an uprising that toppled the Somozoa dictatorship and brought the **Sandinista Front** to power in 1979. The Sandinistas sought to create a socialist-type state in Nicaragua, and **Daniel Ortega** became the nation's leader. The Sandinistas soon faced opposition from the United States. Moreover, the Sandinista government faced serious economic problems brought on by alienating important segments of the agricultural and industrial sectors.

233

Hostility towards the Sandinista government because of its ties to Castro's Cuba, the Soviet Union, and the insurgency in El Salvador led the United States to support the **contra** military forces, which were seeking to overthrow the Sandinistas. The costly civil war in Nicaragua led to large numbers of casualties, increased emigration, and a further deterioration of the Nicaraguan economy.

Political Integration

In 1823, when Spain threatened to try to regain its colonial empire in Latin America, the United States responded with the **Monroe Doctrine.** President James Monroe in a statement issued to Congress declared that the American continents were henceforth not to be considered as subjects for future colonization by European nations. The statement also said that any attempt by European powers to extend their system to this hemisphere would be considered dangerous to the peace and safety of the United States. In addition, the United States declared that it would not interfere in European affairs.

The Monroe Doctrine was favorably received by the Latin American nations. Although the United States did not possess the military force to back up this bold statement, it knew that the British navy would protect Latin America because of Britain's commercial interests in the region.

Prior to the 1860s, the United States did little to protect Latin America from European intrusions. However, in the late 1800s the United States began to play a greater role in the affairs of Latin America. In 1898, the United States defeated Spain in the Spanish-American War and gained control of Puerto Rico and Cuba. Cuba soon gained its independence, but the era of United States' domination of much of Latin America, especially Central America and the Caribbean, had begun.

President Theodore Roosevelt changed the role of the United States from protector to that of an **international police power** in Latin America. In 1904, the **Roosevelt Corollary** to the Monroe Doctrine stated that if the Latin American nations failed to properly maintain their political and financial affairs, the United States would intervene to restore order. This corollary led to interventions in the Dominican Republic, Nicaragua, Haiti, and elsewhere. In addition, the United States' desire to build a canal to connect the Atlantic and Pacific oceans led it to defend Panama's secession from Colombia in 1903. The **Hay-Bunau-Varilla Treaty** negotiated with the newly independent nation to build the Panama Canal was very favorable to United States' interests.

This policy of interference in Latin American affairs caused a growing resentment in the region toward the **"colossus of the north"** as other Presidents continued Theodore Roosevelt's aggressive policy.

President Taft supported **dollar diplomacy,** which encouraged American bankers to make loans to Central America and the Caribbean nations. This led to **intervention** to protect American creditors.

During the 1930s, President Franklin D. Roosevelt sought to modify United States' policy towards Latin America in his **Good Neighbor policy.** Under Roosevelt, the United States succeeded in its economic and security objectives, but the Good Neighbor policy did little to resolve Latin America's fundamental political, social, and economic problems or reduce the region's distrust of the United States.

After World War II, a new **inter-American System,** known as the **Organization of American States** (OAS), was established. At first, it included 20 Latin American nations and the United States, but it has since admitted Canada, Trinidad and Tobaggo, Barbados, and Jamaica. The charter of the OAS provides a legal framework for a permanent inter-American organization. In 1967 a series of changes amended the charter. A **general assembly** of member nations that meets annually was established, and a **secretary general** elected to a five-year term was approved. The amended **charter** stresses economic development, **social justice,** and **regional integration.**

The OAS' record of preserving hemispheric peace has been mixed. The United States has sought to involve the OAS in its attempts to regulate Latin American political affairs. The American-sponsored Bay of Pigs invasion of Cuba in 1961 and the United States' military occupation of the Dominican Republic in 1965 were seen as violations of the OAS charter by many Latin American nations. However, Latin America did support the United States by voting to exclude Cuba from the OAS in the early 1960s.

In the 1980s the United States invaded Grenada and Panama to overthrow dictatorships. The Latin American nations resent these interventions and favor a legal channel for solving international disputes. The Latin American nations also opposed United States' intervention in Nicaragua. The **Contadora** peace plan drafted by a group of Latin American nations, most notably Costa Rica, was an attempt to stop armed conflict and to establish regional peace in Central America. The Nicaraguan election in February 1990, won by **Violeta Chamorro** over the Sandinistas, is a hopeful sign that electoral politics will replace armed conflict in Central America.

The Case of Puerto Rico

United States' rule over Puerto Rico has changed since the Spanish-American War. This **evolutionary process** transformed the original military government in 1898 into a civilian government under the Foraker Act of 1900. The Jones Act of 1917 allowed the popular election of both houses of the **bicameral** legislature and a voice in appointing the governor's cabinet.

The **Muñoz Rivera** and **Muñoz Marín** political dynasty that dominated Puerto Rican politics from 1900 to the mid-1960s was supported
by the United States. The idea of independence did not have much
political support in this period. Under Public Law 600 in 1952, Puerto
Rico became an **associated free state** with full autonomy in internal
matters and its own constitution. As citizens of the United States,
Puerto Ricans share a common currency and the right to defense by
United States government. In 1967, a *plebiscite* (vote) resulted in a
large majority favoring commonwealth status rather than statehood.
Less than one percent of the people voted for independence. In recent
years, although some favor independence the vast majority of the
Puerto Rican people favor either statehood or commonwealth status.

QUESTIONS

Multiple Choice. Select the letter of the answer that correctly completes each statement.

1. All of the following are examples of advanced pre-Columbian civ-
   ilizations EXCEPT the
   A. Mayan
   B. Aztecs
   C. Incas
   D. Tupi-Guarani

2. The Portuguese Empire in America differed from the Spanish Em-
   pire in that the Portuguese
   A. did not practice the Roman Catholic religion
   B. were only interested in agricultural production
   C. did not settle in large numbers in Brazil
   D. treated the Native Americans better than the Spaniards

3. The European nations that colonized Latin America supported
   trade policies that were
   A. mercantilist
   B. laissez faire
   C. unrestrictive
   D. pro free trade

4. Early attempts at unification failed in Latin America after inde-
   pendence because
   A. there were no strong nationalist sentiments
   B. the great leaders of the independence movements did not sup-
      port unification.
   C. the new nations had no common heritage
   D. the landed elites wanted to preserve their local power in Latin
      autonomy

5. All of the following are sources of stability and power in Latin America EXCEPT the
   A. landed elite
   B. military
   C. Roman Catholic Church
   D. liberation theology movement

   Matching. Match the correct hero of the independence of Latin America with the nation liberated in Column 1.

Column 1	Column 2
____ 1. Mexico	A. José San Martín
____ 2. Argentina	B. Pedro I
____ 3. Chile	C. Simón Bolívar
____ 4. Brazil	D. Miguel Hidalgo
____ 5. Colombia	E. Bernardo O'Higgins

ESSAYS

1. Why do the nations of Latin America fear United States interference in Latin American affairs?

2. Why has the military in many Latin American countries seized power so often?

UNIT SIX
WESTERN EUROPE

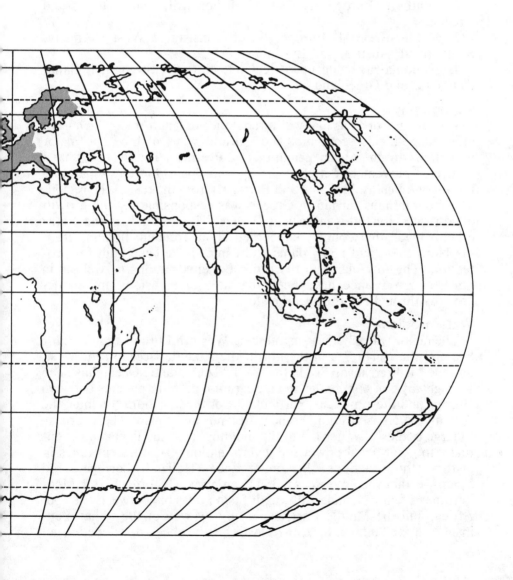

I. Physical Geography (The Physical Setting of Western Europe)

Overview

The region known as Western Europe consists of 20 nations that lie in the western part of the European continent. These nations may be grouped in the following ways:

1. Northwestern Europe, which consists of Ireland, the United Kingdom (England, Scotland, Wales, and Northern Ireland), France, and the Benelux countries (Belgium, the Netherlands, and Luxembourg).

2. Southern Europe, consisting of Portugal, Spain, Italy, and Greece.

3. Middle (Central) Europe, which consists of West Germany, Switzerland, Austria, and Liechtenstein.

4. Scandinavia, made up of Iceland, Norway, Sweden, Finland, Denmark, and Greenland.

Topography

Western Europe has many different kinds of landforms, which have affected political, economic, and cultural ways of life. The major mountains are the **Alps, Apennines,** and **Pyrenees.** The Pyrenees have restricted movement between France and Spain, thereby separating the **Iberian Peninsula** (Spain and Portugal) from the rest of the region. The mountainous terrain in Greece was responsible for the growth of separate city-states in ancient Greece. The lowlands in the Netherlands made that country concerned about frequent flooding from the North Sea, and many dams and canals have been built for protection. The low plains in the other Benelux nations as well as in northeastern France have been the sites of invasions and battlegrounds throughout European history.

Water Bodies

The major water bodies surrounding Western Europe are the **Baltic Sea** and the **North Sea** in the north, the **Atlantic Ocean** in the west, and the **Mediterranean Sea** in the south. The Atlantic Ocean has been a "highway" of commerce and a migration path for peoples between Europe and the Americas, particularly for those nations touching the Atlantic, such as Britain, France, Ireland, and Spain. The nearness to large bodies of water led to the buildup of fishing fleets and eventually to great naval power for several nations. At different times in history, these nations—Britain, France, Holland, Portugal, and Spain—established overseas colonial empires. Historically, the Mediterranean Sea has made cultural diffusion possible between Europe, Africa, and the Middle East, especially by way of the Italian Peninsula. In the 20th century, the North Sea has been developed as an

Western Europe

ICELAND

Reykjavik

ATLANTIC
OCEAN

NORWAY

SWEDEN

FINLAND

NORTH
SEA

Oslo

Stockholm

Helsinki

NORTHERN
IRELAND

SCOTLAND

Edinburgh

IRELAND

Belfast

GREAT
BRITAIN

DENMARK

BALTIC
SEA

Copenhagen

Dublin

NETHERLANDS

Amsterdam

ENGLAND

WALES

London

WEST

Berlin

ENGLISH
CHANNEL

Brussels

BELGIUM

Bonn

GERMANY

Paris

LUXEMBOURG

Vienna

SWITZERLAND

Bern

AUSTRIA

FRANCE

LIECHTENSTEIN

ITALY

PORTUGAL

SPAIN

Madrid

Rome

GREECE

Lisbon

Athens

MEDITERRANEAN SEA

KEY

Central Europe

Scandinavia

Mediterranean Europe

United Kingdom and Ireland

Capital city

important source of oil. The many warm-water ports on these major bodies of water have helped in the movement of goods and people. The Dutch port of Rotterdam, for example, is the largest in Europe and handles more cargo than New York City.

Several navigable rivers are found in the region, providing for easy access between cities and nations. Among these are the **Rhine, Po, Seine, Danube,** and **Thames**.

The **English Channel** separates Britain from the European mainland, and consequently it has provided protection for most of British history.

The **North Atlantic Drift** brings moderate temperature patterns to the Atlantic coast nations. The Mediterranean Sea affects the climate in the nations of southern Europe, causing hot, dry summers.

QUESTIONS

Multiple Choice. Select the letter of the answer that correctly completes each statement.

1. Which of the following is in Northwestern Europe?
   A. Portugal
   B. France
   C. Italy
   D. Austria

2. Norway and Sweden are in a region known as
   A. Central Europe
   B. the Iberian Peninsula
   C. the lowlands
   D. Scandinavia

3. In recent years, the area that has been developed as a source of oil is the
   A. North Sea
   B. Baltic Sea
   C. Mediterranean Sea
   D. Atlantic Ocean

ESSAY

Georgraphy has affected the lives of people in Western Europe. Explain two ways in which each of the following has affected life in Western Europe.

1. Water bodies

2. Mountains

II. Economic Geography (Economic Development of Western Europe)

Agriculture
Europe's farmers, although declining in number in this century, produce large amounts of food. Careful use of land, along with pesticides and modern technology, have contributed to food surpluses in many areas. The major agricultural products are wheat, potatoes, meat, wine, and dairy products.

Industrial Production
Western Europe has long been one of the world's leading areas in manufacturing and industrial development. The large deposits of coal in Britain and West Germany and scientific technology (beginning with the 19th-century Industrial Revolution) have been primary factors in this development. Major industrial products are automobiles, chemicals, electronics, steel, and machinery.

Advances in agricultural and industrial production have resulted in a high standard of living for Western Europe's people. West Germany has the highest GNP (gross national product) on the European continent.

The Marshall Plan
The Marshall Plan is named after George C. Marshall, U.S. Secretary of State, who proposed a way in which the United States could help build up Europe's economy after World War II. His plan was passed by Congress in 1947 and was officially known as the **European Recovery Act**. It made about $12.5 billion in aid available to countries that suffered damage and devastation from the war and called upon the European countries to draw up their own plans for recovery. Most non-Communist European nations accepted the aid offered by the Marshall Plan and as a result achieved much economic progress.

Although the plan included all the European nations, the aid was refused by the Communist nations. Instead, they accepted aid from the Council of Mutual Economic Assistance, a Soviet version of the Marshall Plan.

Economic Systems and Decision-Making
Today, different types of economic systems exist in the Western European nations. An **economic system** is a way of making decisions about such basic economic questions as: What should be produced? Who should produce it? How should it be produced? What should the price be? Who should own the land and the means of production? How is the product to be distributed? To whom should it be distributed?

In a **capitalist system**, most of these economic questions are decided

Europe

ATLANTIC OCEAN

BARENTS SEA

Murmansk

Reykjavik
ICELAND

Narvik

FAEROE ISLANDS (DEN.)

Luleå
Oulu

Trondheim
Vaasa

SHETLAND ISLANDS (U.K.)

NORWAY
SWEDEN
FINLAND

Bergen
Helsinki
Leningrad

Oslo

Stockholm

Moscow

Göteborg

Edinburgh
Ålborg

Belfast
DENMARK
NETHERLANDS

IRELAND
Manchester
Kiel
Copenhagen
Gdansk
Minsk

SOVIET UNION

Dublin

Amsterdam
Berlin
POLAND
Chernobyl

BRITAIN
London
EAST
Warsaw
Kiev

BELGIUM
Bonn GERMANY
Rostov

ENGLISH CHANNEL
Brussels
LUXEMBOURG
L'vov

Brest
WEST
Prague
CZECHOSLOVAKIA

Paris
GERMANY
Odessa

Nantes
LIECHTENSTEIN
Vienna

FRANCE
Munich
AUSTRIA
HUNGARY
Budapest

Bern
ROMANIA
Yalta

Geneva
SWITZ.
Bucharest
BLACK SEA

Milan
Venice
Belgrade

Genoa
YUGOSLAVIA
BULGARIA
Samsun

Bilbao
San Marino
Sofia

PORTUGAL
ANDORRA
Marseille
ADRIATIC SEA
Istanbul

MONACO
Trana
Ankara

Barcelona
CORSICA (FR.)
Vatican City
Rome
ALBANIA
TURKEY

Lisbon
Madrid
ITALY
GREECE
Izmir

SPAIN
SARDINIA (IT.)
Adana

BALEARIC ISLANDS (SP.)
Athens

Malaga
Palermo
RHODES (GR.)
CYPRUS

GIBRALTAR (U.K.)
SICILY (IT.)
CRETE (GR.)

MALTA
MEDITERRANEAN SEA

KEY

Cattle	Corn	Industry	Oil
Citrus	Fish	Iron Ore	Olives
Fruits	Flax	Lumber	Potatoes
Coal	Grapes		

Sheep	Wheat	
Sugar beets	Wine	
Water power	Capital	
	Other city	

miles 0 ... 500
km 0 ... 500

244

on privately and freely by individual citizens. Under capitalism, a society's government has very little to do with making economic decisions. This kind of system permits a free market economy to exist. Societies that have a market economy and economic freedom also allow other kinds of freedom, such as freedom of religion, speech, the press, etc. In *The Wealth of Nations*, written in 1776, Adam Smith provided a good description of a capitalist system.

In a **socialist system**, most of the basic economic issues are decided by the government. A socialist government is freely elected by the people, and its main goal is to improve the conditions of workers. Democratic freedoms are allowed, as are many political parties.

In a **Communist system**, the government makes all the economic decisions. However, Communist governments come to power as a result of violence and revolution. Only one party, the Communist Party, is allowed to exist. *The Communist Manifesto*, written by **Karl Marx** and **Friedrich Engels** in 1848, explained certain aspects of Communist theory. (See also Part IV dealing with the Industrial Revolution.)

The countries in Western Europe today are said to have a **mixed economy**; that is, they have elements of both capitalism and socialism. Each nation has a different degree of government ownership (nationalization) of industries. In the field of health and other social services, some nations, such as England, Denmark, and Sweden, have extensive social welfare programs. For example, the British National Health Service provides free dental and medical benefits. The costs of these programs are paid for by taxes on employers and workers.

Although Communist parties have existed in almost every Western European nation, the Communists have been weak and have never won control of a government. In the late 1970s, a movement called **Eurocommunism** arose. These Communist parties claimed to have somewhat different views from the Soviet and East European Communists, thereby hoping to gain more support. However, this movement was not successful.

Attempts at Economic Cooperation

World War II brought economic ruin to **Western Europe** and also signaled an end to almost 500 years of European economic dominance in the world. During this time, economic rivalry and competition grew among European nations. Since World War II, however, there has been a movement to promote economic unity and cooperation.

The European Economic Community (EEC). Also known as the **Common Market**, this organization was originally created in 1951 as the ECSC (European Coal and Steel Community). Its aim, as stated by French Foreign Minister **Robert Schuman** in his Schuman Plan, was to bring together the coal and steel industries of six nations—Belgium,

France, Italy, Luxembourg, the Netherlands, and West Germany. This group was also known as the "Inner Six."

1. In 1957, the Inner Six agreed to bring together their economies and reduce economic barriers such as tariffs. As a result, there was now more free trade among these nations, and they changed their name from the ECSC to the EEC. They also created **Euratom** to tie together the six nations' research in nuclear power.

2. The EEC came to be known as the **European Community** (EC) and was very successful in increasing economic activity among its members. By 1985, six other nations had been accepted for membership—Denmark, Ireland, England, Greece, Portugal, and Spain.

3. In 1987, the twelve nations of the European Community agreed to bring their economies even closer together by 1992 and to create a "frontier-free Europe." This plan calls for one large common market in which nations can sell their goods more easily to other members; it allows citizens of a member nation to work in any member nation of the EC; and it subjects goods coming into the EC from outside to a high tax (tariff). The EC's twelve nations would thus make up a single economic unit, with 330 million citizens that could compete with the world's two current economic giants—the United States and Japan. Eventually, the twelve nations might join together politically, creating a "United States of Europe." Discussions about this took place in Dublin and Rome in 1990.

The European Free Trade Association (EFTRA). Also known as the "Outer Seven," this organization, which came into existence in 1960, contains seven member nations—Austria, Finland, Iceland, Norway, Sweden, and Switzerland. EFTRA has not established as strong links as the EC, but it has similar economic goals. In time it may ask to be admitted into the EC.

Economic Issues

The term "**post-industrial society**" refers to a society in which more people work in service industries (accounting, health) than in goods-producing industries (steel, textiles). This situation is becoming more and more common in Western Europe, as it is in the United States.

Inflation refers to rising prices, which has caused a decrease in the value of the European currencies. The increase in oil prices charged by the Middle Eastern nations during the 1970s was one reason for **inflation** in Western Europe. Another reason was the attempt by the United States to cut down the flow of European imports into the United States and to increase the flow of American exports. Most Western European nations are dependent on outside areas for raw materials, such as oil from the Middle East.

Of increasing importance to Western Europe in the 1990s will be its economic relations with Japan and the United States, as well as with the Soviet Union and Eastern European nations and the former European colonies in Africa and Asia.

QUESTIONS

Multiple Choice. Select the letter of the answer that correctly completes each statement.

1. Which nation has the highest GNP (Gross National Product) in Western Europe?
   A. France
   B. England
   C. Holland
   D. West Germany

2. The Marshall Plan provided aid that was
   A. cultural
   B. military
   C. financial
   D. agricultural

3. The person most responsible for the growth of the European Common Market was
   A. Karl Marx
   B. Robert Schuman
   C. Friedrich Engels
   D. George Marshall

ESSAY

Show how each of the following has affected or will affect economic activity in Western Europe:

1. The European Community

2. social welfare programs

3. Euratom

4. capitalism

III. Human and Cultural Geography

Overview

Western Europe, with over 300 million people, has a variety of religious, ethnic, and linguistic groups. The largest nations are West Germany (61 million), Italy (57 million), and France (56 million). Overpopulation and overcrowding (high population density) are not problems in Western Europe. In fact, population growth rates are among the lowest in the world. One reason for the absence of demographic (population) problems is that Western Europe is very industrialized and has high standards of living and modern health care. Compared with people in less industrialized areas, such as South Asia and Sub-Saharan Africa, Western Europeans tend to live longer, marry later, and have smaller families. In addition, more women are in the work force. Urbanization—the movement of people from rural to city areas—is also characteristic of Western Europe.

Religion

Christianity is the predominant religion in Western Europe. The majority of people are Catholic, with the largest concentrations in the south, in Spain and Italy. Members of Protestant denominations are found mainly in the north, in nations such as England and Sweden. (Reasons explaining the connection between geography and religion are in Part IV in the section on the Reformation.)

Jews have been a minority in the Western European nations for centuries. They share some basic beliefs with Christians, such as the belief in one God and in the Ten Commandments. The combined basic beliefs and ideals of Jews and Christians make up the **Judeo-Christian tradition**. This tradition has influenced life in Western Europe for the last 2,000 years. It has also influenced life in areas that had the greatest amount of overseas European settlement, such as North and South America. Jews accept the part of the Bible known as the Old Testament; Christians accept both the Old and New Testaments. (For a comparison of Judaism, Christianity, and Islam, see the unit on the Middle East.)

A growing number of Muslims and Hindus are found today in some Western European nations, mostly those nations that once had colonies in Africa and Asia. France's Islamic community comes mainly from Algeria and Morocco. Most Hindus and Muslims in England come from the Indian subcontinent (India, Pakistan, and Bangladesh). The Muslims in West Germany are mainly Turks who have immigrated for economic reasons.

Ethnic Minority Groups

From Outside of Europe. Besides the groups listed above, people from other areas of the world are found throughout Western Europe. They include people from the Caribbean, Africa, the Middle East, and East Asia. With the British colony of Hong Kong scheduled to come under China's rule in 1997, many Hong Kong Chinese are interested in imigrating to England. However, the British have mixed feelings about whether to admit great numbers of Chinese and other non-British people to their nation. Some of this concern in England (as well as in other European nations) results from prejudice against foreigners. This prejudice is rooted in the issues of race as well as competition for employment, and at times it has even led to riots.

248

From Inside of Europe. The more industrialized nations, such as West Germany and France, have "guest workers" from other parts of Europe. These workers often take jobs for short periods of time and send money back to their families. Such workers are from Turkey, Greece, Yugoslavia, Italy, and Portugal. Although there have been attempts by the host countries to assimilate these workers and provide education, instances of ill-feeling and prejudice have also been evident.

Languages

While a variety of languages exist in the Western European nations, many have striking similarities. All languages in Western Europe are written using the Roman alphabet. There are also similarities in the ways some words are put together and are spoken. As a result, people in one nation are frequently able to understand the language of another nation. Because of the similarities between the languages, many Europeans are multilingual. Other reasons for the large numbers of Europeans who are multilingual are the nearness of nations to one another and the frequent travel and economic exchanges between them.

English, French, Spanish, and Italian are Romance languages and have words constructed in a similar pattern. German and Dutch have much in common, while the Scandinavian languages, except for Finnish, are similar. Some nations are officially bilingual because large segments of their populations speak distinct languages. For example, in Switzerland, French and German are spoken, while in Belgium, Flemish and French are used.

Cultural Achievements

Western European achievements in such fields as art, literature, architecture, sculpture, and music have been very extensive. They are treated in the next section, dealing with history and political geography.

QUESTIONS

Multiple Choice. Select the letter of the answer that correctly completes each statement.

1. Which nation has the largest population in Western Europe?
   A. France   C. West Germany
   B. Ireland   D. Italy

2. In which pair of nations is Catholicism the predominant religion?
   A. England and Italy   C. Spain and Portugal
   B. France and Denmark   D. Sweden and Holland

3. Which pair of nations have Romance languages?
   A. Italy and Spain
   B. England and West Germany
   C. France and Holland
   D. Norway and Austria

4. A nation which is officially bilingual is
   A. Finland
   B. Belgium
   C. Sweden
   D. Austria

ESSAY

Overpopulation and high population growth rates are *not* considered to be major problems in Western Europe. Discuss two reasons for this situation.

IV. History and Political Geography (Historic Setting of Western Europe)

Overview

Of all the regions of the world, Western Europe has had the greatest historical influence on the United States. Many of our political, economic, and social ideas resulted from European settlement in the land that became the United States of America. Moreover, more Americans can trace their ancestry to Western Europe than to any other part of the world. In the 20th century, however, important changes have occurred. An increasing number of Americans can now trace their ancestry to Africa, Asia, and Latin America. Our contacts with these regions have increased and, like our contacts with Western Europe, have become more involved and complex. Because of America's special ties to Western Europe, Americans fought in two wars (World War I, World War II) to protect that region from destruction. In the following pages, we will review the history of Western Europe to help understand its past and present, as well as to consider its future.

Ancient Mediterranean Civilizations: Greece and Rome

The time period when the civilizations of Greece and Rome were at their height is called both the **classical period** and the **Age of Antiquity**. For ancient Greece this period was from 750 B.C. to 150 B.C. For Rome it was from 500 B.C. to 200 A.D., even though the Roman Empire lasted until 476 A.D.

Greece. The Greeks were the first people of Western Europe to develop an advanced culture. This was accomplished even though Greece's geography made unity very difficult. Because of the many mountains in the Greek peninsula, the Greek people were isolated from one another and formed individual **city-states**, small governmental units organized around urban centers. Of the hundreds of these city-states dotting the Greek mainland and islands, the most famous were **Athens** and **Sparta**. There were major political, economic, and cultural differences between these two city-states.

Sparta developed as a militaristic city-state. It emphasized military strength and rule by just a few people—the landowners and nobility. The majority of Spartans, including the slaves, or **helots**, had no voice in the government. Sparta could also be called an **aristocracy** because it was ruled by a small number of people. Sparta did not promote individual freedom or progress in the arts and sciences, and thus it had little impact on Western European history.

Athens eventually developed into a **democratic** city-state and had a lasting influence on the history of both Western Europe and the United States. By 450 B.C., Athens had developed the world's first **democracy**, that is, a system in which citizens take part and have a voice in their government. Because Athenian citizens voted directly for or against the laws, this system is called a **direct democracy**. However, there were limitations in Athenian democracy. Women, for example, could not vote for officeholders. Athenian democratic ideals were expressed in the famous "Funeral Oration" of **Pericles**. During the years of Pericles' leadership in the 5th century B.C. (461 B.C.–429 B.C.), Athens made great progress in democracy as well as in the arts and sciences. Consequently, this period, called the **Age of Pericles**, also became known as the **Golden Age of Athens**. Some examples of Greek cultural progress in the **Hellenic period** (750 B.C.–336 B.C.) are:

1. **Philosophy.** The anchient Greeks believed in the ideal of the well-rounded person, that is, one who was intelligent, thoughtful, asked questions, and had a "sound mind in a sound body." According to the famous Greek philosopher **Socrates**, a person should "know thyself." He also said, "The unexamined life is not worth living." **Plato**, his most famous student, wrote *The Dialogues*. One of these dialogues, called *The Republic*, contains Plato's ideas about government. Plato's most famous student was **Aristotle**, whose thoughts on reason, logic, science, ethics, and government are found in his extensive writings, such as the *Nicomachean Ethics* and *Politics*.

2. **Literature.** Drama was the most outstanding Greek contribution in literature. The Greeks invented tragedy and comedy. Some famous Greek writers were **Homer** (*The Iliad* and *The Odyssey*), **Sophocles** (*Oedipus Rex*), and **Aristophanes** (*Lysistrata*). Also notable were the poet **Pindar** and the historians **Herodotus** and **Thucydides**.

251

3. **Mathematics and science**. Noteworthy achievements were made by **Pythagoras** (geometry), **Hippocrates** (medicine), and **Democritus** (matter composed of atoms).

4. **Architecture and sculpture**. The **Parthenon** was a temple built on a hill called the **Acropolis**. As with other Greek buildings, the Parthenon combined balance and symmetry and the use of tall, graceful columns. Many buildings throughout the Western world have imitated Greek architecture. The three basic styles of Greek columns or pillars are called **Doric, Ionic,** and **Corinthian.** Greek sculpture displayed dignity, realism, and simplicity, and it idealized the human form.

5. **The Olympic Games**. These major athletic events were held in honor of the god Zeus, and they are the basis of the modern-day Olympics.

Military conflicts. Although the Greek city-states often quarreled among themselves, they were able to unite against the Persians. In the **Persian Wars** (500–479 B.C.) the Greeks were able to stop the westward expansion of the Persian Empire. Important Greek victories were at the battles of Marathon and Thermopylae.

The **Peloponnesian War** was a conflict between Athens and Sparta. Sparta was victorious and brought Athens under its control but was unable to unite all the Greek city-states.

Eventually, most of the Greek city-states were united by the conquests of **King Philip** of Macedon (a region to the north) in 338 B.C. When he died, his title, power, and lands were passed on to his son Alexander.

Alexander's Empire. Alexander the Great built an empire that extended as far south as Egypt and as far east as India. His conquests were made between 336 and 323 B.C. and resulted in the largest world empire up to that time. Alexander, who had been taught by Aristotle, was an admirer of the culture of Greece, and he spread Greek culture wherever he went. The mixture of Greek culture with the cultures of conquered areas—of Egypt, the Middle East, and South Asia—became known as **Hellenism**. This period of cultural mixing and cultural diffusion lasted beyond Alexander's death in 323 B.C. and is referred to as the **Hellenistic period**. When Alexander died, his empire was divided into three parts, each part ruled by one of his generals. In less than 200 years, these three parts were once again united under the rule of the Roman Empire. Important cultural achievements during the Hellenistic period (336 B.C.–150 B.C.) included:

1. **Philosophy.** During this period, philosphers developed new and different ideas about life. **Diogenes** founded the philosphical school of **Cynics**. The idea of Cynicism included criticism of materialism and social conventions and a distrust of human virtue. **Zeno** founded **Stoicism**, advocating freedom from passions and desires and detachment

from the outside world. **Epicurus** founded **Epicureanism**, advocating the search for pleasure and happiness while maintaining a sense of moderation.

2. **Mathematics and science.** The leading figures were **Aristarchus** (astronomy), **Euclid** (geometry), **Archimedes** (physics), and **Eratosthenes** (geography).

Rome. By 500 B.C. the Latin peoples of central Italy, also known as Romans, had created a **republic**. In a republic, citizens participate in government by electing the rulers who represent them. The early Roman Republic was controlled by a few nobles, the **patricians**, and was thus actually an **aristocracy**. Over the next 200 years, however, important political gains were made by the **plebians**, the farmers and workers, who won the right to become members of the government assembly and to vote for **tribunes**. The tribunes could take action against the patrician-controlled **consuls** and the **Senate**. Plebian gains also included the codification (writing down) of Roman law into the **Twelve Tables**, which enabled all to know what the laws were. Roman law established forms of justice and protection of human rights and property that have influenced legal systems throughout the Western world. In its period as a republic, Rome made progress as a democracy.

The Roman Republic Becomes an Empire (340 B.C.–27 B.C.). After conquering and uniting the Italian peninsula, Rome took control of the lands bordering the western Mediterranean Sea. These lands came under Rome's control after its success in the **Punic Wars** (264 B.C.–146 B.C.) against Carthage, a rival city located in North Africa. Roman forces next turned their attention to the eastern Mediterranean area and conquered the Greek lands that had once been part of Alexander's Empire (Greece, Egypt, the Middle East). The Mediterranean had become "a Roman lake." The Romans admired the Hellenistic culture of the Greeks, and it is said that even though Roman force conquered Greece, Greek culture conquered Rome.

Under **Julius Caesar**, Roman legions conquered most of central and western Europe. Rome now held land on three continents, and by 50 B.C. it had become the largest empire known to the world. However, during this period of conquest, many changes took place in Rome. The Roman army changed from a civilian force to a selectively trained group of professional soldiers. As a result, soldiers were more loyal to their individual generals than to the republican government elected in Rome. As the military commanders gained more power, they fought among themselves in civil wars for control of Rome, and the republic was changed into a dictatorship. In 46 B.C. Julius Caesar became a dictator. He was succeeded by three generals after his death. Among these was **Octavian**, who became the first emperor of Rome when he took the title **Caesar Augustus** and established the Roman Empire. He ruled from 27 B.C. to 14 A.D. The so-called **Augustan Age**, which began with Octavian, was the start of 200 years of stability, peace, and progress in the Roman Empire, a period known as the *Pax Romana*, or "Roman Peace" (27 B.C.–180 A.D.).

The Roman Empire Declines and Falls (180–476). During these years, the Roman Empire slowly declined for several reasons:

1. **Division of the empire.** The emperor **Constantine** moved from Rome and made Constantinople (now Istanbul) his capital in the 4th century A.D. This move split the empire into two parts—the western part, with its capital remaining at Rome, and the eastern part, or the **Byzantine Empire**, headed by Constantine.

2. **Political weaknesses.** The government in Rome became corrupt and because of the size of the empire was unable to keep control over all the territory under its rule.

3. **Economic problems.** The rulers wasted money, and heavy taxation led to anger among the people. A trade imbalance caused by importing many goods lowered the value of Rome's money.

4. **Social factors.** A decline in morality and patriotism was widespread. A rigid class system developed. Many slaves and non-Romans who lived in the major cities were badly treated.

5. **Invasions.** Beginning in the 200s, Germanic tribes invaded Roman lands and eventually were able to defeat Roman armies. In 476, Rome itself was conquered. (The Eastern Roman Empire, however, survived beyond 476. See the unit on the Middle East.)

6. **Impact of Christianity.** The teachings of Christianity conflicted with the dictatorial policies of the emperors.

Achievements of the Ancient Romans. The Romans made many achievements in the arts and sciences and had a lasting impact on the Western world.

1. **Law.** As you read, Roman law was codified in the Twelve Tables. Over the years, many new statutes were added, and Roman law became the basis of the legal systems of Western Europe and South America.

2. **Language.** Latin was the basis for many Romanic (or Romance) languages, such as Spanish, French, and Italian. Many English words also come from Latin.

3. **Literature.** The speeches of **Cicero** and the works of **Vergil** (*The Aeneid*) and **Horace** are well-known. The historians **Livy**, **Plutarch**, and **Tacitus** are still studied today.

4. **Architecture.** Roman-built roads, aqueducts, and buildings were found all over the empire and helped unite the territories. Some structures such as the Colosseum in Rome still stand. The Romans used the arch and were the first to use concrete as a building material.

The Roman Empire: 265 B.C. to 117 A.D.

CASPIAN SEA

BLACK SEA

RED SEA

■ Palmyra

■ Antioch   SYRIA
          ■ Jerusalem

■ Alexandria

ASIA MINOR

PALESTINE

EGYPT

Byzantium
(Constantinople)

■ Athens

MEDITERRANEAN SEA

★ Rome
ITALY

■ Ravenna

SICILY

NORTH AFRICA

■ Carthage

■ Lutetia
(Paris)

GAUL

BRITAIN

Londinium
(London) ■

ATLANTIC
OCEAN

SPAIN

KEY

The Roman Republic in 265 B.C.

The Roman Empire in 117 A.D.

5. **Government administration.** A good civil service of government officials helped to run the far-flung empire. Under the Pax Romana and a strong central government, unity and peace were brought to many areas of Europe. However, when the empire collapsed, disunity and disorder were common in the former Roman lands.

The Middle Ages, 500–1500 A.D.

The time period between the fall of the Roman Empire and the start of the modern era is known as the **Middle Ages,** or the **medieval period.** The first 500 years of this period is sometimes called the **Dark Ages,** due to the disruptive economic and social conditions as well as the absence of a strong and stable central government. During this time, Europe experienced many invasions. The first group of invaders were the Germanic tribes, some of whom eventually settled down and formed kingdoms. Later invaders included the Norse, the Magyars, and the Muslims. These invasions ended about 1000 A.D. Political power was **decentralized,** that is, it was held by several small, weak groups throughout Europe. Among these were the **Franks** (in Gaul, or France), the **Ostrogoths** (in Italy), the **Visigoths** (in Spain), and the **Angles** and **Saxons** (in England). People felt more loyalty to a local ruler in a small territory than to a larger political unit. The protection given by a local ruler, or lord, to people who performed services for him in return was the basis of **feudalism,** which developed in the 800s. This was the form of government prevalent in Europe until the 1400s.

Charlemagne and the Holy Roman Empire. One group of Germans, the Franks, were able to create a strong kingdom by the 5th century. The kingdom of the Franks grew in power during the early Middle Ages. Under **Charles Martel,** the Franks stopped the advance of Muslim forces in 732 at the **Battle of Tours** in France. Martel's grandson was **Charlemagne,** who became the most important ruler in medieval Europe (768–814).

Charlemagne conquered and united lands in central and western Europe, some of which had been part of the Roman Empire. These included parts of present-day Italy, Spain, France, Germany, Czechoslovakia, Austria, Belgium, and Holland. For these efforts and for spreading Christianity, Charlemagne was crowned as the first **Holy Roman Emperor** by **Pope Leo III** in 800. Charlemagne's empire became known as the **Holy Roman Empire.**

Charlemagne built schools and was able to run his empire's provinces with the help of the **missi dominici,** appointed officials who traveled in the provinces and kept Charlemagne informed about various nobles. Consequently, under Charlemagne's rule, a rare example of a stable, centralized government existed in the Middle Ages. After his death, however, the empire was divided and became disunited. His successors were not able to maintain order and stability.

Feudalism. Feudalism developed in Europe in response to the breakdown in central authority in the Frankish empire following Charlemagne's death and also because of the instability and chaos caused by the numerous invasions in the 9th and 10th centuries, especially those of the dreaded Vikings or Norse. Feudalism began in France in the late 800s and spread throughout much of Europe. It was a way of life that involved agreements, promises, and exchanges between different groups of people to help them live together. It involved social, economic, and political relationships.

1. **Social.** A strict class system existed, based on land and military power. Each class had specific rights as well as responsibilities and obligations to the other classes. The classes were **serfs**, knights, and landowning nobles and lords. A code of **chivalry** set rules of behavior that everyone followed, especially the knights and lords.

2. **Economic.** Serfs worked the land on a **manor** (a large estate held by a lord) and supplied food to the landowner, who promised protection and shelter in return. The landowner in turn also promised to fight for a higher noble, such as an overlord or a king, who gave him a piece of land in return. In this relationship, the landowner owed loyalty, or **fealty**, to the king and became a **vassal** of the king. In this manorial system, each manor supported itself economically and was self-sufficient. The three-field system was used for growing food.

3. **Political.** The serfs were bound to the land and had no say in political matters. The king's power rested on his relationship with his vassals. By receiving **a fief** (a grant of land) from the king (as suzerain), in a ceremony called **investiture**, the vassals came under the king's protection and in return owed **homage**, promising allegiance and military service. However, a vassal, the landowning noble exercised great political power in his area because he passed laws, levied taxes, and acted as a judge.

The Role of the Roman Catholic Church. The Christian or Roman Catholic Church was the most powerful and influential institution in Europe in the Middle Ages. It was the only institution able to provide some order amid the chaos in Europe. The Roman Catholic Church was a major force in the lives of people, providing education, the means to salvation, and many services usually provided by governments.

Although early Christians were persecuted in the Roman Empire for almost 300 years after the crucifixion of Jesus, Christianity continued to gain converts and to grow in power. Christianity was spread through the efforts of St. Paul and other followers of Jesus. In 313, the **Edict of Milan**, under the emperor Constantine, permitted religious freedom for Christians. In 392, the emperor Theodosius made Christianity the official state religion of the empire. By this time, the Roman

Empire had split into an eastern part centered in Constantinople and a western part centered in Rome. Different views on religious authority and teachings developed between the Church in Rome (headed by the Pope) and the Church in Constantinople (headed by the Patriarch). Eventually, these differences led to an official division of the Christian Church in 1054 into the **Roman Catholic Church** in Rome and the **Greek Orthodox Church** in Constantinople. While the Greek Orthodox Church divided into several Eastern Orthodox Churches in Eastern Europe, it was the Roman Catholic Church that was to exert a strong influence in Western Europe.

1. **Political.** Besides having the power to crown Charlemagne as Holy Roman Emperor in 800, the Church could use excommunication as a weapon against any ruler or person who did not follow the Church's teachings. A person who was **excommunicated** was no longer considered a member of the Christian faith and was thus denied sal-

Europe in the 14th Century

- ■ Important trading cities

vation. In an era of faith, this was a very strong threat. In the 13th century, the Church created a special court, called the **Holy Inquisition**, to investigate anyone who disobeyed or disagreed with Church teachings. If a person was found guilty as a heretic, that individual could be tortured or put to death.

2. **Economic.** The Church grew wealthy from its many lands and from taxes such as the **tithe**. With this wealth, convents, monasteries, and great cathedrals were built. Many were built in the **Gothic** style. The Church's role in the economy of Western Europe was so great that it was able to forbid usury, the practice of lending money with interest. However, the prohibition on interest was only for Christians; Jews were permitted to become moneylenders and to charge interest. As a result, many Jews created banking houses. Some became wealthy but suffered prejudice because of their financial activities.

3. **Social and cultural.** The Church's teachings were the rules by which most people led their lives. Bishops, priests, and other religious figures were looked to for guidance, especially since they could explain the Bible and were usually the only people who could read and write. Members of the clergy were educated and preserved the classical culture of ancient Greece and Rome. Many members of the clergy encouraged writers, painters, and sculptors to produce works with religious themes. The Church was a stabilizing and unifying influence at a time when Western Europe was going through a period of disorder and confusion.

Since the Jews of Western Europe did not follow Church teachings, they were often the target of prejudice, persecution, and expulsion. Moreover, laws that restricted where Jews could worship and live (ghettos were the result) were frequent (as were forced conversions). These anti-Jewish actions are examples of anti-Semitism.

The Crusades. These were attempts by the Christians of Western Europe to regain control of Jerusalem and other parts of the Holy Land from the Muslims. These "holy wars" lasted for approximately 200 years. There were eight Crusades. The first Crusade came in response to a request from **Pope Urban II** in 1095 and was successful. Other Crusades and fighting between Christians and Muslims continued until 1291, with the Muslims finally emerging victorious. Muslims kept control of the Holy Land until World War I. (For the history of the Holy Land prior to the Crusades, see Unit One on the Middle East.)

Besides hoping to regain the Holy Land in the Crusades, the Church had other goals. It wanted to increase its power and wealth and unite the Western (Roman) and Eastern (Byzantine) branches of Christianity. Although the Crusades failed to achieve these goals, they had important results for European history.

1. **Political.** European kings gained more power, especially since many feudal lords were killed while fighting in the Crusades. Other

lords sold their lands to get money to go on the Crusades. As kings increased their power, they eventually were able to create nation-states, which they ruled.

2. **Economic.** Trade and commerce increased, especially in towns and port cities used by the Crusaders. Goods from the Middle East, such as spices, peppers, and carpets began to appear throughout Europe. Feudalism was weakened, as many serfs joined armies or left their manors to settle in the cities that began to grow because of increased trade.

3. **Social and Cultural.** Europeans learned much from the more advanced culture of the Muslim world at the time of the Crusades. Developments from the "Golden Age of Islam" made their way into Europe. These developments were in such fields as mathematics, science, art, and literature. The Europeans also discovered many Greek and Roman writings that had been lost to them but preserved by Muslim scholars. Classical civilization was reintroduced. The new ideas and new goods brought to Europe because of the Crusades were factors that helped to slowly bring an end to the Middle Ages and led to the period we call modern history. Other factors that brought on this change from medieval to modern times included: the growth of towns and a merchant middle class (the bourgeoisie); increased use of gunpowder and more effective weapons; renewed interest in learning, both about humans and about the world they lived in; increased contact with people outside of Europe; and the rise of nation-states.

The Renaissance

The Renaissance refers to the period between 1400 and 1700 when there was a **great rebirth** of cultural and scholarly activity in Western Europe. This activity began with a revival of interest in the cultures of ancient Greece and Rome. These classical cultures had stressed human endeavor and human conduct, and the Renaissance was marked by a return to the concerns of individual humans and their lives. In addition, the Renaissance had other characteristics.

1. An emphasis on the individual as a reasoning, thinking, and questioning person. Human beings were seen as the center of all things, as was life here on earth. These were **secular**, or worldly, concerns. (This was in direct contrast to the Middle Ages when there was concern with matters of religion, authority, and tradition. Salvation and the "hereafter" received emphasis.)

2. **Humanism** was an important influence in the arts and sciences. This meant that paintings of people were more realistic and "human" than in the Middle Ages. Writers wrote about simple, everyday events. Much writing was done in the **vernacular** languages, that is, in everyday speech in national languages, such as Italian, that were commonly spoken rather than Latin, the language used chiefly by

Church officials and educated people. Scientists questioned traditional ideas about humans and the universe. They used reason and experimentation to try to understand those things that had previously been accepted on faith or because of religious beliefs.

3. The Renaissance began in Italy and was supported by wealthy families who were patrons of the arts. One such family was the Medicis in Florence.

4. The Renaissance gradually spread to other parts of Europe, northward to Holland, Germany, France, and England, and to Spain.

The characteristics described above can be seen in the achievements of several famous people in the fields of art, literature, and science:

Field	Name	Nationality	Achievement
Art	da Vinci	Italian	*The Last Supper*; *Mona Lisa*
	Michelangelo	Italian	Sistine Chapel; the *Pieta*; *David*
	Titian	Italian	*Assumption of the Virgin*
	El Greco	Spanish	*Views of Toledo*
	Rembrandt	Dutch	*The Night Watch*; *The Anatomy Lesson*
Literature	Dante	Italian	*The Divine Comedy*
	Chaucer	English	*Canterbury Tales*
	Erasmus	Dutch	*In Praise of Folly*
	Shakespeare	English	*Macbeth*; *Julius Caesar*; *Hamlet*
	Rabelais	French	*Gargantua and Pantagruel*
	Machiavelli	Italian	*The Prince*
	Cervantes	Spanish	*Don Quixote*
Science	Copernicus	Polish	"The sun is the center of the universe."
	Galileo	Italian	Telescope; law of falling bodies
	Gutenberg	German	Printing press
	Harvey	English	Circulation of blood in the body
	Leeuwenhoek	Dutch	The microscope
	Newton	English	Laws of motion and gravity

The Reformation and Counter-Reformation

The Reformation, which is also called the Protestant Reformation, was a movement to reform or change certain ideas and practices of the Roman Catholic Church. It began in 1517 when **Martin Luther**, a German priest, placed his **Ninety-Five Theses,** or statements, on a church door in Wittenburg, Germany. In this document Luther protested against certain Church practices and also stated his own religious beliefs, which differed from those of the Roman Catholic Church.

1. Luther protested certain Church practices, such as the sale of **indulgences** (paying money for Church pardons), **simony** (selling of Church offices), and **nepotism** (giving Church positions to relatives). He also protested against the worldly and materialistic life led by some Church officials and the power of the Pope to do certain things. Luther saw these practices as Church abuses.

2. Luther believed that the Bible and not the Pope was the final authority on religious matters. He wanted the Bible to be translated into German so that each person could read it and interpret it for himself or herself. Luther believed that salvation was achieved through faith alone, not through both faith and good works as the Church claimed. Faith was a free gift given to humans through God's grace, and it was God's mercy that permitted humans to be saved.

Factors That Led to the Reformation. Luther's protests against Church practices and beliefs about salvation were shared by many people, especially in northern Europe. Besides this, other factors that caused the Reformation were:

1. **Economic.** Some rulers were upset about the economic power and wealth of the Church. This power and wealth came from taxes imposed by the Church as well as from the vast amounts of land that it owned. These rulers hoped to obtain this wealth for themselves and their nation.

2. **Political.** Many felt that the Pope had too much power over political and other secular, or nonreligious, matters. Many rulers challenged the Pope's claim to being supreme in secular as well as religious affairs. They resisted the Church's claim to having power over them and other civil officials and to its interference in political matters concerning their nation.

3. **Renaissance thought.** The Renaissance emphasized the ability of humans to think and reason for themselves. Along with this came the questioning of traditional authority. In this atmosphere, many people during the Renaissance began to disagree with certain Church practices and ideas.

4. **Previous Church problems and reform attempts.** Even before Luther, there had been problems within the Church, such as the "Ba-

bylonian Captivity'' of 1309 to 1377, when the Popes lived in France and were under the control of the king of France. Also the "Great Schism" of 1378 to 1417, when two Popes competed for control of the Church. Other reformers had attacked some of the same practices that Luther protested against. These included **John Wycliffe** (England), **John Hus** (Bohemia), and **Desiderius Erasmus** (Holland).

Immediate Impact of Luther's Actions. Luther established the Lutheran Church in Germany. Lutheranism was the first of the new Protestant religions. It was accepted as a new religion in northern Germany as well as in most of Scandinavia (Norway and Sweden). Other Protestant religions also began as the result of other reformers who challenged the Catholic Church, such as **Ulrich Zwingli** in Switzerland, **John Knox** in Scotland, and **John Calvin**, whose ideas, especially that of **predestination**, won acceptance in Switzerland, Scotland, Holand, England, and parts of France. (According to predestination, God chose certain people, called the elect, to be saved, while those who had not been chosen could never achieve salvation, no matter what they did on earth.)

The Protestant Reformation also spread to England, where **King Henry VIII** broke with the Church because of marriage problems. He defied the authority of the Pope and divorced Catherine of Aragon. During his rule, Parliament passed the Act of Supremacy in 1534, which made the Anglican Church of England independent from the Pope, with the king as its head. Afterwards, Henry took over some Church lands.

The printing press, which was invented in Germany in 1450, helped to spread Luther's ideas as well as those of other reformers throughout Europe.

The Reaction of the Catholic Church. While the Protestant Reformation was underway, the Roman Catholic Church acted to maintain its power and to reform itself. This movement to revise the spiritual mission of the Catholic Church and to stop the spread of Protestantism was called the **Counter-Reformation**. Among the actions it carried out were:

1. Luther was excommunicated.

2. At the **Council of Trent** (1545–1563), the Church upheld its traditional beliefs and practices, including the supreme power of the Pope over the Church and the necessity of both faith and good works for salvation. It also corrected some abuses, banning the sale of indulgences and forbidding simony. It also drew up the Index, or a list of books that Catholics were not allowed to read because they contained heretical ideas.

3. The **Inquisition**, or the Church courts established during the Mid-

dle Ages, took measures against heretics. The Inquisition was very effective in southern Europe, especially in Italy and Spain.

4. The **Jesuit** order was founded. Begun in 1534 by **Ignatius Loyola** and known officially as the **Society of Jesus**, the Jesuits helped to defend and preserve Catholic teachings.

Results of the Reformation. The Reformation shattered the religious unity of Western Europe and led to the development of Protestant religions. By 1600, almost all of Western Europe was divided into Protestants and Catholics, with each group hostile to the other. In the 1600s these feelings erupted into wars. Several religious wars were fought, the most serious of which was the **Thirty Years' War** (1618–1648).

The monarchs of the European nations and local civil officials, especially in central and northern Europe, gained in power and wealth as the strength of the Catholic Church declined. They were able to take over Church lands and taxes.

Progress was made in education and literacy, especially because of the greater interest in reading the Bible.

At first, because of the growing competition between Protestants and Catholics, religious intolerance grew. Some religious conflicts even turned into civil wars, as in France in the 16th century. However, in time, some small steps were made toward religious freedom and tolerance. In the **Edict of Nantes** (1598), France, a Catholic nation, permitted Protestants to practice their faith. In England, the **Toleration Act** of 1689 granted some religious freedom to various Protestant groups.

The Age of Exploration

From the late 1400s to about 1750, the economic life of Western Europe changed greatly. This transformation was caused by an explosion of trade. In time, the search for trade and for alternate routes to Asian markets caused explorers to sail across the oceans, and the Europeans discovered lands which previously had been unknown to them. Spain and Portugal opened up the Age of Exploration and colonization, as they ventured overseas to find new trade routes and markets. The first voyages explored the coast of Africa, and eventually **Vasco da Gama** of Portugal sailed around the Cape of Good Hope to India. **Christopher Columbus**, explorer for Spain, was the first to sail westward, reaching America in 1492. These overseas explorations continued for a period of about 250 years, ending European isolation and eventually leading to European global domination.

Reasons for the Age of Exploration. There were many reasons that the nations of Western Europe undertook these voyages. These included:

1. The Renaissance spirit of inquiry and curiosity, which aroused interest in other parts of the world.

2. Scientific advances in navigational instruments and improved sailing vessels that made such voyages possible.

3. Interest in finding new routes to South and East Asia, stirred by the Crusades and the stories of **Marco Polo**. The Europeans wanted the products of the Asians, such as spices, but they had to pay high prices for them because the Arabs and Italian city-states controlled the routes to the East.

4. The desire for land and resources by the new nation-states of Europe.

5. Many adventurers were stirred by the desires of "gold, God and the glory." Many Europeans who ventured overseas went in search of riches and fame, while others wanted to spread their religion.

The major explorers and their achievements are as follows:

Name	Nation	Achievement/Area of Exploration
Columbus	Spain	North America; the "New World"
da Gama	Portugal	East and west coasts of Africa; India
Magellan	Spain	Philippines; one of his ships circumnavigated the globe, proving that the earth was round.
Cortés	Spain	Conquered Mexico
Pizarro	Spain	Conquered Peru
Cartier	France	St. Lawrence River
Verrazano	France	East coast of North America
Champlain	France	Canada
Cabot	England	Northeast coast of North America; Labrador
Drake	England	Circumnavigation of the world
Hudson	Holland	New York

Results of the Age of Exploration. The European voyages of discovery had many far-reaching effects. One was the establishment of colonial empires. Spain colonized Central and South America, while England colonized North America. Other Western European nations also established colonies. Eventually the rivalry among European nations for control of colonies and for sea routes led to wars. These included the **French and Indian War** in North America (1756–1763) and the defeat of the **Spanish Armada** by England in 1588. As the Europeans colonized overseas areas, they came to dominate native peoples. Also, colonies enabled the nations of Western Europe to acquire sources of raw materials, which they turned into manufactured goods. This made them rich. Finally, the Age of Exploration was made possible by the start of a commercial revolution that was further expanded by the voyages of discovery.

The Commercial Revolution

The term "commercial revolution" refers to the changes in trade and business practices that began in the 1400s and continued throughout the Age of Exploration that were to transform the economies of Europe. This was not a revolution in the way goods were manufactured but in the way goods were bought and sold, and it took place over three centuries.

The changes included:

1. The growth of trade within Western Europe. Also, trade became more worldwide, and goods were traded between Europe and Asia and the Americas.

2. The growth of **capitalism** as an economic system. Under this system, property is privately owned and capital (money) is used to make a profit. A new type of business called a **joint stock** company was formed to undertake risky ventures that required large amounts of capital, such as overseas voyages and establishing colonies. Joint stock companies, such as the Dutch East India Company, were privately owned and sold stock to investors who were willing to risk their money in the hope of making a profit. Capitalism also came to be known as the **free enterprise system**. To meet the needs of this system, a banking system arose. These developments eventually led to the concept of a **market economy**.

3. The Atlantic Ocean replaced the Mediterranean Sea as the center of economic activity. Also, the nations located on the Atlantic Ocean became wealthier and more powerful than the other nations of Europe.

4. The development of **mercantilism**, or the economic theory that claimed it was important for a nation to acquire overseas colonies because they could provide gold, silver, and raw materials that would make that nation wealthy and more powerful. The raw materials obtained from the colonies were used to make manufactured goods, which could be sold at high prices in the colonies. Mercantilists also said that a nation should export more than it imports, thereby achieving a **favorable balance of trade**. This would result in a nation's becoming highly **self-sufficient**.

5. The increase in manufactured goods spurred an increased demand for these goods by consumers.

Effects of the Commercial Revolution. Because of the commercial revolution, the power of several European nation-states and their absolute monarchs increased. (See the following section.) Trade and overseas empires made nations such as England, Spain, and France wealthy and powerful. Also, population shifts occurred. Many Africans were brought as slaves to work in the Americas. Many Europeans left their homelands to settle in the colonies. As a result,

266

European culture was spread to areas around the world. Finally, a new production system, the **domestic system**, was developed in Europe. Under this system, goods were produced in the home rather than in a shop. Although the domestic system was used mainly to produce wool, other items such as buttons and gloves were also made this way. It enabled merchants to increase production. In time, it would be replaced by the factory system.

The Rise of Nation-States; Royal Power and Absolutism

Besides the profound cultural (Renaissance), religious (Reformation), and economic (commercial revolution and exploration) changes that took place in Western Europe between the late 1400s and early 1700s, there also came a series of great political changes. The changes involved the creation of **nation-states** with strong monarchs and centralized governments in England, France, and Spain. The term "nation-state" refers to a specific area of land with fixed boundaries, united under the rule of a central government. The people in a nation-state are usually united by many common factors, such as language, religion, race, and culture. The growth of nation-states in Western Europe began as feudalism declined. Two countries, England and France, had developed into nation-states by the end of the Middle Ages, in 1500. Their governments were under the rule of strong kings, or monarchs. In many nations of Western Europe, the king ruled as an **absolute monarch**, that is, the king had complete or absolute rule over his nation and subjects. Such monarchs are also called **autocrats**, and their governments are referred to as **autocracies**.

England. William the Conqueror, the Duke of Normandy in France, crossed the English Channel with his Norman army and invaded England. After his victory in the **Battle of Hastings** in 1066, he was crowned king of England, and he ruled as a strong monarch. To determine the population and wealth of England, he carried out a survey that listed all the property in England in the **Domesday Book**. William introduced feudalism in England, but he made all the feudal lords and knights take the Salisbury Oath in which they promised allegiance to him. William's successors grew more powerful, uniting England under their control. The Hundred Years' War and the period of Tudor rule increased the power of English monarchs.

The Hundred Years' War (1337–1453) was fought between England and France. Although the British lost their territories in France, they increased their feelings of loyalty to their kings and their homeland. During the period of **Tudor** rule (1485–1603), two monarchs became very popular as they expanded royal power and the nation's prosperity. **Henry VIII** (1509–1547) defied the Pope and helped establish the Anglican Church. His daughter, **Queen Elizabeth I** (1558–1603), defeated the Spanish Armada and encouraged the growth of the British navy and overseas exploration.

Although the Tudor monarchs were powerful, they could not be called absolute rulers. Limitations on their power had been set by the Magna Carta and the British Parliament. However, in the 17th century the Stuart rulers who succeeded the Tudors became absolute rulers and disregarded the traditional limitations on a monarch's powers. (See the section on the growth of democracy.)

France. After the Hundred Years' War, royal power in France became more centralized. **Louis XI** (1461–1483) increased his power by decreasing the power of the rebellious feudal lords, taking their lands and thereby laying the foundation for a strong monarchy. The rulers of France in the 1500s continued to centralize authority in the crown. **Henry IV** (1589–1610), the first **Bourbon** ruler, ended the religious strife and civil wars between French Protestants and Catholics. A Protestant, he adopted Catholicism to avoid bloodshed and issued the Edict of Nantes in 1598, which granted a measure of religious freedom to French Protestants, who were called **Huguenots**. Henry and other members of the Bourbon family ruled France until the Revolution of 1789.

Louis XIII, Henry's son, made **Cardinal Richelieu** (1624–1642) his adviser and chief minister. From 1624 to 1642, Richelieu laid the foundations for a strong French monarchy by weakening the nobles and increasing taxes, which added to royal wealth. Richelieu made the monarchy absolute within France, and his foreign policy made France the strongest power in Europe.

By the mid-1600s **King Louis XIV** (1643–1715), who was known as the "Sun King," ruled as an absolute monarch. Examples of his form of absolutism were:

1. He believed in the **divine right theory** of government, which held that a monarch's power came from God and that the monarch was accountable not to the people he ruled but only to God.

2. He used his wealth for his own benefit rather than for the people. The great palace at Versailles, near Paris, was built at his direction. The construction of the palace seemed to support his statement: "L'état, c'est moi" ("I am the state").

3. He never summoned the Estates-General, a lawmaking body, to meet.

4. He led France into many wars, hoping to gain territory. Few of these were successful, and their major result was to increase the dissatisfaction of the French people because of many deaths and high taxes.

5. His control over the French economy was aided by the actions of his finance minister, **Jean Colbert.**

6. He promoted artistic and musical works to glorify his rule, and he made France the cultural center of Europe. These activities also increased the spirit of French nationalism.

7. He revoked the Edict of Nantes, which was a blow to religious freedom and forced many Huguenots to leave France.

The absolutism in England and France eventually sparked strong political reactions and resulted in important democratic developments.

The Growth of Democracy

A democracy is a system of government that has two basic features:

1. **Popular sovereignty**—the people have the freedom to choose those who govern. Generally, they elect representatives to carry out their wishes.

2. **Equality and respect for the individual**—each person has specific freedoms and rights that are protected by the government.

By the year 1800, democracy had made significant advances in England, France, and the United States.

England—Democratic Progress Up to 1603. Many democratic reforms had been instituted before the 1600s. Generally, they placed limits on the powers of the monarchy and outlined the rights of the English people. These included:

1. **Jury system.** The idea of a trial by jury began under King Henry II (1154–1189).

2. **Limit on royal power.** The **Magna Carta** (Great Charter) was signed by King John in 1215. It placed limits on the king's powers to imprison people and to levy taxes. The king needed the consent of the Great Council, an advisory body composed of England's leading nobles and bishops, in order to levy taxes. The Magna Carta established that the king was not above the law; like his subjects, he had to obey the law.

3. **Legislative power.** The Great Council gained greater power under the rule of King Edward I. In 1295 he decided to include members of the middle class, the burgesses (representatives of the towns), and knights (small landholders). This meeting was the beginning of **Parliament** and became known as the **Model Parliament**. Afterwards, all Parliamentary meetings included representatives of the nobles and "commons." At first, they met together. However, Parliament was eventually divided into two parts, or houses, the House of Commons and the House of Lords. This was the first step toward representative government in England.

4. **Judicial power.** During the later Middle Ages (1000–1500), the verdicts of the judges were written down, collected, and became the basis for future legal decisions. These common practices and legal

decisions, which were based on judges' decisions rather than on a code of laws, formed a body of law known as **common law**.

England—Stuart Absolutism and Its Downfall in the 17th Century.

Following Queen Elizabeth I were the rulers of the **Stuart** dynasty (1603–1642), **James I** and **Charles I**, who ruled as absolute monarchs, believing they should have no limits set on their power to rule. The Stuart rulers did not respect previous democratic traditions and preferred to rule by the "divine right" theory. They came into conflict with Parliament because they disregarded Parliament in raising money, imprisoned people unfairly, and persecuted Puritans. However, the underlying conflict was the question of where power would be centered—in the monarchy or in the Parliament.

In 1628, in exchange for its granting more revenues, Parliament made Charles I agree to the **Petition of Right** (see chart on democratic achievements), which limited the power of the monarch. As soon as he received the money, Charles dissolved Parliament and ruled for eleven years (1629–1640) without Parliament. Ignoring the Petition of Right, Charles appointed special royal courts, such as the Court of Star Chamber, to try individuals who disagreed with him, particularly Puritans. These royal courts ignored the traditional common law.

In 1640 when Scotland invaded England, Charles was forced to call Parliament into session. Led by Puritans, this Parliament, which sat from 1640 to 1660, is known as the **Long Parliament**, and it changed English history by limiting the absolute powers of the monarchy. In 1641 Parliament denied Charles' request for money to raise an army to fight the Irish rebellion. In response, Charles led troops into the House of Commons to arrest some of its Puritan members. Parliament then raised its own army, beginning a civil war.

The English Civil War. This conflict, which lasted from 1642 to 1645, was between the supporters of King Charles, called the **Cavaliers**, and the supporters of Parliament, called the **Roundheads**. The Parliamentary forces emerged victorious under the leadership of **Oliver Cromwell**, a Puritan.

The Puritan Revolution (1642–1660). This period included the Civil War and the rule by Oliver Cromwell, which began in 1649. Under Cromwell's leadership, the Parliament voted to abolish the monarchy, and Charles I was tried and beheaded in 1649. England was now a republic or, as it called itself, a **commonwealth**. However, in 1653, supported by his army, Cromwell took the title of Lord Protector and ruled as a military dictator. His dictatorial policies, which included religious intolerance, strict moral codes, and violence against the Irish, caused resentment. Soon after his death, Parliament invited Charles II, the son of Charles I who was in exile, to take the throne.

The Stuart Restoration (1660–1688). Aware of English democratic traditions and the fate of his father, **Charles II** was careful not to anger Parliament and acknowledged the rights of the people established by the Magna Carta and the Petition of Right. In 1679, he agreed to the **Habeas Corpus Act**. (See Chart.) On his death in 1685, his brother **James II** became king. James angered Parliament because of his pro-Catholic actions and his claim to "divine right" rule. Parliament invited James' older daughter Mary and her husband William of Orange, a Dutch prince who was Protestant, to take the throne.

The Glorious Revolution (1688–1689). **William** and **Mary** accepted Parliament's offer and arrived in England with an army. They were proclaimed king and queen, and King James II fled to France. As a result of this "bloodless revolution," which is known as the "Glorious Revolution," Parliament gained in power and prestige. To protect its newly won supremacy over the monarchy, Parliament passed a **Bill of Rights** that was signed by William and Mary in 1689. (See Chart.) Thus, by the end of the 17th century, England had become a limited, or **constitutional monarchy**, the first in Europe. All of the major decisions were made by Parliament, and the ruler's actions were limited by Parliament. Key steps in this development as well as other democratic advances up to the year 1800 are in the following chart.

Democratic Achievements	Their Importance
Petition of Right, 1628	Parliament's consent needed for taxes; the king could not imprison someone without a trial or quarter soldiers in someone's home without permission.
Habeas Corpus Act, 1679	An arrested person has the right to know the charges against him, to be brought before a judge, and to be given a fair and impartial chance to defend himself.
Bill of Rights, 1689	Strictly limited the power of the monarch in such matters as levying taxes, maintaining an army, and interfering in the affairs of Parliament; basic civil liberties guaranteed to the people, such as a speedy trial, protection from cruel and unusual punishment, and excessive fines and bail.

Democratic Achievements	Their Importance
Toleration Act, 1689	Freedom of worship permitted for all Protestant religions.
Political parties	Two political groups arose in Parliament, each having members with common backgrounds, interests, and goals. They competed peacefully with each other for control of Parliament and became known as political parties. They were the Tories (later called Conservatives) and Whigs (later called Liberals). Political parties are an example of freedom of expression and give voters a chance to choose between different candidates and policies.
Cabinet system	The Cabinet consisted of members of Parliament who became advisers, or ministers, to William and Mary. These ministers eventually came from the majority party, with the leader becoming the prime minister. Over the years, their power increased because they were chosen from the elected officials in Parliament. The monarch became just a figurehead—a symbol of the nation, with the power to reign but not to rule.

Impact of the Growth of Democracy in England. The growth of democracy in England was to have world wide influence.

1. The democratic advances in England influenced political revolutions in the British colonies in North America (1776) and in France (1789). These ideas also influenced the emergence of some democratic nations from imperialism in the 20th century (India, 1947). A major factor in the American Revolution was the emphasis by colonists on their "rights as English subjects." Indeed, many democratic ideas and practices developed in England were included in American documents, such as the Constitution and the first ten amendments, or the Bill of Rights.

2. The writings of **John Locke**, a 17th-century English philosopher, were a source of democratic ideas. They influenced the American

colonists, and had a direct impact on the writing of our Declaration of Independence. Locke's ideas also influenced the leaders of the French Revolution. Locke believed that governments get their power from the consent of the governed (the people) and that the people have the right to change the government when the government abuses its power. For Locke, the chief purpose of any government was to protect the rights of the people. His idea of a **social contract** concerned an exchange of rights and responsibilities between a government and its citizens. Locke's chief work was *Two Treatises on Government*.

The French Revolution

France: Conditions Prior to the Revolution of 1789. The underlying or fundamental causes of the **French Revolution** were the conditions under the **Old Regime**. This term refers to life in France during the 17th and 18th centuries, while the nation was ruled by the Bourbon kings.

1. **Political causes.** The absolute rule of King Louis XIV (see France in the section "The Rise of Nation-States; Royal Power and Absolutism") was continued by **King Louis XVI** (1774–1792) and his wife **Marie Antoinette**. Louis XVI did not permit any criticism of himself and imprisoned without a trial anyone who spoke out against his policies. Imprisonment was often carried out by **lettres de cachet**, letters with the royal seal. He was a poor leader and very unpopular. The population was divided into three classes. The First Estate was the clergy; the Second Estate was the nobles; and the Third Estate was made up of everyone else—city workers, peasants, and the bourgeoisie. (The bourgeoisie were mainly bankers, business people, professional people, and others who made up the middle class.) The Third Estate, which included 90 percent of the population, had little say in the government. In the Estates-General, a lawmaking body, each estate had one vote. The Third Estate felt powerless because the other two estates always voted together.

Most of the French people were aware of the democratic revolutions in England (17th century) and America (18th century) and were impressed with the results of these events.

2. **Economic causes.** The Third Estate was more heavily taxed than the other two estates. Taxes imposed on the Third Estate included the **taille** (a land tax) and the **corvee** (labor on roads). They also paid a **tithe** to the Church and feudal dues to certain lords. The bourgeoisie were upset with strict restrictions on their commercial activities.

3. **Social causes.** The first two estates, although consisting of less than 5 percent of the population, had many more privileges than the Third Estate. They owned much of the land, were exempt from most taxes, and generally lived much better than members of the Third Estate.

4. Influence of the Enlightenment. The **Enlightenment**, also called the **Age of Reason**, was an intellectual movement in the 17th and 18th centuries. It was sparked by the scientific progress of the previous age (the Scientific Revolution). Educated Europeans had learned that natural laws governed the physical universe. They reasoned that similar laws must govern human society as well. If people were able to discover these laws, they might be used to construct a better government and more just societies. The thinkers, philosophers, and writers who examined the political and social problems of the time were known as **philosophes**. They believed that everything, even government and religion, should be open to reason and criticism. They were convinced that through the use of reason, logic, and experience, people could improve their society—its laws, economy, etc. The philosophes claimed that humans had certain natural rights. Traditional royal and Church authority, particularly in France, were in conflict with these rights and had to undergo change. The most important French writers of the Enlightenment are listed in the following chart.

Name	Major Work and Ideas
Montesquieu (1689–1755)	*The Spirit of the Laws*. There should be a separation of powers in government as well as a system of checks and balances. These features would prevent tyranny and absolutism.
Voltaire (1694–1778)	*Letters Concerning the English*. Written in support of the concepts of England's limited monarchy and its ideas on freedom of speech and religion.
Rousseau (1712–1778)	*The Social Contract*. Inequality among people can be ended by citizens' coming together and agreeing to a general will. The general will is what the majority desires and should be carried out by the government.
Diderot (1713–1784)	*The Encyclopedia*. Absolutism and the injustices of the Old Regime were wrong.

There were also other important Enlightenment writers. **Adam Smith** of England (*The Wealth of Nations*) said that people should be free to conduct business without government interference. This was the **laissez-faire** philosophy of economics. The American **Thomas Paine** (*Common Sense*) claimed that it was right and natural for the American colonists to revolt against England, a tyrannical government that was thousands of miles across the Atlantic Ocean. John Locke was also a major Enlightenment writer. (See the section "Impact of the Growth of Democracy.")

The Enlightenment's concern with natural rights and the use of reason, logic, and experience was seen in the field of science as well as in politics and economics. During the 16th and 17th centuries, the way the people of Europe viewed themselves and the universe underwent a dramatic transformation in what was called the **Scientific Revolution**. The discoveries of a succession of astronomers, physicists, and mathematicians undermined many ideas that had been accepted for centuries. A new system of ideas and theories was created, based on the direct observation of nature and a belief in the power of reason. The **scientific method**, based on carefully planned experiments, observation of results, and the formulation of general laws, was the basis of the Scientific Revolution. Scientists such as **Isaac Newton** (1642–1727) of England used the scientific method to investigate nature. Newton, the leading figure in the Scientific Revolution, put forth important theories about gravity and the movement of planets. His famous book was the *Principia Mathematica*.

The French Revolution of 1789: Outbreak and Major Developments. In 1789 King Louis XVI called the Estates-General into session because he needed money to solve France's financial problems. This was the first time this body had been summoned since 1614 (175 years). When the Estates-General met, the Third Estate refused to accept the traditional method of voting—each estate met separately and had one vote—because they would be outvoted by the other two estates. They demanded that all three estates meet together and that each deputy have a vote. When the king refused, the Third Estate, on June 17, 1789, declared itself to be the **National Assembly** and in the **Tennis Court Oath** pledged to write a constitution for the nation. This declaration was the beginning of the French Revolution. On July 14, 1789, the revolution spread as a mob stormed and destroyed the **Bastille**—a prison that was a symbol of the Old Regime. The next day the king recognized the National Assembly. The National Assembly, which was made up of moderates, took power and began to carry out reforms. They passed the **Declaration of the Rights of Man** on August 27, 1789. This document was similar to the American Declaration of Independence and the English Bill of Rights. It stated the following democratic ideals:

1. The class structure and privileges connected with the three estates were ended, abolishing the remains of feudalism.

2. All people were equal before the law and had certain basic freedoms, including freedom of religion, speech, and the press.

3. The spirit of "Liberty, Equality, and Fraternity" was to guide the nation. In 1790, the National Assembly abolished the special taxes and privileges of the Catholic Church in the **Civil Constitution of the Clergy**. It also granted freedom of worship, confiscated all Church land, and placed the Church under the government's control.

The French constitution was written in 1791, and it created a limited, or constitutional, monarchy and established separate executive, legislative, and judicial branches of government.

However, events such as King Louis' unsuccessful attempt to flee the country and war with Austria and Prussia enabled radicals, such as **Robespierre, Danton**, and **Marat**, to take over the revolution. In 1792, delegates were elected by universal manhood suffrage to the **National Convention**, which took the place of the National Assembly and contained more radical members, such as the Jacobins. The first act of the National Convention was to declare France a republic. Louis XVI was brought to trial and executed in 1792.

The National Convention was soon taken over by extremist groups, who formed the **Committee of Public Safety**, which combined the executive, legislative, and judicial powers of government in the hands of a small group of revolutionaries. The committee was given power to conduct the war with France's enemies and to enforce the ideals of the revolution by all means possible. The leading figures were Danton and Robespierre, who began a **Reign of Terror** (1793–1794) in which they executed at the guillotine all enemies of the revolution, that is, nobles or anybody who spoke out against them.

Eventually, more moderate groups, anti-Jacobins, took over the National Convention. Danton and Robespierre were themselves sentenced to die by the guillotine in 1795. The Convention wrote a new constitution in 1795 that made France a republic. It established a five-member **Directory** government that ruled France until 1799, when it was replaced by the military dictatorship of Napoleon Bonaparte. (See the next section.) This return of government to moderate control is called the Thermidorian Reaction.

Importance of the French Revolution. The French Revolution had many important and long-lasting results. It brought about a basic change in the relationship between the government and the governed. Along with the revolutions in England and the United States, the French Revolution advanced democracy by recognizing the value and worth of the individual. Political power passed from a divine-right absolutist monarch and the nobles to the masses of people. A greater sense of nationalism and patriotism developed. Also, the remaining feudal features of French society were removed. The growing power of the bourgeoisie helped France to become a strong capitalist nation.

The Rise and Fall of Napoleon (1799–1815)

Napoleon Bonaparte was an ambitious, brilliant military officer who won many military victories in wars against France's enemies. In 1799 in a coup d'état (a quick, sudden takeover of a government), he came to power in France in a new government called the **Consulate**. The Directory had lost support because of worsening economic problems and its inability to defeat Russia and Austria in the war. The Consulate was headed by three consuls, with Napoleon as First Consul. The new government, France's fourth in ten years, was called a republic, but it was a military dictatorship under the control of Napoleon. He took the title of Emperor Napoleon I in 1804. The French people accepted his ruthless methods because they believed he would bring peace and stability to the nation.

At first, Napoleon was brilliantly successful in his war against France's European enemies. Under Napoleon's leadership, French forces won victories and took large amounts of land in Europe. By 1808, Napoleon dominated Europe, and he reorganized many parts of Europe, making members of his family rulers in Italy, Spain, etc.

The Napoleonic Empire soon became too large to control, however, and in time Napoleon suffered severe military setbacks. His attempt to conquer Russia in 1812 was a failure due to the harsh winter conditions as well as to the scorched-earth and fighting tactics of the Russians. At the **Battle of Waterloo** in 1815, fought near Brussels in Belgium, Napoleon's forces were defeated by a combination of European nations led by **Lord Wellington** of Britain.

Results of the Napoleonic Era. Napoleon made many significant contributions to the governing of France and consolidated many of the achievements of the French Revolution. Both within France and in the areas he conquered, Napoleon sought to carry out the ideals of the French Revolution as he interpreted them. Indeed, he called himself a "son of the Revolution" and carried out the following reforms:

1. The **Code Napoleon** brought all the laws, regulations, and reforms of the revolution into a single system of law. Based on the belief that all people are equal before the law, the Napoleonic Code became the fundamental law of France and the parts of Europe governed by France.

2. The **Concordat of 1801** provided for a peaceful relationship between the French government and the Catholic Church.

3. An efficient, centralized government was created in France, with specific power over the education and banking systems. Government officials were selected based on merit through an examination system, and a public school system was established.

4. Many European monarchs lost their thrones to Napoleon's armies. Peoples in these areas, such as Spain and Italy, learned of the ideals of the French Revolution. At first, some of these people welcomed Napoleon because they believed he had liberated them from foreign and unjust rule. Eventually they turned against Napoleon's dictatorial rule and fought against him. However, as a result of Napoleon's conquests, the ideas of the French Revolution were spread throughout Europe. The ideals of social justice, liberty, and democracy became rallying cries for reformers. Combined with the rise of

the spirit of nationalism, which was stirred by the struggle against Napoleon's armies, the dreams of liberty and equality made many national groups determined to gain self-government in the years after 1815.

The Metternich Age and the Growth of Nationalism, 1815–1871

After Napoleon's defeat, five major European powers—England, Russia, Prussia, France, and Austria—met at the **Congress of Vienna** in 1814 and 1815 to draw up peace plans and settle a number of important territorial questions by redrawing the map of Europe. Under the leadership of Austria's **Count Metternich**, the Congress of Vienna sought to restore political life in Europe, including former rulers and boundaries, to what it had been prior to Napoleon and to maintain peace and stability. Such a policy of restoring past ways and turning the clock back is called **reactionary**. Metternich wanted to wipe out the ideas spread by the Napoleonic era and return to the old days of absolutism and special privilege. The decisions reached at the Congress of Vienna were based on three principles—legitimacy, the balance of power, and compensation. **Legitimacy** meant restoring the ruling families that reigned before the French Revolution to their thrones. **Balance of power** meant that no one nation should be strong enough to threaten the security of the others. To do this, shifts of territory were necessary. This involved **compensation**, or providing one state with territory to pay for territory taken away from that state.

Metternich opposed the French Revolution's ideas of freedom and equality and sought to maintain the status quo. During the Metternich age (1815–1848), there were challenges to the status quo. However, most attempts by European peoples against these reactionary policies in order to achieve national unity were put down by force. These attempts, which led to revolutions in 1830 and in 1848, were inspired by a **nationalistic** spirit, whereby a group of people, such as the Italians, Poles, or Germans, sought to create their own nation and establish self-government. Although most of these revolutions failed, two successful attempts were made in Belgium and Greece in 1830. Although the Congress could not suppress nationalism permanently, it was able to postpone its success for half a century. The unification of Italy and of Germany in the later 1800s were the first break in the territorial settlements of 1815.

The spirit of nationalism influenced the political history of Europe from 1815 to 1914. **Nationalism** is the belief that a group of people who share a common culture, language, and historical tradition should have their own nation in a specific area of land. Once the people accomplish their nationalistic goals and form a nation-state, they can then make their own laws and are said to be **sovereign** and to have **autonomy**. Nationalism was the guiding force that led to the unification of both Italy and Germany in the late 19th century. The Italians, Poles, Hungarians, Turks, and others who were ruled by the large dynastic states that dominated Europe—the Austrian Empire, the Russian Empire, and the Ottoman Empire—all struggled to win freedom and form their own nation-states.

Unification of Italy. In 1815 there was no nation called Italy; Italy was really a "geographic expression." The Italian peninsula was divided among large and small states, such as the Lombardy province and the kingdom of Sardinia-Piedmont. Austria, which controlled the states in the northern part of the Italian peninsula, was against any kind of unity. But by 1861, all the Italian states had become unified into a nation. Those most responsible for bringing unification about were:

1. **Cavour.** Considered the "brain" of unification, he was a successful diplomat who got France to help him fight the Austrians. He also expanded the power of the kingdom of Sardinia-Piedmont by adding to it other Italian states.
2. **Mazzini.** The "soul" of unification, he wrote and spoke eloquently about his desires for Italian unity. He was the founder of the Young Italy movement.
3. **Garibaldi.** The "sword" of unification, he conquered southern Italy and joined it to the state that Cavour had unified under the control of Sardinia-Piedmont in the north.
4. **King Victor Emmanuel.** Formerly the king of Sardinia-Piedmont, he became the king of a united Italy in March 1861.

Unification of Germany. In 1815 there was no nation called Germany. Instead, there were more than 30 independent German states. They acted independently of one another and had their own traditions, laws, and economic regulations. The largest of these states, **Prussia**, located in northern Germany, led the movement for unification. The chief obstacle to Prussia's leadership was Austria. It sought to dominate German affairs and did not want to see the German states unified. But by 1871, under the leadership of Prussia's chief minister, **Otto von Bismarck**, Austria's power was weakened and the German states achieved unification.

Following a policy of "blood and iron," Bismarck used military means to achieve his goal of German unity under Prussia's leadership. Under this policy, Prussia won victories in the Danish War (1864), the Austro-Prussian War (or Seven Weeks' War) (1866), and the Franco-Prussian War (1870–71). As a result of these wars, Prussia was able to gain land, such as Schleswig-Holstein from Denmark and Alsace-Lorraine from France, unite other German states with Prussia, and reduce the influence of Austria in German affairs. King William

I of Prussia became the ruler of a united Germany in 1871 and was called emperor, or kaiser.

Conclusion. Nationalism can be a positive or a negative force. The desire by Italians and Germans to form their own nations brought together people with common ties and histories. The wish of a group of people to achieve sovereignty and self-determination are common themes throughout history and exist even in our own day. However, nationalistic desires can become so intense that hatred and unnecessary bloodshed can result. The "reign of terror" in France was one example; Bismarck's humiliation of France after the Franco-Prussian war was another. Intense nationalism can also be dangerous when it turns into **chauvinism** and excessive **ethnocentrism**. This occurs when a group of people claim to be superior to another group of people. Such claims have often led to prejudice and wars.

The Industrial Revolution

A major upheaval in the way people live, work, and think began about 200 years ago and in many ways is still going on today. This change is called the Industrial Revolution, and it accomplished on a massive scale the replacement of human power and animal power with the power of machines. The Industrial Revolution began in England in the 1750s and involved vast changes in the production of goods. These changes were as follows:

1. From hand-made goods to machine-made goods.

2. From production at home to production in factories (from the domestic system to the factory system).

3. From producing small amounts to producing large amounts (**mass production**).

4. The increased use of science and new forms of energy (steam power, for example) to speed up production and meet human needs. The use of science in these ways is referred to as **technology**.

Causes and Preconditions in 18th-Century England. The Industrial Revolution began in England because of a combination of fortunate conditions that existed at the time.

1. **Natural resources.** Britain was fortunate to have large amounts of coal and iron ore.

2. **Geography.** England had many good harbors, and coastal and river trade was well-developed. England also had relatively good roads and numerous canals for the cheap transport of raw materials and finished goods.

3. **Investment capital.** Entrepreneurs and other private individuals had money which they, as capitalists, were willing to invest and risk in business ventures.

4. **Labor supply.** There were large numbers of skilled workers in the population.

5. **Increased demand.** There was a great demand for British products, both in the domestic market (within the nation) and in foreign or overseas markets.

6. **Transportation and colonial empire.** Britain had a good navy and had built up a shipping industry. Its expanding colonial empire furnished raw materials and markets for goods.

7. **Agricultural changes.** An agricultural revolution that occurred in the 1700s brought changes in farming that made the Industrial Revolution possible. These changes resulted in the production of more food and required fewer farmers to produce the food. Many people left the farms and went to the cities to find work in factories.

8. **Role of government.** Britain had a stable government that had established a good banking system, promoted scientific experimentation, and passed laws to protect business.

9. **Inventions.** The changes in production came first in the cotton textile industry. Several inventors devised inventions that sped up and improved the manufacture of textiles.

Inventor	Invention and its Importance
John Kay	Flying shuttle—speeded up the weaving process
James Hargreaves	Spinning jenny—could spin many threads (up to 24 threads) at one time
Richard Arkwright	Water frame—used water power to increase spinning; first machine to replace human hand power with another power source
Edmund Cartwright	Power loom—used water power to make weaving faster
James Watt	Steam engine—use of steam as a source of power
George Stephenson	Steam locomotive—improved ground transportation

Responses to the Industrial Revolution. The Industrial Revolution fundamentally changed the way people lived. Families moved to industrial cities by the millions to work in the new factories. The first years of adjustment to the new industrial society were a period of severe difficulty for workers. Men, women, and children worked long hours under deplorable conditions in factories. People were crowded into towns and cities that had made little provision for housing or for sanitation. With more people working in factories and living in cities, occupational, health, and housing problems developed. Moreover, even though they were becoming more populated than rural areas, cities had not gained political power. These problems associated with industrialization developed in Britain as well as in other areas of Europe where industrialization took place. In response to workers' protests and reformers' appeals, various reform measures were adopted. These reforms indicated that Europeans had begun to understand the changes in the working and living conditions of those who labored under the factory system. Reform measures in Britain were as follows:

1. **Social and economic reforms.** Harmful working conditions such as child labor, low wages, faulty ventilation, and dangerous equipment were brought to public attention by the Sadler Report on factories and the Ashley Report on mines. In time, members of Parliament became concerned about children as young as five or six working long hours in factories and mines and about the dangerous, unhealthful conditions for all workers in factories. Laws such as the Factory Act (1833) and the Mines Act (1842) were passed to improve conditions for workers. The need for workers to unite to protect and advance their interests led to the formation of **labor unions**.

2. **Political reforms.** The move to reduce property rights for suffrage (the right to vote) and to give cities more representation in Parliament led to the passage of the **Reform Bill of 1832**. This bill also did away with most "rotten boroughs" (areas which no longer had many people but had kept the same amount of representation in Parliament). The middle class, workers, and women were to benefit from the Reform Bill of 1832 and similar legislation passed in the 19th and early 20th centuries. By 1928, for example, Britain had provided for universal suffrage. This meant that both women and men had the right to vote. The expansion of suffrage in Britain and other European countries was partially due to changes brought about by the Industrial Revolution.

The Development of Socialism. Political scientists and philosophers struggled with the problems presented by industrialization, seeking to discover how the political system should respond. One of these solutions was socialism, which was a criticism of capitalism and called for a basic change in the economic system in order to correct these problems. Socialists maintained that it was necessary to transfer ownership of the **means of production** (factories, mines, railroads, land) from private individuals to the state. According to socialist theory, the government, as elected by the people, should own all the means of production and should also make all the key economic decisions. These decisions included: What should be produced? Who should product it? What the price should be? and How should the product be distributed? This kind of **planned** or **command economy**, is in contrast to a **free-enterprise** or **market economy**. In a market economy, according to capitalist principles, the key economic decisions are basically made by private individuals acting on their own.

One group of socialists wanted to create an ideal society, or a utopia. **Utopian socialists** believed that a socialist society would emerge peacefully and that even capitalists would be willing to help create it. Among the utopian socialists of the 19th century were a wealthy British manufacturer, **Robert Owen**, and a French philosopher, **Charles Fourier**.

In contrast to utopian socialists were those who believed in a radically different type of socialism called **scientific socialism** or **communism**. That was a type of socialism based on what they believed were scientific ideas about the way society operates. The leading scientific socialists thinkers were **Karl Marx** and **Friedrich Engels** of Germany. Their ideas were contained in two books: *The Communist Manifesto* (1848) and *Das Kapital* (1867). Their major ideas came to be known as Marxism and included:

1. **Economic interpretation of history.** All history is determined by economic conditions. Whichever group or class controls the means of production will control the government.

2. **Class struggle.** In all societies throughout history, there have been struggles for power between two economic groups—the "haves" and the "have nots." In industrial societies the struggle has taken place between the capitalists, or **bourgeoisie**, and the workers, or **proletariat**.

3. **Surplus value theory.** Surplus value was the difference between the price of a good and the wage paid to a worker. According to Marx, this difference was kept by the capitalists as their profit. For Marx, this was wrong, especially as he felt that workers were paid far too little in wages. Such abuse or exploitation of workers was unjust.

4. **Inevitability of socialism.** Eventually, all of these conditions would lead to depressions and poverty and would result in a violent overthrow by the workers of the government, primarily because the capitalists would not peacefully give up their economic and political power. This **communist revolution** would result in a **dictatorship of the proletariat**, a government that would be more just and would rule on behalf of the working class. The government would operate under the theory of socialism. Eventually, a classless society would emerge, and there would be no need for a government; the government would "wither away."

The Impact of Communism. The history of communism since Marx put forth his ideas shows a wide difference between what Marx said and what has actually happened.

1. His prediction that communist revolutions would occur mostly in Western European industrialized societies was wrong. The first two communist revolutions took place in agricultural societies—Russia (1917) and China (1949).

2. Communism never won control in industrialized societies in Western Europe or in North America. Marx failed to see the growth of unions and their ability to work toward their goals in a free, democratic system. He also did not realize that the living conditions of the workers would improve in the 19th century and that workers would become part of the middle class.

3. As the 1990s began, it was clear that Communist societies have failed to achieve their goals. The continued economic and politial problems in the Soviet Union and Eastern Europe have caused governments there to rethink their strategies for improving the lives of their people. Throughout this century, there have been constant attempts by people in these Communist nations to leave, seeking a better life elsewhere, specifically in non-Communist countries.

Imperialism

Imperialism can be defined as the control by one nation over a weaker area or nation. This control has usually been both political and economic. Since the areas under control are called colonies, the practice of imperialism can be referred to as **colonialism**. There are two distinct periods of imperialism—the "old imperialism" (1500–1800) and the "new imperialism" (beginning in the 1880s). The old imperialism had the following characteristics: concerned with establishing trade routes and obtaining resources; carried on at first by private individuals and companies; took place mainly in the Western Hemisphere, the Americas. (See the unit on Latin America.) The new imperialism had these general characteristics: concerned with establishing trade and markets, obtaining resources, and making large financial investments; carried on by governments as official policy; took place mainly in the Eastern Hemisphere, Africa, and Asia. There were many reasons for the new imperialism.

1. **Economic.** The increased supply of manufactured goods produced by the **Industrial Revolution** encouraged European nations to find new markets for these goods. Investors with surplus capital looked overseas to make investments that would bring them profits. Also, the need for raw materials to produce more goods was another important consideration.

2. **Political.** Nations hoped to gain prestige and glory by expanding their power. These nationalistic desires sparked nations to achieve a **balance of power** with other nations who were also seeking to build colonial empires.

3. **Social.** European nations felt that they were superior to other global areas. They felt that they had both an obligation and a right to spread their culture and way of life into these areas. These feelings of ethnocentrism can be seen in Rudyard Kipling's poem *The White Man's Burden*, which concerns the obligation of carrying Western

civilization to those considered less fortunate. These feelings were also the result of 19th-century notions of white racial superiority and the theory of **social Darwinism**. This was the belief that social progress depended on competition among human beings, resulting in the "survival of the fittest."

Forms of Imperialist Control. Imperialism took many different forms in the 19th century.

1. **Sphere of influence.** A nation gained sole economic power in a region and had exclusive economic rights to trade, to invest, and to develop mines, railroads, or factories. It could not be interfered with by other nations. This form of imperialism was used in China, where each foreign nation—for example, Germany—had economic control in a part of China.

2. **Concession.** This consisted of a foreign nation's obtaining special privileges. An underdeveloped area gave permission to a technologically advanced nation to do something of economic value in the area. (For example, the Arabs let the British drill for oil and build a railroad in the Middle East.)

3. **Protectorate.** A colonial nation allowed the native ruler of an area to remain in office as a figurehead, while in reality the colonial power made all the major decisions (France in Tunisia). The Eastern European **satellite nations** controlled by the Soviet Union after World War II can be thought of as protectorates.

Colonial Policies. The major imperialist nations followed different policies in ruling their empires. These policies influenced the patterns of independence that took place after 1945.

1. **England.** Its policy of **indirect rule** permitted local rulers to retain some power in an area. Nevertheless, because the British felt that their democratic values were superior and should be spread, they sought to educate selected Africans and Asians in English schools. It was hoped that these natives would plant British political and social ideals in their native lands. People who received such an education, such as Gandhi and Nehru in India, eventually led their people to independence in nonviolent ways, based on democratic ideas. Britain was never involved in harsh colonial wars for independence as were some of the other European nations.

2. **France.** Its policy of **direct rule** viewed colonies as if they were actually part of France. Decisions for the colonies were made directly in Paris. Since the French language and culture were assumed to be preferable, all people were to learn them in colonized areas. These attitudes were the basis for France's claim to carry out a "civilizing mission" and to accomplish assimilation of native peoples. Since France viewed areas such as Algeria and Indochina as much a part

of French territory as Paris, the French were unwilling to give into demands for independence that grew after the end of World War II in 1945. Consequently, France fought bitter, unsuccessful colonial wars in these areas. (See the units on the Middle East and Southeast Asia.)

3. **Portugal.** Its policy of **paternalism** viewed colonies as though they were children. Yet, Portugal did little to prepare its colonies for independence. As with France, it looked on its colonies as parts of Portugal. Consequently, it too was unwilling to grant independence to its colonies in Angola and Mozambique without military struggle.

4. **Belgium.** It followed policies of paternalism and **exploitation** in the Congo. Belgium did little to pave the way for independence and left the area amid much bloodshed in 1960. Consequently, this former colony had severe political problems in creating a stable government when it became independent. (See the units on Africa, Asia, and the Middle East for additional information on areas once under European imperialist control.)

Independence and Decolonization. The period after World War II was a time when independence came to almost all areas that had come under European imperialist control. This period of decolonization saw the emergence of over 50 new nations. The end of imperialism after 1945 was a result of many factors: nationalist movements in the colonies grew powerful, gaining support from native people as well as from some people in the imperialist nations; the Western European nations were weary after fighting World War II; the creation of the United Nations was linked to global concern for human rights and recognition of the need for people to achieve self-determination.

Although decolonization was achieved in both peaceful and violent ways, former colonies retain ties today to their former foreign rulers. Many of Britain's colonies, after independence, voluntarily chose membership in the **British Commonwealth of Nations**. The organization meets to discuss matters of mutual interest and provides certain economic privileges for members. Although it no longer exists, the **French Community** was an organization similar to the British Commonwealth. It included France and several of its former colonies. France's interest in its former colonies can be seen in its giving economic aid and in providing military support when requested. For example, in recent years, French forces were sent to the African nations of Chad and Gabon to put down armed opposition to the governments there.

Evaluation of Imperialism. European imperialism had both positive and negative consequences.

Consequence	Positive	Negative
Political	Brought stability and unification; training for independence; promoted the nation-state idea	Colonial wars; discrimination; drew boundaries without consulting native peoples
Economic	Introduced modernization; improved means of transportation and communication; created industries; taught new skills; improved the standards of living; provided employment	Took wealth away from colony; treated workers badly; did not provide for advancement and management for colonized people; destroyed traditional industries and patterns of trade
Social	Introduced Christianity and other aspects of Western culture; built schools and hospitals; modern medicine	Looked down on native cultures; promoted racism and sense of cultural inferiority; introduced Western vices and diseases

World War I

The Congress of Vienna laid the foundation for a century of peace in Europe, broken only by a few brief and local wars (Franco-Prussian, Russo-Turkish, and Crimean). Beginning about 1870, a series of forces combined to move Europe toward war. These forces included a growing spirit of nationalism, increasingly dangerous colonial conflicts, a complex system of entangling alliances, and a rising tide of militarism.

Between 1914 and 1918 war swept across Europe. This war was far more destructive of lives and property than any other previous conflict and was the first total war. Civilian populations became objectives and targets along with soldiers. Terrifying new weapons were used for the first time.

Basic (Fundamental, Underlying) Causes of World War I. Many factors contributed to the start of World War I. All the major powers shared some blame, although historians disagree on whether one nation was more to blame than the others.

1. **Imperialism.** The desire to control other areas led to sharp competition and rivalry among nations of Western Europe. Examples include: Britain and Germany in Africa and the Middle East; France and Germany in Morocco; and Austria-Hungary and Russia in the Balkans. As European nations struggled to claim more territories in Africa and Asia, they approached the brink of war several times.

287

2. **Nationalism.** Strong ties to one's nation and/or ethnic group stirred strong emotions, and many groups of people wanted to be free of the control of other nations. For example, Bosnia and Herzegovina wanted to be free from Austria-Hungary so they could be united with Serbia. Other nationalities in the Balkans also wished to be free of control by Austria or the Ottoman Empire and to create their own nations. The Balkans were called the "tinderbox" of Europe.

3. **Alliances and the Lack of Any World Peacekeeping Machinery.** Two alliances, the **Triple Entente** (France, Russia, and Britain) and the **Triple Alliance** (Germany, Austria-Hungary, and Italy) were formed for defensive purposes, but they soon became two armed camps. At this time no organization existed, such as the United Nations, to foster world peace or to help settle disputes among the major powers.

Europe in 1914

KEY

Allied powers

Central powers

Neutral countries

4. Militarism. As the alliance system divided Europe into two opposing camps, each nation began to increase its military strength. The growth of armies and navies, as well as the development of weaponry, added to the mood of belligerence (war-like attitude) and a tendency to settle disputes by fighting. Manufacturers of arms increased production, as governments sought to build up their military strength. Economic rivalry between Germany and Britain poisoned relations between the two nations. Germany's growing navy was seen by Britain as a threat to its security.

Immediate Cause of the War. The spark that set off World War I was the assassination of the Austrian **Archduke Francis Ferdinand** in June 1914 in the town of **Sarajevo**. The assassin was a Serbian nationalist, **Gavrilo Princip**, who wanted to free Bosnia and Herzegovina from the Austro-Hungarian Empire and unite them with Serbia.

Developments in the War. Austria, backed up by Germany, threatened Serbia. This angered Russia, causing it to get its armed forces ready for war. Because of the alliance system, country after country was drawn into the conflict and all the major powers were soon fighting each other. A local, regional crisis thus became the spark of a major war. The war, known as the "Great War" at first, turned into the most violent European conflict since the Napoleonic War, almost 100 years prior. With neither side able to win, the armies faced one another from trenches. The war was a **stalemate** until 1917. In that year the United States entered the war on the side of the Triple Entente nations, or the **Allies** (Britain, France, and Russia). This helped to bring victory against the **Central Powers** (Germany, Austria-Hungary, and Turkey—a late entrant into the war). The war ended in November 1918, having lasted just over four years.

Results of World War I. The war changed the course of the world's history, causing economic chaos and radical social changes in many countries. Some of the most powerful nations in Europe lost their influence and began to decline. Many monarchs lost their thrones. A Communist government came to power in Russia, and the seeds of a second great conflict (World War II) were sown when World War I ended and the peace treaty was drawn up.

1. **Economic.** The war was very costly to the participants. The losers became debtor nations. Many of the economic problems arising from the war were partly responsible for the worldwide depression that began in 1929.

2. **Social.** Millions were killed and wounded from the fighting. More than 8 million soldiers died, and almost as many civilians were killed. Several deadly weapons were used for the first time in warfare—gas, tanks, airplanes, submarines, and the machine gun. Most Europeans

failed to understand the destructive power of these weapons until they were used and how horrible modern warfare had become.

3. **Political.** The League of Nations was formed in an effort to secure world peace. The political problems and hatreds that emerged in some nations provided a basis for the rise of dictatorships later in Germany and in Italy. There were major territorial changes:

Changes	Taken From
a) Poland recreated, with a "corridor" to the sea	Germany and German-conquered area of Russia
b) Romania enlarged	Austria-Hungary
c) Yugoslavia and Czechoslovakia created as new nations	Austria-Hungary
d) Austria and Hungary become separate nations	Austria-Hungary
e) Finland, Estonia, Latvia, and Lithuania created	Russia
f) Alsace-Lorraine to France	Germany
g) Syria, Lebanon, and Palestine became mandates (see Middle East unit)	Turkey

The Versailles Treaty (1919). The Versailles Treaty officially ended World War I. It was drawn up at the **Paris Peace Conference** by **David Lloyd George** (Britain), **Georges Clemenceau** (France), **Vittoria Orlando** (Italy), and **Woodrow Wilson** (United States). It forced Germany to accept "war guilt" and stripped Germany and Austria-Hungary of much territory (see chart above). Germany was also forced to pay huge amounts of money to the allied victors as **reparations**. It was prohibited from uniting with Austria and required to limit its armed forces (demilitarization). This "diktat" (dictated peace), as it was called by Germany, caused much resentment in that country and was later used by Hitler as propaganda in his rise to power in the 1930s. The treaty also created the **League of Nations**. The League was one of the Fourteen Points that America's Wilson had asked for in an attempt to prevent future wars. The United States Senate refused to ratify (approve) the Versailles Treaty. Therefore, the United States did not become a member of the League. For this reason, as well as the fact that it had no enforcement powers, the League was seen as a weak organization.

The Rise of the Modern Totalitarian State

Totalitarianism is a political philosophy that emerged in the 20th century. Totalitarianism describes governments in which one political party monopolizes all power and exercises complete authority over

Europe in 1919

ICELAND

NORWAY SWEDEN FINLAND

ESTONIA

UNITED KINGDOM

LATVIA

SOVIET UNION

LITHUANIA

IRISH FREE STATE (1922)

NETHERLANDS

E. PRUSSIA

POLAND

GERMANY

BELGIUM LUXEMBOURG

CZECHOSLOVAKIA

FRANCE

AUSTRIA HUNGARY

RUMANIA

SWITZERLAND

YUGOSLAVIA

PORTUGAL

SPAIN

ITALY

BULGARIA

TURKEY

GREECE

ALBANIA

KEY

New countries

Countries with border changes

the people and their activities. It involves total control of all aspects of an individual's life by the government, with both civil and political rights being curtailed. Although various forms of totalitarianism exist in parts of the world today, its earliest examples were in three European nations during the 20-year period following World War I. These nations were the Soviet Union (under communism; see Unit Seven), Italy (under fascism), and Germany (under Nazism). Totalitarian societies look down on individual human rights and civil liberties. The values of democracy are not found in such societies. Totalitarian states emphasize: 1) glorification of the whole community (that is, the state); 2) authoritarian rule by a dictator or by selected members of the one political party allowed to exist; 3) control of the individual citizen's life; 4) belief in the idea that the individual should benefit the state and exists solely to serve the state's interests. In Western Europe, these features of totalitarianism were most characteristic of Germany under the control of **Adolph Hitler** and the **Nazi Party**, from 1933 to 1945. This government, known as the **Third Reich**, arose after the period of the Weimar Republic.

Germany Under the Weimar Republic, 1919–1933. The Weimar Republic was the name of the German government that came to power after World War I. It was a democratic government, with a constitution that was drawn up in the city of Weimar. However, this experiment with democracy in Germany faced many problems, including economic chaos, street violence, and political threats from the left and the right and was not successful for a number of reasons.

1. In the early 1920s the Weimar government printed paper money with little to back it, resulting in severe inflation, which devastated the German economy and resulted in severe unemployment and street violence.

2. When Germany was unable to meet its reparations payments, in 1923, France sent troops to occupy the Ruhr Valley, Germany's chief industrial area.

3. There was terrible unemployment in Germany in the early 1920s and again in the 1930s.

4. The German economy was restored after 1923 and conditions improved. However, in 1929 a worldwide depression that threatened the stability of democratic governments everywhere brought much suffering to Germany. Unemployment rose to 6 million in 1932, and Germans lost faith in their political leaders. This further fueled the bad feelings that had been caused by the Versailles Treaty.

5. The government was unstable because no single party was able to achieve a majority in the Reichstag, the more powerful of the two legislative houses created by the Weimar constitution. As a result, German political leaders seemed helpless to deal with the severe economic problems.

These problems led many Germans to conclude that democracy was ill-suited to their nation and that autocracy was preferable, especially since it had brought Germany political unification, economic growth, and respect as an international power. A strong democratic tradition did not exist in German history.

The Role of Adolph Hitler. Hitler was born in Austria and served in the German army during World War I. He was a founder of the **Nazi Party** (National Socialist German Workers Party). He spoke out against the Weimar government and was arrested for his role in the Munich Putsch of 1923, an unsuccessful attempt to overthrow the government. While imprisoned, he wrote the book *Mein Kampf* ("My Struggle") that contained his ideas for a stronger and more powerful German nation. It also revealed his racist beliefs concerning the alleged superiority of Aryans as a "master race" and the need to eliminate all groups he considered inferior, such as Jews, Slavs, Gypsies, and blacks. Hitler was a stirring and charismatic speaker when addressing large crowds, thereby attracting many people to the Nazi Party.

Rise of the Nazis to Power. In addition to the problems of the Weimar government and the powerful role played by Hitler, a number of other factors led to the rise of the Nazis in Germany:

1. **Economic problems.** The Nazis offered simple explanations for both the causes of Germany's economic problems and its cures. These problems, as described above, affected millions of Germans (6 million workers were unemployed in 1932). The reparations demanded by the Versailles Treaty were condemned as unjust and blamed for causing the economic crisis.

2. **Patriotic appeals.** The Nazi program stirred German nationalism. It called for:

—a large increase in the armed forces;

—the expansion of the German fatherland to include territory in Eruope where people of German descent lived (Austria, parts of Poland, and Czechoslovakia);

—control over educational and cultural institutions to teach Nazi principles of racism and physical fitness for the glory of the state;

—ignoring the Versailles Treaty and refusing to accept the war-guilt clause;

—regaining land that Germany had held in Europe and its overseas colonies prior to World War I;

—the use of violence as a legitimate means to achieve domestic and international goals;

—the importance of looking back to and glorifying the mythical German race (the so-called "Volk") as the source of all strength and power;

The Nazis also claimed that Nordic Germans were destined to rule the world and to eliminate undesirable peoples. They blamed the Weimar government for accepting the Versailles Treaty and said it had been forced to do so by Jews, Communists, and others. Finally, the Nazis claimed that German forces had not been defeated in World War I but had been "stabbed in the back."

3. **Anti-Semitism.** Prejudice towards Jews had existed in Germany for hundreds of years, resulting in exile, loss of life and property, and hatred. However, Hitler's prejudice against Jews was fanatical; he used Jews as scapegoats and blamed them for his own personal failures and also for Germany's problems. These false notions became persuasive parts of Nazi propaganda, especially when they were blended with Hitler's "master race" theories. Hitler claimed that the Aryans (Germans) were a master race who were naturally entitled to

control and rule peoples of less "pure" blood, such as Slavs and Jews. (The Holocaust, in which 6 million Jews were systematically murdered after Hitler came to power, was the tragic consequence of these misguided notions.)

4. **Fear of communism and of Soviet Russia.** The Nazis played upon these fears with much success and portrayed themselves as the only ones capable of protecting Germany from foreign beliefs and potential aggressors. In this way, they were able to win the support of large segments of the German population, such as bankers and industrialists.

5. **Use of private, illegal armed groups.** Many of Hitler's followers were organized into private armies. One such group was the Storm Troopers (S.A.), or the "Brown Shirts," who used scare tactics and violence to terrorize Jews and opponents of the Nazis.

6. **Lack of meaningful opposition.** Few strong voices inside Germany spoke out against the Nazis. Many Germans came to gradually support Hitler, while others were apathetic. Others feared speaking against him, and many who did were intimidated. Internationally, there was little awareness of or concern about the Nazi movement.

The Nazis Come to Power. The formal takeover of Germany by the Nazis took place in January 1933 when the president of the Weimar Republic, Paul von Hindenburg, appointed Hitler as chancellor. By this time, the Nazis had become the largest political party in Germany, and they formed the single largest block in the Reichstag, the German parliament. Yet, they had never won a clear majority in any national election. (In 1932, for example, they won slightly less than 40 percent of the seats in the Reichstag.) Although Hitler promised to preserve the Weimar constitution, he soon carried out policies that destroyed the democracy that had existed under the Weimar Republic. The result was a totalitarian dictatorship that eventually brought about World War II and brought devastation to Germany and to most of Europe. Hitler's distorted ideas, along with his anti-democratic beliefs and tactics, unfortunately found a receptive audience in post-World War I Germany. He was called **der Führer**, or leader.

Italy Under a Fascist Government, 1922–1943. Italy experienced totalitarian rule under a Fascist government headed by **Benito Mussolini**. The word "fascist" comes from the word "fasces," an axe-like weapon that was a symbol of the ancient Roman Empire. Mussolini wanted Italians to feel a strong sense of nationalism and to remember the glory of the Roman Empire. Mussolini and his "Black Shirt" followers came to power for some of the same reasons that led to the rise of the Nazis in Germany.

1. **Economic.** The costs of World War I had been staggering. After the war, there was high unemployment, strikes, and severe inflation.

2. **Political.** The weak and divided parliamentary government of King Victor Emmanuel III was unable to provide leadership or to inspire confidence in its ability to solve the postwar crisis. Also, there was no strong democratic tradition in Italy. Moreover, the fear of communism and a Communist-led revolution was seized upon by Mussolini, who promised to defend Italy and thereby won followers.

3. **Social.** Italy was suffering from low morale, and Mussolini promised the Italian people security, order, and economic progress in exchange for their liberties and freedom.

Mussolini in Power. As a results of his famous **March on Rome** in 1922 supposedly to save Italy from a Communist revolution, Mussolini came to power. Neither the king nor the army opposed him. He soon established a **police state**, destroying civil liberties and demanding that people recognize him as **Il Duce**, the leader. Mussolini reorganized the economy of Italy, establishing Fascist-controlled associations in all industries, and Italy was run as a **corporate state**.

World War II, 1939–1945

Although the war started in Europe, it soon became a global conflict that dwarfed all previous wars in geographical extent and in human and material losses suffered. Fighting took place on three continents—Europe, Africa, and Asia—and on the seas, lands, and oceans around the globe. More nations (over 50) were belligerents (fighters in the war) than in any war in history. The chief antagonists on the **Allied** side were Great Britain, France, the United States, the Soviet Union, and China. On the opposing side were Germany, Italy, and Japan, the so-called **Axis** powers.

Causes. Many of the causes of World War II were similar to those that brought on the first world war. After World War I, many nations hoped to prevent another war by establishing what could be called a "house of peace." The "foundations" of this house included: the Versailles Treaty, the League of Nations, disarmament conferences (held in Washington, D.C., and in London), and the Kellogg-Briand Pact, which attempted to "outlaw" war. Unfortunately, the "house of peace" crumbled for a number of reasons, most of them due to the actions of the Axis powers (Germany, Italy, and Japan). The basic causes of the war were:

1. **Militarism.** Large amounts of money were spent on weapons. Military strength was seen as a source of national pride. The leaders of the Axis nations were always seen in military dress.

2. **Nationalism and racism.** The Axis nations saw themselves as superior to others and with the right therefore to extend their culture and their borders (the German "master race" theory, the Italian wish to revive the ancient Roman Empire, the Japanese self-pride based

on Shinto teachings and the necessity to establish a "new order" in Asia).

3. **Imperialism.** The Axis nations sought to take over other lands for political, racist, and economic reasons. Japan moved into China (1931, 1937); Italy conquered Ethiopia (1938); and Germany annexed Austria (the "Anschluss," or union) and Czechoslovakia (1938, 1939).

4. **Failure of collective security.** The democratic nations of Europe and the United States did little to curb the aggressive policies of Germany, Italy, and Japan. The League of Nations condemned some of these aggressive moves but was unable to take any other action.

5. **Appeasement.** To give in to a potential aggressor, hoping that the aggressor will be content and not commit any further harmful acts is called appeasement. It later came to mean the policy of accepting territorial aggression against small nations in the hope of avoiding a general war. This policy was followed by the British prime minister, **Neville Chamberlain**, at the **Munich Conference** in 1938. Here, he agreed to accept German annexation of the **Sudetenland** portion of Czechoslovakia in return for Hitler's guarantee of independence for the rest of Czechoslovakia. The policy proved to be a failure when Hitler later sent the German army to occupy all of Czechoslovakia in violation of the Munich Agreement.

The Start of the War. The German attack on Poland in September 1939 was the actual start of the war. Britain and France finally realized that they would have to use military force to stop Hitler's aggression and threat to conquer all of Europe. Just prior to its attack on Poland, Germany signed a nonaggression pact with the Soviet Union. Under this agreement, Russia would take over eastern Poland and the Baltic states of Estonia, Latvia, and Lithuania and would not contest Hitler's attempt to take over western Poland. Also, Russia and Germany promised not to fight each other.

Developments in the War. Using **blitzkeig** warfare ("lightning war"), Germany overran most of Europe, except for England, by 1941. In that year, Germany broke its promise not to attack Russia and invaded that nation. The Germans suffered great losses and were driven back. Also, in 1941 the United States entered the war after its navy was attacked by Japan at Pearl Harbor, Hawaii. The nations now fighting the **Axis powers** were known as the **Allies** (U.S., Britain, France, U.S.S.R.). With the invasion of **Normandy** in western France on June 6, 1944, ("**D-Day**"), Allied forces began to retake German-held lands and pushed the Germans eastward. Russian forces entered the German-held eastern European nations and pushed the Germans westward. On May 8, 1945, ("**V-E Day**"), Germany surrendered. In Asia, by 1941 Japan had conquered large areas of East and Southeast Asia. These Pacific areas were slowly retaken by United States forces between 1942 and 1945. In August 1945, the United States dropped two atomic bombs on the Japanese cities of Hiroshima and Nagasaki. On September 2, 1945, ("**V-J Day**"), Japan surrendered.

The Holocaust. This word refers to the intentional persecution and systematic murder of European Jews by the Germans from 1933 to 1945. Six million Jews were exterminated, mostly in concentration camps such as Auschwitz, Dachau, and Treblinka. The planned extermination of a group of people because of their religion, or race, or ethnicity is called **genocide**. The genocidal tactics of the Nazis were a horrible extension of Hitler's anti-Semitic attitudes. The world stood by and did nothing while this happened. There were scattered instances of Jewish armed resistance, such as in the Warsaw Ghetto Uprising in 1943. After the war, at the Nuremberg War Crimes Trials, several Nazis were found guilty of genocide and of "crimes against humanity."

In addition to Jews, other groups of people were labeled as "inferior" by the Nazis and were also sent to the concentration camps. These included homosexuals, Jehovah's Witnesses, Gypsies, Slavs, and mentally retarded people.

Results of World War II. The world of 1945 bore little resemblance to the world of the 1930s. Europe was shattered and lay in ruins, its people facing an uncertain future.

1. **Political.** The United States and the Soviet Union became the two leading **superpowers** and eventually clashed on many issues in what became known as **the Cold War**. Germany was divided up into four zones of occupation—American, British, French, and Soviet. Poland's boundaries with the Soviet Union were changed, adding some to its own land. The Soviets established a sphere of influence, as an imperialist power, in many Eastern European nations. Some of its activities were in violation of the Yalta agreements of 1945. Britain and France lost some of their status as world powers; nationalistic movements in their colonies were to lead to a loss of their empires. The Allies helped to create the United Nations.

2. **Economic.** The war proved to be the most costly ever fought. The loss of life and property in World War II far surpassed that of any previous conflict. The economies of many European nations were destroyed. Communism spread into the nations of Eastern Europe.

3. **Social.** More people, soldiers, and civilians were killed than in any other war. Much of this was due to new highly destructive weapons, as well as to the racist policies of the Axis powers. At war's end, millions of people had become refugees and displaced persons.

4. **Scientific.** The Atomic Age had begun with the dropping of atomic bombs on Hiroshima and Nagasaki.

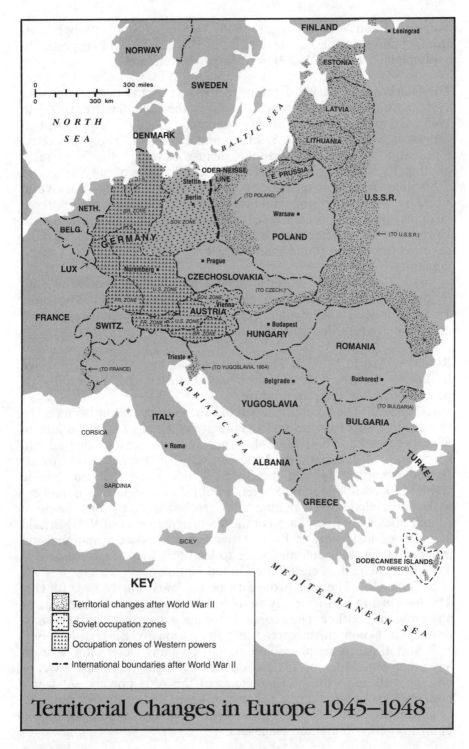

Territorial Changes in Europe 1945–1948

The United Nations

The United Nations was created in 1945. Its founders included the United States and the other World War II Allies. They hoped to make the UN a more effective international peacekeeping organization than the League of Nations had been. The **UN Charter** listed the organization's goals: to maintain peace and prevent war; to fight against hunger, disease, and ignorance; to improve social and economic conditions; and to build friendship and cooperation among nations. To accomplish these goals, the UN is structured as follows:

The General Assembly. The General Assembly has 159 member nations. Each nation has one vote. This figure contrasts with the 50 member nations that signed the UN charter in 1945. The General Assembly meets to consider international problems. It has the power to admit and expel members and to make recommendations to members and to other UN bodies. A decision on important questions requires a two-thirds majority.

The Security Council. The Security Council has 15 members. Five are **permanent members**, while ten are **nonpermanent** members. The five permanent members are the United States, Britain, France, the Soviet Union, and China. The other members are elected by the General Assembly for a two-year term. The Security Council functions as the UN's executive body; it can investigate problems and take action to maintain international peace.

1. Resolutions for action in the Security Council require nine votes, including the votes of **all the five permanent members**. Therefore, each permanent member has **veto power** over Security Council proposals.

2. The most important UN official is the head of the Security Council—the **Secretary-General**. The individuals who have served in that post include **Trygve Lie** of Norway (1946–1953), **Dag Hammarskjöld** of Sweden (1953–1961), **U Thant** of Burma (1961–1971), **Kurt Waldheim** of Austria (1972–1981), and **Javier Perez de Cuellar** of Peru (1981–present).

Specialized Agencies. These are bodies in the UN that carry out specific social and economic tasks. Some of these agencies are **UNESCO** (United Nations Educational, Scientific, and Cultural Organization), **WHO** (World Health Organization), and **FAO** (Food and Agriculture Organization).

Evaluation. The UN has been more successful in dealing with social and economic issues than with political issues. Examples of success can be seen in eliminating smallpox, fighting famines, and drawing attention to women's rights. On political matters, the UN has had mixed results. Examples of effective political action include the following: peacekeeping forces in Cyprus, the Middle East, and South

Asia; truce in the Korean War; overseeing the transition to independence for Namibia. UN resolutions have been disobeyed, however, in other disputes: Soviet troops in Hungary, apartheid in South Africa, India's seizure of Goa.

The Cold War and the Era of the Superpowers

The period after World War II (the postwar period) was marked by the dominance of two superpowers—the United States and the Soviet Union. Each nation had different philosophies about politics, economics, and human rights. Each thought it was superior to the other. Both engaged in a "Cold War" against each other. This was not a shooting war but a war of words and propaganda; it also involved competition in science, weapons, and seeking friends among the new emerging nations in Africa and Asia. Western European nations sided with the United States in what was called the "free world." The Soviet Union occupied the Eastern European nations and, with them, formed the "**Communist Bloc.**" As the 1990s began, however, the Cold War seemed to be over. Evidence of this was seen in the peaceful overthrow of Communist governments in Eastern European nations, such as Poland and Czechoslovakia. In the Soviet Union, President **Mikhail Gorbachev** implied that communism was a failure and promised to begin to reduce Soviet arms and troops in its Eastern European satellite nations. (For more on these developments, see Unit Seven on the Soviet Union and Eastern Europe.) The Cold War era, from 1945 to 1990, was distinguished by certain key events in Western Europe.

NATO. NATO, the **North Atlantic Treaty Organization**, was formed in 1949. It was a defensive alliance consisting of the United States, Canada, and ten Western European nations. It now has sixteen member nations. Its formation was part of the American policy of "containment." Through this policy, the United States and its European allies hoped to prevent the spread of communism by the threat of military power. Two important parts of the containment policy were the **Marshall Plan** (to provide economic aid) and the **Truman Doctrine** (to provide military aid to prevent a Communist takeover in Greece and Turkey). To counter NATO, the Soviet Union and its allies formed the seven-member **Warsaw Pact** in 1955.

The startling political events in Europe in 1990 have influenced and will continue to influence the roles of these two superpower alliances. Warsaw Pact forces have decreased in strength, mostly as a result of the changes in Communist leadership in the Soviet Union and Eastern Europe. In July, for example, Hungary's Parliament voted to leave the Warsaw Pact by 1991 because it felt that the alliance had no reason to exist any longer. Because of the absence of a military threat from the east, the NATO alliance may change from a military to a political organization engaged in promoting East-West peace and cooperation. Such a possibility was the subject of talks among NATO members at a heads-of-state meeting in London in July 1990. Other future issues concerning NATO include the number of troops, equipment, and nuclear weapons needed in Western Europe and the inclusion of a reunified Germany as a member.

Germany. In the years immediately after World War II, the question of what to do about Germany caused much tension between the superpowers. At the end of the war, most of Germany was divided into four occupation zones—the American, British, French, and Soviet. The city of Berlin was also divided into four such zones. Some territories in East Germany were put under Polish control. Since the four Allies were unable to agree on a plan for German reunification, the Western nations permitted their zones to come together in 1949 as the **Federal Republic of Germany** (West Germany), with its capital at Bonn. The Soviet zone became the **German Democratic Republic** (East Germany), with its capital in East Berlin. West Berlin, although surrounded by East Germany, became part of West Germany. The Soviets tried to cut off access to West Berlin in 1948 and 1949 by imposing the **Berlin Blockade**. However, the Western allies sent in food and supplies by plane (**the Berlin Airlift**). The Soviet Union subsequently backed down and ended the blockade.

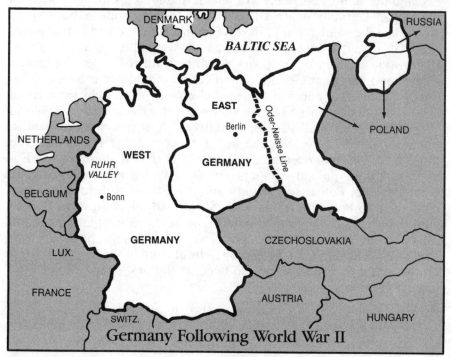

Germany Following World War II

1. **The Berlin Wall.** The Soviets again made Berlin a tension spot in 1961 when they built a wall (the Berlin Wall) along the areas that separated the Western section from the Eastern section. These areas had been used as escape routes for people who wanted to flee from Communist rule. The wall was another example of the Soviet policy of restricting the flow of ideas, goods, and people between the free world and the Communist world. This restrictive policy became known, in the worlds of former British Prime Minister Winston Churchill, as the "**iron curtain.**"

The many historic changes in the European Communist world that occurred in 1989 and 1990 can be thought of as "cracks in the iron curtain." One of these cracks was the destruction of the Berlin Wall by the Communist authorities, making Berlin a more open city. From November 1989 onward, the wall lost its significance as a political, economic, and social barrier.

2. **German reunification.** With the end of the Berlin Wall and the friendlier relationship (**detente**) between the superpowers, the chances of reunifying Germany became a very distinct possibility as the 1990s began. In 1990 itself, free elections were held in East Germany. West German political parties, such as the Christian Democrats and Social Democrats, ran candidates and won the support of some voters. In July 1990, an economic merger occurred when the West German mark became the unit of currency in East Germany. This meant that even though all Germans were still living in two separate nations, they would use the same money. East Germans were allowed to move into West Germany; West German companies were allowed to set up capitalist-style businesses in East Germany. With these developments, it became likely that German reunification would occur by 1991. Indeed, discussions about a reunited Germany were held throughout 1990. Included in these discussions were the four victorious World War II allies, as well as representatives from the two Germanies. Poland wanted to be included in the talks because it had suffered more from German occupation in World War II than any other European nation. Poland wanted assurance that a reunited Germany would respect Polish sovereignty and would not seek to retake any land given to Poland after the war. Specifically, Poland wanted to be sure that the Oder-Neisse boundary line between East Germany and Poland would remain intact. A promise to maintain this boundary was made by West German Chancellor **Helmut Kohl** in the spring of 1990, on the assumption that he would become the first head of a reunited German nation.

Political Issues for the Decade of the Nineties

The consequences of German reunification is one of several political issues that will concern Western European nations in the 1990s. Some of the others are:

Ireland. The Irish question has been a source of controversy between Ireland and England for centuries. By 1600, Protestant England had gained control over Catholic Ireland. From that time until the 20th century, British imperialist treatment of the Irish had been cruel and harsh. During the time in the 17th century when Oliver Cromwell ruled England, many Irish were killed by British forces; in addition, Protestants from England and Scotland took over large areas of land in Northern Ireland. Until the 1800s, Irish Catholics could not hold political office and were taxed to support the Anglican (Protestant) Church.

In 1905, the **Sinn Fein Party** was formed as a nationalist group to press Britain for Irish independence. Its leader was **Eamon de Valera**. Although the **Easter Rebellion** in 1916 against the British was unsuccessful, the Sinn Fein continued its campaign for independence. In 1922, the southern four-fifths of the island of Ireland became a free nation known as the **Republic of Ireland**. The remaining one-fifth, **Northern Ireland**, also known as Ulster, decided to remain as part of the United Kingdom (Great Britain). Catholics in Northern Ireland wanted the area to be united with the Irish Republic to the south, as did the new Republic of Ireland itself. These requests were turned down by Britain, particularly because the majority of Ulster citizens were Protestants and wanted to stay under the British crown. Extremist groups, both Catholic and Protestant, began to fight an undeclared civil war in Northern Ireland. The **I.R.A.** (Irish Republican Army) spoke for many Ulster Catholics and demanded a united Ireland. Militant Protestants, headed by the **Reverend Ian Paisley**, are against unification. British troops have been sent to Ulster since 1976 to help maintain peace and stop the killings and terrorist actions of both sides. These efforts have not been very successful. A 1985 agreement between Ireland and Britain, providing for greater cooperation against extremist groups and for stopping discrimination toward the Catholic minority in the north, has had mixed results.

Political Union and a "United States of Europe." The political unification of European nations is an idea that has been considered by some people since the end of World War II. There already exists a European Parliament, a European Court of Justice, and a European Commission. These organizations have limited powers but stand for some attempts at international cooperation. The twelve-nation **European Community** has made great strides towards economic cooperation. At its meeting in June 1990 in Dublin, the EC agreed to consider proposals for political union. These were to be discussed in future conferences in Rome and elsewhere. French President François Mitterand and West German Chancellor Helmut Kohl have spoken of a single European currency as well as possible political unification. British Prime Minister Margaret Thatcher has been the strongest voice against a "United States of Europe." She has indicated that the present loose grouping of sovereign nations is enough of a political union.

One factor that helped to set the stage for consideration of political and economic cooperation was the **Helsinki Pact of 1975**. This was a treaty signed by the United States, Canada, and 33 European nations, at what was called the **Conference on Security and Cooperation in Europe**. The signing nations agreed to accept the post-World War II boundaries in Europe. They also agreed to recognize the importance of promoting human rights throughout Europe and to investigate any governmental actions that violated such rights. A Helsinki Watch Committee was established to conduct such investigations.

QUESTIONS

Multiple Choice. Select the letter of the answer that correctly completes each statement.

1. The political system of the ancient Roman Empire was characterized by
   A. a strong central government
   B. rule by a coalition of emperors and religious leaders
   C. universal suffrage in national elections
   D. a strict adherence to constitutional ideas

2. Which was a major characteristic of democracy in ancient Athens?
   A. All adult male citizens were eligible to vote.
   B. All residents were given voting rights.
   C. Women were allowed to vote in major elections.
   D. Slaves were permitted to vote in major elections.

3. Which ancient civilization established the basis of Western political thought?
   A. Phoenician
   B. Egyptian
   C. Babylonian
   D. Greek

4. Which statement best describes the role of the Roman Catholic Church in Europe during the Middle Ages?
   A. The Church encouraged individuals to question authority.
   B. Church leaders were involved solely in spiritual activities.
   C. The Church gained influence as the world became more secular.
   D. The Church provided a sense of stability, unity, and order.

5. Which is the most valid generalization about the Crusades?
   A. The Crusades strengthened the power of the serfs in Europe.
   B. The Crusades increased trade between Europe and Asia.
   C. The Crusades brought European influence to Africa.
   D. The Crusades supported the idea of religious tolerance.

6. Which was a result of the Commercial Revolution?
   A. decline in population growth in Europe
   B. shift of power from Western Europe to Eastern Europe
   C. spread of feudalism throughout Western Europe
   D. expansion of European influence overseas

7. Which is a valid conclusion based on a study of European art during the Renaissance in Europe?
   A. Emphasis on artistic creativity can discourage a society from pursuing reforms.
   B. The development of guilds prevented artistic creativity.
   C. The presence of a wealthy leisure class contributes to artistic achievement.
   D. An economy based on subsistence agriculture encourages artistic development.

8. The humanists of the Renaissance differed from the traditional medieval philosophers in their
   A. interest in the spiritual life of the people
   B. lack of interest in ancient Greek and Roman culture
   C. rejection of Christian ideas
   D. emphasis on the importance of the individual

9. An immediate result of the Protestant Reformation was the
   A. breaking of the religious unity of Europe
   B. strengthening of the political power of the Pope
   C. increase in the influence of the Roman Catholic Church
   D. restoration of political unity to Western Europe

10. Martin Luther's Ninety-five Theses were a call for
    A. religious revolt against the German princes
    B. reforms within the Roman Catholic Church
    C. greater Papal authority
    D. crusades to spread Christianity

11. The theory of laissez-faire capitalism advocates
    A. government control of the economy
    B. noninvolvement of the government in the economy
    C. government regulation of big business
    D. government sponsorship of labor unions

12. One important result of the French Revolution was that
    A. France enjoyed a lengthy period of peace and prosperity
    B. the Church was restored to its former role and power in the French government
    C. political power shifted to the bourgeoisie
    D. France lost its spirit of nationalism

13. In Europe, which group benefited most from the industrialization of the 19th century?
    A. rural farmers
    B. middle class
    C. factory workers
    D. clergy

14. A main idea of Karl Marx and Friedrich Engels' *Communist Manifesto* is that the proletariat
    A. would need foreign help to achieve its revolutionary ends
    B. had to cooperate with the capitalists to gain economic rewards
    C. should allow the capitalists to control the means of production
    D. must unite to overthrow the capitalist class

15. Which statement best reflects the theories of Karl Marx and Friedrich Engels?
    A. Workers can expect that working conditions will improve as a result of government legislation.
    B. Owners of businesses will eventually realize that conditions for workers must be improved.
    C. Workers will experience an improved standard of living as capitalism matures.
    D. Workers will change working conditions by revolutionary means.

16. The Magna Carta, the Reform Bill of 1832, and the Parliament Act of 1911 were all steps by which Great Britain
    A. evolved toward democratic principles
    B. extended British imperialism
    C. created a classless society
    D. promoted socialist policies

17. Which was a major effect of European rule in Africa?
    A. decreased dependence of African nations on imports
    B. development of subsistence agriculture
    C. improved transportation and communication systems
    D. increased use of barter

18. Which group suffered from anti-Semitism during the Hitler era?
    A. Czechs   C. Muslims
    B. Jews   D. Aryans

19. The Helsinki Conference sought to establish secure boundaries and protect human rights several years after
    A. the Napoleonic Wars
    B. the Franco-Prussian War
    C. World War I
    D. World War II

ESSAYS

1. Throughout Europe's history, several individuals have acted in ways that have had a major impact on one or more nations.

   Alexander the Great
   Caesar Augustus
   Martin Luther
   Elizabeth I
   Robespierre
   Metternich

   Select any five of the above. For each one chosen:
   1. State the nation or homeland of the person.

   2. Describe one title the person had.

   3. Describe something this person did that had a major historical impact.

   4. Explain one reason why the person acted this way and one result of that action.

2. Nationalism has been a major force in shaping world events.

   Nationalistic Struggles

   French Revolution (1789–1815)
   Unification of Germany (1860–1871)
   World War I (1914–1918)
   Unification of Italy (1850–1861)
   The Irish Question (1650–present)

   Choose *three* of the nationalistic struggles listed. For each nationalistic struggle chosen:

   1. Identify *one* nationalistic leader or group involved in the struggle

   2. Describe *one* nationalistic goal of the leader or group

   3. Describe *one* action taken by the leader or group to achieve the goal

UNIT
SEVEN

THE SOVIET UNION AND EASTERN EUROPE

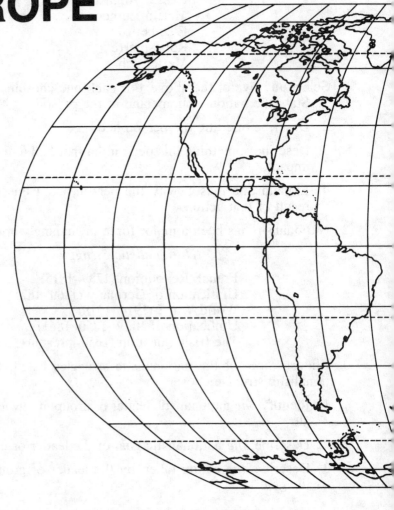

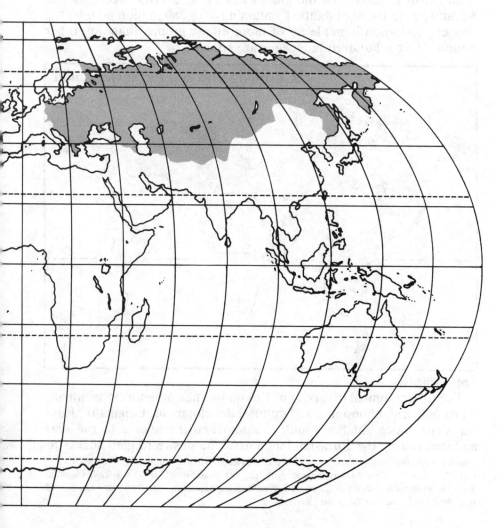

I. Physical Geography (The Physical Setting of the Soviet Union

Overview

Russia* (presently the Union of Soviet Socialist Republics or U.S.S.R.) is an immense nation that is more than two and one-half times the physical size of the United States. The U.S.S.R. is the largest country in the world today. Located in both Europe and Asia, the Soviet Union occupies a large part (two-fifths) of the continent or landmass referred to as Eurasia. This geographic location of the Soviet Union in both Europe and Asia was often reflected in political and cultural developments in Russian history. Russia's great size (more than a quarter of the globe) has brought both problems and advantages to its inhabitants. Containing over 280 million people, the Soviet population is made up of more ethnic groups than any other nation. Over a hundred languages are spoken.

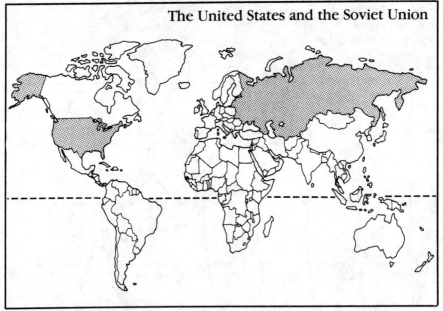

The United States and the Soviet Union

Topography

The topographical diversity of Russia has had an enormous impact on its political, economic, and cultural development. Originally, Russia was a much smaller country, landlocked (no access to the sea) and isolated by the Eurasian landmass. The desire to gain access to

* In this unit, the terms "Russia," "Union of Soviet Socialist Republics," "Soviet Union," and "U.S.S.R." are used interchangeably. Before 1917, the Soviet Union was called Russia. Today it is officially called the Union of Soviet Socialist Republics, and Russia is one of its 15 republics. (See chart on the Soviet Republics.)

The Soviet Republics

Republic	Entry into Union	Major Ethnic Group (%)	Total Population (Millions)	Area (1000 sq. mi.)
Russian	Original member, 1922	Russians (83)	145.3	6,593
Byelo-Russian	Original member, 1922	Byelorussian (79)	10.1	80
Ukranian	Original member, 1922	Ukranians (74)	51.2	232
Turkmen	Formed from parts of Turkestan, Bokhara, and Khiva, 1925	Turkmens (68)	3.4	188
Uzbek	Formed from parts of Khiva and Bokhara, 1925	Uzbeks (69)	19.0	174
Tadzhik	Formed from parts of Bokhara and Turkestan, 1929	Tadzhiks (59)	4.8	55
Azerbaijanis	Formed from division of Transcausacian Republic, 1936	Azerbaijanis (78)	6.8	33
Armenian		Armenians (88)	3.4	12
Georgian		Georgians (69)	5.3	27
Kazakh	Formed from provinces within RSFSR, 1936	Russians (41)	16.2	1,048
Kirghiz	Autonomous region in RSFSR until entry in 1936	Kirghis (48)	4.1	77
Estonian	Annexed in World War II, 1940	Estonians (65)	1.6	17
Latvian	Annexed in World War II, 1940	Latvians (54)	2.6	2.5
Lithuanian	Annexed in World War II, 1940	Lithuanians (80)	3.6	25
Moldavian	Formed from parts of Moldavian Autonomous Republic and Bessarabia (ceded from Rumania), 1940	Moldavians (64)	4.2	13

Source: USSR '88 © Novosti Press Agency, 1988.

the sea for trading purposes led many Russian rulers to adopt a policy of expansion. This goal of gaining warm-water ports has been central to Russian foreign policy until the present day. The numerous rivers that run throughout Russia long served as its only connections to the outside world. It was through these water trade routes that the Kievian princes made contact with the Byzantine or Eastern Roman Empire, which eventually gave Russia its religion and culture. Invasions from both Europe and Asia made it clear to later Russian rulers that if Russia did not gain access to the sea, it would be absorbed by other nations and cease to exist as a nation. As a result, the Russian kings, called **tsars**, followed an expansionist policy. First they set out on a path of conquest to the North and White seas, then south to the Black Sea, and finally east through Siberia to the Pacific Ocean. Yet, despite the acquisition of several thousand miles of coastline by the early 20th century, Russia's access to the Mediterranean, which carried the great bulk of commerce, was limited. Russian ships must leave from a port on the Black Sea and travel through the Dardanelles and the Sea of Mamara to reach the Mediterranean. Moreover, the ports gained by the Soviet Union were cold-water ports and were locked in ice during the winter.

The plain of northern Eurasia consists of several thousands miles of flat land, often referred to as the **Northern European Plain**. This area stretches from the Atlantic Ocean, across Western Europe and Eastern Europe until it reaches Russia, where it becomes the **Siberian Plain**. Only some mountain ranges, such as the **Urals** (the traditional dividing line between Europe and Asia), interrupt the plain. This geographic feature made Russia open to invasion. For example, during the Middle Ages, Russia suffered attacks by the Teutonic knights as well as by Swedish and Polish armies from the west, while Mongols and Tartars invaded from the east.

The **Great Caucasus**, the highest mountains in the European part of Russia, stretch between the Black and Caspian seas. A series of mountain ranges, which run eastward from the Great Caucasus along the borders of Iran, Afghanistan, Pakistan, and India and then north along Tibet and China, separate Russia from its southern neighbors. Although these mountains are an obstacle, they have not prevented Russian attempts at expansion.

Bodies of Water

As you have read, the rivers of Russia have played an important role in its history and development. In the European part of Russia, the **Volga** (the longest river in Europe), **Dneiper, Dvina**, and **Don** rivers were essential for internal trade and commerce. The **Neva** River still serves as an important link between the U.S.S.R.'s industrial centers and the Baltic Sea. In the Asian part of Russia, the **Ob, Yen,** and

Lena rivers have recently become valuable as sources for hydroelectric industrial power.

Russia's seas and lakes also have great importance. The **Caspian Sea** (the largest inland body of water in the world) provides food and a passageway for commerce. The **Black Sea** also provides an important trade route. Russia's fresh-water lakes, such as **Lake Baikal** (the deepest lake in the world) and **Lake Ladoga** (the largest inland body of water in Europe), also provide important links in a generally land-locked country.

Vegetation Belt

The vegetation belts of Russia consist of three zones: the **Tundra**, the **Taiga**, and the **Steppes**. The northern rim, including the islands of the Arctic Circle, is known as the Tundra and covers about 10 percent of the country. It consists of a thick layer of permanently frozen ground, called **permafrost**. Its severe climate makes the Tundra uninhabitable.

The Taiga, which covers nearly half of Russia, is a great forest that provides wood and limited crops. These conditions have kept the population there small.

The Steppes is a very fertile region that has attracted both farmers and nomadic tribes. The southwestern region of the Steppes, called the **Ukraine**, is an important agricultural area known as the "Bread-basket of Russia." It has the most fertile land in the Soviet Union. Because it has no natural barriers, the Steppes has always served as an invasion route for armies from both the west and the east.

The territories between the Steppes and frontier mountains of the southeast are mainly uninhabited desert. The majority of people in Russia have always lived in European Russia, particularly in the Steppes region. Only recently have large numbers of people moved north and east, largely to exploit the natural resources in these areas. Russia's vast size has always presented great obstacles for travel, communication, and trade. However, it has also helped to save the Russians from invaders. For example, the invasions of both Napoleon and Hitler were defeated by Russia's vast size and harsh climate. The relative isolation of much of the population has resulted in the often stubborn and conservative nature of the Russian people.

Climate

The climate of Russia has played an important role in shaping the character of its people. The lack of warming ocean winds and the cool Arctic blasts make Russia's winters the coldest in the populated world. Even Russia's warmest areas have a climate similar to that of the Great Lakes or Canada. The harsh winters and short growing season have made the Russians both patient and able to endure great hardships.

QUESTIONS

Multiple Choice. Select the letter of the answer that correctly completes the statement.

1. The U.S.S.R. is physically
   A. twice the size of the United States
   B. more than two and a half times the size of the United States
   C. half the size of the United States
   D. larger than Europe, but less than the United States

2. Until the 18th century, Russia
   A. was landlocked and isolated by the Eurasian landmass
   B. only had ports on the Black Sea
   C. had Baltic ports with limited use
   D. had easy access to the Mediterranean via the Black Sea

3. The most fertile region of Russia that attracted both farmers and nomadic tribes is the
   A. taiga
   B. steppe
   C. tundra
   D. plain

4. Covered with permafrost and uninhabitable, Russia's northern rim is
   A. taiga
   B. tundra
   C. steppe
   D. plain

5. Which of the following rivers has not been important in the development of Russia?
   A. Dnieper
   B. Neva
   C. Sava
   D. Volga

ESSAY

The geography of Russia has been extremely important to its development.
   A. To what extent did Russia's diverse topography (mountains, plains, vegetation belts) influence its development? (5)
   B. How have Russia's rivers shaped its economic development? (5)
   C. How has Russia's diverse and often extreme climate affected the development of the Russian people? (5)

II. Economic Geography (Economic Development of the Soviet Union)

Agriculture

Until the 20th century, Russia's economy was almost completely agricultural. Southern Russia, in particular the **Ukraine** (southwest), has been the primary source of crops. Called the "Breadbasket of Russia," the Ukraine has been able to grow enough grain to supply the entire Russian nation with enough surplus to make it a major food-exporting nation of Europe. Southern Russia still produces wheat, rye, barley, cabbage, and potatoes. The Caucasus region supplies cotton, tea, and subtropical fruit such as oranges and grapes.

However, certain traditional geographic conditions are harmful to Russia's agricultural production. These include droughts that severely affect crop production and Russia's vast size, which makes the transportation of goods difficult.

In addition to these geographic factors, there are other conditions that have affected agricultural production in Russia. The policy of forced **Collectivization** (a Soviet government policy that made farmers work together on state land in accordance with Communist philosophy) under Stalin reduced agricultural output. State control of the Soviet economy (the government decides what is produced, who should produce it, and how much it should cost) has interfered with the farmers' free choice and has not always responded to the demands of the population. Also, in 1986 the nuclear power plant at **Chernobyl** near Kiev exploded. As a result, much of the soil in the Ukraine was contaminated and the produce was not safe for humans. For that reason, the Soviet Union has been dependent on outside sources, especially the United States, for much of its wheat.

Industrial Production Resources

Major Resources. Southwest Russia, particularly the Ukraine, is rich in coal, iron ore, manganese, natural gas, and other minerals, especially metallic ores and precious and semi-precious stones. It is also a major source of oil. Siberia supplies the U.S.S.R. with 90 percent of its coal and half of its natural gas. Siberia also has a huge supply of oil and immense deposits of iron and other minerals. However, the severe climatic conditions make these resources difficult to obtain. In addition, Siberia provides over 60 percent of all Soviet hydroelectric power. The rich forests of the Taiga provide the U.S.S.R. with timber and fur. The Pacific Ocean in the Far East yields one-third of the Soviet fish supply, while the Baltic and Black seas regions provide the balance.

Major Industries. The U.S.S.R. is the world's largest producer of coal. The most important centers of this production are in the Ukraine, Urals, and eastern Siberia. Petroleum is also an important part of the Soviet economy. The largest oil-producing area is the Volga-Ural region, which provides over 70 percent of the Soviet Union's oil, followed by Azerbaijan and western Siberia. Most natural gas is produced in the Volga-Ural region as well. The U.S.S.R. is also the world's largest producer of iron and manganese, the Ukraine serving as the major center of this industry. The production of chemicals, essential to Soviet technology, is also centered in the Volga-Ural region.

Guns vs. Butter Controversy. The gross national product (total value of goods and services produced in a country) of the U.S.S.R. has been severely strained by its large military expenditures. It is estimated that between 16 and 20 percent of the total Soviet GNP is spent on national defense. Recently, this has led to a "Guns vs. Butter" controversy, that is, a disagreement over whether more of the GNP should be spent on the military or on food production and consumer goods. For example, much of the iron produced in the U.S.S.R. is used to manufacture tanks rather than consumer goods. As a result, few consumer goods are available. It also lowers the general standard of living for most Soviet citizens.

Perestroika. In the 1980s, the Soviet Union faced an enormous economic crisis. It had become evident that the Communist system had failed. In an effort to revive the Soviet economy, **President Gorbachev** (who had taken power in 1985) began a series of economic reforms known as "**Perestroika**" ("Restructuring"). Beginning with an attempt to improve the quality of products, Gorbachev decentralized Soviet industrial and agricultural management (the **Enterprise Law of 1987**). Factory and farm managers were given greater control over determining both production and distribution of profits. Worker incentives, such as a pay increase for greater individual productivity, were adopted. The goal of this law is to make factories and farms independent, self-sufficient, and profitable so that they no longer need government subsidies (money to make up losses). The **Law of Cooperatives of 1987** allowed Soviet citizens to set up private businesses, free of state control, and keep the profits. The goal of this law is to encourage more production and better products or services by beginning a system of individual enterprise. The **Agricultural Reform Law** of 1988 broke up the state and collective farms, replacing them with a private leasing system. Individual farmers can now own and profit from their farms after paying off a long-term lease. The goal of this reform is to promote greater productivity through private ownership of land.

While the purpose of Perestroika has been to restructure and thereby improve the Soviet economy, it faces many problems. These include:

1. The Soviet people are used to a state-dependency system that provides security and undemanding work, not individual initiative and productivity.
2. Consumers expect immediate improvements (greater availability of goods and services), while Perestroika needs time in order to be effective.
3. Opposition by conservatives, especially government officials and party members who have benefited from the Communist system, have made it difficult to carry out the reforms.

QUESTIONS

Multiple Choice. Select the letter of the answer that correctly completes the statement.

1. Called the "Breadbasket of Russia," the greatest agricultural output has always come from
   A. Byelo-Russia
   B. Georgia
   C. Siberia
   D. Ukraine

2. The Soviet government's policy of forcing farmers to work on state farms is known as
   A. Collectivization
   B. Cooperatives
   C. Russification
   D. Perestroika

3. The Guns vs. Butter Controversy is a disagreement over
   A. the quality of arms and food production
   B. whether or not to nationalize heavy and light industries
   C. whether or not to decentralize industry
   D. the amount of the GNP spent on arms as opposed to consumer goods

4. In 1986, Mikhail Gorbachev began a series of reforms designed to "restructure" the Soviet economy known as
   A. Glastnost
   B. Perestroika
   C. N.E.P.
   D. Collectivization

5. Both the Enterprise Law of 1987 and the Law of Cooperatives are examples of
   A. capitalist incentives
   B. Marxist economic principles
   C. a command economy
   D. economic nationalism

ESSAY

Can Perestroika solve the U.S.S.R.'s economic problems?
A. What economic problems have the Communists faced since taking power in 1917? (5)
B. To what extent have Communist economic principles created problems in the Soviet economy? (5)
C. How have Gorbachev's reforms attempted to resolve these problems? Are they successful? (5)

III. Human and Cultural Geography

Demography

The population of the U.S.S.R. is approximately 280 million, slightly more than that of the United States. However, when one considers that Russia is more than twice the physical size of the United States, it is really underpopulated. In fact, Russia's population density is only 33 people per square mile, compared with 68 persons

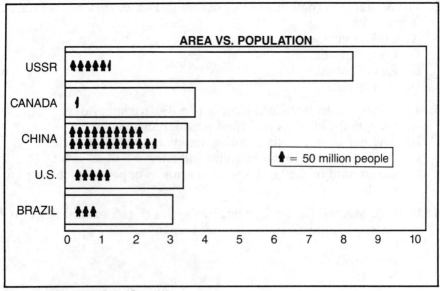

Source: *World Almanac and Book of Facts,* 1989

per square mile in the United States and over 288 people per square mile in China. Yet, most of the population is located in the Steppes region of European Russia. The small populations in Siberia, the Taiga, and the Asian part of the Soviet Union have only grown slightly in the present century. Most of this increase in largely due to industrialization in these areas.

Ethnic Groups and Languages

There are many ethnic groups in the Soviet Union. The largest of these, the **Great Russians**, **Ukrainians**, and **Byelo-Russians**, share a common cultural and religious heritage. They also have common linguistic roots in **Slavonic**, the ancient language of the Slavic Eastern Orthodox Churches. The **Georgians**, while distinct in cultural and linguistic origins, also share the Orthodox Christian faith with the Slavic majority. The **Armenians** come from what was the eastern Anatolian nation, which was forced into Russia by Turkish aggression between 1915 and 1923. The **Azerbaijanis**, **Turkmen**, **Uzbeks**, and **Kazakhs** are descended from the Turkish invaders of Russia in the Middle Ages. The **Tartars** are the descendants of the Mongols, who ruled Russia from 1237 to 1450. The peoples of the Baltic region—**Latvians**, **Estonians**, and **Lithuanians**—also share common linguistic, cultural, and/or religious experiences.

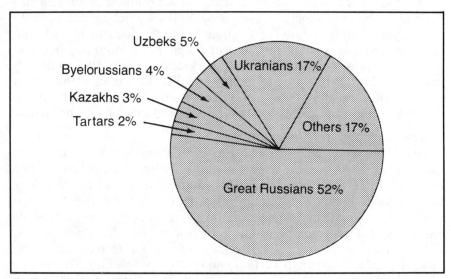

(Source: *The Information Please Almanac, 1989*)

The Orthodox Church

Christianity came to Eastern Europe and Russia from the Byzantine Empire. It played an essential role in the development of the Russian language, culture, art and architecture.

319

In 988, **Prince Vladimir** of Kiev adopted Eastern Orthodox Christianity and had the entire Russian nation baptized along with him. The **Russian Orthodox Church** dominated the culture of Russia until the 18th century. It continued to play a major role in the life of most Russians until the Communist Revolution in 1917. The Russian language is written in **Cyrillic** letters and was influenced greatly by the Slavonic language used by the Church. Russian folk music and polyphony (using four-part harmony) was incorporated in Church hymns. The building of churches became the chief objective of Russian architects, who developed a distinctive "Onion Dome" style. The painting of holy pictures, or **icons**, depicting Jesus, the Virgin Mary, and the saints, became Russia's major art form. Monasticism became very popular in Russia, and soon large monasteries were centers of spirituality and pilgrimages.

The Russian Orthodox Church is an independent institution with strong ties to the other Orthodox Churches throughout the world. It is headed by a bishop known as the **Patriarch of Moscow**. Unlike the Pope of the Roman Catholic Church, who is supreme in religious matters, the Patriarch is one of many bishops who consult together regularly to decide important church matters.

Historically, the Russian Orthodox Church was often pressured and controlled by the tsars. Since the Russian Revolution of 1917, it has been the subject of violent persecution by the Soviet government. In recent years, the hostility of Communist authorities to the Church has lessened and a small measure of religious freedom has been allowed. Despite the years of great persecution, many Russians remained faithful. While precise figures are difficult to obtain (the Soviet state is still officially atheist), the majority of Russians, Ukrainians, Byelo-Russians and Georgians have remained Orthodox Christians.

Other Religions in Russia

The Armenians, who are also Eastern Orthodox Christians, have their own church, which differs slightly in ritual and practice. The majority of Roman Catholics in Russia are Uniates, or Eastern Rite Catholics (Orthodox in ritual but officially under the authority of the Pope). Most Uniates are located in the Ukraine. Otherwise, Lithuania has the only large Roman Catholic population. The other Baltic states, Estonia and Latvia, are primarily Lutheran. The Azerbaijanis, Turkmen, Uzbeks, Kazakhs, Tartars, and other peoples of Turkish or Mongol origin are mainly Muslims. Finally, there is a sizable minority of Jews living in the U.S.S.R.

Cultural Achievements

Russia's culture had two great influences—Byzantium and Western Europe. From the 10th to the 17th centuries, the Byzantine Empire, and consequently the Orthodox Church, were the main influences on the development of Russian art, architecture, music, and literature. Religion played the key role in the early development of these forms. Most art was religious, usually in the form of icons, while Russian architects distinguished themselves building churches. (See "The Orthodox Church" in Section III.) Russian composers were usually monks who devoted themselves to writing church hymns, often based on traditional folk music. The ban on the use of musical instruments by the Orthodox Church encouraged the development of á cappella (without instrumental accompaniment) choirs. Literature, written in Slavonic, the language of the Church, consisted for the most part of **chronicles** (narratives that combined history and legend) and **hagiography** (the lives of saints). As with music, literature was also almost exclusively written by monks.

At the beginning of the 17th century, **Tsar Peter the Great** carried out a policy of Westernization that drastically changed the direction of Russian culture. Combining traditional Russian themes while imitating Western European styles, uniquely Russian schools of art, architecture, music, and literature developed. Artists painted portraits and landscape series as well as icons, while architects created lavish palaces and churches that combined the best of Western European and Russian styles. It was, however, in music and literature that the Russians most distinguished themselves. Russia's best known composers in the Tsarist period were **Aleksandr Borodin** (1833–1887), **Modest Moussorgskii** (1839–1881), **Piotr Illich Tchaikovskii** (1840–1893), and **Nikolai Rimskii-Korsakov** (1844–1908). These musical giants composed operas, choral works, symphonies, concertos, and chamber music that featured traditional Russian melodies. This tradition was continued in the Soviet period by composers such as **Sergei Prokofiev** (1891–1953), **Dimitrii Shostakovich** (1906–1975), and **Aram Kachaturian** (1903–1978). Certain composers, such as **Sergei Rachmaninov** (1873–1943) and **Igor Stravinskii** (1882–1971), forced into exile by the Russian Revolution in 1917, continued to create and win acclaim for their work.

Russia's literary giants also brought a unique perspective to their work. These include: **Aleksandr Pushkin** (1799–1837), best known for his poetry and short stories; **Nikolai Gogol** (1809–1852), noted for his short stories and novel *Dead Souls* (which criticized serfdom); **Ivan Turgenev** (1818–1883), famous for his novels, particularly *Fathers and Sons*; **Theodor Dostoievskii** (1821–1881), whose psychological novels *Crime and Punishment* and *The Brothers Karamazov* won him worldwide acclaim; **Count Lev Tolstoy** (1828–1910), author of the masterpiece novels *Anna Karenina* and *War and Peace*; and **Anton Chekhov** (1860–1904), whose plays (*The Cherry Orchard, The Seagull, The Three Sisters*) have become world theatre classics. In the Soviet period, most distinguished writers have been dissidents, often punished for their work. One of the most famous of these, **Boris Pasternak** (1890–1960), was forced by the government to reject the Nobel Prize in Literature for his novel *Doctor Zhivago*. Another is **Aleksandr Solzhenitsyn** (1918–), whose stories ("One Day in the Life of Ivan Denisovich"), novels (*Cancer Ward*), and history of the Soviet concentration camps (*The Gulag Archipelago*) brought him arrest, prison, and exile.

QUESTIONS

Multiple Choice. Select the letter of the answer that correctly completes the statement.

1. Most of the Soviet Union's population lives
    A. in Central Asia
    B. in European Russia
    C. in Siberia
    D. in the Far East

2. The largest ethnic group in the U.S.S.R. is
    A. the Kazakhs
    B. the Georgians
    C. the Slavs
    D. the Armenians

3. In 988, Russia adopted
    A. Eastern Orthodox Christianity and Medieval Latin culture
    B. Roman Catholicism and Medieval Latin culture
    C. Eastern Orthodox Christianity and Byzantine culture
    D. Roman Catholicism and Byzantine culture

4. The spiritual leader of the Russian Church is
    A. the Patriarch of Constantinople
    B. the Pope of Rome
    C. the Metropolitan of Kiev
    D. The Patriarch of Moscow

5. Russia's most notable cultural achievements were in
    A. art and architecture
    B. literature and art
    C. music and art
    D. literature and music

6. Match the correct author and work.
    A. Nikolai Gogol, *War and Peace.*
    B. Count Lev Tolstoy, *Dead Souls.*
    C. Theodor Dostoievskii, *The Brothers Karamazov.*
    D. Aleksandr Solzhenitsyn, *Fathers and Sons.*

7. Russia's architecture is characterized by the
   A. Baroque style
   B. Basilica style
   C. Onion Dome style
   D. Classical style

ESSAY

Religion played a major role in the development of Russia.
A. Discuss the role of religion in the creation of the Russian language, literature, art and architecture. (5)
B. To what extent did religion hold various ethnic groups and nationalities together in the Russian Empire? In what ways did it divide? (5)
C. In what ways did the Church reinforce the social order through its teachings, institutions and administration? (5)

IV. History and Political Geography (Historical Setting of Russia)

Early Rus' (862–879)

The earliest settlers in Russia were **Slavic tribes** who migrated there between 600 and 700. Depending on trade (furs, beeswax, and honey) rather than agriculture, their settlements grew from towns into prosperous cities. These cities depended upon the Vikings (whom the Slavs called Varangians) to protect the trade routes. The **Varangians** soon became a ruling class, intermarrying with the Slavs, founding both a royal dynasty known as the **House of Rurik** and a new state called Rus'.

The Kievian State (879–1240)

By 879, the center of trade (and therefore power) in the state of Rus' had become the city of **Kiev** in the Ukraine. Kiev's location in the most fertile region of Rus', with excellent river transportation to encourage trade, made it wealthy and powerful. The Kievian princes led a loose federation of Russian cities for mutual protection and the expansion of trade. Kiev's prosperity and prominence brought it into a close relationship with the **Byzantine Empire**. In 988, the Kievian **Prince Vladimir** was converted to **Orthodox Christianity**, bringing both Kiev and all Rus' with him. With the adoption of Byzantine religion came new political and social ideas. New artistic and cultural forms were also introduced (See "The Orthodox Church" in Section III). In addition, this brought Rus' into the political orbit of Byzantium and its Eastern European allies. (See Section IV of Eastern Europe.)

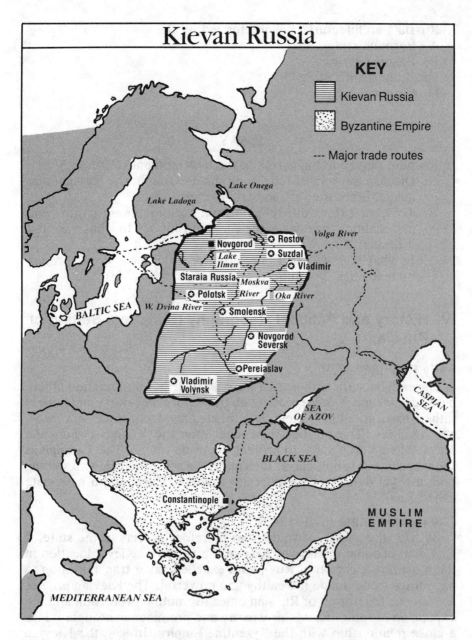

Kievan Russia

KEY

Kievan Russia

Byzantine Empire

--- Major trade routes

Lake Onega

Lake Ladoga

Volga River

■ Novgorod   ⊙ Rostov

Lake Ilmen   ⊙ Suzdal

⊙ Vladimir

Staraia Russia   *Moskva River*

⊙ Polotsk   *Oka River*

BALTIC SEA   *W. Dvina River*

⊙ Smolensk

⊙ Novgorod Seversk

⊙ Pereiaslav

⊙ Vladimir Volynsk

CASPIAN SEA

SEA OF AZOV

BLACK SEA

Constantinople ■

MUSLIM EMPIRE

MEDITERRANEAN SEA

The Mongol Period (1237–1450)

In 1237, Kievian Russia was invaded by Mongol armies under the leadership of **Batu Khan**, a grandson of Genghis Khan. (See "The Mongols in the China" section.) Called **Tartars** by the Russians, these nomadic warriors on horseback conquered Russia and ruled it for more than 200 years. The **Khanate of the Golden Horde**, as the Mongol princes who ruled Russia were called, exercised control from their capital city of **Sarai**, located in the Steppes. Mongol rule was indirect and usually consisted of no more than collecting tribute from the local inhabitants. Frequently, local Russian princes served as representatives for the Mongol government and ruled their principalities with little, if any, interference. Only **Novgorod**, city of the legendary Rurik, was able to repulse the Mongols (as well as the Swedes and Germanic Crusaders who attacked from 1240 to 1242) and remain free of Mongol rule. Mongol domination of Russia did not last as the armies of Tamerlane and uprisings by Russian princes soon overextended Mongol military forces. By 1395, every major Mongol city, including Sarai, had been destroyed. Between 1450 and 1480, the last remains of Mongol rule were wiped out by the princes of **Moscow**.

The Rise of Moscow (1450–1685)

Moscow's position as the headquarters of the Russian Orthodox Church after the fall of Kiev greatly contributed to its rise to prominence. The support of the Patriarch enhanced Moscow's image as the leading city of Russia. When the Byzantine Empire fell to the Ottoman Turks in 1453, **Prince Ivan III** declared Moscow to be the "Third Rome," or the center of the Eastern Orthodox Church (Constantinople took the title of "Second Rome" after the fall of the original capital of the Roman Empire was overrun by Germanic tribes in 476). (See "Roman Empire" in the Western European section.) In 1462, Ivan III married **Sophia Paleologos**, niece of the last Byzantine emperor, and adopted her family's symbol (the double-headed eagle), declaring himself "**Tsar**" or "Caesar" (emperor) of all the Russias. From Ivan III's reign (1462–1505) until the fall of the monarchy in 1917, Russia's tsars considered themselves the defenders of the Orthodox Church.

Under **Tsar Ivan IV** (1533–1584), often referred to as "the Terrible," Russia's government became centralized. Often using brutal and ruthless force, Ivan ended the independent authority of local princes and **boyars** (nobles), making the aristocracy subservient to an autocratic central monarchy. He also created a new "service nobility" that was loyal only to the tsar. Ivan had extended Moscow's control over most of European Russia by the year of his death.

Ivan's weak successor, **Theodor**, died without an heir in 1598, ending the House of Rurik and beginning a period of anarchy known as the "Time of Troubles." This ended in 1613 with the selection by the **Zemskii Sobor** (Council of Nobles) of a new tsar, **Mikhail Romanov**, and the establishment of a new dynasty. Under the early **Romanovs**, the power of the monarchy grew even stronger, while Russia's borders (particularly in the Ukraine) were expanded.

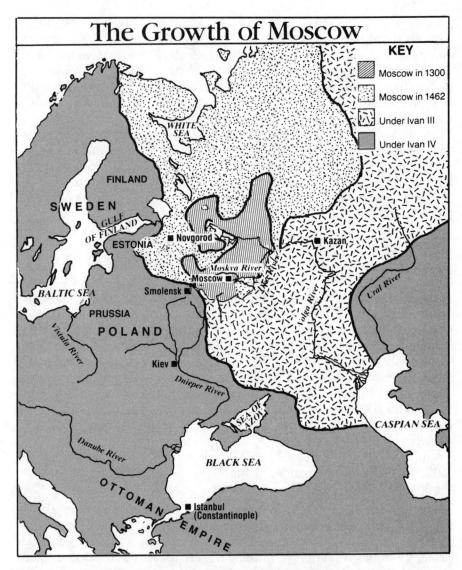

The Growth of Moscow

KEY

- Moscow in 1300
- Moscow in 1462
- Under Ivan III
- Under Ivan IV

WHITE SEA

FINLAND

SWEDEN

GULF OF FINLAND

ESTONIA

■ Novgorod

■ Kazan

Moskva River

Moscow ■

Smolensk ■

BALTIC SEA

PRUSSIA

POLAND

Vistula River

Volga River

Ural River

Kiev ■

Dnieper River

Danube River

SEA OF AZOV

CASPIAN SEA

BLACK SEA

OTTOMAN EMPIRE

■ Istanbul (Constantinople)

Peter the Great and Westernization (1685–1725)

Under Piotr or **Peter I**, usually referred to as "the Great," Russia underwent important changes. Following a policy of Westernization in order to modernize his nation, Peter forced the nobility and upper classes to imitate their counterparts in Western Europe socially and culturally. A Western European-style bourgeoisie, or urban middle class was also created. An enormous civil service and government bureaucracy was established that drew from both the upper and middle classes. Peter encouraged the development of new industries and the importation of Westerners to train Russians. A new capital city,

St. Petersburg, was built on the Baltic. Known as the "Window to the West," St. Petersburg was modeled after Western European cities. The Patriarchate was abolished and replaced with the **Synod** (Council) **of Bishops** under the control of a **Procurator** (one of the tsar's ministers). The education system, once administered by the Church, was also taken over by the state. The army was modernized, the latest weapons technology imported, and a navy was created. Under Peter, Russia expanded westward to the Baltic and southeast to the Black Sea. For the first time in history, the nation of Russia was no longer landlocked, although both water routes were limited. While most of the population, who were peasants, remained unaffected by the so-called "**Petrine Reforms**," Russia was transformed into a modern world power.

Expansion and Modernization Under the Tsars (1725–1905)

Under the tsars and tsaritsas who succeeded Peter I, Russia continued to expand its empire and its involvement with Western Europe. During the reign of Ekaterina or **Catherine II** (1762–1796), usually referred to as "the Great," Russia regained the parts of the Ukraine and Byelo-Russia lost under the last Rurik tsars, as well as Lithuania. In the southeast, the last of the Tartar tribes were defeated, thus gaining the entire Crimea and much of the northern coast of the Black Sea at the expense of the Ottoman Turks. This began a traditional policy that was pursued by the Soviet government as well as the later tsars—to gain Constantinople (modern-day Istanbul) and the straits that connect the Black Sea with the Aegean and the Mediterranean (the Dardanelles) in order to have access to major trade routes. In addition, much of Siberia was explored and settled by Russia.

Tsar Aleksandr or **Alexander I** (1801–1825) was credited as the monarch who defeated Napoleon. This victory was due to the "**scorched earth**" policy (retreating and burning anything that could not be taken rather than leaving it for the enemy) that the Russians adopted in response to Napoleon's invasion. A lack of supplies and the severe Russian winter devastated the French army, and thousands died during the chaotic retreat. (See the "Napoleonic Wars" in the Western Europe section.) At the Congress of Vienna, Russia acquired most of Poland. Alexander also gained Finland from Sweden in 1809.

Under the strongly autocratic rule of Nikolai or **Nicholas I** (1825–1855), Russia was unsuccessful in further expansion. Greatly shaken by the **Decembrist Revolt** of 1825 (in which officers favoring democratic reforms tried to overthrow Nicholas), the tsar fought any movement for change. Fearing that reform would undermine his authority, Nicholas followed repressive policies at home and abroad (he earned the title "Policeman of Europe"). Yet, Russia's defeat in the **Crimean War** (1854–1856) revealed the need for both reform and modernization.

327

Russian Expansion in Europe

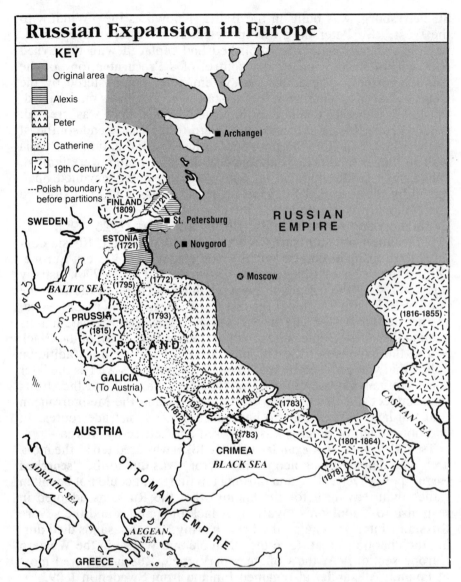

KEY

- Original area
- Alexis
- Peter
- Catherine
- 19th Century

---Polish boundary
before partitions

FINLAND
(1809)

SWEDEN

ESTONIA
(1721)

St. Petersburg

Novgorod

Archangel

**RUSSIAN
EMPIRE**

Moscow

BALTIC SEA (1795) (1772)

PRUSSIA (1793)

(1815)

P O L A N D

(1816-1855)

GALICIA
(To Austria)

(1792) (1783) (1783)

(1812)

AUSTRIA

(1783)

(1801-1864)

CRIMEA
BLACK SEA

CASPIAN SEA

(1878)

ADRIATIC SEA

OTTOMAN EMPIRE

AEGEAN
SEA

GREECE

Alexander II (1855–1881), the son of Nicholas I, made many of the necessary changes that his father would not. Known as the "Tsar Liberator," Alexander ended the institution of serfdom (peasants were bound to the land they farmed and therefore practically enslaved to the landowner), which held back the expansion of Russian agriculture and promoted many abuses and social evils. Industrialization was also started in order to make Russia competitive with other European nations. Finally, Alexander instituted reforms in government, education, and the military that ended many abuses and cruelties and modernized the Russian system. Despite the many changes made by Alexander II, new problems were created by the reforms themselves.

1. The liberation of the serfs created many small independent farmers who could not pay off their debts. This resulted in mass foreclosures and enormous migrations of unskilled labor to the cities.

2. The abundance of unskilled labor gave factory owners the opportunity to exploit (take advantage of) the workers, or **proletariat**.

3. Widespread exploitation of workers resulted in poverty, slums, and unsafe working conditions in Russian cities and industrial centers.

4. The exploited workers became strong supporters of revolutionary ideas and parties, particularly the Socialists, Communists, and Anarchists. The assassination of Alexander II in 1881 resulted in the end of reform and a renewal of repression.

Alexander III (1881–1894) reacted to his father's murder by enforcing strict control over his subjects. Instituting a policy of "**Russification**" (forcing Russian language, culture, and religion on all peoples in the Russian Empire), Alexander created resentment and revolutionary feelings.

The Russian Revolution (1905–1917)

The reign of **Nicholas II** (1894–1917) saw Russia make its greatest strides toward reform, modernization, and, ironically, revolution. From 1894 to 1905, Nicholas followed his father's (Alexander III) policies in opposing reform. Despite great gains made in the industrialization program under the direction of **Finance Minister Sergei Witte**, the conditions in urban slums and factories were still terrible. After the embarrassing defeat in the **Russo-Japanese War** (1904–1905) and the massacre of peaceful demonstrators in St. Petersburg in January of 1905, known as "**Bloody Sunday**," uprisings broke out in every major Russian city and industrial center. Known as the "**1905 Revolution**," this series of revolts frightened the government into making reforms, most notably the creation of a **Duma**, or parliament. While Russia technically became a constitutional democracy, the Duma was little more than an advisory body that could be dissolved by the tsar at will.

In 1906, the monarchy instituted its own reforms in order to restore public confidence. Under the guidance of **Prime Minister Piotr Stolypin**, a program of industrial expansion, foreign investment, and land reform (which made millions of peasants private landowners) was instituted. The **Stolypin Reforms** helped to overcome revolutionary feelings and restored a strong base of support for the monarchy, especially in the countryside.

In 1914, Russia entered World War I (1914–1918), a conflict that it was neither militarily nor economically prepared to fight. For three years the Russians suffered defeats by the technologically superior

German forces. (See "World War I" in the Western Europe section.) Enormous casualties and government inefficiency led to widespread dissatisfaction with the conduct of the war. Scandal within the royal family also hurt the prestige of the monarchy. **Tsaritsa Alexandra** had fallen under the influence of a fraudulent "holy man," Grigory Efimovich **Rasputin**, who was able to control the **Tsarevich** (Prince) **Alexis'** hemophilia (probably through hypnosis).

While the Tsar was away at the front running the war, Rasputin exercised a destructive domination over the German-born tsaritsa, who was already suspected by many as a spy. His interference produced corruption and even greater inefficiency. By February of 1917, food shortages and an outbreak of strikes and riots led to the collapse of the Tsar's authority in St. Petersburg and other cities. Nicholas II was forced to abdicate, and a provisional (temporary) democratic government was formed by the Duma, headed first by **Prince Georgii L'vov** and later by **Aleksandr Kerenskii**.

The **Provisional Government** attempted to make Russia a democracy by instituting political reforms. By October of 1917, however, the Provisional Government had been overthrown by force and the **Bolshevik** (Communist) **Party** had taken power. There were a number of reasons for this:

1. Kerenskii's decision to continue fighting the war was very unpopular.

2. Russia did not have a democratic tradition. Most of the Provisional Government's goals were not understood and irrelevant to the majority of the population.

3. The war continued to create shortages and strain the economy. Conditions in the cities did not improve and unrest began again.

4. The Bolsheviks capitalized on the unpopularity of the war. They undermined support for the Provisional Government through antiwar propaganda.

5. The monarchy had held the Russian Empire together. With the traditional symbol of unity (the tsar) gone, the Provisional Government could provide no equivalent institution.

6. Kerenskii was experimenting with democracy in a nation with no democratic heritage during a war, a time when most democracies temporarily suspend civil liberties.

7. The war wasted the best troops the Provisional Government had. The regiments that remained to protect the Provisional Government were poorly trained and unreliable.

8. The Bolshevik leader **Lenin** promised "bread, peace, and land" as well as a "worker's state," promises that were better understood than the democratic principles put forth by the Provisional Government.

9. The Bolsheviks influenced the **soviets,** or local committees, that represented workers, soldiers, and farmers. Closely linked throughout Russia, they became influential, especially in the cities.

Lenin (1917–1924)

Born Vladimir Illich Ulianiov, **Lenin** founded the **Bolshevik,** or "Majority," Party at a 1903 Socialist Party Conference in London. While the Bolsheviks were never a majority, they were "professional revolutionaries" who ruthlessly pursued revolution, using any means necessary in order to succeed. The other Russian Socialists, the **Men-**

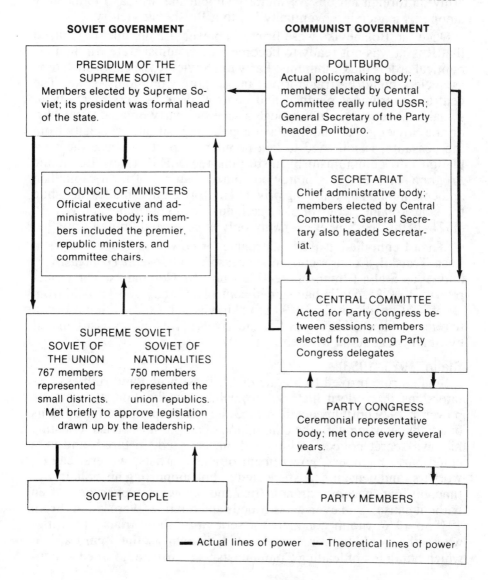

sheviks, or "Minority," favored gradual, peaceful change, without the violence and terror advocated by the Bolsheviks.

When the Bolsheviks seized power in 1917, Lenin immediately made peace with Germany and took Russia out of the war. Giving away sizable parts of Russia in a peace treaty (Treaty of **Brest-Litovsk**) and having no widespread support, the Bolsheviks soon faced strong opposition throughout Russia. A civil war followed (1918–1921) in which the Bolsheviks, or "**Reds**," fought the combined forces of anti-Communist groups, or the "**Whites.**" The dependence of the White army on foreign nations for military supplies as well as the disunity among its leadership eventually led to a Bolshevik victory.

Once the Bolsheviks were firmly in power, Lenin quickly realized that Russia was not ready to become a Communist state. In the new political order, the Communist Party ran Soviet Russia until such time as society could be transformed into a pure Communist state. The central government planned and controlled all aspects of political, social, and economic life through a series of party organs. (See chart on the Soviet government.) Facing great opposition, especially from the peasants, Lenin tried to win popular support and ease the population into communism by instituting the **N.E.P.** (New Economic Program) in 1921. This policy combined features of both capitalism and communism by allowing private enterprise on a small scale while the state retained control of large industries. Yet, under the N.E.P. (1921–1928), the Soviet economy only experienced limited growth.

When Lenin died in 1924, a struggle for power developed between **Leon Trotskii**, Lenin's chosen successor, and Joseph Dzhugashvili, known as **Stalin** ("man of steel"), who was Communist Party Secretary. By 1925, Stalin had gained control and removed Trotskii from all official positions. In 1929, Trotskii was deported as Stalin began to remove all possible opposition and rivals (Trotskii was assassinated by Stalin's agents in Mexico in 1937).

Stalin (1925–1953)

Stalin's rule proved to be one of the most brutal and ruthless dictatorships in modern history. From his consolidation of complete power in 1929 until his death in 1953, he was responsible for millions of deaths, starting with the elimination of all possible rivals. Creating his own secret police, Stalin spied on, arrested, tortured, and executed party members, government officials, artists, writers, clergy, workers, and peasants he suspected of not supporting his policies. In time, his fears became paranoia (fear and suspicion of everyone, often without cause), and even close friends and relatives were killed. From 1935 to 1936, Stalin conducted a series of "show trials" (hearings where the verdicts were pre-decided) known as the "**purges**," in which hundreds of leading Communists were arrested, forced to confess to crimes they had never committed, and executed.

In 1928, dissatisfied with the slow growth rate of Soviet industry, Stalin abandoned Lenin's N.E.P. in favor of centralized economic planning. Goals for agriculture and industry (often unrealistically high), as well as the means for achieving them, were laid out in a series of **Five Year Plans**. These were designed to make the U.S.S.R. "catch up" with the other industrialized nations by emphasizing the industrial development of steel, iron, coal, and oil. The population was expected to sacrifice and do without consumer goods until the Soviet Union could reach the level of industrial development attained by capitalist nations. Opposition to these plans was quickly and brutally put down. In order to pay for the importation of the technology needed to institute the Five Year Plans, farms were collectivized. (See "Economic Policy" in the Economic Geography Section of this unit.)

To end the opposition of peasants to collectivization, Stalin began a series of **genocides**, or mass killings (1932–1937), claiming that he was eliminating the **kulaks** (wealthy peasants who supposedly exploited their neighbors). In fact, few of the 14.5 million peasants who died by execution, perished in Siberian labor camps, or starved in Stalin's human-made famine in the Ukraine (1932–1933) were kulaks. While outright opposition was finally crushed by these genocides, the peasants did not fully cooperate, and the collectivization program failed to achieve its goal. When World War II interrupted the Third Five Year Plan in 1941, only heavy industry had made any progress. The loss of life and human suffering that this modest gain had cost was enormous. It is no wonder that many, especially the Ukrainians, first saw the invading German armies as liberators.

When Nazi Germany invaded the Soviet Union in 1941, the population was once again forced to resort to the "scorched earth" policy used so effectively against Napoleon. (See "Expansion Under the Tsars" in this section.) By 1944, overextension of supply lines, the harsh Russian climate, and stiff military resistance by the Russians, despite heavy losses, had worn down the German forces. By 1945, the Red army had pushed the Nazis out of Russia and Eastern Europe into Germany and occupied the eastern portion of that nation. Despite an agreement made with the Allies earlier that year (the **Yalta Conference**) that the Soviet Union would occupy Eastern Europe only temporarily, Soviet forces remained. Instead of holding free elections for self-determination in each Eastern European nation, Stalin placed "puppet" Communist governments throughout Eastern Europe. These countries became "**satellites**," controlled by the Soviet government. By Stalin's death in 1953, Eastern and Western Europe were divided by ideological differences and mutual fear. This last legacy of Stalin became known as the "Iron Curtain."

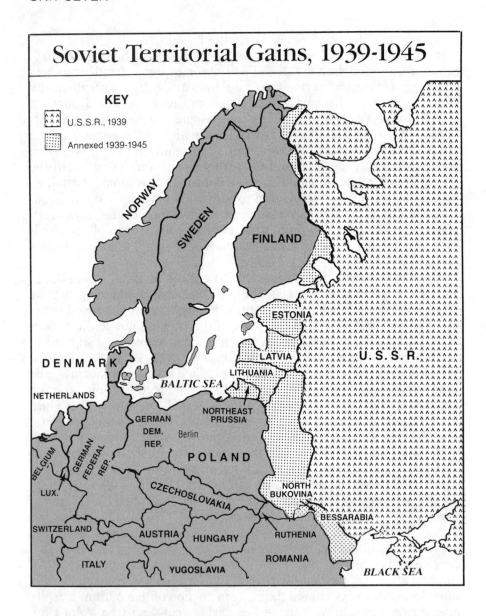

Soviet Territorial Gains, 1939-1945

KEY

U.S.S.R., 1939

Annexed 1939-1945

NORWAY

SWEDEN

FINLAND

DENMARK

ESTONIA

LATVIA

LITHUANIA

U.S.S.R.

NETHERLANDS

BALTIC SEA

BELGIUM

GERMAN
DEM.
REP.

Berlin

NORTHEAST
PRUSSIA

GERMAN
FEDERAL
REP.

LUX.

P O L A N D

CZECHOSLOVAKIA

NORTH
BUKOVINA

SWITZERLAND

AUSTRIA

HUNGARY

RUTHENIA

BESSARABIA

ITALY

YUGOSLAVIA

ROMANIA

BLACK SEA

The Cold War (1953–1990)

As a result of the division of Europe, a Cold War (political, economic, and diplomatic conflict without open military conflict) developed. In 1949, the countries of Western Europe and the United States formed a military alliance, **NATO** (North Atlantic Treaty Organization), in response to Stalin's takeover of Eastern Europe and his unsuccessful attempts to install Communist governments in Greece, Turkey and Iran. The Allied policy, called "**containment**"

The Division of Europe

KEY

NATO Countries
Other NATO members include:
Canada, Iceland, and the
United States

Warsaw Pact
Countries

0   200   400

(to limit the spread of communism to areas where it already existed),
was answered by the U.S.S.R. with the creation of the **Warsaw Pact**,
an alliance of the Soviet Union and the Eastern Bloc or satellite countries. The military buildup that resulted from the Cold War put an
even greater strain on the Soviet economy, which was still suffering
from the devastation of the war. The U.S.S.R.'s new superpower
status was expensive to maintain, and Soviet consumers bore the
burden.

With the death of Stalin, there was a period of readjustment from
the fear and suffering the Soviet dictator's rule had brought. This

"**Great Thaw**" from Stalinism (1953–1958) allowed some freedom of political and cultural expression (mostly denouncing Stalin). However, this was short-lived. When **Nikita Khrushchev** (1958–1964) took power as First Secretary and Premier, these freedoms ended. Khrushchev attempted to increase industrial and agricultural production through a series of reforms, particularly productivity incentives and an expansion of agricultural development into thinly populated areas ("**Virgin Lands**" Program). Khrushchev's policies failed due to the inefficiency of the bureaucratic Soviet system, the lack of incentives to produce in the factories and on the collective farms, inefficiency of central planning, and the severe forces of nature in Russia. Many conservatives from the Stalinist period resented Khrushchev. They used his setback in the Cuban Missile Crisis and the failures of his economic reforms to oust him from power in 1964.

Khrushchev was succeeded by **Leonid Brezhnev** (1964–1982), who, unlike Stalin or Khrushchev, did not have complete power and was answerable to top party officials. Despite the great need for change that had prompted Khrushchev's programs, Brezhnev feared that reform would undermine the authority of the Communist Party. The policy of concentrating on heavy industry was therefore continued, except for one unsuccessful experiment to expand consumer goods production in the Ninth Five Year Plan (1971–1975). By 1972, the antagonism between the Soviet Union and Communist China and the fear produced by improved relations between China and the United States forced Brezhnev to adopt a policy of **Detente** ("Understanding") with the United States and Western Europe. This "first thaw" in the Cold War also resulted in the first of two SALT (Strategic Arms Limitation Talks) Agreements, in which both NATO and the Warsaw Pact nations agreed to restrict the development of antiballistic missile systems. These were followed by START (Strategic Arms Reduction Talks) in the Gorbachev era. Despite Detente, Brezhnev continued to suppress dissent and oppose any domestic reform.

Gorbachev (1985–)

After the brief period of rule by **Yurii Andropov** (1982–1984) and **Konstantin Chernenko** (1984–1985), **Mikhail Gorbachev** became General Secretary of the Communist Party. He quickly consolidated his power by removing the older, more conservative members of the U.S.S.R.'s ruling **Politboro** (chief political committee of the Communist Party) and replacing them with younger reformers like himself. The stagnation of the Soviet economy had reached a crisis, and Gorbachev proposed sweeping reforms. (See "Perestroika" in Economic Geography section of this unit.) Gorbachev also adopted a policy called **Glasnost** ("Openness"), which was aimed at destroying the secrecy and suspicion of Soviet life. Public criticism and suggestions

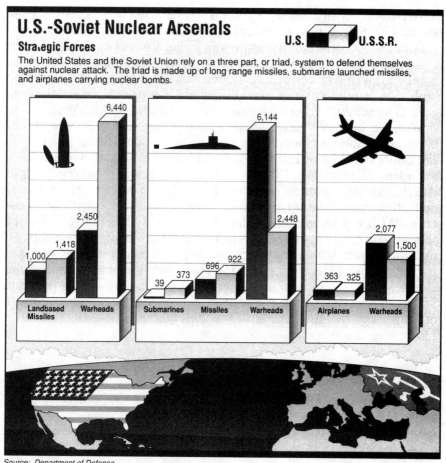

U.S.-Soviet Nuclear Arsenals
Strategic Forces

U.S. ▮▯ U.S.S.R.

The United States and the Soviet Union rely on a three part, or triad, system to defend themselves against nuclear attack. The triad is made up of long range missiles, submarine launched missiles, and airplanes carrying nuclear bombs.

Source: Department of Defense

about national problems were encouraged as well as opposing ideas that had previously been censored. Literature, films, music, and art that had been banned were now reinstated as cultural life was given new freedoms. As the Russian Orthodox Church celebrated his millennium (1,000-year anniversary), Gorbachev lifted many of the restrictions on Orthodox Christianity and the practice of religion in general.

From 1988 to 1990, Gorbachev reorganized the entire Soviet political system. Communist Party control over the government was reduced, a popularly elected assembly (the **Congress of People's Deputies**) was established, a structure for a multi-party system, and a presidency with control over domestic and foreign affairs was created. In March of 1989, the Soviet Union held its first elections in which many non-Communist Party candidates were elected. When the Congress first met in June, it elected a smaller body (the **Supreme**

337

Soviet) to deal with daily legislation. It also elected Mikhail Gorbachev as the U.S.S.R.'s first president.

Gorbachev also greatly improved relations between the Soviet Union and the West. In 1987, the U.S.S.R. and the United States agreed to an INF (Intermediate Range Nuclear Forces) treaty in which both sides would destroy two classes of nuclear weapons. Many regard Gorbachev's administration as the end of the Cold War.

With Gorbachev's new policies, many of the U.S.S.R.'s republics are now demanding independence. The most outstanding example is the Baltic republic of Lithuania, which voted to secede and establish an independent nation. Ethnic rivalries have brought the republics of Azerbaijan and Armenia into bloody conflict. Similarly, the Ukraine and other republics are now considering a move toward independence. With a growing nationalist movement within the Republic of Russia, led by its president **Boris Yeltsin**, there is a great possibility that the Soviet Union may separate into sovereign nations that are part of a loose federation. With the independence of Eastern Europe (see the following section on Eastern Europe) and growing impatience within the Soviet Union for change, Gorbachev faces even greater challenges in the last decade of the 20th century.

QUESTIONS

Multiple Choice. Select the letter of the answer that correctly completes the statement.

1. The first ruling group in Russia was the
    A. Varangians
    B. Georgians
    C. Mongols
    D. Kazakhs

2. The period of Mongol domination
    A. resulted in the mass conversion of the Russians to Islam
    B. divided the nation into Christian and Muslim parts
    C. gave local princes greater autonomy
    D. restored the powers of the Kievian princes

3. The Petrine Reforms
    A. gave Russia its first democratic government
    B. restored the power of the Autocracy
    C. transformed Russia into a modern world power
    D. began a period of Russian isolation from the rest of the world

4. A traditional problem both Imperial Russia and the U.S.S.R. have faced in the expansion of trade is
   A. limited ports and lack of access to the Mediterranean
   B. aggressive attacks from Poland
   C. Chinese imperialism in the East
   D. lack of navigable rivers

5. The liberation of the serfs
   A. created a new middle class
   B. marked the beginning of democracy in Russia
   C. resulted in the mass migrations of impoverished farmers to the cities
   D. increased the number of productive farms in Russia

6. Which event did NOT lead to the Russian Revolution of 1917?
   A. The "Bloody Sunday" massacre
   B. The Russo-Japanese War
   C. Participation in the First World War
   D. The creation of the Duma

7. One reason for the overthrow of the Provisional Government was that it
   A. did not appeal to the peasants
   B. had no army
   C. continued an unpopular war
   D. did not guarantee civil rights

8. Lenin's New Economic Program (N.E.P.) attempted to revive the Russian economy by
   A. combining features of capitalism with communism
   B. re-creating a capitalist system in Russia
   C. transforming Russia's economy into a free market system
   D. strictly applying Marxist economic principles

9. Starting with Brezhnev, the U.S.S.R. followed a policy of Detente or
   A. Understanding with the West
   B. Openness with the West
   C. Standing Firm to the West
   D. Suspicion of the West

10. Gorbachev's policy of Glasnost is aimed at creating greater
    A. job opportunities and work incentives
    B. efficiency, especially in industry
    C. openness with an end to the secrecy and suspicion in Soviet society
    D. patriotism and faith in Communism

ESSAY

Throughout Russian history, determined individual rulers have significantly changed their nation's course.
A. Choose three Russian rulers:
   1. Prince Vladimir of Kiev
   2. Tsar Ivan IV ("the Terrible")
   3. Tsar Peter I ("the Great")
   4. Tsar Alexander II ("the Tsar Liberator")
   5. Vladimir Illich Ulianov (Lenin)
   6. Joseph Dzhugashlivi (Stalin)
   7. Leonid Brezhnev
   8. Mikhail Gorbachev
B. Describe each ruler's most important policies and goals. Evaluate the success of each (10)
C. Discuss how each individual significantly altered the course of Russian history. (5)

I. Physical Geography (The Physical Setting of Eastern Europe)

Overview

Eastern Europe consists of the nations located between Western Europe and Russia. Common religious, ethnic, and/or cultural ties distinguish the Eastern European countries. Despite a diverse mixture of peoples and influences, the Eastern European nations of Albania, Bulgaria, Czechoslovakia, Hungary, Poland, Romania, and Yugoslavia have similar historical roots and have had similar experiences. Containing approximately 126 million people, with a wide range of languages and religions, these nations seem to have been constantly brought together by historical events.

Topography

Its topography and location have made Eastern Europe an invasion route throughout history. This has resulted in the mixing of many peoples, languages, and cultures. Mountains have played the most influential role in the development of Eastern Europe's nations. They have acted as barriers and trade routes, both protecting and/or unifying peoples in this region. Eastern Europe's mountains are low and relatively accessible when compared with other ranges in the world. The **Carpathians** are the longest mountain range (stretching through Romania, Hungary, Czechoslovakia, and Poland), followed by the **Balkans** (which run from northern Bulgaria to Yugoslavia). Other important ranges are the **Rhodopes** (in Southern Bulgaria), the **Bohemian** and **Sudetens** (in Czechoslovakia), and the **Julian** and **Dinaric Alps** (running through Albania and Yugoslavia).

340

Plains have also had a profound effect on the history of Eastern Europe. The **Northern Plain** stretches from the Atlantic Ocean across Western Europe through the north of Germany into Poland and continues across Eastern Europe into Russia (see "Topography" in Russia section). This has served as a major invasion route for armies from both the east and west for centuries. The **Great Hungarian Plain**, located in the center of Eastern Europe, is both an agricultural and horse-breeding region and has also attracted invaders.

Bodies of Water

Rivers have played an important role in the development of Eastern Europe. They have served as major trade routes, linking the nations of Eastern Europe with the rest of Europe, and particularly with Byzantium. The **Danube** is the most important of these waterways, connecting Hungary, Yugoslavia, Bulgaria, and Romania. In addition to trade, it has always been a source of fish, irrigation, and, in modern times, hydroelectric power. Other important rivers are: the **Morava** (linking Austria with Czechoslovakia and Yugoslavia), the **Drava** (flowing from Hungary to Yugoslavia), the **Vandar** (flowing from Yugoslavia to Greece), the **Prut** (which connects Romania to the U.S.S.R.), and the **Bug** (which runs from Poland to the U.S.S.R.). There are also several rivers that have been essential to trade and communication within countries: the **Tisza** (Hungary), the **Vitava** (Czechoslovakia), the **Vit** (Bulgaria), the **Sava** (Yugoslavia), and the **Vistula** (Poland). In addition there are many scenic lakes throughout Eastern Europe, the most important of which is **Lake Balton** in Hungary. Both Yugoslavia and Albania are located on the Adriatic coast, while Bulgaria and Romania have access to the Black Sea. The latter countries have experienced the same problems as the Russians (see "History" in Russia section), their only access to the Mediterranean being the Black Sea. Yugoslavia has exploited its coastal advantage in trade, fishing, and tourism. Poland's access to the Baltic has been as limited and full of problems as the Russian's access since the 18th century.

Vegetation Belts

As a whole, the region of Eastern Europe is mountainous. Yet, there are areas of abundant vegetation: in Yugoslavia, the **Pannonian Plain** (located in the provinces of Serbia and Montenegro); in Hungary, parts of the **Great Hungarian Plain** (particularly near Debrecen on the Romanian border); in Czechoslovakia, the **Danube Valley**, the provinces of Moravia, Bohemia, and Slovakia (in the eastern part of the country); in Bulgaria, the **Maritsa Valley**, known as "Bulgaria's California" (located between the Balkan and Rhodope mountains), and the Balkan Plateau (in the north bordering Romania); in Romania,

341

Western Transylvania as well as the river valleys of the Danube and Prut; and in Poland, the Silesian region (southern plain).

There are also extensive forests in the uplands of Yugoslavia (along the coast of the Adriatic) and the northern plain of Poland. The exception is Albania, whose poor soil and lack of resources have only compounded other problems, making it an extremely poor nation.

Climate

The harshest climates of Eastern Europe are in Czechoslovakia and Poland, where very cold winters and cool summers have traditionally shortened growing seasons and lengthened peoples' endurance. There are less severe winters but warmer summers in Hungary, Bulgaria, and Romania. With hot, dry summers and milder winters (especially by the Adriatic coast), Yugoslavia has benefited from its climate by expanding agriculture and developing tourism. Albania's problems make its climate (the same as Yugoslavia) of little use.

II. Economic Geography (Economic Development of Eastern Europe)

Agriculture

Eastern Europe's economy was almost completely agricultural until the 20th century. Due to larger growing areas and richer soil, Yugoslavia, followed by Bulgaria and Romania, provide the greatest agricultural output. Yugoslavia produces grains, fruits, tobacco, and wood; Bulgaria provides grains, fruit, rose oil, and tobacco; and Romania grows corn, wheat, and timber. Poland produces limited grain and timber, while Hungary provides grain and wine. Czechoslovakia's production is almost completely industrial, and Albania's rigid Communist system, combined with its other problems, make its agricultural output barely self-sufficient.

Industrial Production/Resources

Czechoslovakia is Eastern Europe's most industrialized nation. Rich in coal and atomic energy ores, it produces beer, glass, china, machinery, and light aircraft. Poland, with its wealthy deposits of iron ore, coal, zinc, and sulphur, provides iron, automobiles, textiles, and chemicals. Romania, rich in oil (for which it became a target in World War II), produces textiles, machinery, and metals in addition to exporting oil, its greatest resource. Hungary provides steel, iron, aluminum, machinery, and railway equipment. Yugoslavia's industrial output is steel, copper, lead, zinc, chrome, and wood products. Bulgaria's production is limited to machinery and chemicals. Albania's state-controlled industrial production is limited to domestic consumption.

"Guns vs. Butter" Controversy

As in the Soviet Union, the "Guns vs. Butter" Controversy (see Section II on Russia) also rages in Eastern Europe. While varying in degree, the question of whether to produce consumer goods or weapons for the military and defense has become very important, especially as most Eastern European nations have started to reject Communist economic doctrines and develop democratic governments. (See "History" in this section.)

QUESTIONS

Multiple Choice. Select the letter of the answer that correctly completes the statement.

1. Eastern Europe's topography and location have made it
   A. well protected from invaders
   B. an invasion route throughout history
   C. isolated and culturally homogeneous
   D. dominant in the affairs of Western Europe

2. All of the following are important Eastern European rivers EXCEPT
   A. Danube
   B. Don
   C. Vistula
   D. Bug

3. The nations which provide the largest agricultural output are
   A. Yugoslavia, Bulgaria, Romania
   B. Poland, Romania, Yugoslavia
   C. Bulgaria, Hungary, Czechoslovakia
   D. Albania, Bulgaria, Yugoslavia

4. The most industrialized Eastern European nation is
   A. Czechloslovakia
   B. Hungary
   C. Poland
   D. Romania

5. Which is NOT true of Eastern Europe?
   A. It consists of nations located between Western Europe and the U.S.S.R.
   B. There is a diverse mixture of peoples
   C. It contains approximately 126 million people
   D. There is a unity of religious belief.

343

ESSAY

The topography of Eastern Europe has been important to its development.

A. To what extent did Eastern Europe's diverse topography (mountains, valleys, plains) influence its development? (5)

B. What role did Eastern Europe's rivers play in its economic development? (5)

C. To what extent has Eastern Europe's geography made its nations interdependent? (5)

III. Human and Cultural Geography

Demography

The population of Eastern Europe is approximately 126 million people. A comparison of the population and area of each individual nation illustrates the breakdown: Hungary, about the size of Indiana, has approximately 11 million people; Czechoslovakia, about the size of New York State, has a population of approximately 16 million; Albania, slightly larger than Maryland, has roughly 3 million; Yugoslavia, about the size of Wyoming, has approximately 24 million; Bulgaria, as large as Ohio, has a population of about 10 million; Romania, twice the size of Pennsylvania, has a little over 23 million; and Poland, roughly the size of New Mexico, has a population of about 39 million.

Ethnic Groups and Languages

While many ethnic and linguistic groups make up the population of Eastern Europe, the largest and most dominant are the **Slavs** (approximately 85 million). This ethnic grouping includes Great Russians, Byelo-Russians, Ukrainians, the Polish, Serbians, Croatians, Bulgarians, Slovenes, Slovaks, and Czechs. The larger non-Slavic groups in Eastern Europe are the Magyars (proper name for Hungarians), Romanians, Albanians, Greeks, Balts, Lats, Lithuanians, Germans, Tartars, Turks, and Gypsies. Each nation is divided ethnically and linguistically as follows:

ALBANIA:
ETHNIC GROUPS: Albanian 96 percent, Greek 4 percent
LANGUAGES: Albanian, Greek

BULGARIA:
ETHNIC GROUPS: Bulgarian 85 percent, Turkish 8 percent, Greek 7 percent
LANGUAGES: Bulgarian, Turkish, Greek

CZECHOSLOVAKIA:
ETHNIC GROUPS: Czech 64 percent, Slovak 31 percent, Magyar, German, Ukrainian, and Polish 5 percent
LANGUAGES: Czech, Slovak, Magyar, German, Ukrainian, Polish

HUNGARY:
ETHNIC GROUPS: Magyar 94 percent, German 3 percent, Gypsy 3 percent
LANGUAGES: Magyar, German, Serbian, Croatian, Slovak, Romanian

POLAND:
ETHNIC GROUPS: Polish 98 percent, Ukrainian and Byelo-Russian 2 percent
LANGUAGES: Polish, Ukrainian, Byelo-Russian

ROMANIA:
ETHNIC GROUPS: Romanian 90 percent, Magyar 8 percent, German 2 percent
LANGUAGES: Romanian, Magyar, German

YUGOSLAVIA:
ETHNIC GROUPS: Serbian 40 percent, Croat 20 percent, Bosnian Muslim 9 percent, Slovene 8 percent, Macedonian 6 percent, Albanian 6 percent, others 11 percent
LANGUAGES: Serbian, Croatian, Slovenian, Albanian

Religion in Eastern Europe
While most governments in Eastern Europe are still officially atheist (denying the existence of God and prohibiting religious worship), the situation is changing, and religious freedom is growing stronger as communism diminishes. The majority of Eastern Europeans are and have always been **Eastern Orthodox Christians**. With the exception of Poland and Hungary, which were converted by German Roman Catholic missionaries, the bulk of Eastern Europe's peoples were Christianized by the Orthodox Church and came under the influence of the Byzantine Empire. A large group of **Uniates** (Orthodox in practice while nominally under the Pope), Protestants, and Muslims also exist in Eastern Europe.

ALBANIA:
Muslim 60 percent, Christian (Eastern Orthodox and Roman Catholic) 40 percent

BULGARIA:
Eastern Orthodox 90 percent, Muslim 10 percent

CZECHOSLOVAKIA:
Roman Catholic 65 percent, Eastern Orthodox and Uniate 35 percent

345

HUNGARY:
Roman Catholic 70 percent, Protestant 25 percent

POLAND:
Roman Catholic 94 percent, Eastern Orthodox 6 percent

ROMANIA:
Eastern Orthodox 85 percent, Roman Catholic 10 percent, Muslim 5 percent

YUGOSLAVIA:
Eastern Orthodox 60 percent, Roman Catholic 30 percent, Muslim 10 percent

QUESTIONS

Multiple Choice. Select the letter of the answer that correctly completes the statement.

1. The largest and most dominant ethnic group in Eastern Europe is
   A. the Romanian
   B. the Slavic
   C. the Magyar
   D. the Albanian

2. The Eastern European nation that is composed of many smaller nations that were formally independent is
   A. Romania
   B. Hungary
   C. Yugoslavia
   D. Czechoslovakia

3. The religion of the majority of Eastern Europeans is
   A. Eastern Orthodox Christianity
   B. Roman Catholicism
   C. Protestantism
   D. Islam

4. Most Eastern European governments are officially
   A. Eastern Orthodox
   B. Roman Catholic
   C. Unitarian
   D. atheist

5. Uniates are
   A. Roman Catholics who support the union of all Christian churches
   B. Eastern Catholics who are Orthodox in practice, but nominally under the Pope

346

C. Christians married to Muslims
D. Orthodox Christians who want union with the Roman Catholics

ESSAY

Religion has played a major role in the development of Eastern Europe.
A. Select three Eastern European nations. (2)
B. Discuss the role of religion in the creation of each nation's language, literature and culture. (8)
C. Examine the extent to which religion has acted as a disunifying factor for the nations of Eastern Europe. (5)

IV. History and Political Geography (Historical Setting of Eastern Europe)

Early Migrations

The earliest settlers in Eastern Europe were the descendants of the modern-day Romanians and Albanians, who were first influenced by the ancient Romans. They were followed by waves of Slavic tribes migrating to present-day Byelo-Russia, the Ukraine, and eastern Poland. A second group of Slavs later settled in western Poland and Czechoslovakia. A third wave migrated to present-day Yugoslavia, Bulgaria and Albania. Nomadic tribes from Central Asia followed the Slavs, settling throughout Eastern Europe, most notably the Magyars in Hungary and the Bulgars in Bulgaria (where they mixed and were absorbed by the Slavs living there).

Conversion to Christianity and the Byzantine Commonwealth (863–1453)

The conversion of the peoples of Eastern Europe to Orthodox Christianity and the adoption of elements of Byzantine culture created a sense of religious and cultural unity throughout the entire region. These factors gave the people of Eastern Europe a new identity. The work of two Byzantine missionaries, **Cyril** (826–869) and **Methodius** (815–885), was instrumental in the conversion of the Slavs. Preaching and conducting worship in the **vernacular** (the common spoken language), the brothers Cyril and Methodius were very successful in converting tribes of Slavs in Moravia (present-day Czechoslovakia). Cyril created an alphabet (**Cyrillic**), based on Greek and Coptic letters, and grammar for the spoken Slavic language. This evolved into Church Slavonic, the liturgical language that unified early Slavic literature and culture. While the mission of Cyril and Methodius was confined to Moravia, their followers soon converted both Slavic and non-Slavic nations throughout Eastern Europe: Bulgaria, 865; Serbia, 874; Romania, 900; Rus'/Ukraine, 988. Poland and Hungary were converted by German missionaries and came under the influence of the Roman Catholic Church.

By the year 1000, the Byzantine Empire and its Orthodox satellites (including Hungary) formed the **Byzantine Commonwealth**, an alliance to promote trade and economic expansion in Eastern Europe as well as to provide a common defense against the Arabs, Turks, and Germans. It was also a political triumph for the Greek East over the Latin West in developing Eastern Europe as a sphere of influence. Poland joined forces with the Baltic peoples, particularly the Lithuanians, and became a Roman Catholic rival to the nations of the Byzantine Commonwealth, especially the Russians.

Turkish Domination (1453–1821)

Despite the establishment of the Byzantine Commonwealth, by 1450 the Ottoman Turks had captured much of the Byzantine Empire and Eastern Europe. The behavior of the Latin West, especially the Crusaders, created suspicion and hatred of both the papacy and Western Europe among Greeks and Slavs.

In 1453, when Constantinople was conquered by the Ottoman Turks, Moscow claimed leadership of the Orthodox Church. (See "The Rise of Moscow" in Russia section.) During the period of Turkish domination, a struggle developed between the Russian tsars (Romanovs) and the Austrian emperors (Habsburgs) to lead the Slavs out of Turkish rule. Each claimed to be the rightful heir to the Byzantine Empire (they both used the double-headed eagle in their coat-of-arms). Not surprisingly, the Orthodox nations favored the Russians, while the Catholic nations favored Austria.

Independence and Pan-Slavism (1821–1914)

The Greek struggle for independence in 1821 touched off a movement throughout Eastern Europe to end Turkish domination in that region. As revolutions broke out in each country, the rivalry between Russia and Austria intensified. The other major European powers became involved, trying to maintain the balance of power. In 1683, the Habsburgs defeated the Turks and captured Hungary. In 1815, Russia and Austria divided Poland at the Congress of Vienna after the Napoleonic Wars. (See Western Europe section.) By 1900, Austria had also gained Bohemia (Czechoslovakia) and Croatia. Both Russia and Austria had great interest, therefore, in the shape of the new independent Eastern European states.

Throughout the 19th century, Russia supported and financed wars for independence in Greece, Serbia, Bulgaria, and Romania. Developing the concept of "Pan-Slavism" (political, religious, and cultural unity of all Slavs and/or Orthodox Christians), Russian tsars came into conflict with the British, Germans, and French, as well as the Austrians and Turks. The modern nation of Albania was created at the Congress of Berlin in 1878, as a compromise between Russia and the other Western powers concerning Serbian expansion. By 1914, tensions had grown so great in Eastern Europe, especially in the Balkans, that it was called the "tinderbox of Europe." The incident that set off World War I (the assassination of the Austrian Archduke Franz Ferdinand by a Serbian nationalist) was one further example of how explosive the tension of Eastern Europe had become.

War and Communism (1914–1945)

With the exception of the Bulgarians, who fought with the Greeks, Serbians, and Romanians over territory from 1912 to 1913 (the Balkan Wars), the Slavic/Orthodox nations joined Russia against Austria in World War I. When the war was over, the Russian Empire had collapsed and was involved in a bloody civil war (1918–1921). The Ukraine (retaken by Soviet Russia in 1921) and Poland were independent, as were the Baltic states of Finland, Lithuania, Latvia, and Estonia. While Bulgaria and Romania remained as they were, three new nations were created by the Versailles Treaty: the independent states of Hungary and Czechoslovakia (Bohemia and the Sudentenland) from the Habsburg Empire, and Yugoslavia (Serbia, Croatia, Slovenia, Macedonia, Montenegro and Bosnia-Herzegovina).

Eastern Europe developed constitutional monarchies and democratic governments between the wars. During World War II, fascist governments were set up in the nations of Eastern Europe under the Nazis. During the war, the Soviet army pushed the Nazis out of Eastern Europe. Puppet Communist governments were established by the Soviet Union to replace the fascist governments, as Stalin occupied Eastern Europe. (See "Stalin" in Russia section.) The only exception was Yugoslavia, where **Marshall Josip Broz** (known as **Tito**) established an independent Communist government. Once again, the nations of Eastern Europe were satellites.

The Soviet Bloc (1945–1990)

Unlike the Byzantine Commonwealth or the Pan-Slavic alliances of the 19th century, the creation of the Communist Eastern bloc was forced on the nations of Eastern Europe by Stalin. The Bloc consisted of Hungary, Czechoslovakia, Bulgaria, Albania, Poland, Romania, and East Germany. From the start, Yugoslavia under Tito refused to take orders from Moscow. The formation of NATO in 1949 and the subsequent creation of the Warsaw Pact (see "Stalin" in Russia section) in 1955 once again divided Europe into two camps, the East and the West.

Starting with riots after Stalin's death in 1953, the nations of the Eastern bloc began to oppose control by the U.S.S.R. In 1956 a revolution overthrew the puppet Communist government in Hungary, but Soviet troops were sent in to restore it. In 1961, Albania's extremist Communist government left the sphere of Soviet domination and allied itself with Communist China. In East Berlin, a wall was built to stop the embarrassing flow of East Germans and Eastern Europeans from the East to the West. In 1968, after the Czechoslovakian government under **Alexander Dubcek** tried to initiate democratic reforms, Soviet troops invaded that nation and installed a government more obedient to Moscow. From 1970 to 1980, food riots and worker unrest in Poland grew, as the trade union **Solidarity** was formed under the leadership of **Lech Walesa**. In 1981, the puppet Polish government began a series of moves (pressured by Moscow) to crush Solidarity, but it was unsuccessful. By 1989, Solidarity had been legalized. In addition, domestic and international pressure forced the Polish government to hold elections, in which the Communists were swept out of power. Solidarity formed a new government, with Solidarity leader **Tadeusz Mazowiecki** as prime minister. Encouraged by Mikhail Gorbachev's reforms (see "Perestroika" and "Glasnost" in Russia section) and his policy not to interfere in Eastern Europe, other countries began to break away from the Communist bloc.

In the fall of 1989, Hungary allowed thousands of East Germans to escape through that nation. Faced with enormous protest and pressure, both internal and external, the East German government allowed free travel by the winter, and citizens began to dismantle the Berlin Wall. Realizing that their authority had gone when Gorbachev refused to support them, the East German Communists resigned their monopoly of power. A non-Communist government was elected, and plans for reunification with West Germany began. In the manner of dominoes, Hungary, followed by Czechoslovakia, began reforms and free elections. By 1990, both nations ousted the Communist governments and established democracies, electing former dissident writers **Arpad Goncz** (Hungary) and **Vaclav Havl** (Czechoslovakia) to lead the new governments. In Romania, a major uprising overthew the Communist dictator **Nicolai Ceaucescu**, executing him and his closest followers and establishing a fragile democracy. After Tito's death in 1980, the independent Communist government of Yugoslavia began to allow civil liberties unheard of in the Eastern bloc. Yet, despite these, a poor economy often caused riots and strikes, forcing several governments to resign. Presently, Yugoslavia's new leadership has started to completely overhaul the economy and to deal with the movements of ethnic groups (particularly the Serbians) to break up the nation. Bulgaria's Communist government also started to make concessions to reform following Gorbachev's lead but seemed to stop short of making real changes. Bulgarian Communist Party leader **Todor Zhivkov** tried to overcome criticism by launching a campaign to nationalize or oust the nation's Turkish Muslim minority. However, Zhivkov was forced to resign, and a parliament was elected. Finally, the most hard-line xenophobic (fear of foreigners), isolated, and ruthless Communist regime, Albania, showed the first sign of change as it allowed thousands of Albanians to leave the country for the first time.

By the summer of 1990, it seemed that the Communist Eastern Bloc had ended. On July 6, 1990, NATO issued an official statement proclaiming that the Cold War was over and that efforts to disarm Europe should be sped up. Only two years before the projected date of Western European unity (1992) (see "European Community" in Western European section), a new Eastern Europe alliance appeared to be on the horizon.

QUESTIONS

Multiple Choice. Select the letter of the answer that correctly completes the statement.

1. The earliest settlers in Eastern Europe were the descendants of modern day
   A. Byelo-Russians and Poles
   B. Albanians and Bulgarians
   C. Romanians and Albanians
   D. Bulgarians and Serbians

2. The mission of Cyril and Methodius was responsible for all of the following EXCEPT the
   A. creation of a Slavic alphabet and grammar
   B. unity of Slavic literature and culture
   C. conversion of the Slavic peoples to Christianity
   D. introduction of Classical learning

3. The Eastern European nations seeking independence in the 19th century were divided in their support of
   A. Russia and France
   B. Austria and Germany
   C. Great Britain and France
   D. Austria and Russia

4. Before World War I, Eastern Europe was known as the "tin-
   derbox of Europe" because
   A. tensions in that area had grown great and there was a danger
      of war
   B. it had many forests and provided Europe with lumber
   C. it was at odds with Western Europe and there was a danger
      of war
   D. it was very arid and susceptible to forest fires

5. After World War I, the nations of Eastern Europe developed
   A. constitutional monarchies and democratic governments
   B. autocratic monarchies
   C. fascist dictatorships
   D. communist regimes

6. After World War II, Stalin occupied Eastern Europe establishing
   puppet communist governments EXCEPT for
   A. Bulgaria
   B. Yugoslavia
   C. Albania
   D. Romania

7. The formation of N.A.T.O. in 1949 resulted in the creation of an
   Eastern European communist military alliance under Soviet dom-
   ination known as
   A. S.E.A.T.O.
   B. E.E.C.
   C. the Eastern Bloc
   D. the Warsaw Pact

8. The two Eastern European nations that unsuccessfully attempted
   to free themselves of Soviet domination in 1956 and 1968 were
   A. East Germany and Czechoslovakia
   B. Hungary and Poland
   C. Hungary and Czechoslovakia
   D. Poland and Czechoslovakia

9. The Polish Communist Party was forced out of power in 1989
   largely due to
   A. the Polish Liberation Army
   B. the trade union Solidarity
   C. N.A.T.O.
   D. Detente between the U.S.S.R. and the U.S.

10. Democratic reform and ethnic struggles began in Yugoslavia after the death of
   A. Josip Broz (Tito)
   B. Nicolae Ceaucescu
   C. Joseph Stalin
   D. Alexander Dubček

ESSAY

The history of Eastern Europe is one of interdependence.
A. Select three Eastern European nations. (2)
B. Discuss how each nation's history and politics is influenced by its neighbors. (8)
C. Explain why alliances between the nations of Eastern Europe keep recurring in their history. (5)

UNIT
EIGHT
THE WORLD TODAY

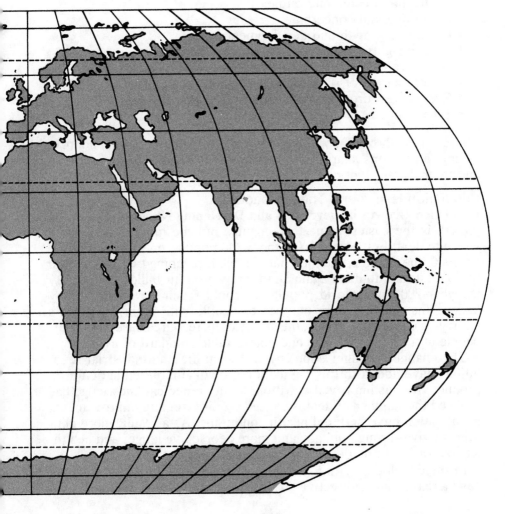

Global Issues

Today's world could be considered a "global village," tied together by the ease of rapid travel and nearly instant communication. These ties create **interdependence** among culture regions and countries. Examples of this interdependence include: agricultural and industrial products are traded; knowledge and ideas flow from one region to another; and political alliances provide mutual help and support.

Most importantly, however, our "smaller" world is united by the need to address common problems and concerns. All regions are challenged by several major world issues. These world issues are:

- War and peace
- Population
- Hunger and poverty
- Political and economic refugees
- Environmental concerns
- Economic growth and development
- Human rights
- World trade and finance
- Determination of political and economic systems
- Energy: resources and allocation
- Terrorism

These issues show that we live in a world of global interdependence. Today, all regions share the possibility for sharing and cooperation and the progress that can result.

Population Issues and Their Impact

Population Growth in Developed and Developing Nations. Population growth is the easiest issue to recognize but the most difficult with which to deal. In the year 1800, the world population was one billion. By 1900, the world population had doubled, reaching two billion, and by 1975, it had doubled again and there were four billion people. By the year 2000, the world population could reach six billion. Many believe that such a large number of people will strain the earth's "carrying capacity," that is, the ability of its resource base to support people at a reasonably safe and comfortable standard of living.

The changes brought about by the scientific and industrial revolutions have added to this population growth. Increased agricultural productivity has improved nutrition; modern medical knowledge has reduced the number of deaths caused by disease; and improvements in sanitation have bettered health conditions. As a result, more children survive through infancy and more people live longer and healthier lives in both the developed and developing nations.

In the developed nations where the production of material goods has increased and protective social and governmental services have been introduced, people have generally decided to have fewer children. Most of these nations have low population growth rates, and some have even reached zero percent population growth. Demographers (social scientists who study population patterns) and politicians agree that developing nations must make special efforts to control population growth.

Consequently, the governments of many developing nations have begun family planning or birth-control programs. They use many techniques, such as advertising and educational campaigns, economic incentives, and restrictive legislation to convince their citizens to have fewer children. China's "one-child family" law, India's "transistor radios for vasectomies" campaign, and Singapore's free education only for the first two children policy are examples of the different approaches that have been used.

Reducing the birth rate in many developing nations has proved to be difficult, however. Often cultural factors have worked against limiting population growth. In some cultures, economic and social conditions as well as religious beliefs lead to the desire, even the necessity, for large numbers of children. Children may be needed to help with the family farm or business, to provide care for elders, or to contribute income from outside jobs. They may also be needed for religious ceremonies (especially funerals), to enhance a family's prestige, or to inherit the family occupation and property and carry the family name into the future.

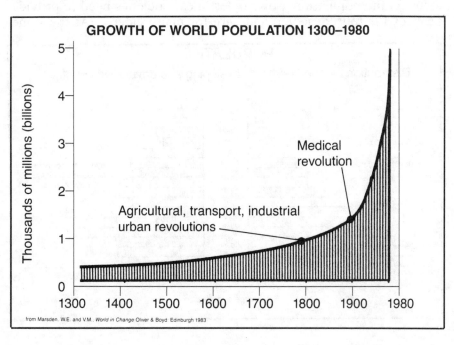

GROWTH OF WORLD POPULATION 1300–1980

Thousands of millions (billions)

Medical revolution

Agricultural, transport, industrial urban revolutions

from Marsden. W.E. and V.M., *World in Change* Oliver & Boyd: Edinburgh 1983

In some areas, other factors also make limiting population growth difficult. Geographic and historical circumstances have created an uneven distribution of population. Fertile river valleys and coastal plains are capable of producing vast amounts of food grain, and such production requires large labor forces. Consequently, dense populations are both possible and desirable. Eastern China, coastal Japan, and South Asia's Indo-Gangetic Plain are examples of this circumstance.

At the same time, modern agricultural technology has made areas that previously provided only small amounts of food extremely productive with small labor forces. The Great Plains of North America and the North European Plain are two such areas, and they help to provide Americans and Europeans with an abundant food supply and a high standard of living.

Urbanization stimulated by the Industrial Revolution has also contributed to uneven population distribution. Today, over 40 percent of the world's population lives in cities. Cities need workers for industries and services. Moreover, urban areas provide many economic and cultural opportunities for their inhabitants. As a result, people migrate from the rural agricultural areas to further crowd and congest urban areas, helping to create squalid, crime-ridden, and unhealthy slums. This trend of rural migration is continuing today.

Population can also be unequally distributed by age. In the developed nations, more people live longer and couples have fewer children. As the population grows older, these societies need to provide services for retired people and care for many elderly. At the same

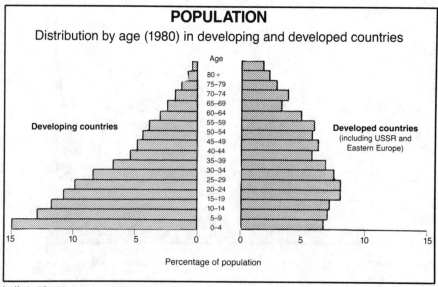

POPULATION

Distribution by age (1980) in developing and developed countries

Developing countries

Developed countries (including USSR and Eastern Europe)

Age: 80+, 75–79, 70–74, 65–69, 60–64, 55–59, 50–54, 45–49, 40–44, 35–39, 30–34, 25–29, 20–24, 15–19, 10–14, 5–9, 0–4

Percentage of population

from Marsden, W.E. and V.M., *World in Change* Oliver & Boyd: Edinburgh 1983

358

time, there are fewer wage-earners to provide tax revenues for such services.

Developing nations, with their growing populations, are faced with large numbers of school-age children. However, they do not have the money to fund education. This deprives young people of the skills and knowledge necessary to compete for jobs in modernized sectors of the economy and results in large numbers of young people being unemployed or underemployed.

World Hunger. Although population growth is an underlying cause of hunger and malnutrition in many parts of the world and the increasing numbers of people put a strain on food supplies, the issue is more complex. Many nations do not grow enough food crops. This is often because of policies carried out by former European colonial powers. In these areas, food production was frequently replaced by the production of cash crops for the European market. Also, in some areas, especially in Africa, borders were drawn without regard to natural and traditional agricultural ecosystems (the living community and nonliving environment working together in a cooperative ecological system).

Since independence, the governments of some developing nations have ignored the development of agriculture. Instead, leaders have often emphasized industrialization and the growth of cities, hoping to build political support among city workers, the growing middle class, and the educated elite.

Climatic conditions and changes affect the food supply in some areas. Droughts (a long period of dryness as in Africa's Sahel) often force people to overuse and damage the environment by digging deeper wells, which lower the water table, by allowing herds to strip sparse vegetation, or by cutting down trees and bushes for firewood. Floods and storms (as in Bangladesh) can wipe out harvests, ruin arable land, and destroy storage and transport facilities.

Although the developed nations produce a large enough food surplus to ease shortages in crisis areas, a number of obstacles prevent an equal distribution of these surpluses. First of all, simply giving vast amounts of food to needy nations creates dependencies. It also interferes with agricultural prices in other areas. Political differences and policies may hamper the distribution of both food aid and local food supplies (as in Ethiopia/Eritrea). Moreover, corruption, hoarding, and price fixing are often part of the political and economic systems of developing countries.

Finally, many developing nations do not have or cannot afford to develop the factories to produce technological innovations (new ideas) which could bring about higher crop yields. They also are unable to purchase those items from more developed countries. New, improved seed varieties, chemical fertilizers, pesticides, and farm machinery are all expensive. Also, prices for fuels used in small engines that power farm machinery have increased.

Education—a Growing Gap. Development in Third World nations depends on information and technical skills. Education is necessary to make use of these resources. However, as communication and information technology leap ahead in the industrialized nations, the developing nations are losing ground in gaining access to these essentials. This is due in part to the shortage of funds that are available for schools, colleges, and educational media. Also, social or economic limitations often take children out of the educational system. For example, they may be needed to contribute to family care or earnings, or tradition may exclude the participation of females. Also, governments sometimes ignore or attempt to eliminate long-standing methods or institutions, which makes it difficult for citizens to adapt to new ways.

Population pressure is not limited to particular culture regions, nor is the issue simply that of numbers of humans or even birth or population growth rates. It involves decisions about fairness and equity and how nations will deal with one another in the future. Developing nations react to criticisms of their high birth rates by criticizing how much of the world's natural resources are consumed by the industrialized countries.

Increased World Trade. As it relates to the network of world trade, the population issue involves developing relationships that promote fairness in the prices paid for natural resources and agricultural products provided by developing nations. Increased prices for these products would help provide money for these nations to improve education, skill training, industrial capacity, transportation, and communication. These items make up a nation's **infrastructure**, a necessity for improving living standards and enabling societies to effectively deal with poverty, hunger, and population growth.

Economic Development and World Trade

Interdependence brought about by scientific, technological, and industrial progress has carried the message of economic development to every nation on earth. Every government strives to improve the standard of living of its citizens in a variety of ways. Improved health, sanitation, and nutrition; broader educational training, and employment opportunities; better housing, clothing, and other basic necessities; affordable entertainment, reasonably priced consumer goods, and more leisure time—all of these are elements of economic development.

Accomplishing these things requires the investment of money and human effort, both of which may be strained by the great need. Po-

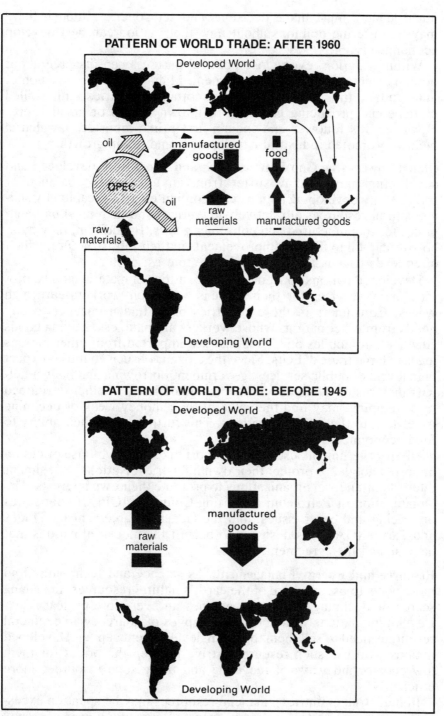

PATTERN OF WORLD TRADE: AFTER 1960

Developed World

oil

manufactured goods

food

OPEC

oil

raw materials

raw materials

manufactured goods

Developing World

PATTERN OF WORLD TRADE: BEFORE 1945

Developed World

raw materials

manufactured goods

Developing World

from Nixon, Brian, *World Contrasts* Bell & Hyman: London 1986

361

litical leaders must make decisions and set policies although there may be differing opinions about how their nation can best develop economically.

Within a nation, even close political partners can disagree about how to achieve economic development. Mahatma Gandhi's vision of independent India saw a nation of cottage industries with skilled craftspeople producing goods in their own homes or small shops. However, his follower and India's first prime minister, Jawaharlal Nehru, promoted industrial development and urban growth.

Global Power—the Gap Between Rich and Poor. Both developed and developing nations may suffer from an unfavorable balance of trade. Many developing nations earn foreign-exchange capital by selling natural resources at relatively low prices and then must pay high prices for manufactured and consumer goods. In addition, they must borrow capital to finance improvements in their infrastructure, which often leads to massive debts and huge interest costs.

Developed nations consume large quantities of material goods, provide many services for their citizens, and their workers earn high wages. Consumers in these countries often find it cheaper to buy goods from other nations whose workers are paid less. Buying goods such as automobiles and TV's that are imported from other nations leads to large trade deficits. Since the citizens of such countries expect high levels of public services, government borrowing and budget deficits may result. Nations with debts and deficits, whether developed or developing, may find the value of their money weak or declining in relation to that of other nations. This further limits their ability to fund economic development.

Often governments use **tariffs** (import taxes), which raise prices on imported goods, to protect their own industries. Nations with similar interests often form organizations to promote their own interests. The Organization of Petroleum Exporting Countries (OPEC) cooperates on pricing and other issues, and the General Agreement on Trades and Tariffs (GATT) is designed to benefit the industrial nations that have signed the agreement.

Resource and Energy Management. As science and technology find more ways to use up more of the earth's natural resources, managing scarce or declining resources becomes an ever-more critical issue. Developing nations with abundant supplies of nonrenewable mineral resources need to sell them to obtain development capital. Developed nations who use such resources strive to keep the prices for them low and to find ways of recycling and using such resources more efficiently.

In industrial countries, financial resources may be spent on excessive amounts of consumer goods or lost to corruption or inefficiency

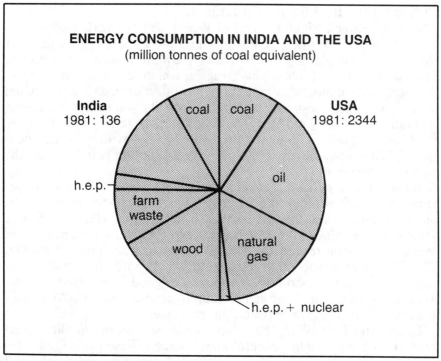

ENERGY CONSUMPTION IN INDIA AND THE USA
(million tonnes of coal equivalent)

India
1981: 136

USA
1981: 2344

coal   coal

h.e.p.

oil

farm
waste

wood   natural
gas

h.e.p. + nuclear

from Nixon, Brian, *World Contrasts* Bell & Hyman: London 1986

(as in some Communist nations). Developing countries are often forced to use much of their capital to pay off their debts and the interest on their loans.

Human resources are also crucial to development. Many African and Asian societies have suffered a so-called "brain drain," as many of their educated, skilled, or financially prosperous citizens have emigrated to developed nations for better opportunities. And the lack of money for investment in education means that developing nations cannot fully develop the potential of the remainder of their population.

Tradition and Modernization: Finding a Balance. As developing nations look for ways to improve living standards for their citizens, they often find that modern techniques disrupt or conflict with established cultural patterns. For example, family-planning programs may violate religious beliefs (as with the Roman Catholic Church in Latin America); migration from rural areas to urban areas upsets established social structures (for instance, India's caste system); changing roles for women threatens the traditional male-female relationships (as in some Islamic nations); and changing governmental structures may clash with centuries-old economic patterns (China's communes versus family farms).

Changing Political Power Structures

The Superpowers. Since the end of World War II, world politics has been dominated by the so-called "superpower" struggle, which pits the Communist ideology of the Soviet Union against the capitalist ideas of the United States. This struggle, which has involved military, political, and economic competition, has often been called the "Cold War," and each nation has attempted to build and extend its power and influence. The Cold War was an icy state of tension and hostility between the Soviet Union and the United States without armed conflict. Their rivalry never broke out into a shooting war between the two superpowers.

Although competition between the superpowers has been worldwide, it has often focused on Europe, where their two opposing alliances faced one another across the "iron curtain." Here, the Soviet Union and its allies (the satellite states of Eastern Europe) in the **Warsaw Pact** confronted the United States and its allies in **NATO**. The Cold War led to an arms race in which both sides built more sophisticated and destructive weapons designed to maintain a "balance of terror," or "mutually assured destruction" (MAD), preventing all-out warfare between the two sides.

During the Cold War, there have been periods of stability when both sides have sought peaceful coexistence. These periods of "detente" (easing of hostility) have alternated with times of heightened tensions, such as during the Cuban Missile Crisis of 1961 and the Soviet invasion of Afghanistan in 1979. From time to time, summit meetings have been held between leaders of the two nations in order to improve communication and to seek conflict resolution.

Each of the superpowers has attempted to extend its influence to other areas of the world. At times, the United States has supported military or dictatorial governments opposed to communism, often at the expense of real democracy in those countries. The Soviet Union has supported "national liberation" movements in some nations, often resorting to sabotage and terrorism.

Recently, however, dramatic political changes, especially in Eastern Europe, have disrupted this nearly 50-year-old pattern of relationships. The ideology of communism and its reliance on totalitarian control has been discredited and found ineffective in meeting people's economic and emotional needs. The desires for self-expression and self-determination of the people of Eastern Europe are coupled with a need for higher material standards of living. How these political changes will affect East-West relationships and political and economic structures will shape human history for the next few decades.

The Third World. Many African, Asian, and Latin American nations have held a different world view, that of a "multi-polar" or many-sided pattern of power. The concept of **nonalignment** for nations that did not wish to be too closely allied with either the West or the Eastern bloc was formulated by Nehru of India. The first meeting of nonaligned nations was held by Sukarno in Indonesia in 1955.

Arms and the Third World

from Morrish. Michael, *Development in the Third World* Oxford University Press 1983

The superpowers have often become involved in regional conflicts and disputes. They have never been involved in direct military conflict but have fought against each other through proxy or client states. At times, these involvements have led to direct superpower confrontations, while at other times, the Soviet Union and the United States have been only minimally involved, supplying only weapons or aid. The Korean War pitted Communist North Korea and China directly against the United States and its allies. American military involvement in Southeast Asia brought massive Russian support for North Vietnam. The Soviet invasion of Afghanistan brought American weapons and money to aid Afghan mujaheddin (freedom fighters) who were resisting Soviet control.

One area in which the superpowers have not been able to greatly influence events is the Middle East. Although the superpowers have been involved in the Arab-Israeli dispute, they have not been able to greatly influence events or bring about desired changes. President Carter's efforts brought about the **Camp David Accords**, settling some differences between Egypt and Israel, but the two superpowers have had little success in solving this long-standing dispute. Bitterness between Iran and Iraq created a prolonged war in the 1980s, and social and religious differences have all but destroyed Lebanon as a nation. Superpower efforts to work out agreements in these disputes also failed.

Elsewhere, many conflicts have been regional in nature and have not involved the United States or the Soviet Union. India and Pakistan have engaged in hostilities over Kashmir, and in early 1990 the dispute broke out once more. Argentina and Great Britain engaged in a brief but bloody war in Los Islas Malvinas (the Falkland Islands) in the South Atlantic, and hostilities have broken out between Vietnam and China even though both are Communist nations.

Arms Control. The presence of nuclear weapons in the arsenals of the superpowers has led to a constant search for ways to reduce the massive sums of money spent on their development and deployment. Likewise, the potential for other nations to develop or acquire such weapons has led to efforts to control their spread.

During the 1960s, the **Limited Test Ban Treaty** (1963), the **Nuclear Non-Proliferation Treaty** (1968), and similar agreements were the focus of control efforts. Nations without nuclear capability, however, have claimed the right to it for both peaceful means (energy) and to protect themselves against enemies who already possess such weapons. India's 1974 nuclear test possibly spurred Pakistan's quest for an "Islamic bomb."

The United States and the Soviet Union have had many arms-control discussions, some of which have been successful. The 1970s saw limitations placed on certain types of missiles as a result of the first **Strategic Arms Limitation Treaty** (**SALT**), while **SALT II** set limits on the kinds of warheads, missile weights, and types of delivery vehicles. More recently, discussions have focused on **Strategic Arms Reduction Treaties** (**START**), designed to "build down" (decrease) the numbers and types of weapons each nation possesses.

Terrorism as a Political Weapon. Today, some groups frustrated by what they feel to be oppression by their own government or the policies of other governments often turn to terrorism. They use violence or the threat of it to publicize their grievances or to press their demands. Terrorism involves the use of violence against unarmed, innocent civilians. Its special horror lies in the fact that innocent men, women, and children are killed.

Terrorism can involve kidnapping or hijacking, assassination, random murder, or mass killing. It is usually carried out by small groups of highly dedicated, even fanatical individuals who believe they can obtain concessions, frustrate governments, or just gain revenge. Some believe in violence as the only way to fight conditions they view as evil, but most have specific goals.

Among those who have turned to terrorism to publicize their demands are the Palestinians, who have carried out global attacks against Israel and its supporters, especially the United States. Branches of the Irish Republican Army who are against Britain's role in Northern Ireland and groups like the Tuparmaros of Uruguay and Shining Light in Peru have used terrorist tactics to bring down the governments of those nations. State supported terrorism has also become a problem. Countries such as Libya and Syria have provided money and training for terrorist groups and have supported their activities.

Environmental Issues

As humans increase their capacity to use the earth's resources through technology, they are also increasingly capable of destroying and polluting the very environment that sustains human and all other life. Human activities can now affect the ecology and even the climate of the entire planet. As President George Bush said, "Environmental problems respect no borders."

Chief among the environmental concerns are possible climate changes caused by the "greenhouse effect." Carbon dioxide and other gases produced by modern industries trap more of the sun's heat and energy within the earth's atmosphere, causing global warming. While scientists disagree on the effects of global warming, many feel that even a slight increase in the earth's temperatures worldwide could melt the polar ice cap, raise sea levels, submerge coastal areas, and change growing seasons and agricultural production.

Associated with climate change is the issue of the destruction of forests, especially the tropical rain forests. Increasingly, the developing nations are clearing large areas of tropical rain forests. They are exporting timber to obtain foreign capital, converting forests to farm land to grow cash crops such as rubber, and attempting to develop more land for settlement and to raise food crops. It is estimated that 3,000 acres of tropical rain forest are destroyed every hour. At this rate, in 100 years the rain forests could all be gone.

The destruction of the forests adds to the greenhouse effect because it decreases the number of trees and plants on the earth to change carbon dioxide to oxygen. In addition, thousands of plant and animal species may become extinct, reducing the earth's biological diversity, and possibly its capacity to sustain other kinds of life. If the rain forests vanish, 40 percent of all living species will be destroyed. This means that millions of species, many of which we have not yet even been discovered, will vanish. Finally, changing natural patterns can destroy the usefulness of the soil and the effectiveness of the water supply, thus defeating the original purpose of the attempted change in land use. The soil of the tropical rain forest is extremely poor and can only sustain agriculture for a short time. As a result, farmers move on and cut down more forest.

Also at issue is the need to protect endangered species and to conserve the wildlife of the earth. Animals such as leopards and alligators (for their skins), elephants and rhinos (for their tusks and horns), and ostriches (for their feathers) have been hunted to the verge of extinction to provide luxury consumer goods. The nets used by the tuna-fishing industry have endangered dolphins. Several nations have depleted the whale population for industrial purposes, and the spread of human settlement and recreation areas have reduced the land available for animals and plants.

Increased industrialization means increased pollution and an increased threat to human health. Pollution creates carcinogens that cause cancer. Respiratory diseases result from unhealthful substances in the air we breathe, and chemicals in the water supply and food chain create additional threats. Chlorofluorocarbons used in aerosol sprays and refrigeration units contribute to the depletion of the ozone layer, the part of the earth's atmosphere that filters out some of the most harmful of the sun's rays.

The waste byproducts of energy production are another threat. Acid rain is caused by the burning of fossil fuels and has the capacity to wipe out fish and aquatic plant life when it accumulates in bodies of water. Used-up radioactive fuel from nuclear power plants and other hazardous waste products must be disposed of and their transport across international borders regulated.

Safeguards must be developed to prevent industrial disasters such as those that occurred in Chernobyl and Bhopal. Radiation from the accident at the Chernobyl nuclear power plant in the Soviet Union killed Soviet citizens and spread across northwestern Europe. A poisonous gas leak from an American chemical factory in Bhopal, India, killed and injured thousands.

Governments around the world are beginning to cooperate in dealing with these environmental issues, though opinions differ about what to do in specific cases. For example, Brazilians see the clearing of the rain forest as essential to their nation's development. They consider American criticism unfair since the United States has been clearing forest lands for over a century. Agreements over the use of the resources of the oceans and areas such as Antarctica may establish patterns for dealing with global environmental issues in the future.

Human Rights

Along with the industrial and scientific revolutions of the past several centuries has come the democratic revolution. Fundamental to this has been the idea that all human beings possess certain political, social, and economic rights. In 1948 the United Nations adopted the *Universal Declaration of Human Rights*, which states the basic right to dignity for all people, as well as the rights to freedom of speech, freedom of assembly, and the right to an adequate standard of living.

In 1975, thirty-three nations of Europe along with the Soviet Union and the United States signed the *Helsinki Accords*. This agreement included a statement of basic human rights. In spite of these documents, however, human-rights abuses continue around the world. Organizations such as Amnesty International monitor and publicize such abuses.

Recent Violations of Human Rights

Apartheid in South Africa. South Africa's government denies political rights to all citizens of native African background and has attempted to establish "homelands" for blacks. This policy denies the black population the use of much of the land and resources of the nation. It has severely limited economic opportunities for blacks and preserved the white minority's control of the economy.

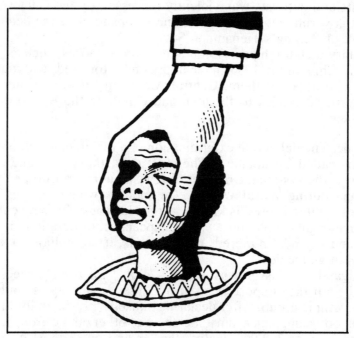

from MacLean, Kenneth, and Norman Thompson, *World Environmental Problems* Bartholomew/Holmes McDougal: Edinburgh 1981

The South African system also severely limits the rights of those of Asian or mixed backgrounds and extends full political participation only to those of European ancestry. Efforts by the black majority to gain political rights, including the Freedom Charter of the 1950s as well as demonstrations, have often led to violent repression. Several hundred blacks were killed by police at Sharpeville in 1965. Students protesting educational changes were gunned down in 1976, and protests and activism in the 1980s led to continued violence.

Individuals who criticized or campaigned against apartheid have suffered "banning," that is, restriction in their travel and contacts, or imprisonment. Black leader Nelson Mandela was released in 1990 after 30 years in jail. Some, such as Stephen Biko who died in police custody, have been murdered.

Totalitarian Governments. Such governments are known for their violations of human rights. The Soviet Union has suppressed and imprisoned dissidents, those who have criticized the Communist Party or the government. Forced labor camps and psychiatric wards have been used to punish those who spoke out or wrote critical articles or books.

In the spring of 1989, the democracy movement started by Chinese students and activists was violently repressed by the Chinese Communist government. It sent tanks and troops to clear the demonstrators out of Beijing's Tienanmen Square.

Military dictatorships in Latin American countries, such as Argentina and Chile in the 1980s have imprisoned, tortured, and murdered those who opposed them. Central American "death squads" have used terrorist tactics to threaten and eliminate those who disagree with them.

Genocide. The deliberate extermination of a racial, cultural, or ethnic group is called "genocide." The most devastating example of genocide was the systematic murder of Jewish people in Europe by Nazi Germany during World War II. This policy, which resulted in the death of 6 million Jews, is known as the **Holocaust.** Two recent cases of human-rights violations warrant special consideration. In Cambodia and Uganda, hundreds of thousands, if not millions, were the victims of genocide.

In Uganda, the issue was ethnic. Colonel Idi Amin seized power in 1971 with the support of an army largely made up of soldiers of his own ethnic group. After declaring himself "president for life," he led a bloody campaign against members of other ethnic groups, which resulted in over 300,000 deaths, the emigration of most citizens of Asian background, and eventually an invasion by the army of neighboring Tanzania in 1979.

The Cambodian tragedy was even more horrible. The fanatical Communist Khmer Rouge, led by Pol Pot, gained control in 1977 after the turmoil of the Communist takeover in Vietnam. The Khmer Rouge forced the people to leave the cities and killed the educated, the middle class, Buddhist priests, and anyone else of power, authority, or uniqueness in the society. By the time Vietnam helped establish an opposition government in the capital of Phnom Penh in 1985, it is estimated that some 4 million Cambodians had died.

Technology

The post-Industrial Revolution refers to changes that have taken place in this century. These changes were in such fields as the gathering of information, communication, and the manufacture of products. These changes have accelerated contact and diffusion among culture regions and promoted global interdependence. This has, in turn, widened the impact of machines and medical technology on the life styles, work patterns, and standard of living of people in all societies.

The Silicon Chip. Computers have been the key to the changes of the post-Industrial Revolution. The tiny low-cost silicon chip has brought the most important change in human communication since the printing press. A silicon chip makes it possible to perform millions of calculations in a second and to store vast amounts of information. Today's largest computers can perform as many as 800 million calculations a second and store 4 million words. This stored data can be retrieved instantly and transmitted to any location on earth or even into space. Computers today are used in many areas of human activity. These include: international financial and banking transactions and investments; automation of industrial production and product distribution; informational data storage, analysis, sharing, and retrieval; news gathering and spreading via electronic telecommunication; and weapons development, monitoring, and control.

The "Green Revolution." The developing nations need to increase their agricultural production to keep up with the population increases in their nations. The efforts of scientists and government leaders to find ways to do this have produced a "Green Revolution," that is, they have increased the amount of agricultural production from land already under cultivation and expanded farming onto previously non-productive land.

The basis of these improvements has been the development by agronomists (agricultural scientists) of high-yielding plant varieties. These are seeds that can produce greater amounts of crops (especially food grains such as rice and wheat) from an area of land than traditional seeds could produce. However, the new grains are not always as hardy as the older ones, and they need chemical fertilizers, more water, and pesticides to protect them from diseases and insects. Different farming techniques are also necessary to use them effectively.

The Green Revolution needs government support to be carried out. Governments must provide education and information as well as loans to enable farmers to buy the new seeds and the necessary pesticides and fertilizers. They must also build irrigation and transportation systems and provide price supports to guarantee that farmers can sell

371

FACT SHEET: THE GREEN REVOLUTION IN INDIA

Growth rate of agricultural production
1900–47	0.3%
1951–79	2.7%

Production of food grains (rice, wheat and other cereals) (million tonnes)
1950–1	55
1977–8	126.4
1978–9	131.4
1979–80	109.7

Average yields (kg per ha)
	1950–1	1977–8
Wheat	655	1480
Rice	668	1308

Land growing high yield varieties of crops (million ha)
1979–80	43
1985	56

Total irrigated area (million ha)
1950–1	22
1978–9	58.5
1985	68

Use of chemical fertilizers (million tonnes)
1961	0.3
1979–80	5

from Graves, Norman, John Lidstone, and Michael Naish, *People and Environment: A World Perspective* Heinemann Educational Books, Ltd.: London 1987

their products at a profit. In addition, governments must carry out land reform, distributing land in a more equal fashion. Finally, the technology of the Green Revolution (appropriate farm machines and techniques) that are useful in small areas at low cost must be developed and made available.

Without such government support, the risk is too great for most farmers to try the new methods. One of the criticisms of the revolution in agriculture has been its failure to reach poorer farmers. Only those who already make a profit have the money to invest in new methods and techniques. Another criticism is that some of the changes create threats to the environment—irrigation may disrupt normal water systems; internal combustion engines in machinery as well as fertilizers and pesticides pollute the air and water; and overuse of the land can wear it out.

Medical Breakthroughs. The advances in medical technology over the past century have prolonged human life and increased its quality. Vaccinations have helped make humans immune to many deadly diseases, while new treatment techniques have increased survival rates for many others. Likewise, improved treatment of wounds and injuries, as well as organ transplants and artificial body parts, have enabled people to live full lives where in the past they might have been severely disabled.

Attitudes have also changed. People are now seen as "physically challenged" rather than handicapped, and encouraged to strive to reach their potential. "Accessible" public facilities and special activities and support groups have helped to enrich the lives of those with physical disabilities.

Preventing diseases has also become an important medical concern. Scientists have researched the effects of most human activities from smoking to jogging, from eating red meat to living near nuclear power plants. Although there is not always agreement on the implications of such studies, the information does provide people with knowledge and possible choices.

Biotechnology and genetic engineering hold both a promise and a threat for the future. The development of new organisms (biotechnology) may help control diseases or pollutants, but long-term effects may be hard to predict. And the capacity to alter human genes (genetic engineering) that control a person's individual makeup raises ethical as well as medical issues.

Underlying all of this is the issue of cost. Medical treatment grows ever more expensive, even in developed nations. In the developing nations, it is one more factor that must be considered in making decisions regarding use of limited money resources.

Transportation and Communication

One aspect of our modern world is increased mobility — mobility of resources, manufactured goods, ideas and techniques, and of human beings themselves. While the horizons of the average North American, Western European, or Japanese have been expanded by the automobile, the telephone, and satellite television, in Asia and Africa the bicycle or motorbike, the train or mini-bus, and the transistor radio have had a similar impact.

Improved transport systems move oil by supertanker from the Middle East to Japan's industries and move Korean technicians and engineers by jumbo jet to Saudi Arabian oil fields. Paved roads move fertilizer to the rural farms of India's Punjab and rural workers in search of jobs to the cities of Latin America.

China manufactures and uses more bicycles than any other nation. More people ride more trains over more miles in India than anywhere else. Job opportunities for rural Indonesians are increased by their ability to commute to a factory in a nearby town on small Japanese-built motorcycles and bus-vans.

Communication technology also improves people's standards of living. The American investor gathers data using cable TV and buys and sells using a computer. The Philippine farmer listens to the agricultural and weather reports; the Thai craftsperson watches traditional religious dramas on the government television station.

However, improved transportation and communications can also have negative effects. The massive oil spill from the ship Exxon *Valdez* in 1990 damaged Alaska's coastline and disrupted its economy. Tokyo commuters wear masks to keep air-borne chemicals out of their lungs, and London cab drivers average only 9.2 miles per hour, hoping gridlock will not bring a complete standstill.

Terrorists hijack and destroy airliners. Computer hackers develop the potential to disrupt financial, informational, and perhaps even governmental communications systems. Smugglers make millions using boats and airplanes to transport illegal drugs. Each technological innovation also creates the possibility of dishonesty and abuse.

Space Exploration

The "space race" began in 1957 when the Soviet Union launched "Sputnik," the first artificial satellite. One of the highlights of the space race was the landing of American astronauts on the moon in 1969. Today, the space program continues to be the focus of much attention and requires huge amounts of money and resources. Achievements in this area bring great prestige to the nations involved, but some think that the money could be more effectively used elsewhere.

Effects on Global Communication and International Relations. Electronic communication by satellite links has had important effects on both civilian and military aspects of human culture. News and entertainment can be shown live or almost immediately, and nations with "spy-in-the-sky" satellites can monitor the actions and movements of potential enemies.

International crises can develop more quickly but can often be dealt with more easily because of rapid communication. Moreover, when emergencies or disasters occur, aid and relief can be dispatched sooner and with greater effect.

Applications of Space and Space-based Technology. Both the United States and the Soviet Union have applied rocket technology from their space programs to the development of intercontinental ballistic missiles (ICBMs) for use as carriers of atomic weapons. The American "star wars," or Strategic Defense Initiative (SDI), is an attempt to apply satellite techniques to the destruction of missiles in flight.

Astronomers have profited from satellites' ability to look into the depths of space without the interference of the earth's atmosphere. Deep space probes to the farthest reaches of the solar system have extended scientific knowledge in a number of fields.

Meteorology and the analysis and prediction of weather patterns have been changed by satellite radar and photography. Such knowledge benefits travelers, businesspeople, farmers, and those threatened by storms or droughts. Other fields, too, may gain knowledge from the opportunity to conduct experiments in the weightlessness of an orbiting space vehicle. Many consider space the latest human frontier.

Mutual Impact and Influence: Euro-American and Afro-Asia

Much of the history of the past 500 years has focused on the relationships between culture regions that experienced the direct effects of the Industrial Revolution and those that received those effects secondhand. The regions that directly experienced the Industrial Revolution, principally the nations of Europe and North America, are also areas whose cultures are based on the Judeo-Christian and Greco-Roman traditions.

The regions that did not directly experience the Industrial Revolution, such as the Indian cultures of the Americas, the ethnic groups ("tribes") of Africa, the Islamic, Hindu, Buddhist, and Confucian societies of Asia, have been dominated by the West because of its technical and economic power for much of those 500 years. During this period, there has not been much recognition of the contributions of the non-Western cultures to the development of Europe and America.

Europe's reaction to the availability of trade and resources in Africa, Asia, and the Americas was colonialism and imperialism. The technology of the Industrial Revolution provided the weapons and tools and the development of capitalism provided the financial resources for Europe to colonize these areas of the world and to dominate them. This dominance profoundly affected European attitudes, resulting in feelings of cultural superiority, prejudice, discrimination, ethnocentrism, and racism.

In time, the cultures that came under European control reacted with an awakening of pride in their own cultures. As nationalism developed, Americans, Africans, and Asians often used European ideas of political revolution, democracy, and self-determination against the European colonial powers.

The political and economic policies carried out by the colonial powers often disrupted traditional patterns and weakened institutions in the colonies' cultures. Negative elements that already existed in colonized areas were also sometimes made worse—ethnic and social

375

groups vied for power, corruption in government and the economy hurt development, and autocratic elites failed to use human and natural resources effectively.

Most of these difficulties that began in the colonial period have continued to hold back developing nations even after achieving independence from the colonial powers. Old dependencies have continued and are referred to as **neocolonialism**—that is, continued economic dependence on developed nations because of weaknesses in the economies of developing nations.

Stimulated by media images of the developed world, people in the developing nations have experienced a "revolution of rising expectations." Consumer goods such as bicycles and radios, entertainment like rock music and movies, and clothing styles have prompted desires for a higher standard of living. So, too, has knowledge of the possibility of new technologies for increased production in agriculture and industry.

This interaction among culture regions has had a profound impact on both sides. The mutual impact has accelerated and broadened as a result of modern technology, global interdependence, and increased cultural diffusion. This stimulates changes in customs, beliefs, and institutions, often creating conflict between cultures and within cultures.

QUESTIONS

Multiple Choice. Select the letter of the answer that correctly completes each statement.

1. People experiencing the "revolution of rising expectations" today are
   A. eager to accept democracy as the answer to political problems.
   B. not interested in receiving assistance from developed nations.
   C. dissatisfied with some aspects of their present way of life.
   D. determined to follow all of their traditional ways of living.

2. Rapid population growth in a developing nation is due mainly to
   A. a high standard of living for most families.
   B. the availability of medical and health care services.
   C. a booming economy and many employment opportunities.
   D. the number of marriages among younger teenagers.

3. Nations have formed international organizations such as the European Economic Community, the Organization of Petroleum Exporting Countries, and the Organization of African Unity in order to

A. provide for increased military security and national defense.

B. insure that they receive a sufficient supply of natural resources.

C. carry out the decisions of the United Nations Security Council.

D. further their own national interests and improve their situation.

4. Political leaders in both the United States and Great Britain have often spoken in favor of peaceful resolution of international conflicts. Yet during the 1980s the armed forces of both nations have been involved in military encounters outside their own national boundaries. This observation best supports which of the following conclusions?

A. Most armed conflicts are deliberately started by one side or the other.

B. Industrialized nations tend to be more aggressive than developing ones.

C. A popularly elected government must be warlike to satisfy its citizens.

D. Nations often place greater value in their self-interest than in peace.

5. "Acid Rain Destroys North American Forests"
"Chemical Leak in Bhopal, India Kills Thousands"
"Nuclear Accident at Soviet Power Plant in Chernobyl"
The above headlines best support which of the following conclusions?

A. Communist nations produce more pollution than capitalist nations.

B. Developing nations are responsible for most pollution in the world.

C. Protecting the environment is an issue of worldwide importance.

D. The United Nations is responsible for solving pollution problems.

6. A modern well-organized infrastructure is necessary for the economic development of a nation. Which of the following factors would be included in a nation's infrastructure?

A. A network of transportation and communication.

B. A written organizational plan for development.

C. A technological system for using infrared rays.

D. A strong system of family support and unity.

COMPARISON OF INTERNATIONAL INEQUALITIES

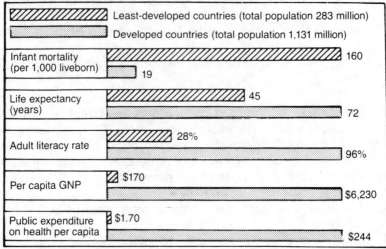

Note: The figures are weighted averages based on data for 1980 or latest available year.
Source: United Nations Children's Fund (UNICEF)

7. A valid conclusion that can be made from the chart above is that nations with a low per capita GNP have
   A. greater life expectancy
   B. greater public expenditure on health per capita
   C. a high infant mortality rate
   D. a high adult literacy rate

Base your answers to question 8 on the chart below.

WHAT AMERICANS BUY FROM AFRICANS* *1982 U.S./sub-Saharan Africa trade ($ value in millions)	
Crude petroleum	$9,900
Coffee beans	$599
Platinum	$352
Aluminum	$292
Diamonds (non-industrial)	$286
Uranium	$200
Cocoa beans	$137
Iron alloys (for steel)	$119

8. Most of the exports from Africa to the United States can be described as
   A. high-technology components
   B. consumer goods
   C. raw materials
   D. agricultural products

9. Global issues such as overcrowding and pollution are a direct result of
   A. high unemployment
   B. an agricultural based economy
   C. population growth
   D. an imbalance in world trade

10. During the 1970s and 1980s, attempts have been made by the United States and the Soviet Union to
    A. share advances in military technology
    B. bring democracy to Eastern Europe
    C. form an alliance against Israel
    D. limit the build up of nuclear weapons

11. In developing countries, the major reason that people move from rural areas to urban areas is to
    A. gain more political power
    B. escape dangerous chemical fertilizers
    C. find better job opportunities
    D. enjoy more varied entertainment

12. Terrorism in the 1980s has been used by certain groups primarily to
    A. find a peaceful way of settling international conflicts
    B. draw the attention of the world to their causes
    C. increase humanitarian aid to their people
    D. put pressure on the superpowers to end the arms race.

13. Which is most characteristic of a nation whose economy is dependent upon the production of one commodity?
    A. The economy is self-sufficient
    B. The nation has a subsistence economy
    C. Economic well-being is closely tied to world market prices
    D. Industrialization makes it possible to export a variety of goods

14. A policy of non-alignment may be attractive to a developing nation because it allows that nation to
    A. become a strong military power in its own right
    B. develop an overseas empire
    C. concentrate on domestic problems
    D. gain benefits from both sides in the super-power competition

15. Which has been an important result of improved means of communication and travel?
    A. Changes in one part of the world can greatly affect other areas
    B. Countries have become more nationalistic
    C. Barriers to international trade have been abolished
    D. There is less need for international organizations

ESSAYS

1. "Our world has become a 'global village.' What happens in one country not only affects the people in that nation, but also those in neighboring nations and possibly those on the other side of the planet."
   Choose one of the hypothetical issues listed below and explain

   a) its possible impact on the people of the nation in which it occurred;
   b) how it might affect neighboring nations;
   c) what impact it might have on distant nations.

   Issues

   The government of Brazil decides to clear 1 million acres of rain forest.

   Britain's Ministry of Industry issues strict rules limiting emissions from coal-burning power plants.

   The Indian Ministry of Family Planning is abolished

   The government of South Africa grants equal rights to all residents

   A cyclone kills thousands and destroys crops in Bangladesh

2. The human rights of certain groups of people have been violated through official government policy and/or by traditional social patterns

Groups

Blacks in South Africa
Untouchables in India
Inhabitants of Cambodia (Kampuchea)
Jews in Europe
Palestinian refugees in the Middle East
Political dissidents in the Soviet Union

Choose THREE of the groups from the list. For EACH group chosen:

—Describe a specific violation of human rights that the group suffered or is suffering
—Describe the efforts that were made or are being made to overcome or compensate for the violations of that groups' human rights

3. In the 20th century, technological developments have had both positive and negative effects.

Technological Developments

Space technology
Nuclear energy
Computer revolution
Advanced medical techniques
Green revolution
Internal combustion engine

Choose THREE technological developments from the list above. For EACH technological development chosen, discuss one positive effect and one negative effect of that technological development on 20th century society. In your answer, include ONE specific example of EACH technological development.

Answer Key

INTRODUCTION

pages 8–9
1. C   4. C   7. D
2. C   5. D   8. C
3. C   6. A   9. A

UNIT ONE

pages 15–16
Multiple Choice
1. B   4. B
2. C   5. C
3. B   6. D

Fact or Opinion
1. F   2. O   3. O

pages 21–22
1. C   5. B
2. D   6. D
3. A   7. C
4. C

page 27
1. C
2. C

pages 46–47
Matching
1. E   4. C
2. B   5. D
3. A

Timeline
1. 4   5. 4   8. 5
2. 1   6. 4   9. 5
3. 4   7. 5   10. 5
4. 2

Issues
1. B   4. B   7. C
2. C   5. A   8. B
3. A   6. B   9. B

UNIT TWO

page 53
Fact or Opinion
1. F   3. F
2. O   4. F

True – False
1. T   4. Arabian Sea
2. Himalayas   5. T
3. Pakistan

pages 58–59
1. B   4. C
2. C   5. D
3. C

page 67
1. A   4. C   6. A
2. D   5. D   7. C
3. B

pages 75–76
Matching
1. D   3. F   5. E
2. C   4. B   6. A

Multiple Choice
1. A   2. D   3. B

page 83
1. D   4. C
2. C   5. C
3. B   6. D

page 86
1. B   3. A
2. B   4. B

page 91
1. A   4. C
2. B   5. B
3. C

UNIT THREE

pages 99–100
Multiple Choice
1. A   2. B   3. D

Fact or Opinion
1. O   3. F
2. O   4. O

pages 105–106
1. D   3. A
2. C   4. D

pages 110–111
1. C   4. B
2. A   5. C
3. B

pages 123–124
1. B   4. B
2. B   5. A
3. A

page 128
1. C   4. A
2. B   5. D
3. B

pages 132–133
1. C   3. A
2. B   4. A

pages 138–139
1. A   3. D   5. C
2. A   4. C   6. B

pages 151–152
1. D   3. B   5. B
2. A   4. C   6. B

UNIT FOUR

page 165
Multiple Choice
1. A   4. A
2. C   5. C
3. D

Matching
1. A   3. D
2. C   4. A

page 171
1. B   3. B
2. B   4. C

pages 177–178
Multiple Choice
1. B   4. B
2. B   5. A
3. D   6. C

Fact or Opinion
1. O   3. F   5. O
2. O   4. F

pages 196–197
1. C   4. C   6. C
2. C   5. B   7. A
3. C

UNIT FIVE

pages 205–206
Multiple Choice
1. A   4. A
2. A   5. A
3. A

Matching
1. D   4. B
2. E   5. C
3. A

pages 213–214
Multiple Choice
1. A   4. D
2. A   5. D
3. A

Matching
1. B   4. C
2. A   5. E
3. D

pages 218–219
Multiple Choice
1. D   4. C
2. A   5. A
3. D

Matching
1. E   4. B
2. D   5. A
3. C

pages 236–237
Multiple Choice
1. D   4. D
2. C   5. D
3. A

Matching
1. D   4. B
2. A   5. C
3. E

UNIT SIX

page 242
1. B   2. D   3. A

page 247
1. D   2. C   3. B

pages 249–250
1. C   3. A
2. C   4. B

pages 304–307
1. A   6. D   11. B   16. A
2. A   7. C   12. C   17. C
3. D   8. D   13. B   18. B
4. D   9. A   14. D   19. D
5. B   10. B   15. D

UNIT SEVEN

page 314
1. B   3. B   5. C
2. A   4. B

pages 317–318
1. D   3. D   5. A
2. A   4. B

pages 322–323
1. B   4. D   6. C
2. B   5. D   7. C
3. C

pages 338–339
1. A   5. C   8. A
2. C   6. D   9. A
3. C   7. C   10. C
4. A

page 343
1. B   4. A
2. B   5. D
3. A

pages 346–347
1. B   4. D
2. C   5. B
3. A

pages 351–352
1. C   5. A   8. C
2. D   6. B   9. B
3. D   7. D   10. A
4. A

UNIT EIGHT

pages 376–380
1. C   3. D   5. C   7. C   9. C   11. C   13. C   15. A
2. B   4. D   6. A   8. C   10. D   12. B   14. D

REGENTS EXAMINATIONS

Part I (55 credits)

Answer all 48 questions in this part.

Directions (1–48): For each statement or question, write on a separate answer sheet the *number* of the word or expression that, of those given, best completes the statement or answers the question.

1 The geographic isolation of a people frequently reinforces
1 a traditional way of life
2 the development of scientific investigation
3 the need for higher education
4 a process of cultural diffusion

2 Nationalism is most likely to develop in an area that has
1 land suited to agriculture
2 adequate industry to supply consumer demands
3 a moderate climate with rivers for irrigation
4 common customs, language, and history

3 Which generalization about the geography of Latin America is accurate?
1 Geographic features prevented foreign imperialism.
2 Harsh climatic conditions have prevented the development of large-scale agriculture.
3 The lack of geographic barriers facilitated the development of transportation and communication systems.
4 Great variations in latitude and land forms resulted in a diversity of climates.

4 Which factor best accounts for the existence of cash-crop production as the major form of agriculture in many Central American nations today?
1 demand of world markets for such crops
2 lack of modern agricultural technology
3 inadequate supply of water and other natural resources
4 peasant ownership of most farmlands

5 Which has been an important factor that has discouraged investment in the economic development of many Latin American nations?
1 lack of natural resources
2 history of colonial dependence
3 declining birth rate
4 political instability

6 Which statement best describes the Roman Catholic Church in most Latin American countries in the 1980's?
1 The activities of the Church are controlled by the national governments.
2 The Church has confined its activities to religious issues.
3 The Church has become active in social and human rights issues.
4 Most people see the Church as having little influence in daily life.

7 The major goal of the Organization of American States (OAS) is to
1 develop trade between Europe and the nations of Latin America
2 provide a peaceful way to settle disputes in the Western Hemisphere
3 encourage political, economic, and social changes in Latin America
4 promote United States investment in South America

8 Which statement best describes the effects of the geography of Africa?
1 Geography has encouraged physical mobility throughout Africa.
2 The geography of Africa has hindered economic development.
3 The geography of Africa has stimulated political and cultural unity.
4 The geography of Africa has resulted in most African countries having similar economic and social systems.

9 A major result of the development of civilization in ancient Egypt was the
1 conquest and settlement of Western Europe by the Egyptian Empire
2 establishment of a democratic system of government in Egypt
3 establishment of trade routes between Egypt and other kingdoms
4 decline of agriculture as an important occupation in Egypt

Base your answer to question 10 on the table below and on your knowledge of social studies.

MINERAL RESOURCES - REPUBLIC OF SOUTH AFRICA
(Averages, in percent, 1981-84)

	Industrial diamond stones	Platinum group metals	Chromium	Vanadium	Manganese	Uranium	Gold
Share of U.S. imports originating in South Africa	67	67	56	38	33	24	n.a.
South Africa's share of world reserves	7	81	84	47	71	14	55.1
South Africa's share of world production	14.8	43.2	n.a.	42.2	14.7	14.8	47.0

Sources: U.S. Department of Commerce; U.S. Bureau of Mines; Organization for Economic Cooperation and Development

10 Which is the most valid statement about the Republic of South Africa that can be made based on the information in the table?
1 Most of South Africa's trade is with other African countries.
2 Trade with the United States is not important to South Africa.
3 South Africa is the single most important producer of manganese in the world.
4 The export of mineral resources is an important part of the economy of South Africa.

---

11 During the 1950's and 1960's, the history of most African countries was characterized by
1 colonization by imperialist nations
2 the achievement of political independence
3 a sharp decrease in the birth rate
4 the development of economic self-sufficiency

12 The term "Pan-Africanism" can best be defined as a movement whose purpose is to
1 promote African unity
2 support cultural diversity
3 encourage European investment in Africa
4 advocate a return to colonial conditions

13 A valid statement concerning the caste system in India is that it has
1 been weakened by urbanization
2 been reinforced by aid from the United States
3 been strengthened by government legislation
4 become a cohesive force for national unity

14 The government of Great Britain built railroads, schools, and irrigation systems in colonial India primarily to
1 prepare India for independence
2 strengthen its political and economic control in India
3 secure favorable trading arrangements with different Indian leaders
4 help India maintain its traditional cultural systems

15 Which generalization best explains the creation of the nations of India and Pakistan in 1947?
1 Armed conflict is necessary for independence movements to succeed.
2 Religious conflicts may have a strong influence on political events.
3 Industrialization needs to reach a high level before a nation can become independent.
4 Similar geographical and historical conditions may promote unity between nations.

Base your answer to question 16 on the cartoon below and on your knowledge of social studies.

Now, remove that and fix this one.

IBH Publishing Company, Bombay.

16 The cartoon illustrates India's problems with
  1 an inadequate transportation system
  2 inefficient government agencies
  3 conflict between religious groups
  4 the monsoon cycle

17 In traditional Chinese culture, which philosophy had the greatest influence on the development of social order and political organization?

1 Taoism
2 Shintoism
3 Confucianism
4 Marxism

18 Which statement best describes the status of women in most traditional Asian societies?

1 Women were encouraged to obtain an education.
2 Women were expected to run for political office.
3 Women were expected to dedicate their lives to their families.
4 Women were encouraged to work outside the home.

19 The Boxer Rebellion of the early 20th century was an attempt to

1 eliminate poverty among the Chinese peasants
2 bring Western-style democracy to China
3 restore trade between China and European nations
4 remove foreign influences from China

20 Which statement about the economy of China in the 1980's is most accurate?

1 China surpassed the Soviet Union in steel production.
2 China's economy slowed down because of a lack of natural resources.
3 China increased its industrial capacity and foreign trade.
4 China's economy suffered from overproduction of consumer goods.

21 In Japan, a major economic problem has been the lack of

1 natural resources
2 investment capital
3 skilled labor
4 experienced management

Base your answers to questions 22 and 23 on the cartoon below and on your knowledge of social studies.

"Don't worry, I'll only use it if I fall behind."

22 What is the main idea of the cartoon?

1 The Japanese should trade only with the United States.
2 The United States has threatened to use tariffs to protect its industries from Japanese competition.
3 Sports competition between the United States and Japan can have an effect on reducing tariffs.
4 United States tariffs have hurt post-war Japanese economic development.

23 Which situation led to the idea presented in the cartoon?

1 the unfavorable United States balance of trade with Japan
2 the superior quality of goods made in the United States
3 takeover of Japanese businesses by Americans
4 the Japanese defeat in World War II

24 Which geographic feature has been most responsible for the population distribution in the Middle East?
1 abundance of oil deposits
2 location of water
3 presence of high plateaus
4 availability of natural harbors

25 Which has been a serious problem for many nations of the Middle East since World War II?
1 renewed colonial conquest by Europeans
2 cutbacks in foreign aid from the United States
3 increased world demand for oil
4 conflicts between traditionalists and modernists

26 The primary goal of the Palestine Liberation Organization (PLO) has been to
1 establish a home state for Palestinian Arabs
2 eliminate communist influence in the Arab nations
3 bring about a peaceful settlement of the conflicts between Egypt and Palestinian Arabs
4 control the Organization of Petroleum Exporting Countries (OPEC)

27 In most of the oil-rich Arab nations, the wealth generated by oil has affected the way of life in that
1 most people have adopted a Western lifestyle and given up their traditional ways
2 oil money has been used by the religious institutions, but not for educational and health facilities
3 technological modernization has occurred, but traditional laws and customs continue
4 women have been given political and social rights equal to those of men

28 Which statement best explains why many Jews left Russia during the late 1800's?
1 There was tremendous overcrowding in the regions of Russia where most of the Jews lived.
2 The Jews experienced many forms of discrimination and persecution.
3 The climate of Western Europe was better suited to the Jews' tradition of farming.
4 The Jews were forced to work in Russian factories.

29 The political reorganization of Russia after the Communist Revolution of 1917 resulted in
1 the establishment of a two-party political system
2 increased political power for ethnic minorities
3 a limited monarchy with the Czar as a figurehead
4 a federation of socialist republics

30 The events that took place in Hungary in the 1950's and in Czechoslovakia in the 1960's demonstrated the Soviet Union's
1 support of nationalism among satellite nations
2 influence on the economies of developing nations
3 determination to maintain political control over Eastern Europe at that time
4 attempts to promote its artistic and literary achievements in Western Europe

31 During the 1980's in the Soviet Union, a major element of the economic policy of *perestroika* was
1 increased collectivization of farms
2 more reliance on local and regional decision-making
3 the expanded use of national five-year plans
4 an emphasis on the redistribution of wealth

32 "All things were under its domain . . . its power was such that no one could hope to escape its scrutiny."

Which European institution during the Middle Ages is best described by this statement?
1 the guild   3 the Church
2 knighthood   4 the nation-state

33 Which was a major result of the Reformation?
1 New Christian denominations emerged.
2 Religious teachings were no longer allowed in the universities.
3 The Crusades were organized.
4 The power of the Pope was strengthened.

34 Karl Marx believed that a proletarian revolution was more likely to occur as a society became more
1 religious   3 industrialized
2 militarized   4 democratic

Base your answers to questions 35 and 36 on the maps below and on your knowledge of social studies.

EUROPE BEFORE AND AFTER WORLD WAR I

Europe Before World War I   Europe After World War I

35 The boundaries of which two countries were most changed by World War I?

1 France and Italy
2 Germany and Belgium
3 Austria-Hungary and Russia
4 Greece and Bulgaria

36 Which is the most valid conclusion that can be drawn from a study of these maps?

1 European boundaries more closely reflected ethnic patterns after World War I.
2 Communist expansion into Eastern Europe began in 1919.
3 The end of World War I brought the need for military alliances.
4 The new boundaries resulted in an end to ethnic conflicts in Europe.

37 Which was a result of the Industrial Revolution in England during the 19th century?

1 The number of farmers increased as the demand for wool in the textile industry rose.
2 Democratic principles were weakened as the power of the working class increased.
3 Workers became more secure in their jobs and less dependent on employers.
4 The structure of society changed to include a growing middle class.

38 The major factor that enabled Western Europe to dominate large parts of Asia and Africa in the 19th and early 20th centuries was the

1 technological and military superiority of European nations
2 acceptance of Christianity by many Asians and Africans
3 desire of Asians and Africans for European raw materials
4 refusal of Asians and Africans to fight against European imperialism

39 Global problems of uneven economic development, environmental pollution, and hunger reflect the need for
1 a return to policies of economic nationalism
2 increased military spending by all nations
3 a reduction in foreign aid provided by industrialized nations
4 increased international cooperation

40 Eighteenth-century Russia and nineteenth-century Japan were similar in that both countries
1 began the process of modernization after a long period of isolation
2 developed democratic governments after years under absolute monarchies
3 refused to accept Western technological ideas
4 adopted socialist economic systems after capitalism had failed

41 The French Revolution of 1789 and the Cuban Revolution of 1959 were similar in that both were caused primarily by the
1 desire of the people to be free from foreign rule
2 pressure of religious leaders for government reform
3 failure of the government to meet the needs of the people
4 ambition of the upper class to attain wealth and property

42 A major cause of the continued conflicts in Northern Ireland and Lebanon has been
1 opposing dynastic claims
2 religious differences
3 interference from the superpowers
4 industrial rivalry

43 Which statement is most characteristic of totalitarian governments?
1 Local media report a variety of opinions concerning government policies.
2 The judiciary is independent of the executive branch of government.
3 Human rights are constitutionally guaranteed for all people.
4 Loyalty is measured by the extent to which a person agrees with government policy.

44 Feudalism in Western Europe was similar to feudalism in Japan in that
1 power was based on class relationships
2 the national government controlled the nobility
3 social mobility was easily achieved
4 most of the people lived in cities

Base your answers to questions 45 and 46 on the passage below and on your knowledge of social studies.

"... But there come some occasions ... when he considers certain laws to be so unjust as to render obedience to them a dishonor. He then openly and civilly breaks them and quietly suffers the penalty for their breach. ..."

45 This passage supports the use of
1 military force   3 appeasement
2 civil disobedience   4 retaliation

46 Which leader based his actions on the philosophy expressed in this passage?
1 Vladimir I. Lenin
2 Simón Bolívar
3 Yasir Arafat
4 Mohandas K. Gandhi

47 Which was characteristic of France under Napoleon's rule and Germany under Hitler's rule?
1 Democratic ideas and diversity were encouraged.
2 Authoritarian control and a strong sense of nationalism prevailed.
3 Peaceful relations with neighboring countries were fostered.
4 Artistic and literary freedom flourished.

48 The best example of nationalism is
1 the people of India demanding independence from Great Britain
2 a medieval lord raising an army to protect his manor
3 the peacekeeping forces of the United Nations patrolling in Lebanon
4 Spain deciding to join the North Atlantic Treaty Organization (NATO)

In developing your answers to Part II, be sure to

    (1) include specific factual information and evidence whenever possible
    (2) keep to the questions asked; do not go off on tangents
    (3) avoid overgeneralizations or sweeping statements without sufficient proof; do not overstate your case
    (4) keep these general definitions in mind:

        (a) discuss means "to make observations about something using facts, reasoning, and argument; to present in some detail"
        (b) describe means "to illustrate something in words or tell about it"
        (c) show means "to point out; to set forth clearly a position or idea by stating it and giving data which support it"
        (d) explain means "to make plain or understandable; to give reasons for or causes of; to show the logical development or relationships of"

Part II

ANSWER THREE QUESTIONS FROM THIS PART.   [45]

1 Many problems of regions and nations of the world are related to geography.

Geographic Characteristics
Climate
Location
Mountains
Lack of natural barriers
Scarcity of water
Scarcity of mineral resources

Select *three* geographic characteristics from the list and for *each* characteristic:

    • Discuss how that characteristic has created a problem for a specific region or nation selected from Africa, Asia, Europe, the Middle East, or Latin America [You must use a different region or nation for each characteristic discussed.]
    • Explain an action the region or nation has taken to adapt to or modify the effect of the geographic characteristic   [5,5,5]

2 Throughout history, the lives of people have been shaped by the forms of government under which they live.

Forms of Government
Nazi totalitarianism
Communist totalitarianism
Constitutional democracy
Absolute monarchy

Select *one* of the forms of government from the list.

    a Discuss *two* factors that led to the establishment of this form of government in a specific nation. [You may *not* select the United States for your answer.]   [6]
    b Describe *two* ways the lives of the people in the nation identified in part *a* were affected following the establishment of this form of government.   [4]
    c Discuss the extent to which this form of government improved or hindered the political, economic, or social development of the nation.   [5]

3 A strong leader acts decisively not only to influence events within his or her nation but also to influence relations with other nations.

Leaders

Corazón Aquino
Peter the Great
Ayatollah Khomeini
Deng Xiaoping
Fidel Castro
Napoleon Bonaparte
Indira Gandhi
Jomo Kenyatta

Select *three* leaders listed and for *each* leader:
- Identify the nation in which the leader acted
- Discuss *one* domestic policy or *one* foreign policy of the leader
- Discuss a method used by the leader to put his or her policies into effect   [5,5,5]

4 Since World War II, the 20th century has been a period of increased interdependence. International organizations reflect this interdependence.

International Organizations

European Economic Community (EEC)
North Atlantic Treaty Organization (NATO)
Warsaw Pact
Organization of Petroleum Exporting Countries (OPEC)
United Nations
Organization of African Unity (OAU)

Select *three* of the organizations listed and for *each* organization:
- Describe the organization
- Identify a major goal of the organization
- Discuss a problem faced by the organization in attempting to achieve this goal
  [5,5,5]

5 ·Throughout history, both men and women have had an impact on their times. They have played various roles.

Roles

Scientist
Political reformer
Social reformer
Writer
Revolutionary

a Select *two* roles from the list and for *each* role selected, identify *one* man or woman who played the role in a specific African, Asian, Latin American, Middle Eastern, or European nation. [You must identify a different person for each role.] [5]

b Describe an action, discovery, or work of *each* individual identified in part *a*, and discuss the individual's impact on the political, economic, or social development of his or her nation or society.   [10]

6 Throughout history, great civilizations have existed in different areas of the world.

Civilizations

Ancient Mesopotamia
Ancient Africa
Golden Age of Athens
Golden Age of China
Ancient Latin American Empires
Golden Age of Muslim Culture

Select *three* of the civilizations listed and discuss *two* specific characteristics or achievements of each civilization.   [5,5,5]

7 Nations and regions often adopt ideas and practices from other parts of the world. The nations listed below have experienced cultural diffusion.

Japan from China
Mexico from Spain
Rome from Greece
Europe from Africa
Russia from the Byzantine Empire
Southeast Asia from India

Select *three* of the examples listed and for *each* example:

- Describe one idea or practice that was acquired by the first nation or region from the second
- Discuss the effect of the idea or practice on the nation or region that adopted it
      [5,5,5]

Part I (55 credits)

Answer all 49 questions in this part.

Directions (1–49): For each statement or question, write on a separate answer sheet the *number* of the word or expression that, of those given, best completes the statement or answers the question.

1 The river valleys of the Tigres-Euphrates, the Nile, and the Indus were centers of civilization because they
  1 had rich deposits of iron ore and coal
  2 were isolated from other cultural influences
  3 were easy to defend from invasion
  4 provided a means of transportation and irrigation

2 Which statement about nationalism is most accurate?
  1 It becomes a unifying force among a people.
  2 It encourages diversity within nation-states.
  3 It prevents the rise of militarism.
  4 It eliminates the ethnic identities of different groups.

3 Cultural diffusion occurs most rapidly in societies that
  1 adhere to traditional social values
  2 have extended families
  3 come into frequent contact with other groups
  4 have a strong oral history

4 The geographic features of the African Continent are partly responsible for the
  1 use of French or English as the official language of many African nations
  2 diversity of cultures found in Africa
  3 decline of the slave trade in the 19th century
  4 recent advances in technology in African nations

5 Which is a major characteristic of traditional African art?
  1 African art contains a great deal of symbolism.
  2 The human form is represented very realistically in African art.
  3 Painting is the primary medium for African art.
  4 African art reflects a highly urban culture.

6 Jomo Kenyatta and Kwame Nkrumah were African leaders opposed to
  1 militarism   3 nationalism
  2 socialism   4 colonialism

7 In the Republic of South Africa, the government's apartheid policy has been based primarily on the concept of
  1 justice under the law
  2 nativism
  3 racial segregation
  4 economic specialization

8 Future economic development of sub-Saharan Africa will most likely be centered around Africa's
  1 handicraft traditions
  2 mineral resources
  3 rich agricultural soil
  4 highly developed transportation systems

9 In traditional India, the caste system and the Hindu beliefs in karma and dharma most directly resulted in
  1 the establishment of a set of rules for each individual in the society
  2 the rapid industrialization of the economy
  3 a strong emphasis on the acquisition of wealth
  4 a strong belief in the importance of education

10 Which was a major reason for the creation of the separate nations of India and Pakistan in 1947?
  1 India was economically dependent on Great Britain, while Pakistan was economically self-sufficient.
  2 The two nations favored vastly different forms of government.
  3 The religious and cultural patterns of the two areas were in serious conflict.
  4 Natural geographic features of the Indian subcontinent divided the two areas.

11 Which development was a result of the other three?
  1 West Pakistani government administrators being appointed in East Pakistan
  2 the creation of the nation of Bangladesh
  3 the existence of cultural and economic differences between East and West Pakistan
  4 rioting in East Pakistan in 1971

12 Which is a result of India's policy of nonalignment?
1 India has kept its defense spending at a low level.
2 The Indian government has been successful in limiting population growth.
3 The Indian government has worked to reduce religious conflicts.
4 India has accepted aid from both the United States and the Soviet Union.

Base your answers to questions 13 and 14 on the cartoon below and on your knowledge of social studies.

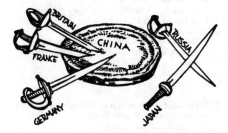

13 The cartoon depicts the
1 ethnocentrism of the Chinese during the Manchu Ch'ing dynasty of the 17th century
2 separation of China into spheres of influence by 19th-century imperialist nations
3 military aid given to the Chinese revolutionaries by the Soviet Union during the 1940's
4 favored trading-partner status awarded to China by many Western European countries in the 1980's

14 The situation depicted in the cartoon was brought about by the
1 economic agreements with Western nations signed by Deng Xiaoping
2 low level of cultural and economic development in China throughout its history
3 military weakness of China and the European desire for expansion
4 alliance of the Soviet Union with the Communists and the aid given to the Nationalists by Western Europe

15 Which segment of Chinese society gave the most support to the Communists during the Revolution?
1 peasants   3 landowners
2 religious leaders   4 bureaucrats

16 During the 1980's, a major goal of China was to
1 accelerate economic growth
2 encourage the growth of traditional religions
3 establish a federal system of government
4 protect individual liberties

17 Which value was common to traditional society in both China and Japan?
1 pacifism   3 individualism
2 family loyalty   4 materialism

18 Which was a major justification used by Japan for empire building in the 1930's and 1940's?
1 revenging attacks by aggressive neighbors
2 promoting immigration of foreigners
3 spreading the Buddhist religion
4 obtaining food and raw materials

19 Since World War II, which development has occurred in the Japanese economy?
1 Japan has become self-sufficient since it now possesses adequate resources.
2 Japan has achieved a favorable balance of trade.
3 Japan has returned to a strong emphasis on agriculture.
4 Japan has a shortage of skilled workers.

20 Which statement about Latin America is an opinion rather than a fact?
1 African slaves were imported because there was a scarcity of workers.
2 Roman Catholicism is the dominant religion of the area.
3 Enormous diversity exists in the physical environment of Central and South America.
4 The people of this area are less resistant to change than people in other developing areas.

21 Which group has most frequently opposed social and economic changes in Latin America?
1 landowners   3 liberation priests
2 students   4 peasants

22 Which is the main purpose of the Good Neighbor policy, the Alliance for Progress, and the Organization of American States (OAS)?
  1 to establish democracy among newly independent Latin American nations
  2 to provide mutual military support for Latin American nations
  3 to develop cooperation among nations of the Western Hemisphere
  4 to eliminate all barriers to trade between member nations

Base your answer to question 23 on the cartoon below and on your knowledge of social studies.

23 The main idea of the cartoon is that in the early part of the 20th century
  1 South Americans asked the United States to protect them
  2 international cooperation maintained peace in South America
  3 the Monroe Doctrine was no longer enforceable
  4 the United States forcefully extended its influence into South America

24 The Middle East has been a crossroads for trade from Asia, Africa, and Europe. Which is a major result of this fact?
  1 Most of the Middle East's natural resources have been exhausted.
  2 The Middle East has become a wealthy area with a high standard of living.
  3 Many different cultures can be found in the Middle East.
  4 The Middle East has experienced a strong sense of national unity.

25 Which generalization is best supported by a study of the Middle East?
  1 Illiteracy has become almost nonexistent.
  2 Religious differences have led to serious conflicts.
  3 Oil wealth has led to economic equality.
  4 Industrial development has urbanized the area.

26 Which factor has served as a bond among Arab countries in the Middle East?
  1 similarity of government
  2 unity under a military leader
  3 reliance on the United States for aid
  4 hostility toward Israel

27 The Organization of Petroleum Exporting Countries (OPEC) was formed primarily to
  1 give member nations more influence in world markets
  2 force developing countries to abandon policies of nonalignment
  3 help Middle Eastern nations form alliances with Western powers
  4 allow the Soviet Union to develop greater influence in the Middle East

28 In Middle Eastern society, women have increasingly been at the center of a conflict between the forces of modernization and the
  1 values of traditional Islamic culture
  2 pressure for a Palestinian homeland
  3 shortage of capital for industrial development
  4 need to reduce the birth rate

29 The art, music, and philosophy of the medieval period in Europe generally dealt with
1 human scientific achievements
2 religious themes
3 materialism
4 classic Greek and Roman subjects

30 Which statement best describes the result of the Crusades?
1 Europeans maintained a lasting control over much of the Middle East.
2 Islamic influence dominated Europe.
3 Europeans developed tolerance of non-Christian religions.
4 Trade between Europe and the Middle East was expanded.

31 Which societal condition was basic to the development of Greek philosophy and Renaissance art?
1 rigid social classes
2 emphasis on individualism
3 religious uniformity
4 mass education

32 The writers and philosophers of the Enlightenment believed that government decisions should be based on
1 fundamental religious beliefs
2 the concept of divine right of kings
3 laws of nature and reason
4 traditional values

33 In France, which was a major result of the French Revolution?
1 The King was restored to unlimited power.
2 The clergy dominated government.
3 The middle class gained political influence.
4 The tax burden was carried by the lower classes.

34 Which statement best describes Europe just before World War I?
1 The formation of opposing alliance systems increased international distrust.
2 European leaders resorted to a policy of appeasement to solve international disputes.
3 The communist nations promoted violent revolution throughout Western Europe.
4 The isolationist policies of England and France prevented their entry into the hostilities.

35 Which situation contributed to Adolf Hitler's rise to power in Germany after World War I?
1 support of Hitler's radical policies by the Social Democrats in the Reichstag
2 strong feelings of resentment and nationalism built up by economic and political crises
3 refusal by the League of Nations to admit Germany as a member
4 violence and terrorism promoted by Germany's former enemies

36 Which has been a major change in the political situation in Western Europe in the last half of the 20th century?
1 Nationalism has increased rivalry between Western European nations.
2 Western European nations have gained power through control of world oil resources.
3 Western European nations have worked cooperatively for security and prosperity.
4 Powerful dictatorships have emerged throughout Western Europe.

37 Which term best describes the political system in Russia before the 20th century?
1 constitutional republic
2 absolute monarchy
3 parliamentary democracy
4 military dictatorship

38 The Russian peasants supported the Bolsheviks in the 1917 revolutions mainly because the Bolsheviks promised to
1 establish collective farms
2 maintain the agricultural price-support system
3 bring modern technology to Russian farms
4 redistribute the land owned by the nobility

39 Which statement best describes the political situation in the Soviet Union immediately after Lenin's death in 1924?
1 The nation adopted a constitutional monarchy.
2 Trotsky and his followers assumed full control of the Communist Party.
3 Popular elections were held to choose a new General Secretary.
4 A power struggle developed among Communist Party leaders.

Base your answer to question 40 on the quotation below and on your knowledge of social studies.

"From Stettin in the Baltic to Trieste in the Adriatic, an iron curtain has descended across the Continent. Behind that line lie all the capitals of the ancient states of central and eastern Europe. Warsaw, Berlin, Prague, Vienna, Budapest, Belgrade, Bucharest and Sofia, all these famous cities and the populations around them lie in what I might call the Soviet sphere, and all are subject, in one form or another, not only to Soviet influence, but to very high, and in some cases increasing measure of control from Moscow."

— Winston Churchill

40 What is the main idea of this quotation?
  1 The Soviet Union has expanded its influence throughout eastern Europe.
  2 The Soviet Union has helped the nations of eastern Europe improve their standard of living.
  3 The democratic nations of western Europe have stopped the expansion of Soviet influence in the world.
  4 The Soviet Union will support communist revolutions in Southeast Asia.

41 During the 1980's, the Soviet Union experimented with modifications of its command economy by
  1 eliminating central planning
  2 allowing private ownership of major industries
  3 introducing some market economy strategies
  4 legalizing independent trade unions

42 In a number of European countries in the 1800's, which situation occurred as a result of the influence of the French Revolution?
  1 increase in religious conflict
  2 rise of nationalistic movements
  3 decentralization of governmental power
  4 economic depression

43 Dr. Martin Luther King, Jr.'s ideas on nonviolence were most directly influenced by the
  1 sayings of Confucius
  2 teachings of Buddha
  3 principles of Mohandas K. Gandhi
  4 philosophy of Socrates

44 The concept of mercantilism is best illustrated by the
  1 political structure of China during the Chou dynasty
  2 social kinship system of the Ashanti people
  3 military strategies of the armies of the Roman Empire
  4 economic relationship between Spain and its Latin American colonies

45 A study of untouchables and Brahmins in India and a study of Indians and people of European descent in some Central American nations indicates that
  1 class systems exist in many parts of the world
  2 low levels of technology create divisions between people
  3 there is a new unity among the poor of the world
  4 people live as equals throughout the world

46 The European concept of the divine right of kings and the Chinese belief in the mandate of heaven were both based on
  1 the principle of democratic election of rulers
  2 the division of power between the nobility and the king
  3 the idea that political power comes from a Supreme Being
  4 a constitution that defines individual rights

47 Gamal Abdel Nasser, Mao Zedong, and Simón Bolívar were similar because they
  1 promoted nationalism among their peoples
  2 believed in Marxist principles
  3 modeled their political actions on religious doctrine
  4 encouraged terrorism and violence in their revolutions

48 During the 1970's and 1980's, India and China attempted to improve the quality of life for their people and to increase economic growth by
  1 changing the political structure
  2 adopting policies to limit population growth
  3 encouraging farmers to move to the cities
  4 seeking overseas colonies

49 A valid statement about technology in the 20th century is that technology has
  1 eliminated famine and disease throughout the world
  2 delayed economic progress in developing countries
  3 led to the adoption of free trade policies
  4 accelerated the pace of cultural diffusion

In developing your answers to Part II, be sure to

(1) include specific factual information and evidence whenever possible
(2) keep to the questions asked; do not go off on tangents
(3) avoid overgeneralizations or sweeping statements without sufficient proof; do not overstate your case
(4) keep these general definitions in mind:
    (a) <u>discuss</u> means "to make observations about something using facts, reasoning, and argument; to present in some detail"
    (b) <u>describe</u> means "to illustrate something in words or tell about it"
    (c) <u>show</u> means "to point out; to set forth clearly a position or idea by stating it and giving data which support it"
    (d) <u>explain</u> means "to make plain or understandable; to give reasons for or causes of; to show the logical development or relationships of"

Part II

ANSWER THREE QUESTIONS FROM THIS PART. [45]

1 Geographic factors have influenced the development of many nations of the world. Some pairs of nations whose development has been influenced by geographic factors are listed below.

Pairs

Soviet Union and China
West Germany and Japan
India and Italy
Egypt and Brazil
Poland and Great Britain
Nigeria and Mexico

Choose *three* of the pairs of nations listed. For *each* pair chosen, use specific examples to show how geographic factors have had similar *or* different effects on the economic *or* political *or* cultural development of the two paired nations. [5,5,5]

2 The relationships between colonialism, imperialism, and nationalism have formed an important part of the world's history.

  a Identify a European nation that established colonies during the 17th, 18th, or 19th century. Identify an area colonized by that nation and discuss specific reasons that the European nation colonized the area. [5]

  b Discuss *two* effects that the European nation identified in part *a* had on the people of the colonized area. [5]

  c Describe how nationalist movements within the colonized area discussed in parts *a* and *b* led to independence from the European nation. [5]

3 Major events or movements in history are sometimes described in terms of cause-and-effect relationships.

Events/Movements

Fall of Rome
Arab Conquest of the Middle East
Renaissance in Europe
Industrial Revolution in Europe
Meiji Restoration in Japan
Opium War in China
Mau Mau Uprising in Kenya
Cuban Revolution

Choose *three* of the events or movements listed above. For *each* one chosen:

- Describe the major causes of the event or movement
- Discuss the impact of the event or movement on a specific nation or region   [5,5,5]

4 The actions or ideas of one person often have a profound effect on the actions or ideas of another person.

Pairs

Mohandas K. Gandhi and Jawaharlal Nehru
Mao Zedong and Chiang Kai-shek
Adolf Hitler and Winston Churchill
Karl Marx and Vladimir Lenin
Anastasio Somoza and Daniel Ortega
Shah Pahlevi and Ayatollah Khomeini

Choose *three* of the pairs listed above. For *each* pair chosen, use specific examples to show how the actions or ideas of one person in the pair affected the actions or ideas of the other person.   [5,5,5]

5 Human interaction has often resulted in conflict between groups and cultures. Some groups and cultures that have experienced conflict are listed below.

Groups and Cultures

Israelis and Arab Palestinians in the Middle East
Sandinistas and Contras in Central America
Blacks and whites in the Republic of South Africa
Shiite Muslims and Sunni Muslims in the Middle East
Hindus and Sikhs in India
Catholics and Protestants in Northern Ireland

Select *three* of the groups or cultures from the list. For *each* one selected, discuss a major cause of the conflict and the effects of the conflict on the groups involved.   [5,5,5]

6 Some of the principal aims of the United Nations are listed below.

Maintaining international peace and security
Fostering and promoting human rights
Promoting social progress and better standards of life

For *each* aim listed:

- Describe a specific action taken by the United Nations between 1945 and the present to achieve this aim
- Describe a major obstacle the United Nations has faced in trying to achieve this aim
- Discuss the extent to which the United Nations has been successful in achieving this aim   [5,5,5]

7 The drawing below depicts an economic situation in the world today.

a Describe the economic situation illustrated by the drawing.   [3]

b For *each* of the two sections of the world pictured, describe a specific economic problem that has resulted from the situation.   [6]

c Discuss how nations or regions within *one* of the sections of the world pictured have attempted to change the situation.   [6]

Part I (55 credits)

Answer all 48 questions in this part.

Directions (1–48): For each statement or question, write on the separate answer sheet the *number* of the word or expression that, of those given, best completes the statement or answers the question.

1 Early civilizations developed mainly in
  1 areas with abundant mineral resources
  2 valleys near rivers
  3 areas with climatic diversity
  4 mountainous areas

2 Both the ancient Romans and the ancient Chinese viewed foreigners as barbarians. This is an example of
  1 cultural diffusion   3 imperialism
  2 materialism   4 ethnocentrism

3 Which is a feature of most traditional societies?
  1 political equality of men and women
  2 extended family system
  3 ease of upward social mobility
  4 involvement of all adults in decisionmaking

4 Which situation generally occurs in a society as a result of urbanization?
  1 Opportunities for social mobility increase.
  2 Ties to extended families are strengthened.
  3 Poverty in rural areas is eliminated.
  4 Employment opportunities in the cities decrease.

5 The main purpose of a written constitution, regardless of the political system to which it applies, is to
  1 guarantee protection of civil liberties
  2 regulate trade and commerce
  3 describe the relationship between citizens and their government
  4 define the status of religious and ethnic minorities

6 When the Indian subcontinent became independent of Great Britain, the subcontinent was partitioned because of
  1 religious differences between Hindus and Muslims
  2 unresolved territorial claims of local princes
  3 ethnic problems between Punjabis and Bengalis
  4 economic conflicts between rural and urban dwellers

7 Which has been one effect of the traditional caste system in India?
  1 It has provided many opportunities for upward social mobility.
  2 The nation's wealth has been shared equally among the people.
  3 It has provided people with a sense of identity.
  4 Basic political rights have been extended to all people.

8 During the 1980's, a major problem in India was
  1 widespread rejection of the policy of nonalignment
  2 the decline of the Hindu religion
  3 the threat of invasion from Pakistan
  4 violence resulting from cultural differences

9 Europeans were able to dominate much of south and southeast Asia in the 19th and 20th centuries primarily because
  1 Christianity appealed to the people of the region
  2 Europeans had more advanced technology
  3 this region lacked political organization
  4 few natural resources were found in the region

Base your answers to questions 10 and 11 on the cartoon below and on your knowledge of social studies.

ACTUALLY, OUR COUNTRIES HAVE A UNIQUE RELATIONSHIP. WE PROTECT JAPAN'S STRATEGIC AND OIL INTERESTS FROM EXTERNAL THREATS, AND JAPAN PROTECTS ITS DOMESTIC MARKETS FROM U.S. IMPORTS!

© 1987 H. PAYNE—SCRIPPS HOWARD

10 The main idea of the cartoon is that the current relationship between the United States and Japan
1 may lead to a destruction of Japan's traditional culture
2 has prevented trade with other countries
3 has been more beneficial to Japan than to the United States
4 has had a negative impact on the economies of both countries

11 Which person would be most likely to agree with the point of view expressed in the cartoon?
1 an American importer of Japanese cars
2 an unemployed American factory worker
3 a prosperous Japanese farmer
4 the Japanese Minister for Economic Affairs

12 Japan's present-day industrial success is based primarily on
1 dependence on loans from Western European nations
2 abundant natural resources of iron and petroleum
3 cultural adaptation and modern technology
4 strong military forces and imperialism

13 Confucianism in traditional China and communism in modern-day China are similar because both emphasize that
1 the needs of the group are more important than those of the individual
2 the pursuit of individual wealth is a necessary and desirable goal
3 a nation must give up its old traditions if it wants to be strong
4 there is wisdom in adopting foreign ways to meet the needs of the nation

14 Both the Taiping Rebellion and the Boxer Rebellion attempted to rid China of
1 Mongol control
2 illegal drug traffic
3 communist influence
4 foreign domination

15 The Chinese Communists were successful in their revolution during the 1930's and 1940's mainly because the Communists
1 gave factory workers leadership positions in the Communist Party
2 accepted advanced military technology from Western nations
3 emphasized the needs of the rural peasant population
4 provided for universal suffrage and free elections

Base your answer to question 16 on the cartoon below and on your knowledge of social studies.

16 The cartoon suggests that the system of white minority rule in the Republic of South Africa will be most affected by
1 military intervention by Western European nations
2 democratic reforms taken by neighboring African nations
3 human rights resolutions passed by the United Nations
4 economic actions taken by black South Africans

17 Which is often a characteristic of traditional African art?
1 African art forms reflect society's desire to become industrialized.
2 African works of art are an important part of religious life.
3 African art forms generally support government-approved objectives.
4 African works of art primarily commemorate important battles and victories.

18 In Africa, a major result of World War II was
1 an increase in feelings of nationalism
2 a general decline in the standard of living
3 an increase in colonization by European nations
4 a rapid decline in population

Base your answers to questions 19 and 20 on the table below and on your knowledge of social studies.

ECONOMIC CONDITIONS IN LATIN AMERICA

Nation	Population (in millions)	Per capita GNP (in dollars)	Infant Mortality (per 1,000)	Literacy (percent)	Years until Population Doubles	Urban Population (percent)	Life Expectancy (years)
Bolivia	6.9	1,217	142	75	25	46	51
Brazil	144.4	2,002	75	74	30	68	63
Costa Rica	2.9	1,400	38	90	27	48	73
Haiti	6.3	290	107	23	30	28	53
Mexico	83.5	2,590	54	74	27	70	66
Venezuela	18.8	3,726	36	86	25	76	69

19 Which nation has the greatest problem in the area of public health?
1 Bolivia
2 Costa Rica
3 Mexico
4 Venezuela

20 Which statement is most accurate based on the information in the table?
1 Mexico has the largest population in Latin America.
2 Brazil has the highest literacy rate in Latin America.
3 Most of the people of Venezuela live in cities.
4 Costa Rica has the highest per capita GNP in Latin America.

21 Which is a valid generalization about Latin America?
  1 Most Latin Americans live in isolated farm villages.
  2 The majority of the governments in Latin America are communist.
  3 Most Latin Americans are descendants of immigrants from Africa.
  4 Latin America is a region of racial and cultural diversity.

22 Which was a major trend in Latin American politics during the 1980's?
  1 Civilian governments replaced military governments in many countries.
  2 Monarchies were returned to power throughout the region.
  3 Most countries supported United States intervention in Cuba.
  4 Many countries rejected the policies of the Organization of American States.

23 The Ten Commandments and the Five Pillars of Wisdom are similar in that they
  1 established a class structure for society
  2 are guidelines for living
  3 consist of prayers for salvation
  4 promise a happy and easy life

24 Which has been a major goal of both the Zionists and the Palestinian Arabs in the Middle East?
  1 to unite the Middle East under their religion
  2 to improve their relations with the Soviet Union
  3 to become leaders in the world economy
  4 to have their own independent country

25 During the Renaissance, which development contributed most to the Protestant Reformation?
  1 interest in ancient Greece and Rome
  2 advances in mathematics and science
  3 questioning of traditional authority
  4 attention to realism and detail

Base your answer to question 26 on the map below and on your knowledge of social studies.

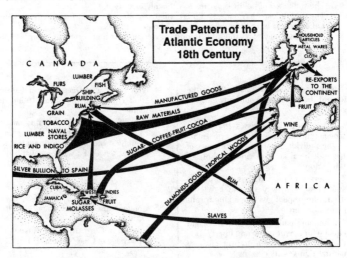

26 The map illustrates the concept of
  1 mercantilism   3 socialism
  2 isolationism   4 feudalism

27 In Western Europe, which development was the cause of the other three?

  1 the increase in the size and number of cities
  2 fewer people living and working on farms
  3 the Industrial Revolution
  4 the existence of severe air and water pollution

28 Which statement best explains why democratic governments failed in many European nations after World War I?
  1 The governments were unable to solve serious economic problems in these nations.
  2 The working classes were put in control of industrial production in these nations.
  3 These nations were constantly threatened by attacks from the victors of the war.
  4 The United States openly interfered in European political affairs.

29 The Holocaust in Europe and the treatment of Armenians in the Ottoman Empire have both been cited as examples of

1 genocide 3 imperialism
2 socialism 4 divine right

30 In which way were the results of World War I and World War II similar?

1 Hereditary monarchs were exiled and replaced by elected officials throughout Europe.
2 Harsh peace treaties prevented economic recovery and led quickly to war in Europe.
3 United States foreign aid programs helped rebuild European economies.
4 The political boundaries of Central and Eastern European nations changed significantly.

Base your answer to question 31 on the table below and on your knowledge of social studies.

SOCIAL ORIGINS OF MEMBERS OF THE BRITISH CABINET
(19th and 20th centuries)

Class	1868-1886	1886-1916	1916-1935	1935-1955	1955-1970
Aristocracy	55%	49%	23%	21%	13%
Middle class	45	49	57	58	72
Working class	—	3	19	21	14

31 Which generalization is supported by the information in the table?

1 The influence of political parties has steadily increased.
2 The middle class has played an increasingly significant role in British government.
3 Labor unions have little influence on Cabinet decisions.
4 The aristocracy plays the most important role in British government today.

Base your answers to questions 32 and 33 on the speakers' statements below and on your knowledge of social studies.

Speaker A: Good government stresses the importance of the nation and accepts the rights of the individual only if the interests of the individual are the same as those of the nation.

Speaker B: The person of the king is sacred and to attack him in any way is to attack religion itself. The respect given to a king is religious in nature.

Speaker C: All human beings are born free and equal with a right to life and liberty. It is the duty of government to protect these natural rights of its citizens.

Speaker D: Our goal will not be achieved by democracy or liberal reforms, but by blood and iron. Only then will we be successful. No nation achieves greatness or unity without the traumatic experiences of war.

32 Which speaker's statement expresses the idea of divine right?

(1) A (3) C
(2) B (4) D

33 Which speaker's statement best reflects the ideas of the Enlightenment?

(1) A (3) C
(2) B (4) D

34 Which was a characteristic of Germany under Adolf Hitler and the Soviet Union under Josef Stalin?

1 an official foreign policy of isolationism
2 governmental control of the media
3 public ownership of business and industry
4 the absence of a written constitution

35 A major cause of the Russian Revolution of 1917 was the

1 defeat of Germany in the Russian campaign
2 marriage of Czar Nicholas II to a German princess
3 existence of sharp economic differences between social classes
4 appeal of Marxism to the Russian nobility

36 Which statement best describes most Eastern European countries immediately after World War II?

1 They adopted democratic reforms in their political systems.
2 They became satellite states of the Soviet Union.
3 They became dependent on aid provided by the Marshall Plan.
4 They emerged as world economic powers.

37 The economic policies of the Soviet Union have traditionally emphasized the production of
1 automobiles for export
2 building materials for luxury housing
3 consumer goods
4 heavy industrial goods

38 The Soviet Union's reaction to the 1968 revolt in Czechoslovakia was to
1 permit limited political and economic reforms in Czechoslovakia
2 withdraw Soviet troops from Eastern Europe
3 send Soviet troops to occupy Czechoslovakia
4 bring the matter to the attention of the United Nations

39 Which statement best describes the political situation in Eastern Europe during the 1980's?
1 Nationalism has often been a strong force for change.
2 Communist governments have gained power through democratic elections.
3 Ethnic rivalries have been eliminated throughout the region.
4 United States influence has been used to keep communist governments in power.

40 A nation that is nonaligned and economically developing would be most likely to
1 enter into an exclusive trade agreement with the United States
2 join the other members of the Warsaw Pact
3 form a military alliance with the Soviet Union
4 accept aid from both the Soviet Union and the United States

41 Many Muslims live in Egypt, Nigeria, Pakistan, and Indonesia. Based on this information, which conclusion is valid?
1 Most Muslims tend to support repressive governments.
2 Islam is practiced by people of many different cultures.
3 Most Muslims live in areas that are sparsely populated.
4 Islamic nations produce surplus food for export.

42 Technological changes in economically developing countries have most often resulted in
1 mass migrations from urban to rural areas
2 fewer educational and employment opportunities
3 weakening of traditional values and family patterns
4 decreased use of natural resources

43 Which is the best example of an element of a command economy?
1 large, modern corporations in Japan
2 cottage industries in India
3 subsistence agriculture of Southeast Asia
4 Five-Year Plans in the Soviet Union

44 Feudal societies are generally characterized by
1 an emphasis on social order
2 a representative government
3 many economic opportunities
4 the protection of political rights

45 The North Atlantic Treaty Organization, the Cuban Missile Crisis, and the Korean War are examples of
1 attempts to prevent the spread of communist power
2 United States efforts to gain foreign territory
3 the failure of capitalism and free market economies
4 United Nations interference in the internal affairs of member nations

46 A study of revolutions would most likely lead to the conclusion that prerevolutionary governments
1 are more concerned about human rights than the governments that replace them are
2 refuse to modernize their armed forces with advanced technology
3 attempt to bring about the separation of government from religion
4 fail to meet the political and economic needs of their people

47 The withdrawal of France from Indochina, the involvement of the Soviet Union in Cuba, and the United States support of the Contras in Nicaragua illustrate that nations
1 consistently discard traditional foreign policy goals after changes in administration
2 tend to base foreign policy decisions on what they believe to be their self-interests
3 no longer use warfare as a means to resolve international conflict
4 tend to refer foreign policy conflicts to the United Nations

48 Which generalization is best supported by developments in trade such as Japanese investments in Southeast Asia, the sale of United States grain to the Soviet Union, and the reliance of many Western European nations on oil from the Middle East?
1 Most of the nations of the world are adopting socialist economies.
2 Nations that control vital resources are no longer able to influence world markets.
3 The goal of the world's economic planners is to decrease national self-sufficiency.
4 The nations of the world have become interdependent.

Answers to the following questions are to be written on paper provided by the school.

Students Please Note:

In developing your answers to Parts II and III, be sure to

(1) include specific factual information and evidence whenever possible
(2) keep to the questions asked; do not go off on tangents
(3) avoid overgeneralizations or sweeping statements without sufficient proof; do not overstate your case
(4) keep these general definitions in mind:
    (a) <u>discuss</u> means "to make observations about something using facts, reasoning, and argument; to present in some detail"
    (b) <u>describe</u> means "to illustrate something in words or tell about it"
    (c) <u>show</u> means "to point out; to set forth clearly a position or idea by stating it and giving data which support it"
    (d) <u>explain</u> means "to make plain or understandable; to give reasons for or causes of; to show the logical development or relationships of"

Part II

ANSWER THREE QUESTIONS FROM THIS PART.   [45]

1 Geographic features such as topography, climate, or resources have influenced the development of many nations.

Nations

China
Great Britain
India
Israel
Japan
Panama
Republic of South Africa
Soviet Union

Choose *three* nations from the list above, and for *each* one chosen, discuss how a specific geographic feature has influenced the nation's political, economic, or historical development.   [5,5,5]

2 Imperialism was the dominant force in world politics during the 19th century (1801–1900).

a Explain *three* reasons nations become imperialistic.   [9]

b Choose *one* former 19th-century colony and describe *one* positive and *one* negative effect of imperialism during its colonial period.   [6]

3 Throughout history, leaders have had to deal with problems affecting their nations or people.

Leaders

Martin Luther
Elizabeth I
Mao Zedong
Anwar el-Sadat
Mother Teresa
Bishop Desmond Tutu
Fidel Castro
Lech Walesa

Choose *three* of the leaders listed above and for *each* leader chosen:

- Explain a problem affecting his or her nation
- Describe a method he or she used to deal with the problem   [5,5,5]

4 Many problems face the nations of the world today. Some of these problems are listed below.

Problems

Air pollution
Deforestation
Disposal of nuclear waste
Endangered species
Human rights violations
Overpopulation
Refugees
World hunger

Choose *three* problems from the list and for *each* problem chosen:

- Using a specific example, explain why it is a problem
- Describe *one* way governments or groups of people have attempted to solve the problem   [5,5,5]

5 Changes within various societies or nations are brought about by a variety of factors.

Society — Factor

Europe following the Crusades — cultural diffusion
Britain from 1200 to 1950 — political evolution
18th-century France — political revolution
20th-century Japan — impact of war
20th-century India — civil disobedience
20th-century Middle East — influence of religion

Choose *three* pairs from the list and for *each* one chosen:

- Describe a change that occurred because of the factor
- Describe the impact of the change on the society or nation   [5,5,5]

6 Religion and philosophy have played important roles in the development of many nations. The list below pairs a religion or philosophy with an area that it has influenced.

> Confucianism — China
> Hinduism — India
> Islam — Iran
> Judaism — Israel
> Protestantism — Germany
> Russian Orthodoxy — Russia
> Shintoism — Japan

Choose *three* of the pairs listed and explain how *each* religion or philosophy chosen has influenced the development of the nation with which it is paired.   [5,5,5]

7 When controversial topics are examined, there are always opposing viewpoints. Each statement below expresses a viewpoint about a controversial topic.

Statements

Industrialization was beneficial to the people of 18th-century England.

The Palestinians have a right to a homeland.

Demonstrations have been successful in bringing about change in China and in Eastern Europe.

The Treaty of Versailles was a good treaty.

Terrorism is an appropriate means to bring about change.

The United Nations has had little success in achieving world peace.

The Chinese Government has a right to limit family size.

The European Economic Community (Common Market) has been successful in unifying Western Europe.

Choose *three* statements from the list. For *each* statement chosen, discuss *one* argument for and *one* argument against the statement.   [5,5,5]

INDEX

A

Abbasids, 32-33
Absolute monarch, 267
Abu Bakr, 30
Acropolis, 252
Afghanistan War (1979-1989), 45
Africa, 5
  economic geography, 166-171
  history and political geography, 179-196
  human and cultural geography, 172-177
  physical geography, 156-164
Africanization, 192
African National Congress, 191
African nationalism, 188-189
Afrikaaners, 190
Age of Antiquity, 250
Age of Exploration, 264-265
Age of Pericles, 251
Age of Reason, 274-275
Agricultural Reform Law, 316
Agriculture:
  Africa, 170-171
  East Asia, 100-103, 131
  Eastern Europe, 342
  Latin America, 208-209
  Middle East, 17
  South Asia, 54-56
  Southeast Asia, 79
  Soviet Union, 315
  Western Europe, 243
Agriculture diversification, 209
Ahaggar Mountains, 159
Ahimsa, 66
Ainu, 133, 137
Akbar, 69
Alexander I (1801-1825), 327
Alexander II (1855-1881), 328-329
Alexander III (1881-1894), 329
Alexander (the Great), 28, 252
Algeria, 35
Ali, 30
Allah, 23
Allies, 289, 295, 296
Alps, 240
Altai Mountains, 98
Amazon River, 205
Amritsar Massacre, 71
Andes Mountains, 203
Andropov, Yurii, 336
Angles, 256
Angola, 196
Animism, 85
Anthropologists, 179
Anti-Semitism, 36, 293-294
Apartheid, 190-191, 369-370
Apennines, 240
Appeasement, 296
Aquino, Corazon, 90
Arabian Peninsula, 13
Arabian Sea, 13
Arabic, 172
Arab-Israeli conflict:
  Arab views, 42
  background of, 36-37
  four Arab-Israeli wars, 37-41
  Israeli views, 42-43
  since 1973, 41-42
Arab League, 45
Arab nationalism, 35
Arabs, 23
Arab sovereignty, 36
Arafat, Yasir, 41

Archeological evidence, 179
Archimedes, 253
Archipelagoes, 77
Argentina, 228, 231-232
Aristarchus, 253
Aristocracy, 251, 253
Aristophanes, 251
Aristotle, 251
Armenians, 319
Arms control, 366
Artifacts, 179
Artisans, 107
Aryans, 68
ASEAN (Association of Southeast Asian
  Nations), 79
Ashoka, 68
Asia Minor, 12
Assad, Hafez el-, 45
Assimilation, 186
Associated free state, 236
Aswan High Dam, 160
Atacama Desert, 203
Ataturk, Mustapha Kemal, 27, 35
Athens, 251
Atlantic Ocean, 240
Atlas Mountains, 13, 159
Atomic bombs, 148-149
Audiencia, 224
Augustan Age, 254
Augustus, 253-254
Aurangzeb, 69
Autocracy, 267
Axis powers, 295, 296
Axum civilization, 180-181
Azerbaijanis, 319
Aztecs, 220

B

Babur, 69
Baghdad, 32
Balance of power, 278
Balfour Declaration, 37
Balkan Mountains, 340
Baltic Sea, 240
Bandeiras, 224
Bangladesh, 74
Bantu, 172
Bastille, 275
Batista, Fulgencio, 233
Battle of Hastings (1066), 267
Battle of Tours, 256
Battle of Waterloo (1815), 277
Batu Khan, 324
Begin, Menachem, 41
Belgian Congo, 194
Belgium, 286
Ben Bella, Ahmed, 35
Bengali, 62
Berlin Airlift, 301
Berlin Blockade, 301
Berlin Wall, 302
Bhagavad Gita, 64
Bhutto, Benazir, 73-74
Bhutto, Zulfikar Ali, 73
Biafra, Republic of, 193
Bicameral legislature, 235
Bill of Rights, 271
Birth rate, 61, 170
Bismarck, Otto von, 279
Black Sea, 13, 313
Blitzkreig, 296
"Bloody Sunday," 329
Blue Nile, 159

Bodhissatva, 85
Boers, 190
Bohemian Mountains, 340
Bolivar, Simon, 227-229
Bolshevik Party, 330-332
Bonaparte, Napoleon I (1799-1815), 276-278
Borodin, Aleksandr, 321
Botha, P.W., 191
Bourbons, 268
Bourgeoisie, 283
Boyars, 325
Brahma, 63
Brahmans, 64
Brahmaputra River, 51
Brazil, 229
Brazilian Highlands, 203
Brezhnev, Leonid, 336
British Commonwealth of Nations, 194, 286
British East India Company, 69-70
British mandate, 37
British Raj rule (1760-1947), 69
Buddha, 66, 85
Buddhism, 66, 85, 108-109, 134
Bug River, 341
Bunraku, 135
Bush-fallow, 170
Byelo-Russians, 319
Byzantine Commonwealth, 348
Byzantine Empire, 29, 254, 323

C

Caesar, Julius, 253
Caliph, 30
Caliphate, 30
Calvin, John, 263
Camp David Accords, 365
Capital investment, 207
Capitalist system, 243, 245, 266
Capital reserves, 168
Caribbean, 229
Carpathian Mountains, 340
Cash crops, 168
Caspian Sea, 13, 313
Caste system, 64
Castro, Fidel, 233
Catherine II, "the Great" (1762-1796), 327
Caudillo, 230, 231
Cavaliers, 270
Cavour, Camillo Benso di, 279
Ceaucescu, Nicolai, 350
Centralist form of government, 232
Central Powers, 289
Chad, 195
Chamberlain, Neville, 296
Chamorro, Pedro, 233
Chamorro, Violeta, 235
Chang River, 98-99
Chao Phraya River, 78
Charlemagne (768-814), 256-258
Charles I (1625-1649), 270
Charles II (1660-1685), 271
Chauvinism, 280
Chekhov, Anton, 321
Chernenko, Konstantin, 336
Chernobyl disaster, 315
Chiang Kai-shek, 117-118, 121
Chile, 228
Chimu, 220
China:
    economic geography, 100-105
    history and political geography, 112-123
    human and cultural geography, 106-110
    physical geography, 96-99
    See also People's Republic of China

China Proper, 98
China's Golden Age, 113
Ch'in dynasty. See Qin dynasty
Ch'ing dynasty. See Qing dynasty
Ch'in Shih-Huang-ti. See Qin Shi Huang
Chivalry, 257
Chou dynasty. See Zhou dynasty
Chou En-lai, 118
Christianity, 175, 248
Chronicles, 321
Cicero, 254
Citizenship, 231
Civil Constitution of the Clergy, 275
Civil service system, 113
Clan, 176
Classical period, 250
Clemenceau, Georges, 290
Clive, Robert, 69-70
Code Napoleon, 277
Colbert, Jean, 268
Cold War, 297, 300-302, 334-336
Collective farms, 103
Collectivization, 315
Colonialism, 284
"Colossus of the north," 234
Columbus, Christopher, 264
Commercial agriculture, 209
Commercial revolution, 266-267
Committee of Public Safety, 276
Common law, 270
Common Market, 245
Commonwealth, 270
Communalism, 65, 75
Communes, 103
Communication, 374
Communism, 245, 283-284
Communist Bloc, 300, 349-351
Communist Manifesto, The (Marx and
    Engels), 283
Concessions, 18, 115, 285
Concordat of 1801, 277
Conference on Security and Cooperation in
    Europe, 304
Confucianism, 106-107, 109-110
Confucius, 106-107
Congo River, 160
Congo (Zaire), 194-195
Congress of People's Deputies, 337
Congress of Vienna (1814, 1815), 278
Congress Party, 70
Consensus, 149
Constantine, 28-29, 254
Constitutional monarchy, 271
Constructive engagement, 196
Consulate, 276
Consuls, 253
Contadora peace plan, 235
Continents, 1
Contras, 234
Cooperative farms, 103, 169
Corporate state, 295
Corvee, 273
Council of the Indies, 224
Council of Trent (1545-1563), 263
Counter-Reformation, 263-264
Coup d'etat, 230
Craftspeople, 144
Credit, 207
Creole, 227
Crimean War (1854-1856), 327
Cromwell, Oliver, 270
Crusades, 33, 259-260
Cuban Revolution, 233
Cultural diffusion, 6-8, 51, 176, 201

Cultural Revolution, 104, 120
Culture, 6-7, 60
Culture areas, 4-8
Cynics, 252
Cyril (826-869), 347
Cyrillic alphabet, 320, 347

D

Da Gama, Vasco, 264
Daimyo, 141
Danton, Georges Jacques, 276
Danube River, 242, 341
Danube Valley, 341
Dark Ages, 256
Dasht-i-Kavir, 13
Das Kapital (Marx and Engels), 283
"D-Day," 296
Death rate, 61
Debt crisis, 208
Debt interest payments, 212
Deccan Plateau, 51
Decembrist Revolt, 327
Declaration of the Rights of Man, 275
Decolonization, 286
deKlerk, F.W., 191
Delhi Sultanate (1206-1526), 69
Democracy, 251, 269-273
Democratic city-state, 251
Democratic traditions, 231
Democritus, 252
Demographic growth, 215
Demography, 60
Deng Xiaoping, 103-105
Desert, 13, 164
Desertification, 161, 166
Dessalines, Jean-Jacques, 227
Detente, 302, 336
Dharma, 63
Dialects, 224
Diaspora, 36
Diaz, Porfirio, 232
Dinaric Alps, 340
Diogenes, 252
Direct democracy, 251
Directory government, 276
Direct rule, 285-286
Diversified economic relationships, 213
Divestment and sanctions, 196
Divine right theory, 268
Division of labor, 176
Dneiper River, 312
Dollar diplomacy, 235
Domesday Book, 267
Domestic system, 267
Don River, 312
Dostoievskii, Theodor, 321
Drakensberg Mountains, 159
Drava River, 341
Dravidians, 68
Dubcek, Alexander, 350
Duma, 329
Dvina River, 312

E

East Asia, 5
    economic geography, 100-105, 129-132
    history and political geography, 112-123,
        140-151
    human and cultural geography, 106-110,
        133-138
    physical geography, 96-99, 125-127
Eastern Europe, 5
    economic geography, 342-343
    history and political geography, 347-351
    human and cultural geography, 344-346
    physical geography, 340-342
Eastern Ghats, 51
Eastern Orthodox Church, 29, 345
Easter Rebellion, 303
East Jerusalem, 39
Ecological balance, 168
Economic development:
    Africa, 166-171
    East Asia, 100-105, 129-132
    Eastern Europe, 342-343
    Latin America, 206-213
    Middle East, 17-21
    South Asia, 54-58
    Southeast Asia, 79-82
    Soviet Union, 315-317
    Western Europe, 243-247
Economic opportunity, 212
Economic system, 243
Edict of Milan, 28-29, 257
Edict of Nantes (1598), 264
Education, 360
Egypt, 28, 35
Elburz Mountains, 13
Elites, 217
Elizabeth I (1558-1603), 267-268
Encomienda, 222
Endogamy, 62
Energy resources, 211-212
Engels, Friedrich, 245, 283
England:
    colonial policies, 285
    growth of democracy in, 269-273
    Industrial Revolution in, 280-282
    rise as nation-state, 267-268
English Channel, 242
English Civil War (1642-1645), 270
Enlightenment, 226, 274-275
Enterprise Law of 1987, 316
Environmental conditions, 215
Environmental issues, 367-368
Epicureanism, 253
Epicurus, 253
Erasmus, Desiderius, 263
Eratosthenes, 253
Ershad, Hussain Mohammed, 74
Estonians, 319
Ethics, 106
Ethiopia, 195
Ethiopian Highlands, 159
Ethnic diversity, 216
Ethnic groups, 85, 176, 344-346
Ethnocentrism, 280
Euclid, 253
Euphrates River, 14, 28
Euratom, 246
Eurocommunism, 245
European Community, 246, 303
European Economic Community (EEC),
    194, 245-246
    See also European Community
European Free Trade Association (EFTRA),
    246
European imperialism, 185-188
Europeanization, 216
European Recovery Act, 243
Exchange rates, 208
Excommunication, 258-259
Exploitation, 286
Export value, 209
Extended family, 176
Extraterritoriality, 115

F

Factors of production, 17
FAO (Food and Agriculture Organization), 299
Farsi, 26
Favorable balance of trade, 266
Fealty, 257
Federal Republic of Germany, 301
Federation of Central America, 230
Feudalism, 141, 257
Fief, 257
Five-Year Plans, 57, 333
Food staple crops, 209
Forced labor, 186
Foreign imports, 208
Foreign investment, 207
Fossils, 179
Fourier, Charles, 283
"Four Modernizations," 103
Four Noble Truths, 85
France:
    colonial policies, 285-286
    French Revolution, 273-276
    Napoleonic Era, 276-278
    rise as nation-state, 268-269
Francis Ferdinand, Archduke, 289
Franks, 256
Free enterprise system, 266
French and Indian War (1756-1763), 265
French Community, 286
French Revolution, 273-276
Fujiwara, 141
Fulani, 193
Funan Empire, 87

G

Gandhi, Indira, 70, 72
Gandhi, Mohandas "Mahatma," 70-71
Gandhi, Rajiv, 72
Ganges River, 51
Garibaldi, Giuseppe, 279
Gaza, 39
General assembly (OAS), 235
General Assembly (U.N.), 299
Genocide, 297, 333, 370
Georgians, 319
German Democratic Republic, 301
Germany:
    after WWII, 301-302
    reunification of, 302
    rise of Nazis to power, 293-294
    under Weimar Republic, 292
    unification of, 279-280
Ghana, 181
Ghettoes, 36
Glasnost, 336-337
Global environment, 1
Global interdependence, 1
Global studies, 5
Glorious Revolution (1688-1689), 271
Gobi Desert, 98
Gogol, Nikolai, 321
Golan Heights, 39
Golden Age of Athens, 251
Goncz, Arpad, 350
Good Neighbor policy, 235
Gorbachev, Mikhail, 300, 316, 336-338
Gothic style, 259
Government of India Act, 71
Gran Colombia, 228-230
Great Caucasus, 312
"Greater East Asia Co-Prosperity Sphere," 146
Great Hungarian Plain, 341
Great Leap Forward, The, 103

Great Rift Valley, 159
Great Russians, 319
"Great Thaw," 336
Great Wall, 112
Greece, 251-253
Greek Orthodox Church, 258
"Green Revolution," 55, 171, 371-372
Grito de Dolores, 227
Growth rate, 60-61
Guiana Highlands, 203
Gulf War, 44
"Guns vs. Butter" controversy, 316, 343
Guptas, 68

H

Hacienda, 222, 232
Hagiography, 321
Haiti, 227
Han dynasty, 113
Harambee, 192
Hausa, 172, 193
Havl, Vaclav, 350
Hay-Bunau-Varilla Treaty, 234
Hebrew, 26
Hegira, 24
Heian period (794-1185), 141
Hellenic Period (750-336 B.C.), 251-252
Hellenistic period (336-150 B.C.), 28, 252
Helots, 251
Helsinki Pact (1975), 304
Henry IV (1589-1610), 268
Henry VIII (1509-1547), 263, 267
Herodotus, 251
Herzl, Theodore, 36
Hidalgo, Father Miguel, 227
Himalayas, 50-51, 98
Hinayana, 85
Hindi, 61
Hinduism, 63-65
Hindustan Plain, 51
Hippocrates, 252
History:
    Africa, 179-196
    East Asia, 112-123, 140-151
    Eastern Europe, 347-351
    Latin America, 219-236
    Middle East, 27-46
    South Asia, 68-75
    Southeast Asia, 86-91
    Soviet Union, 323-338
    Western Europe, 250-304
Hitler, Adolph, 292-293
Ho Chi Minh, 88
Hokkaido, 126
Holocaust, 37, 297, 370
Holy Inquisition, 259
Holy Roman Empire, 256
Holy war (jihad), 32
Homage, 257
Homer, 251
Homogeneous people, 133
Hong Kong, 115, 123
Honshu, 126
Horace, 254
House of Rurik, 323
Hsia dynasty. See Xia dynasty
Hsi or West River. See Xi River
Huanghe River, 98-99
Huguenots, 268
Huitzilopochtli, 220
Humanism, 260-261
Human rights, 217, 222, 368-370
Hundred Schools of Thought, 112
Hundred Years' War (1337-1453), 267

Hunger. *See* World hunger
Hus, John, 263
Hussein, Saddam, 44
Hwang-Ho or Yellow River. *See* Huanghe
  River
Hydroelectric power, 159

I

Iberian Peninsula, 240
Ibn Saud, 35
Icons, 320
Ideographs, 109
Imams, 30
Imperialism, 284-286, 287
Incarnation, 63
Incas, 220-222
Independence movements, 226-236, 348-349
India:
  economic geography, 54-58
  history and political geography, 68-75
  human and cultural geography, 60-66
  physical geography, 50-51
Indian National Congress, 70
Indirect rule, 185, 285
Indo-Gangetic Plain, 51
Indulgences, 262
Indus River, 51
Industrialization, 177
Industrial production:
  Eastern Europe, 342
  Latin America, 207-208
  Middle East, 17-19
  South Asia, 56
  Southeast Asia, 79
  Soviet Union, 315-316
  Western Europe, 243
Industrial Revolution, 280-282
Inflation, 246
Infrastructures, 207, 208, 216
Inner Mongolia, 98
Inquisition, 263-264
Intendancy system, 226
Inter-American System, 235
Interdependence, 356
International Monetary Fund (IMF), 194
International organizations, 194
International police power, 234
Intervention, 235
Intifada, 41
Investiture, 257
I.R.A. (Irish Republican Army), 303
Iran, 43-44
Iran-Iraq War, 44
Iraq, 35
Irawaddy River, 78
Ireland, 304
"Iron curtain," 302
Islam, 23-26, 30-33, 64-65, 173-174
Islamic fundamentalists, 26, 43-44
Israel, 35-36
Istanbul, 12, 33
Italy:
  under Mussolini, 294-295
  unification of, 279
Iturbide, Agustin de, 227
Ivan III, Prince, 325
Ivan IV, Tsar, 325

J

Jainism, 66
Jajmani, 62
James I (1603-1625), 270
James II (1633-1701), 271

Japan:
  economic geography, 129-132
  history and political geography, 140-151
  human and cultural geography, 133-138
  physical geography, 125-127
Jati, 64
Jesuits, 264
Jewish sovereignty, 36
Jinnah, Mohammed Ali, 70-71, 73
Joao VI, 229
Joint stock, 266
Jomon culture, 140
Jordan, 35
Jordan River, 15
Juarez, Benito, 232
Judeo-Christian tradition, 248
Judicial power, 269-270
Julian Alps, 340
Jury system, 269
Justicialismo, 231
Justinian, 29
Justinian Code, 29

K

Kabbah, 24
Kabuki drama, 135
Kachaturian, Aram, 321
Kalahari, 161, 164
Kanto, 126
Karma, 63
Kashatriyas, 64
Katanga, 194
Kazakhs, 319
Kenya, 192-193
Kenya African National Union (KANU), 192
Kenya African Union, 192
Kenyatta, Jomo, 192
Kerenskii, Aleksandr, 330
Khan, Gen. Mohammed Ayub, 73
Khanate of the Golden Horde, 324-325
Khmer empire, 87
Khmer Rouge, 89
Khoisan, 172
Khomeini, Ayatollah, 26, 44
Khrushchev, Nikita, 336
Khyber Pass, 51
Kibbutz, 17
Kiev, 323-325
Knox, John, 263
Kohl, Helmut, 302
Kojiki, 140
Koran, 24
Korean War (1950-1953), 121
Kuang Hsu, 115-116
Kublai Khan, 113
Kulaks, 333
Kung Fu-tzu. *See* Confucius
Kuomintang, 116, 117
Kush civilization, 180
Kyushu, 126

L

Laissez-faire, 274
Lake Baikal, 313
Lake Balton, 341
Lake Chad, 162
Lake Chapala, 205
Lake Kariba, 160
Lake Ladoga, 313
Lake Malawi, 162
Lake Maracaibo, 205
Lake Nasser, 160
Lake Tanganyika, 162

Lake Titicaca, 205
Lake Victoria, 162
Land reform, 209
Languages:
  Africa, 172
  Eastern Europe, 344-346
  Latin America, 200
  Middle East, 26-27
  South Asia, 61-62
  Southeast Asia, 84
  Soviet Union, 319
  Western Europe, 249
Lao-tzu, 107
La Plata, 224
Las Casas, Bartolome de, 222
Latifundio, 209, 222, 230
Latin America, 5
  economic geography, 206-213
  history and political geography, 219-236
  human and cultural geography, 215-218
  physical geography, 200-205
Latvians, 319
Law of Cooperatives of 1987, 316
Leached soil, 166
League of Nations, 290
Leakey family, 179
Lebanon, 35
  civil war in, 44-45
Legalism, 108
Legend, 4
Legislative power, 269
Lena River, 313
Lenin, Vladimir Illich, 330-332
Leo III, 256
Lettres de cachet, 273
Liberal Democratic Party, 149
Liberation theology, 231
Libya, 45
Limited Test Ban Treaty (1963), 366
Lineage, 176
Lithuanians, 319
Liu Shaoqi (Liu Hsao Ch'i), 120
Livy, 254
Lloyd George, David, 290
Locke, John, 272-273
Lome Convention, 194
Long Parliament, 270
Louis XI (1461-1483), 268
Louis XIII (1601-1643), 268
Louis XIV (1643-1715), 268-269
Louis XVI (1774-1792), 273
L'Ouverture, Toussaint, 227
Loyola, Ignatius, 264
Luther, Martin, 262-263
L'vov, Prince Georgii, 330

M

MacArthur, Gen. Douglas, 147-148
Machismo, 216
Magna Carta (1215), 269
Mahabharata, 64
Mahayana, 85
Mahdi, 30
Mali, 181-182
Manchukuo, 147
Manchuria, 97
Mandate, 34
Mandate of heaven, 107
Mandela, Nelson, 191
Manor, 257
Mansur, 32
Mao Zedong (Mao Tse-tung), 101-103, 117-121
Maps, 2-4

Marat, Jean Paul, 276
March on Rome (1922), 295
Marcos, Ferdinand, 90
Marie Antoinette, 273
Marin, Munoz, 236
Maritsa Valley, 341
Market economy, 266, 282
Marshall Plan, 243, 300
Martel, Charles, 256
Marx, Karl, 245, 283
Mary II (1689-1694), 271
Mass production, 280
Matrilineal descent, 177
Mau Mau, 192
Maurya, Chandragupta, 68
Maurya dynasty, 68
Mayans, 219-220
Mazowiecki, Tadeusz, 350
Mazzini, Giuseppe, 279
Means of production, 282
Media, 177
Medical breakthroughs, 373
Mediterranean climate, 164
Mediterranean Sea, 13-14, 240
Mekong River, 78
Mensheviks, 331-332
Mercantilism, 168, 226, 266
Mercenaries, 195
Merchants, 107, 144
Mesopotamia, 14, 28
Mestizos, 223
Methodius (815-885), 347
Metternich, Count, 278
Mexico, 227-228, 232-233
Middle Ages (500-1500 A.D.), 256-260
Middle East, 5
  economic geography, 17-21
  history and political geography, 27-46
  human and cultural geography, 22-27
  physical geography, 12-15
Middle Kingdom, 96
Migration, 212
Militarism, 289, 295
Military dictator, 230, 231
Militia, 45
Minamoto, 141-142
Minerals, 209-212
Ming dynasty, 113-114
Miranda, Francisco, 227
Missi dominici, 256
Missions, 223-224
Mita, 222
Mixed economy, 57, 103, 245
Model Parliament, 269
Modernization, 177
Mohammed, 23-26
Moi, Daniel Arap, 192
Moksha, 63
Monogamy, 176
Monotheism, 23
Monroe Doctrine, 234
Monsoon, 51, 97
Montagu-Chelmsford Reforms, 71
Morava River, 341
Morelos, Father Jose, 227
Moscow, 325
Moussorgskii, Modest, 321
Mt. Everest, 50
Mt. Kenya, 159
Mt. Kilimanjaro, 159
Mubarak, Hosni, 41
Mughal (Mogul) dynasty (1526-1760), 69
Mujahadeen, 45
Mulattos, 223

Multinational corporations, 169, 194, 213
Munich Conference (1938), 296
Muslim League, 70
Mussolini, Benito, 294-295
Muswiyah, 30

N

Nafud, 13
Namib, 161, 164
Nanak, 66
Napoleon. *See* Bonaparte, Napoleon
Nasser, Gamal Abdel, 39, 46
National Assembly, 275
National Convention, 276
National Diet, 149
Nationalism:
  Africa, 188-189
  Latin America, 231-234
  Middle East, 35-36
  Western Europe, 278-280, 288
  See also Independence movements
Nationalist Party, 116
Nationalized industries, 169, 232
Nation-states, 267
NATO (North Atlantic Treaty
  Organization), 300-301, 334, 364
Nazis, 293-294
Near East, 12
Negev, 13
Nehru, Jawaharlal, 70-72
Neocolonialism, 169, 193, 376
N.E.P. (New Economic Program), 332
Nepotism, 262
New Granada, 224
New Spain, 224
Newton, Isaac, 275
Nicaragua, 233-234
Nicholas I (1825-1855), 327
Nicholas II (1894-1917), 329-330
Niger delta, 161
Nigeria, 193
Niger River, 160-161
Nihongi, 140
Nile delta, 159
Nile River, 14-15, 28, 159-160
1956 War, the, 39
Ninety-Five Theses, 262
Nirvana, 85
Nixon, Richard, 122
Noh drama, 135
Nomads, 13, 219
Nonaligned nations, 75, 193, 365
North Atlantic Drift, 242
North China, 97
Northern European Plain, 312, 341
Northern Ireland, 303
North Sea, 240
Novgorod, 325
Nuclear Non-Proliferation Treaty (1968),
  366
Nyerere, Julius, 169

O

Oases, 161
Ob River, 312
Oceans, 1
Octavian. *See* Augustus
O'Higgins, Bernardo, 228
Oil industry, 17-19
Old Regime, 273
Old Silk Road, 109
Oligarchy, 145, 232
Olympic Games, 252
One-crop economies, 209

OPEC (Organization of Petroleum
  Exporting Countries), 18, 194
Open Door Policy, 115
Opium War, 114
Oral tradition, 179
Organization of African Unity, 190, 194
Organization of American States (OAS), 235
Orinoco River, 205
Orlando, Vittoria, 290
Ortega, Daniel, 233
Osman, 33
Ostrogoths, 256
Ottoman Empire (1453-1918), 33-35
Ottoman Turks, 29, 33-35
Owen, Robert, 283

P

Pahlavi, Mohammed Reza, 43
Paine, Thomas, 274
Paisley, Rev. Ian, 303
Pakistan, 72-74
Pakistan People's Party, 73
Paleologos, Sophia, 325
Palestine, 28
Pan-Africanism, 190
Pan-Arabism, 46
Panchayat, 62
Pannonian Plain, 341
Pan-Slavism, 348-349
Paris Peace Conference, 290
Parliament, 269
Parthenon, 252
Pasternak, Boris, 322
Paternalism, 186, 286
Patriarch of Moscow, 320
Patricians, 253
Pearl Harbor attack, 147
Peasants, 107, 144
Pedro I, 229
Peloponnesian War, 252
Peninsulars, 223
People's Republic of China, 118-123
  See also China
Perestroika, 316-317
Pericles, 251
Permafrost, 313
Peron, Eva, 231
Peron, Juan D., 231
Perry, Comm. Matthew, 144
Persian Wars (500-479 B.C.), 252
Peru, 224
Peter I, "the Great" (1685-1725), 321,
  326-327
Petition of Right, 270
"Petrine Reforms," 327
"Petro-dollars," 18-19, 21
Phalange Party, 44
Philip (King of Macedon), 252
Philosophes, 274
Pictographs, 109
Pindar, 251
Planned economy, 282
Plan of Iguala, 228
Plantation economy, 226
Plateau, 158
Plato, 251
Plebians, 253
Plebiscite, 236
Plutarch, 254
Pogroms, 36
Politboro, 336
Political map, 4
Polo, Marco, 265

Polygamy, 176
Polytheism, 220
Population:
  Africa, 172
  China, 110
  Eastern Europe, 344
  India, 60
  Japan, 135-136
  Latin America, 215-216
  Middle East, 20, 23
  Southeast Asia, 84
  Soviet Union, 318-319
Population density, 60
Population growth, 356-359
Po River, 242
Portugal, 224, 286
Post-industrial society, 246
Pot, Pol, 89
Predestination, 263
PRI, 232-233
Princip, Gavrilo, 289
Procurator, 327
Prokofiev, Sergei, 321
Proletariat, 283, 329
Protective tariffs, 208
Protectorate, 285
Provisional Government, 330
Prussia, 279
Prut River, 341
Puerto Rico, 235-236
Punic Wars (264-146 B.C.), 253
Purges, 332-333
Puritan Revolution (1642-1660), 270
Pushkin, Aleksandr, 321
Pyrenees, 240
Pythagoras, 252

Q

Qaddafi, Col. Muammar, 45
Qin dynasty, 112-113
Qing dynasty, 114
Qinling Mountains, 98
Qin Shi Huang, 112
Quipu, 222

R

Rachmaninov, Sergei, 321
Rahman, Sheik Mujibur, 74
Rain forest, 163-164
Ramayana, 63-64
Rasputin, Grigory, 330
Reactionary, 278
Red Guards, 120
Red River, 78
"Reds," 332
Red Sea, 13
Reformation, 262-264
Reform Bill of 1832, 282
Regions, 4-8
Reign of Terror (1793-1794), 276
Reincarnation (samsara), 63
Religions:
  animism, 85
  Buddhism, 66, 85, 108-109, 134
  Christianity, 175, 248
  Confucianism, 106-107, 109-110
  Eastern Orthodox Christians, 345
  Hinduism, 63-64
  Islam, 23-26, 30-33, 64-65, 173-174
  Jainism, 66
  Russian Orthodox Church, 320
  Shinto, 134
  Sikhism, 66

  Taoism, 107-108
  traditional beliefs, 172-173
  Uniates, 345
Renaissance (1400-1700 A.D.), 260-261
Reparations, 290
Republic, 253
Republican form of government, 231
Republic of Ireland, 303
Resource and energy management, 362-363
Rhine River, 242
Rhodope Mountains, 340
Richelieu, Cardinal (1624-1642), 268
Rimskii-Korsakov, Nikolai, 321
Rio de la Plata, 205
Rivera, Munoz, 236
River basins, 158
Robespierre, Maximilien, 276
Roman Catholic Church, 230-231, 257-259
Roman Empire (340 B.C.-476 A.D.),
  28-29, 253-256
Romanov, Mikhail, 325
Rome-Berlin-Tokyo Axis, 147
Roosevelt Corollary, 234
Rosas, Juan Manuel de, 231
Roundheads, 270
Rub-al Khali, 13
Rurales, 232
Russian Orthodox Church, 320, 323
Russian Revolution (1905-1917), 329-330
"Russification," 329
Russo-Japanese War (1904-1905), 146, 329
Ruwenzori Mountains, 159

S

Sadat, Anwar, 41
Sahara, 13, 161, 164
Sahel, 161
St. Petersburg, 327
Samurai, 141, 144
Sandinista Front, 233-234
Sankin-kotai, 144
San Martin, Jose de, 227, 228
Sanskrit, 87
Sanskritization, 64
Santa Anna, Antonio, 232
Santander, Francisco, 229
Sarai, 325
Satellite nations, 285, 333
Saudi Arabia, 35
Savanna, 164
Sava River, 341
Saxons, 256
Scale, 4
Scholars, 107
Schuman, Robert, 245
Scientific method, 275
Scientific Revolution, 275
Scientific socialism. *See* Communism
"Scorched earth" policy, 327
Secretary general, 235
Secularism, 260
Security Council (U.N.), 299
Seine River, 242
Selassie, Haille, 195
Seljuk Turks, 33
Semites, 22
Sen, Hun, 89
Senate, 253
Sepoy Mutiny (1857), 70
Serfs, 257
Shah Jahan, 69
Shang dynasty, 112
Sharpeville Massacre, 191

Shatt-al-Arab, 14
Shi'ite Muslims, 30
Shikoku, 126
Shinto, 134
Shiva, 63
Shostakovich, Dimitrii, 321
Shotoku, Prince, 134
Shudras, 64
Siberian Plain, 312
Siddhartha Gautama (Buddha), 66, 85
Sierra Madre del Sur, 203
Sierra Madres, 203
Sihanouk, Prince Norodom, 89
Sikhism, 66
Silicon chip, 371
Simony, 262
Sinai, 13
Sinai Peninsula, 39
Singh, Vishwanath Pratap, 72
Single-crop usage, 209
Sinhalese, 62
Sinn Fein Party, 303
Sino-Japanese War (1894-1895), 146
Six-Day War (1967), 39
Slave trade, 182-185
Slavonic, 319
Slavs, 323, 344
Smith, Adam, 274
Social contract, 273
Social Darwinism, 285
Socialism, 245, 282-283
Socrates, 251
Solidarity, 350
Solzhenitsyn, Aleksandr, 322
Song dynasty, 113
Songhai, 182
Sophocles, 251
South Africa, 190-192, 369-370
South Asia, 5
    economic geography, 54-58
    history and political geography, 68
    human and cultural geography, 60-66
    physical geography, 50-52
Southeast Asia, 5
    economic geography, 79-82
    history and political geography, 86-91
    human and cultural geography, 84-85
    physical geography, 77-79
Southern China, 97
Sovereignty, 36
Soviets, 331
Soviet Union:
    economic geography, 315-317
    history and political geography, 323-338
    human and cultural geography, 318-322
    physical geography, 310-313
Space-based technology, 374-375
Space exploration, 374
Spanish Armada, 265
Spanish colonial empire, 222-224
Sparta, 251
"Spheres of influence," 115, 285
Squatter settlements, 216
Srivijaya empire, 87
Stalin, Joseph, 332-333
State-supported terrorism, 45
Steppes, 164, 313
Stoicism, 252-253
Stolypin, Piotr, 329
Stolypin Reforms, 329
Strait of Malacca, 78
Strategic Arms Limitation Treaty (SALT), 366
Strategic Arms Reduction Treaties
    (START), 366

Stratified social structure, 220
Stravinskii, Igor, 321
Stuart Restoration (1660-1688), 271
Stuarts, 270
Subcontinent, 50
Sub-Saharan Africa. See Africa
Subsistence farmers, 170
Sucre, Antonio Jose de, 229
Sudan, 164
Sudetenland, 296
Sudeten Mountains, 340
Suffrage, 216
Sugar-plantation economy, 226
Sukarno, Ahmed, 88
Suleiman (the Magnificent), 33
Sung dynasty. See Song dynasty
Sunni Muslims, 30
Sun Yat-sen, 116-117
Superpowers, 168, 300, 364
Supreme Soviet, 337-338
Swahili, 172
Synod of Bishops, 327
Syria, 35

T

Tacitus, 254
Taiga, 313
Taika Reforms, 140
Taille, 273
Taiping Rebellion, 116
Taiwan, 118, 121
Tale of Genji, The (Lady Murasaki), 135
Tamil, 61
Tang dynasty, 113
Tao, 108
Taoism, 107-108
Tariffs, 362
Tartars, 319, 324
Tassili-N-Ajjer Mountains, 159
Taurus Mountains, 13
Tchaikovskii, Piotr Illich, 321
Technology, 55, 207, 217, 280, 371-375
Tennis Court Oath, 275
Terrace farming, 209
Terrorism, 366-367
Thames River, 242
Thar Desert, 51
Theodor, 325
Theodora, 29
Third World, 364-366
Thirty Years' War (1618-1648), 264
Thucydides, 251
Tibesti Mountains, 159
Tibet, 98
Tienanmen Square massacre, 122
Tien Shan Mountains, 98
Tigris River, 14, 28
Tisza River, 341
Tithe, 259, 273
Tito, Marshal (Josip Broz), 349
Tlaxcalans, 220
Tokugawa, 143-144
Toleration Act (1689), 264
Tolstoy, Count Lev, 321
Tombalbaye, Francois, 195
Tomb period, 140
Topographical map, 4
Totalitarianism, 290-295, 370
Tourism, 213
Trade. See World trade
Traditional African art, 175-176
Traditional African religions, 172-173
Tradition vs. modernization, 363

Transportation, 373
Treaty of Brest-Litovsk, 332
Treaty of Nanking, 115
Treaty of Portsmouth, 146
Treaty of Shimonoseki, 146
Treaty of Tordesillas, 222
Tribunes, 253
Tribute states, 113, 220
Tripartite Pact, 147
Triple Alliance, 288
Triple Entente, 288
Trotskii, Leon, 332
Truman Doctrine, 300
Tsars, 312
Tshombe, Moise, 194
Tudors, 267-268
Tundra, 313
Turgenev, Ivan, 321
Turkey, 35
Turkish, 26-27
Turkmen, 319
Twelve Tables, 253, 254
"Twenty-One Demands," 146
Tzu-hsi, 115-116

U

Ujamaa, 169
Ukraine, 313, 315
Ukrainians, 319
Umayyad clan, 30, 32, 36
UN Charter, 299
Unequal treaties, 115
UNESCO (United Nations Educational,
    Scientific and Cultural Organization), 299
Unfavorable balance of trade, 362
Uniates, 345
United Nations, 194, 299-300
Untouchables, 64
Upanishads, 63
Urals (mountains), 312
Urban areas, 176
Urban II, 259
Urbanization, 215
Urdu, 62
Utopian socialists, 283
Uzbeks, 319

V

Vaishyas, 64
Valera, Eamon de, 303
Vandar River, 341
Varangians, 323
Varnas, 64
Vassal, 257
Vedas, 63
"V-E Day," 296
Veldt, 164
Vergil, 254
Vernacular, 260-261, 347
Versailles Treaty (1919), 290
Vertical climate, 164
Viceroys, 224
Victor Emmanuel, 279
Village, 62-63
"Virgin Lands" program, 336
Vishnu, 63
Visigoths, 256
Vistula River, 341
Vitava River, 341
Vit River, 341
"V-J Day," 297
Vladimir, Prince, 320, 323
Volga River, 312

W

Walesa, Lech, 350
War for Independence (1948-1949), 37-39
Warring States, 112
Warsaw Pact (1955), 300, 335, 364
Wars of independence, 227
Water bodies:
    Africa, 159-162
    East Asia, 98-99
    Eastern Europe, 341
    Latin America, 205
    Middle East, 13-15
    South Asia, 51
    Southeast Asia, 77-78
    Soviet Union, 312-313
    Western Europe, 240, 242
Wellington, Lord, 277
West Bank, 15, 39
Western Europe, 5
    economic geography, 243-247
    history and political geography, 250-304
    human and cultural geography, 247-249
    physical geography, 240-242
Western Ghats, 51
Wheel of life, 63
White Man's Burden, The (Kipling),
    284-285
White Nile, 159
"Whites," 332
WHO (World Health Organization), 299
William III (1689-1694), 271
William the Conqueror, 267
Wilson, Woodrow, 290
Witte, Sergei, 329
World Bank, 168, 194
World hunger, 359-360
World trade, 360-362
World War I, 287-290
World War II, 147, 207, 295-297
Wycliffe, John, 263

X

Xia dynasty, 112
Xinjiang, 98
Xi River, 98-99

Y

Yalta Conference, 333
Yangtze River. *See* Chang River
Yayoi culture, 140
Yeltsin, Boris, 338
Yen River, 312
Yoga, 63
Yom Kippur War (1973), 40-41
Yoruba, 193
Yuan dynasty, 113

Z

Zaibatsu, 129, 145
Zaire, 195
Zambezi River, 160
Zemskii Sobor, 325
Zen Buddhism, 134, 135
Zeno, 252
Zhivkov, Todor, 351
Zhou dynasty, 112
Zia, Gen. Mohammed, 73
Zionism, 35-36
Zwingli, Ulrich, 263